Workshop on Arabic Natural Language Processing

(ANLP 2014)

Held at the Conference on Empirical Methods in Natural Language Processing (EMNLP 2014)

Doha, Qatar
25 October 2014

ISBN: 978-1-63439-479-6

Printed from e-media with permission by:

Curran Associates, Inc.
57 Morehouse Lane
Red Hook, NY 12571

Some format issues inherent in the e-media version may also appear in this print version.

Printed by Curran Associates, Inc. (2014)

For permission requests, please contact the Association for Computational Linguistics at the address below.

Association for Computational Linguistics
209 N. Eighth Street
Stroudsburg, Pennsylvania 18360

Phone: 1-570-476-8006
Fax: 1-570-476-0860

acl@aclweb.org

Additional copies of this publication are available from:

Curran Associates, Inc.
57 Morehouse Lane
Red Hook, NY 12571 USA
Phone: 845-758-0400
Fax: 845-758-2634
Email: curran@proceedings.com
Web: www.proceedings.com

Introduction

Welcome to Arabic Natural Language Processing Workshop at EMNLP 2014 in Doha, Qatar.

There has been a lot of progress in the last 15 years in the area of Arabic Natural Language Processing (NLP). In particular, the TIDES, GALE, and BOLT programs provided a significant boost to Arabic NLP, both in generating new language and speech resources on a large scale, and in advancing the state-of-the-art in morphological processing, parsing, named entity recognition, information retrieval, speech recognition, and machine translation. The substantial investment done through these projects reflect the fact that the Middle East continues to grow in its political and economic importance. We also observe that countries in the Middle East invest substantially into higher education and into building an ecosystem, which fosters new research initiatives. This creates the hope that our own research field, NLP, and especially Arabic NLP will continue to grow, will continue to attract students both in the region and in top international universities, and that new job opportunities will open up not only in the well established language service providers, but also through start-ups offering innovative solutions.

A number of Arabic NLP (or Arabic NLP-related) workshops and conferences have taken place, both in the Arab World and in association with international conferences. The Arabic NLP workshop at EMNLP 2014 follows in the footsteps of these previous efforts to provide a forum for researchers to share and discuss their ongoing work. The Arabic NLP workshop also includes a shared task on Automatic Arabic Error Correction, which was designed in the tradition of high profile NLP shared tasks such as CONLL's grammar/error detection and correction shared tasks in 2011-2013, and numerous machine translation campaigns by NIST/WMT/MEDAR, among others. The challenge chosen for the shared task is highly relevant, not only to spelling correction while composing a text, but also to developing techniques for automatically correcting errors in the far-from-perfect outputs of NLP technologies such as speech recognition or machine translation.

We are happy to have received 40 submissions. Unfortunately, not all the papers could be included in the workshop due to time limitations. The acceptance rate is 50%. The papers cover a wide range of topics: building language resources for standard and dialectal Arabic, language identification, sentiment analysis, named entity disambiguation, and machine translation for dialectal Arabic, etc. Twelve papers were selected for oral presentation and were organized under the general topics Corpora (four papers), Text Mining (four papers), Translation & Transliteration (three papers) and one paper describing the shared task. The remaining eight papers were selected to be presented in a poster session. There is no difference in quality between the oral and poster presentations.

The shared task was a success. We received 18 systems submissions from nine teams in six countries, representing a diverse set of approaches. Nine shared task system description (short) papers are included in the proceedings to document the shared task systems, but were not reviewed with the rest of the papers of the main workshop. These papers will be presented as posters.

The quantity and quality of the contributions to the main workshop, as well as the shared task, are strong indicators that there is a continued need for this kind of dedicated Arabic NLP workshop. We would like to acknowledge all the hard work of the submitting authors and thank the reviewers for their diligent work and for the valuable feedback they provided. We are also thankful to the work of the shared task committee, website committee and the publication co-chairs.

It has been an honor to server as program co-chairs. We hope that the reader of these proceedings will find them stimulating and beneficial.

Nizar Habash and Stephan Vogel, Arabic NLP Workshop, EMNLP 2014.

Organizers:

Program Co-Chairs

Nizar Habash, New York University Abu Dhabi

Stephan Vogel, Qatar Computing Research Institute

Publication Co-chairs

Nadi Tomeh, Université Paris 13, Sorbonne Paris Cité

Houda Bouamor, Carnegie Mellon University Qatar

Website Committee

Noura Farra, Columbia University

Kareem Darwish, Qatar Computing Research Institute

Shared Task Committee

Behrang Mohit (co-chair), Carnegie Mellon University Qatar

Alla Rozovskaya (co-chair), Columbia University

Wajdi Zaghouani, Carnegie Mellon University Qatar

Ossama Obeid, Carnegie Mellon University Qatar

Nizar Habash (advisor), New York University Abu Dhabi

Program Committee:

Abdelmajid Ben-Hamadou, University of Sfax, Tunisia
Abdelhadi Soudi, Ecole Nationale de l'Industrie Minérale, Morocco
Abdelsalam Nwesri, University of Tripoli, Libya
Achraf Chalabi , Microsoft Research, Egypt
Ahmed Ali, Qatar Computing Research Institute, Qatar
Ahmed Rafea, The American University in Cairo, Egypt
Alexis Nasr, University of Marseille, France
Ali Farghaly, Monterey Peninsula College, USA
Almoataz B. Al-Said, Cairo University, Egypt
Alon Lavie, Carnegie Mellon University, USA
Aly Fahmy, Cairo University, Egypt
Azadeh Shakery, University of Tehran, Iran
Azzeddine Mazroui, University Mohamed I, Morocco
Bassam Haddad, University of Petra, Jordan
Bayan Abu Shawar, Arab Open University, Jordan
Behrang Mohit, Carnegie Mellon University Qatar, Qatar
Eric Atwell, University of Leeds, UK
Farhad Oroumchian, University of Wollongong, Australia
Ghassan Mourad, Université Libanaise, Lebanon
Hassan Sawaf, eBay Inc., USA
Hazem Hajj, American University of Beirut, Lebanon
Hend Alkhalifa, King Saud University, Saudi Arabia
Houda Bouamor, Carnegie Mellon University Qatar, Qatar
Imed Zitouni, Microsoft Research, USA

Joseph Dichy, Université Lyon 2, France
Karim Bouzoubaa , Mohammad V University, Morocco
Karine Megerdoomian, The MITRE Corporation, USA
Katrin Kirchhoff, University of Washington, USA
Kemal Oflazer, Carnegie Mellon University Qatar, Qatar
Khaled Shaalan, The British University in Dubai, UAE
Khaled Shaban, Qatar University, Qatar
Khalil Sima'an, Universiteit van Amsterdam, Netherlands
Lamia Hadrich Belguith, University of Sfax, Tunisia
Michael Rosner, University of Malta, Malta
Mohamed Elmahdy, Qatar University, Qatar
Mohsen Rashwan, Cairo University, Egypt
Mona Diab, George Washington University, USA
Mustafa Jarrar, Bir Zeit University, Palestine
Nada Ghneim, Higher Institute for Applied Sciences and Technology, Syria
Nadi Tomeh, Université Paris 13, Sorbonne Paris Cité, France
Ossama Emam, IBM, USA
Otakar Smrž, Charles University , Czech Republic
Owen Rambow, Columbia University, USA
Preslav Nakov, Qatar Computing Research Institute, Qatar
Ramzi Abbes, TECHLIMED, France
Salwa Hamada, Cairo University, Egypt
Shahram Khadivi, Tehran Polytechnic, Iran
Sherri Condon , The MITRE Corporation, USA
Taha Zerrouki, University of Bouira, Algeria
Violetta Cavalli-Sforza, Al Akhawayn University, Morocco

Table of Contents

Conference Program

Saturday, October 25, 2014

Session 1: Corpora

9:00–9:20 *Using Twitter to Collect a Multi-Dialectal Corpus of Arabic*
Hamdy Mubarak and Kareem Darwish

9:20–9:40 *The International Corpus of Arabic: Compilation, Analysis and Evaluation*
Sameh Alansary and Magdy Nagi

9:45–10:05 *Building a Corpus for Palestinian Arabic: a Preliminary Study*
Mustafa Jarrar, Nizar Habash, Diyam Akra and Nasser Zalmout

10:05–10:25 *Annotating corpus data for a quantitative, constructional analysis of motion verbs in Modern Standard Arabic*
Dana Abdulrahim

10:30–11:00 ***Break / Poster setup***

Shared Task

11:00–11:30 *The First QALB Shared Task on Automatic Text Correction for Arabic*
Behrang Mohit, Alla Rozovskaya, Nizar Habash, Wajdi Zaghouani and Ossama Obeid

11:30–11:45 *Shared Task: 1-minute Summary for Shared Task Participants*
Shared Task participants

11:45–12:15 *Shared Task: Panel*
Group Discussion

12:15–12:30 *Main Workshop Poster Teaser 1-minute Summary*
Main Workshop participants

12:30–14:00 ***Lunch / Main and Shared Task Poster Session***

Saturday, October 25, 2014 (continued)

Main and Shared Task Poster Session

12:30–14:00 *Main Workshop Posters*
Main Workshop participants

A Framework for the Classification and Annotation of Multiword Expressions in Dialectal Arabic
Abdelati Hawwari, Mohammed Attia and Mona Diab

Al-Bayan: An Arabic Question Answering System for the Holy Quran
Heba Abdelnasser, Maha Ragab, Reham Mohamed, Alaa Mohamed, Bassant Farouk, Nagwa El-Makky and Marwan Torki

Automatic Arabic diacritics restoration based on deep nets
Ahmad Al Sallab, Mohsen Rashwan, Hazem M. Raafat and Ahmed Rafea

Combining strategies for tagging and parsing Arabic
Maytham Alabbas and Allan Ramsay

Named Entity Recognition System for Dialectal Arabic
Ayah Zirikly and Mona Diab

Semantic Query Expansion for Arabic Information Retrieval
Ashraf Mahgoub, Mohsen Rashwan, Hazem Raafat, Mohamed Zahran and Magda Fayek

Transliteration of Arabizi into Arabic Orthography: Developing a Parallel Annotated Arabizi-Arabic Script SMS/Chat Corpus
Ann Bies, Zhiyi Song, Mohamed Maamouri, Stephen Grimes, Haejoong Lee, Jonathan Wright, Stephanie Strassel, Nizar Habash, Ramy Eskander and Owen Rambow

Tunisian dialect Wordnet creation and enrichment using web resources and other Wordnets
Rihab Bouchlaghem, Aymen Elkhlifi and Rim Faiz

12:30–14:00 *Shared Task Posters*
Shared Task participants

A Pipeline Approach to Supervised Error Correction for the QALB-2014 Shared Task
Nadi Tomeh, Nizar Habash, Ramy Eskander and Joseph Le Roux

Arabic Spelling Correction using Supervised Learning
Youssef Hassan, Mohamed Aly and Amir Atiya

Saturday, October 25, 2014 (continued)

Autocorrection of arabic common errors for large text corpus
Taha Zerrouki, Khaled Alhawiti and Amar Balla

Automatic Correction of Arabic Text: a Cascaded Approach
Hamdy Mubarak and Kareem Darwish

CMUQ@QALB-2014: An SMT-based System for Automatic Arabic Error Correction
Serena Jeblee, Houda Bouamor, Wajdi Zaghouani and Kemal Oflazer

Fast and Robust Arabic Error Correction System
Michael Nawar and Moheb Ragheb

GWU-HASP: Hybrid Arabic Spelling and Punctuation Corrector
Mohammed Attia, Mohamed Al-Badrashiny and Mona Diab

TECHLIMED system description for the Shared Task on Automatic Arabic Error Correction
Djamel MOSTEFA, Omar ASBAYOU and Ramzi ABBES

The Columbia System in the QALB-2014 Shared Task on Arabic Error Correction
Alla Rozovskaya, Nizar Habash, Ramy Eskander, Noura Farra and Wael Salloum

Session 2: Text Mining

14:00–14:20 *A Large Scale Arabic Sentiment Lexicon for Arabic Opinion Mining*
Gilbert Badaro, Ramy Baly, Hazem Hajj, Nizar Habash and Wassim El-Hajj

14:20–14:40 *Evaluating Distant Supervision for Subjectivity and Sentiment Analysis on Arabic Twitter Feeds*
Eshrag Refaee and Verena Rieser

14:45–15:05 *Arabic Native Language Identification*
Shervin Malmasi and Mark Dras

15:05–15:25 *AIDArabic A Named-Entity Disambiguation Framework for Arabic Text*
Mohamed Amir Yosef, Marc Spaniol and Gerhard Weikum

15:30–16:00 ***Break***

Saturday, October 25, 2014 (continued)

Session 3: Translation & Transliteration

Closing Session

17:10–18:00 *Workshop Group Discussion*
Group Discussion

Using Twitter to Collect a Multi-Dialectal Corpus of Arabic

Hamdy Mubarak, Kareem Darwish
Qatar Computing Research Institute
Qatar Foundation
{hmubarak,kdarwish}@qf.org.qa

Abstract

This paper describes the collection and classification of a multi-dialectal corpus of Arabic based on the geographical information of tweets. We mapped information of user locations to one of the Arab countries, and extracted tweets that have dialectal word(s). Manual evaluation of the extracted corpus shows that the accuracy of assignment of tweets to some countries (like Saudi Arabia and Egypt) is above 93% while the accuracy for other countries, such Algeria and Syria is below 70%.

1 Introduction

Arabic is a morphologically complex language (Holes, 2004). With more than 380 million people whose mother tongue is Arabic, it is the fifth most widely spoken language. Modern Standard Arabic (MSA) is the lingua franca amongst Arabic native speakers, and is used in formal communications, such as newspaper, official speeches, and news broadcasts. However, MSA is rarely used in day to day communication. Nearly all the Arabic speakers use dialectal Arabic (DA) in everyday communication (Cotterell et al., 2014). DA may differ from MSA in morphology and phonology (Habash et al., 2012). These dialects may differ also in vocabulary and spelling from MSA and most do not have standard spellings. There is often large lexical overlap between dialects and MSA. Performing proper Arabic dialect identification may positively impact many Natural Language Processing (NLP) application. For example, transcribing dialectal speech or automatically translating into a particular dialect would be aided by the use of targeted language models that are trained on texts in that dialect. This has led to recent interest in the automatic collection large dialectal corpora and the identification of different Arabic dialects (Al-Mannai et al., 2014; Elfardy et al., 2013; Cotterell et al., 2014; Zaidan et al., 2014).

There are many varieties of dialectal Arabic distributed over the 22 countries in the Arabic world. There are often several variants of a dialect within the same country. There is also the difference between Bedouin and Sedentary speech, which runs across all Arabic countries. However, in natural language processing, researchers have merged dialectal Arabic into five regional language groups, namely: Egyptian, Maghrebi, Gulf (Arabian Peninsula), Iraqi, and Levantine (Cotterell et al., 2014; Al-Sabbagh and Girju, 2012).

In this paper, we use geographical information in user Twitter profiles to collect a dialectal corpus for different Arab countries. The contributions of this paper are:

1. We show that we can use Twitter as a source for collecting dialectal corpra for specific Arab countries with reasonable accuracy.

2. We show that most Arabic dialectal words are used in more than one country, and cannot be used separately to collect a dialectal corpus per country.

The paper is organized as follows: Section 2 surveys pervious work on dialect classification; Section 3 describes dialectal Arabic and some of the possible ways to breakdown Arabic dialects; section 4 describes how tweets are collected and classified; section 4 shows how to extract dialectal words and shows that many of them are used in more than one country; Section 5 describes our evaluation approach and reports on evaluation results; and Section 6 contains conclusion and future work.

Proceedings of the EMNLP 2014 Workshop on Arabic Natural Langauge Processing (ANLP), pages 1–7,
October 25, 2014, Doha, Qatar.

2 Previous Work

Previous work on Arabic dialect identification uses n-gram based features at both word-level and character-level to identify dialectal sentences (Elfardy et al., 2013; Cotterell et al., 2014; Zaidan et al., 2011; Zaidan et al., 2014). Zaidan et al. (2011) created a dataset of dialectal Arabic. They performed cross-validation experiments for dialect identification using word n-gram based features. Elfardy et al. (2013) built a system to distinguish between Egyptian and MSA. They used word n-gram features combined with core (token-based and perplexity-based features) and meta features for training. Their system showed a 5% improvement over the system of Zaidan and Callison-Burch (2011). Later, Zaidan et al. (2014) used several word n-gram based and character n-gram based features for dialect identification. The system trained on word unigram-based feature performed the best with character five-gram-based feature being second best. A similar result is shown by Cotterell et al. (2014) where word unigram model performs the best. Recent work by Darwish et al. (2014) indicates that using a dialectal word list to identify dialectal Egyptian tweets is better than training on one of the existing dialect corpora.

All of the previous work except Cotterell et al. (2014)[1] evaluated their systems using cross-validation. These models heavily rely on the coverage of training data to achieve better identification. This limits the robustness of identification to genres inline with the training data. In this paper, we exploit geographic information supplied by users to properly identify the dialect of tweets.

There is also increasing interest in the literature to geotag tweets due to its importance for some applications such as event detection, local search, news recommendation and targeted advertising. For example, Mahmud et el. (2012) (Mahmud et al., 2012) presented a new algoritm for inferring home locations of Twitter users by collecting tweets from the top 100 US cities using the geo-tag filter option of Twitter and latitude and longitude for each city using Googles geo-coding API. Bo Han et al. (2014) (Han et al., 2014) presented an integrated geolocation prediction framework and investigated what factors impact on prediction accuracy. They exploited the tweets and profile information of a given user to infer their primary city-level location.

3 Dialectal Arabic (DA)

DA refers to the spoken language used for daily communication in Arab countries. There are considerable geographical distinctions between DAs within countries, across country borders, and even between cities and villages as shown in Figure 1. According to Ethnologue (http://www.ethnologue.com/browse/names), there are 34 variations of spoken Arabic or dialects in Arabic countries in addition to the Modern Standard Arabic (MSA).

Some recent works (Zbib et al., 2012; Cotterell et al., 2014) are based on a coarser classification of Arabic dialects into five groups namely: Egyptian (EGY), Gulf (GLF), Maghrebi (MGR), Levantine (LEV), and Iraqi (IRQ). Other dialects are classified as OTHER.

Zaidan and Callison-Burch (2014) mentioned that this is one possible breakdown but it is relatively coarse and can be further divided into more dialect groups, especially in large regions such as Maghreb. The goal of this paper is to collect a large, clean corpus for each country and study empirically if some of these dialects can be merged together.

We found that there are very few dialectal words that are used in a country and not used in any other country. For example, we took the most frequent Egyptian dialectal words in the Arabic Online Commentary Dataset (AOCD) described in Zaidan and Callison-Burch (2014) according to what they call the dialectness factor, which is akin to mutual information. The AOCD contains comments from newspapers from dialect groups and these comments were classified into different dialects using crowd souring. We examined whether they appear in different dialects or not. As shown in Table 1, most Egyptian dialectal words are being used in different dialects.

With this finding, we realized that unique dialectal words for each country are not common in the sense that they are few and in the sense that relying on them to filter tweets would likely yield a small number of tweets. Thus, we opted not to use such

[1]Zaidan et al. (2014) applied their classifier to a different genre but did not evaluate it's performance.

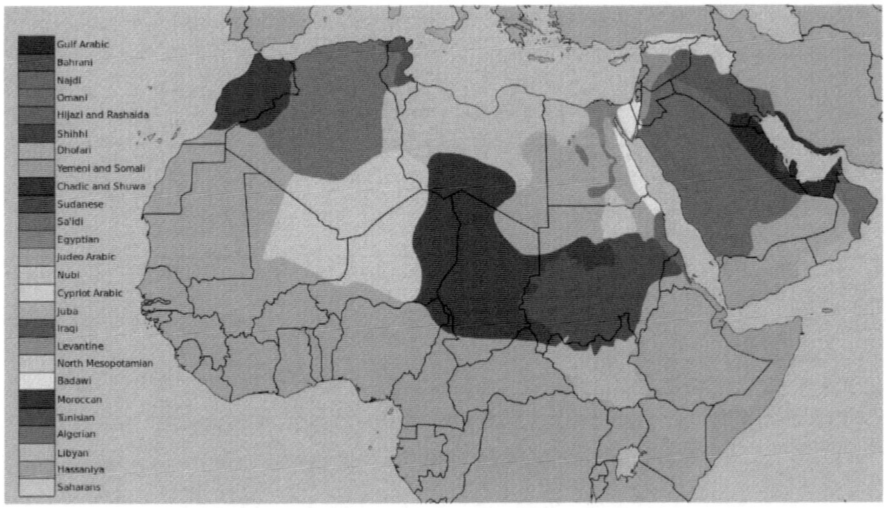

Figure 1: Different Arabic Dialects in the Arab World (`http://en.wikipedia.org/wiki/Arabic_dialects`)

Word	Word in Tweet	Dialect
دي (dy)	الشمس الايامات دي شغالة اوفر تايم عديل كده	Sudan
ده (dh)	كلام كتير داير تقوله لكن بيقيف في طرف لسانك! ده الطبيعي بتاعي	Sudan
عشان (E$An)	انخلقنا عشان نبني لنا مكان في الجنة هذي هي الخلاصة	Gulf
تاني (tAny)	وبعدين ماحكا شي تاني هيك اظن	Levantine

Table 1: Egyptian dialectal Words in other Dialects. We use Buckwalter transliteration in this paper

words to extract tweets for each dialect. From the AOCD, we extracted all unique uni-grams, bigrams, and trigrams, and counted the occurrence of these n-grams from the comments that were marked to belong to different dialects and also in a large MSA corpus composed of 10 years worth of Aljazeera articles, containing 114M tokens [2]. We retained the n-grams that appeared at least 3 or more times in either the dialectal comments. In all, we extracted roughly 45,000 n-grams. The n-grams were manually judged as dialectal or not, and also to which dialect they are most commonly used in. The judgments were performed by one person who is a native Arabic speaker with good exposure to different dialects.

Table 2 lists some words along with their frequencies and to which dialect (or MSA) they belong. Since MSA words compose more than 50% of the words in dialectal text, it is not surprising that words that appear frequently in the corpora of different dialects are indeed MSA. Further, we found that Aljazeera articles contain many dialectal words. Upon further investigation, we found the articles contain transcripts of interviews, where often times the interviewees used dialects, and quotes within articles, where the quoted persons used dialectal utterances. We also found that this was not unique to Aljazeera articles.

When we examined the Arabic GigaWord corpus [3], which is a commonly used MSA corpus, we found that it contains many dialectal words as well. For example, the word كده (kdh) is mentioned 2,574 times and the word علشان (El$An) is mentioned 974 times). This was the main motivating factor for manually judging n-grams as dialectal or not. Of the n-grams we manually tagged, approximately 2,500

[2]`http://aljazeera.net`

[3]`https://catalog.ldc.upenn.edu/LDC2011T11`

Word	EGY	LEV	GLF	IRQ	MGR	MSA	Classification
دي (dy)	541	1	3	0	7	98	EGY
ليه (lyh)	380	23	73	0	22	3734	EGY
ليش (ly$)	28	218	193	18	12	6118	LEV
هيك (hyk)	20	348	9	0	2	4891	LEV
ايش (Ay$)	10	53	87	2	2	87	GLF
يبي (yby)	1	3	99	1	2	21	GLF
شنو ($nw)	0	1	5	5	1	850	IRQ
اكو (Akw)	1	0	1	4	0	0	IRQ
واش (wA$)	2	8	32	5	477	0	MGR
كيما (kymA)	4	3	3	0	246	0	MGR
حاجة (HAjp)	317	8	10	0	120	24468	MSA
صار (SAr)	24	153	79	3	16	12348	MSA

Table 2: Dialectal Words Frequencies in AOCD and MSA (Aljazeera)

were dialectal. We assumed that if a sentence contained one of these n-grams, then the sentence is dialectal. This assumption is consistent with recent published work by Darwish et al. (2014). The distribution of these dialectal n-grams was: 54% unigrams like مش (m$), 39% bigrams like هم دول (hm dwl), and 7% trigrams such as ما أنا عارف (mA >nA EArf). We plan to make the list of dialectal n-grams available to the research community.

Based on interaction with people at Twitter, the estimated number of Arabic microblogs on Twitter is in excess of 15 million per day. The ubiquity of Arabic tweets has been one of the strongest motivations for us to investigate the building of an Arabic dialectal corpus from tweets. Also, tweets are more similar to verbal utterances than formal text, which may be helpful in building language models that are better suited for dialectal Arabic speech recognition.

4 Collecting and Classifying Tweets

4.1 Tweets Collection

We collected 175 M Arabic tweets in March 2014 (5.6M tweets per day) by issuing the query lang:ar against Twitter API [4]. Each tweet has a user ID, and following this ID we can extract the following information from users profile: user name, user time zone, and **user location**. The user location has the user declared geographical location. This could be in the form of a city name, country name, landmark name, country nickname, etc. Such information is available for roughly 70% of tweets. Precise geotagging of tweets, namely latitude and longitude, was available for a very small percentage of tweets. Further, due to the fact that some countries, particularly in the Gulf region, have large expat communities, geo-tagging of tweets only indicate where the tweet is authored but cannot reliably indicate the dialect. By retaining tweets where the user declared a location, we were left with 123M tweets, i.e. 70% of the tweets.

4.2 Tweet Normalization

Tweets and user locations were normalized and cleaned in the manner described in Darwish et al. (2012) by mapping frequent non-Arabic characters and decoration to their mappings, handling repeated characters, etc. Below in an example that shows a tweet before and after normalization:

[4] `http://dev.twitter.com`

Before: مبرووووووك يا باشا mbrwwwwwwk yA bA$A.
After: مبروك يا باشا mbrwk yA bA$A.
Translation: Congratulations sir.

4.3 User Locations

By looking at user locations, we found that the top unique 10K user locations cover 92M tweets. This is approximately 75% of tweets that have user locations. We used the GeoNames [5] geographical database, which contains eight million place names for each country, to initially assign a user location to one of the Arab countries.

GeoNames has many places without Arabic transliteration, and also users write their locations in Arabic or English, in full or abbreviated forms, and using formal or informal writings. Thus, we manually revised mapping that matched in GeoNames and attempted to map non-matching ones to countries. Examples of such mappings are shown in Table 3.

There were some cases where we could not map a user location to a single Arab country because it is not unique to a particular Arab country or it is not indicative of any country. Such examples include: الوطن العربي الكبير "Great Arab Homeland," الجزيرة العربية "Arabian Peninsula," or الشرقية "the Eastern." In all, approximately 3,500 user locations were mapped to specific countries and the remaining were not. By excluding tweets with non-deterministic user locations, we were left with 62M tweets that have deterministic mappings between user locations and Arab countries. We plan to make the manually reviewed list of user locations publicly available.

4.4 Filtering on Dialectal Words

We used the aforementioned list of dialectal n-grams that we manually extracted to filter the tweets, by retaining those that contain at least one of the n-grams. By doing so, we extracted 6.5M tweets (i.e. 3.7% of the original tweets). Their by-country breakdown is as follows: 3.99M (61%) from Saudi Arabia (SA), 880K (13%) from Egypt (EG), 707K (11%) from Kuwait (KW), 302K (5%) from United Arab Emirates (AE), 65k (2%) from Qatar (QA), and the remaining (8%) from other countries such as Morocco and Sudan. The distribution of tweets per-country is shown in Figure 2.

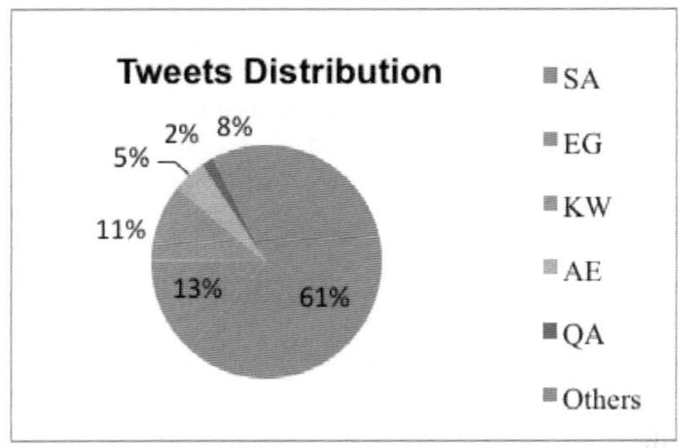

Figure 2: Dialectal Tweets Distribution

5 Evaluation of Dialectal Tweets

To evaluate the accuracy of tweets belonging to the dialect commonly spoken in the different countries that they were assigned to, we randomly extracted 100 tweets per dialect to be manually tagged for dialect.

We used CrowdFlower crowd-sourcing website [6] to evaluate the dialects of tweets. We asked people from the countries associated with each of the associated tweet to judge whether the tweets indeed match the dialect in their country or not. We asked for 3 judgments per tweet. We utilized 20 challenge questions to verify that the judges were doing a good job. We were able to get a sufficient number of judges to finish task for some countries but not all. For example, we were not able to find judges from Qatar and Bahrain. Table 4 lists the accuracy of classification using dialectal words filter and user location.

Errors occurred because some words are mostly used in dialects but less frequently used in MSA

[5] http://www.geonames.org/

[6] http://www.crowdflower.com/

User Location in Profile	Country
الرياض (AlryAD), Riyadh, Saudi Arabia, KSA, الحجاز (AlHjAz)	Saudi Arabia
الكويت (Alkwyt), Q8, kwt, الجهراء AljhrA, كويت العز kwyt AlEz	Kuwait
Egypt, مصر (mSr), Cairo, Alex, أم الدنيا >m AldnyA, جيزة jyzp	Egypt

Table 3: Mapping User Location to Arab Countries

(like تطلع (tTlE)), and the second reason is sometimes a user profile has user location that was mapped to an Arab country, but the user writes tweets using another dialect that is different than one for the stated country.

Examples of tweets that were tagged as Egyptian correctly and incorrectly are shown in table 5.

Dialect	Accuracy
Saudi	95%
Egyptian	94%
Iraqi	82%
Lebanese	75%
Syrian	66%
Algerian	60%

Table 4: Per country classification accuracy

6 Conclusion

Twitter can be used to collect dialectal tweets for each Arab country with high accuracy for some countries and average accuracy for other countries using the geographical information associated with Twitter user profiles. We were able to find dialectal tweets belonging to different dialects with good accuracy by identifying tweets where users used dialectal word n-grams and declared their user locations to belong to particular countries. We tabulated a list of roughly 2,500 dialectal n-grams and 3,500 countries/user locations pairs that we used for identification. We plan to release them publicly. Also, we showed that cross-dialect dialectal words overlap is common, which adds to the complexity of identifying tweets that belong to specific dialects. Thus, using geographical information can greatly enhance dialect identification.

For future work, we plan to analyze the correctness of users' claims on their locations by different methods like tweet geographical information (latitude and longitude), collecting dialectal words for each country, etc. Also, we plan to empirically reexamine the dialect conflation schemes that are commonly used in the literature. Existing schemes for example tend to conflate dialects of all Gulf countries, include Saudi Arabia, Kuwait, Bahrain, Qatar, United Arab Emirates, and Oman. We believe that the dialect spoken in the Western part of Saudi Arabia is sufficiently different from that in Kuwait for example. We would like to study the overlap between dialects spoken in different countries to ascertain dialects of which countries can be safely conflated.

References

Kamla Al-Mannai, Hassan Sajjad, Alaa Khader, Fahad Al Obaidli, Preslav Nakov and Stephan Vogel. 2014. Unsupervised Word Segmentation Improves Dialectal Arabic to English Machine Translation. Arabic Natural Language Processing Workshop, EMNLP-2014.

R. Al-Sabbagh and R. Girju. 2012. YADAC: Yet another Dialectal Arabic Corpus. In LREC. pp. 28822889.

Leo Breiman. 2001. Random Forests. Machine Learning. 45(1):5-32.

Ryan Cotterell and Chris Callison-Burch. 2014. A Multi-Dialect, Multi-Genre Corpus of Informal Written Arabic. LREC-2014, pages 241–245.

Kareem Darwish, Walid Magdy, Ahmed Mourad. 2012. Language Processing for Arabic Microblog Retrieval. CIKM-2012, pages 2427–2430.

Kareem Darwish, Hassan Sajjad, Hamdy Mubarak. 2014. Verifiably Effective Arabic Dialect Identification. EMNLP-2014.

Heba Elfardy, Mona Diab. 2013. Sentence Level Dialect Identification in Arabic. ACL-2013, pages 456–461.

Habash, Nizar, Ramy Eskander, and Abdelati Hawwari. 2012. A morphological analyzer for Egyptian Arabic. Proceedings of the Twelfth Meeting of the Special Interest Group on Computational Morphology and Phonology, Association for Computational Linguistics, 2012.

Tweet	User Location	Is EGY?
الّي ماعاش حياته ايام المدرسه ده فاته نص عمره	Cairo Egypt	Yes
احساس صعب اوي لما يكون معاك دقايق مجانيه وموش لاقي حد تكلمه :(	Masr	Yes
من ادرك ركعة من الصبح قبل ان تطلع الشمس	Alex	No (MSA)
انا عارف فيه ناس كتير عايزة تعرف المعاد بس مكسوفة	Egyptian	Yes
محرك الستة اسطوانات مايقدرش ايدير قوة حصانية زي محرك الثمانية	cairo	No (MGR)

Table 5: Examples of Collected Egyptian Tweets

Han, Bo, Paul Cook, and Timothy Baldwin. 2014. Text-Based Twitter User Geolocation Prediction. Journal Artificial Intelligence Res.(JAIR) 49 (2014): 451-500.

Clive Holes. 2004 Modern Arabic: Structures, functions, and varieties. Georgetown University Press, 2004.

Mahmud, Jalal, Jeffrey Nichols, and Clemens Drews. 2012. Where Is This Tweet From? Inferring Home Locations of Twitter Users. ICWSM. 2012.

Omar F. Zaidan, Chris Callison-Burch. 2011. The Arabic Online Commentary Dataset: An Annotated Dataset of Informal Arabic with High Dialectal Content. ACL-11, pages 37–41.

Omar F. Zaidan, Chris Callison-Burch. 2014. Arabic Dialect Identification. CL-11, 52(1).

Rabih Zbib, Erika Malchiodi, Jacob Devlin, David Stallard, Spyros Matsoukas, Richard Schwartz, John Makhoul, Omar F. Zaidan, Chris Callison-Burch. 2012. Machine translation of Arabic dialects. NAACL-2012, pages 49–59.

The International Corpus of Arabic: Compilation, Analysis and Evaluation

Sameh Alansary
Bibliotheca Alexandrina, P.O. Box 138, 21526, El Shatby, Alexandria, Egypt.
Department of Phonetics and Linguistics, Faculty of Arts, Alexandria University , El Shatby, Alexandria, Egypt.
Sameh.alansary@bibalex.org

Magdy Nagi
Bibliotheca Alexandrina, P.O. Box 138, 21526, El Shatby, Alexandria, Egypt.
Computer and System Engineering Dept. Faculty of Engineering, Alexandria University, Alexandria Egypt.
Magdy.nagi@bibalex.org

Abstract

This paper focuses on a project for building the first International Corpus of Arabic (ICA). It is planned to contain 100 million analyzed tokens with an interface which allows users to interact with the corpus data in a number of ways [ICA website]. ICA is a representative corpus of Arabic that has been initiated in 2006, it is intended to cover the Modern Standard Arabic (MSA) language as being used all over the Arab world. ICA has been analyzed by Bibliotheca Alexandrina Morphological Analysis Enhancer (BAMAE). BAMAE is based on Buckwalter Arabic Morphological Analyzer (BAMA). Precision and Recall are the evaluation measures used to evaluate the BAMAE system. At this point, Precision measurement ranges from 95%-92% while recall measurement was 92%-89%. This depends on the number of qualifiers retrieved for every word. The percentages are expected to rise by implementing the improvements while working on larger amounts of data.

1. Introduction

Arabic is the largest member of the Semitic language family, most closely related to Aramaic, Hebrew, Ugaritic and Phoenician. Arabic is one of the six official languages of the United Nations[1] and it is the main language of most of the Middle East countries. Arabic ranks fifth in the world's league table of languages, with an estimated 206 million native speakers, 24 million as 2nd language speakers to add up to total of 233 million and World Almanac estimates the total speakers as 255 million. Arabic language is the official language in all Arab nations as Egypt, Saudi Arabia and Algeria. Moreover, it is also an official language in non-Arab countries as Israel, Chad and Eritrea. It is also spoken as a 2nd language in other non-Arab countries as Mali and Turkey[2].

The formal Arabic language, known as Classical Arabic is the language in which the Qur'an is written and is considered to be the base of the syntactic and grammatical norms of the Arabic language. However, today it is considered more of a written language than a spoken one. Modern Standard Arabic (MSA) is similar to Classical Arabic, but it is an easier form. It is understood across the Arab world and it is used by television presenters and politicians, it is the form used to teach Arabic as a foreign language. There are different MSA varieties as the rate of similarity between every Arab country version of MSA and Classical Arabic differs. This is one of the issues that this paper will present.

Due to the fact that the need for Arabic corpus is increasing as well as the fact that the trials to build an Arabic corpus in the last few years were not enough to consider that the Arabic language has a real, representative and reliable corpus, it was necessary to build such an Arabic corpus that is capable of supporting various linguistic research in Arabic. Thus, ICA was inspired by the difficulties that encountered Arabic Language researches as a result of the lack of publicly available Arabic corpora.

Bibliotheca Alexandrina (BA) has initiated a big project to build the "International Corpus of Arabic (ICA)", a real trial to build a representative Arabic corpus as being used all over the Arab world to support research in Arabic. The International Corpus of Arabic is planned to contain 100 million words. The collection of samples is limited to written Modern Standard Arabic, selected from a wide range of sources and designed to represent a wide cross-section of Arabic; it is stimulating the first systematic investi-

[1] http://www.un.org/en/aboutun/languages.shtml

[2] http://www.vistawide.com/languages/top_30_languages.htm

Proceedings of the EMNLP 2014 Workshop on Arabic Natural Langauge Processing (ANLP), pages 8–17,
October 25, 2014, Doha, Qatar. ©2014 Association for Computational Linguistics

gation of the national varieties as being used all over the Arab world (Alansary, et al. 2007).

There were some trials for building Arabic corpora. Some of them were annotated corpora and others were raw texts corpora. Annotated corpora trails as Penn Arabic Treebank (PATB). The LDC was sponsored to develop an Arabic POS and Treebank of only 1,000,000 words. This corpus doesn't contain any branched genres except 600 stories from the ANNAHAR News Agency. The POS only annotated version of this ANNAHAR corpus was released in 2004[3]. The output from Buckwalter's Arabic Morphological Analyzer is used as the starting point for the morphological annotation and POS tagging of Arabic newswire text (Maamouri M., 2004). Arabic Gigaword Corpus is an archive of newswire text data that depends on press only; it has been compiled from Arabic news sources by LDC[4]. The data coverage is limited, it was compiled from Egypt, Lebanon, Tunisia, Saudi Arabia and from outside the Arab world such as England. NEMLAR Annotated Written Corpus consists of about only 500, 000 words of Arabic text from 13 different categories, aiming to achieve a well-balanced corpus that offers a representation of the variety in syntactic, semantic and pragmatic features of modern Arabic language[5]. The accuracy of the automatic analysis is around 95% (Atiyya M. et al, 2005). Its analysis features are limited, moreover its use is restricted; it is not accessible for commercial use[6]. KALIMAT is a free multipurpose Arabic corpus, consists of 18,167,183 annotated words representing 20,291 Arabic articles collected only from the Omani newspaper Alwatan. A morphological analysis process on the data collection using AL Khalil[7] morphological analyser was conducted to reach an accuracy of 96% (El-Haj M., 2013). Prague Arabic Dependency Treebank (PADT) version 1.0 distribution comprises over 113,500 tokens of data annotated analytically and provided with the disambiguating morphological information. In addition, the release includes complete annotations of MorphoTrees resulting in more than 148,000 tokens, 49,000 of which have received the analytical processing[8].

The raw text corpora trails as (KACST) King Abdul-Aziz City for Science and Technology Corpus[9] contains 732,780,509 words representing 869,800 text files and 7,464,396 distinct words. It contains a lot of classical Arabic texts; however, it is neither analyzed nor well planned. ArabiCorpus[10] is a corpus that was developed by Dilworth Parkinson. It is a large corpus that could be accessed, but it is not analyzed. Words can be searched for in Arabic or Latin script. The website provides detailed instructions on the search. It contains 173,600,000 words in five main categories or genres: Newspapers, Modern Literature, Nonfiction, Egyptian Colloquial, and Premodern.

In what follows, Section 2 reviews the ICA data design, how it is compiled, discuss the copyrights issue and what is the current ICA statistics. Section 3 describes the analysis stage of ICA, the tool that is used in the analysis, why was it chosen followed by ICA evaluation and a comparison with another morphological disambiguator. Section 4 gives a brief review on the ICA website for the researchers to query its data. Conclusions and suggestions for further work are given in section 5.

2. ICA Design & Compilation Stage

The ICA is similar to the International Corpus of English (ICE) in terms of concept rather than in design. They are similar in trying to include the varieties of the language; the Modern Standard Arabic (MSA) includes publications from every Arab country that uses Arabic as official language and it has been decided to include Arabic publications from outside the Arab nations. However, they are different in terms of corpus design criteria and data compilation. For example, on the one hand, Egyptian Modern Standard Arabic is the most widespread variety that is used to represent MSA in ICA corpus. On the other hand, in building ICE[11] a fixed size from each variation was taken from any country that uses English as official language (one million words); however, balance in size does not always mean fixing a number of words for each variation as will be clarified in the next section.

[3] https://catalog.ldc.upenn.edu/LDC2005T20
[4] https://catalog.ldc.upenn.edu/LDC2003T12
[5] http://catalog.elra.info/product_info.php?products_id=873
[6] http://catalog.elra.info/product_info.php?products_id=873
[7] http://alkhalil-morpho-sys.soft112.com/
[8] https://catalog.ldc.upenn.edu/LDC2004T23
[9] http://www.kacstac.org.sa/Pages/default.aspx
[10] http://arabicorpus.byu.edu/search.php
[11] http://ice-corpora.net/ICE/INDEX.HTM

It is important to realize that the creation of ICA is a "cyclical" process, requiring constant reevaluation during the corpus compilation. Consequently, we are willing to change our initial corpus design if there are any circumstances would arise that requires such changes.

2.1 ICA Design

ICA genre design relied on Dewey decimal classification of documents; however, this has been further classified to suit clear genre distinction rather than classifications for libraries. For example, Dewey decimal classification combines history and geography in one classification, while in ICA they are separated into two sub genres related to humanities genre. It has been designed to reflect a more or less real picture of how Arabic language exists in every field and in every country rather than relying on a theoretical image.

ICA is designed to include 11 genres, namely; Strategic Sciences, Social Sciences, Sports, Religion, Literature, Humanities, Natural Sciences, Applied Sciences, Art, Biography and Miscellaneous which are further classified into 24 subgenres, namely; Politics, Law, Economy, Sociology, Islamic, Pros etc. Moreover, there are 4 sub-sub-genres, namely; Novels, Short Stories, Child Stories and plays. As shown in Figure 1.

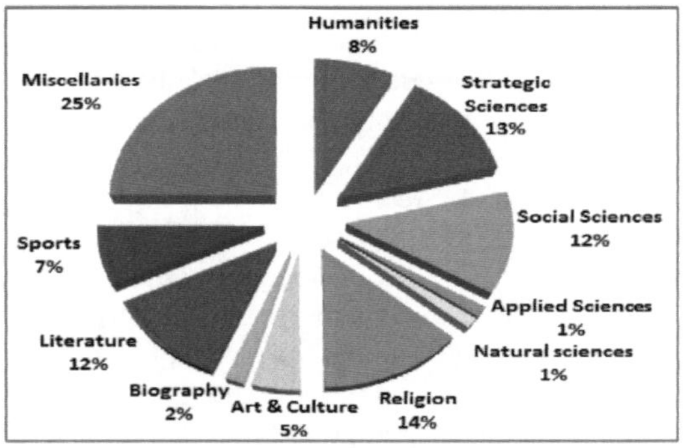

"Figure 1: ICA Genres"

Planning of ICA data collection is based on some criteria related to corpus design such as representativeness, diversity, balance and size that were taken into the consideration. In collecting a corpus that represents the Arabic Language, the main focus was to cover the same genres from different sources and from all around the Arab nations. However, we decided to add Arabic data that belongs to the Arabic language even if they had been published outside as al-Hayat magazine which is published in London[12].

Size criterion in the corpus design focuses on the number of words. However, issues of size are also related to the number of texts from different genres, the number of samples from each text, and the number of words in each sample. Such decisions were taken based on how common the genre or the source is. Balance in a corpus has not been addressed by having equal amounts of texts from different sources or genres. It has been addressed by the factual distribution of the language real use. For example, Literature genre represents 12% and biography genre represents 2% from the corpus data distribution.

2.2 Text Compilation and Categorization

The International Corpus of Arabic has been compiled manually, and that enabled the corpus compilers to select all and only the MSA data rather than the colloquial Arabic data. Also, the ICA text categorization has been done manually according to the topic of the text and the distinct semantic features for each genre. These features keep the ICA data categorization objective rather than being subjective; depending on the compiler intuition. Accordingly, ICA texts can be considered as a good training data for text categorization system. ICA is planned to contain 100 million words. However, currently it is still around 80 million words.

ICA data is composed of Modern Standard Arabic (MSA) written texts. There are different resources for compiling the data. It has been decided to compile all available Arabic data written in MSA. ICA will be composed of four sources, namely; 1. Press source which is divided into three sub-sources, namely; (a) Newspapers, (b) Magazines which had been compiled from the official magazines along with newspapers that are written in MSA such as Al Ahram from Egypt, Addstour from Jordan, Al Hayat from Lebanon … etc. finally the publications that have a printed copy as well as a soft electronic copy through world wide web such as (http://www.ahram.org.eg/), and (c) Electronic Press which had been compiled from magazines and newspapers that are written in MSA and have only soft electronic copy through world wide web. (2) Net articles which were compiled from forums and blogs that are also written in MSA. (3) Books which had been compiled from

[12] http://alhayat.com/AboutWebsite

all available books that are written in MSA and have a soft copy. (4) Academics which had been compiled from the scientific papers, researchers thesis, PhDs etc..

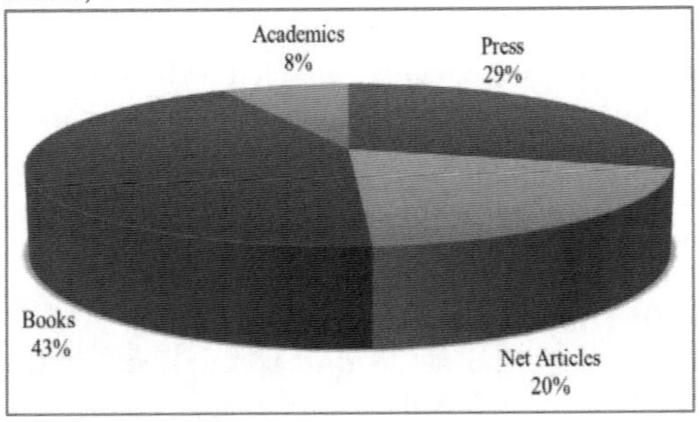

"Figure 2: ICA Sources"

2.3 Metadata

Each compiled text has its own text encoding. This coding process for the text file names will customize the search scope at which level of the corpus this file belongs. For example, the following filename coding [AH10-A1.1.1_140207] can be clarified as shown in Table1:

AH10	AH: Indicate the source of the text which is Ahram newspaper. 10: This attached number that indicates that this file is the 10th article in that newspaper with the same genre, subgenre and date.
A1.1.1	Contains three pieces of information: Newspaper source (A1), Strategic science "genre" (A1.1) and Politics "sub-genre" (A1.1.1).
140207	Contains three pieces of issuing information: The day (14), the month (02) and the year (2007).

"Table 1: An example of filenames coding"

ICA Metadata covers the needed information related to Corpus for each compiled text as data source providers, Text code name, Text size, Website, date of publishing, publisher (name and country), writer (name, gender, age, nationality and educational level) and Collection/Annotation Specifications.

2.4 Copyrights

One of the serious constraints on developing large corpora and their widespread use is national and international copyright legalizations. According to copyright laws, it is necessary and sensible to protect the authors as well as the publishers rights of the texts that they had produced. ICA data Copy rights and publishing issues are in progress by Bibliotheca Alexandrina Legal Affairs. For that reason, the ICA data is not available to be downloaded but the researchers can search the ICA data via the ICA website[13].

2.5 ICA statistics

Corpus analysis is both qualitative and quantitative. One of the advantages of corpora is that they can readily provide quantitative data which intuitions cannot provide reliably. The use of quantification in corpus linguistics typically goes well beyond simple counting.

Table 2 shows some of the numbers of ICA data coverage. It must be noted that total number of "Tokens" refers to all word forms except numbers, foreign words and punctuations to reflect the real size of the used word forms before the analysis stage. Coverage interval starts from 1993 up to 2014; however, there is a compilation problems as result of the data availability since the size of the data was not equal throughout the years. Balance is considered as an issue for the ICA current situation. It deals with the coverage of texts over the years rather than balance according to time span and that will remain as issue in the future.

Statistics	Total Number
No. of texts	70,022
No. of words	79,569,384
No. of Tokens	76,199,414
No. of unique words	1,272,766
No. of ICA sources	4
No. of sub sources	3
No. of genres	11
No. of sub genres	24
No. of sub sub-genres	4
No. of countries	20
No. of covered years	22
No. of writers	1021

"Table 2 : Shows qualitative linguistic analysis for ICA statistics"

[13]http://www.bibalex.org/ica/ar/

3. ICA Analysis stage

The first stage of linguistic analysis of the International corpus of Arabic is to analyze the 100 million words morphologically.

The stem-based approach "concatenative approach" has been adopted as the linguistic approach. There are many morphological analyzers for Arabic; some of them are available for research and evaluation while the rest are proprietary commercial applications. Buckwalter Arabic Morphological Analyzer (Buckwalter, 2004) is a well-known analyzer in the field`s literature and has even been considered as the "most respected lexical resource of its kind" (Hajič et al, 2005). It is used in LDC Arabic POS-tagger, Penn Arabic Dependency Treebank, and the Prague Arabic Dependency Treebank. It is designed to consist of a main database of word forms that interact with other concatenation databases. Every word form is entered separately, and the stem is used as the base form. The word is viewed as to be composed of a basic unit that can be combined with morphemes governed by morph tactic rules. It makes use of three lexicons: a Prefixes lexicon, a Stem lexicon, and a Suffixes lexicon.

Buckwalter Arabic Morphological Analyzer (BAMA) has been selected since it was the most suitable lexical resource to our approach. (Alansary, et al. 2008).

Although it has many advantages including its ability to provide a lot of information such as Lemma, Vocalization, Part of Speech (POS), Gloss, Prefix(s), Stem, Word class, Suffix(s), Number, Gender, Definiteness and Case or Mood, it does not always provide all the information that the ICA requires, and in some cases, the provided analyses would need some modification. Its results may give the right solution for the Arabic input word, provide more than one result that needs to be disambiguated to reach the best solution, provide many solutions but none of them is right, segment the input words wrongly without taking the segmentation rules in consideration or provide no solutions. Consequently, solutions enhancement is needed in these situations.

Number, gender and definiteness need to be modified according to their morphosyntactic properties. Some tags had been added to Buckwalter's analyzer lexicon, some lemmas, glossaries had been modified and others had been added. In addition, new analysis and qualifiers had been added as root, stem pattern and name entities. (Alansary, et al. 2008)

Due to all these modifications, there are some clear differences between the tool adopted by ICA and BAMA 2.0 as:

- There are 44,756 distinct lemmas in ICA lexicon while they are 40,654 in BAMA 2.0.
- The root feature has been added to ICA lexicon representing 3,451 distinct roots, the pattern feature has been added to ICA lexicon representing 782 distinct stem patterns and they will be increased to cover all Arabic roots.
- There are 191 distinct tags in ICA while they are 167 in BAMA 2.0. Table 3 shows some tags that have been added to ICA lexicon that are not found in BAMA:

Tag	Description
NOUN(ADV_M)	Adverb of Manner
NOUN(ADV_T)	Adverb of Time
NOUN(ADV_P)	Adverb of Place
NOUN(VERBAL)	Verbal noun
NOUN_PROP(ADV_T)	Proper nouns that refer to adverb of time
NOUN(INTERJ)	The vocative nouns

"Table 3: Added Tags in ICA lexicon"

- Table 4 shows some tags that are added to prefixes and suffixes:

Sample of Added Prefixes and suffixes	
CV_SUBJ:2FP	Prefixes
CV_SUBJ:2FS	
CV_SUBJ:2MP	
CV_SUBJ:2MS	
wa/PREP	
la/PREP	
>a/INTERROG_PART	
hAt/NSUFF	Suffixes
NSUFF_SUBJ:2MS	
CVSUFF_SUBJ:2MD	
CVSUFF_SUBJ:2FP	
CVSUFF_DO:3FS	
CVSUFF_DO:3FS	

"Table 4: Sample of added prefixes and suffixes."

Moreover, new features have been added in number as well as in definiteness qualifiers as the plural broken (PL_BR) and the EDAFAH features.

These modifications and other new features were used in disambiguating two million words to be used as a training data extracted from the

ICA corpus to represent a sample of Arabic texts. After disambiguating the training date, some linguistic rules had been extracted, depending on the contexts, to help in the automatic disambiguation process of Bibliotheca Alexandrina Morphological Analysis Enhancer (BAMAE) as will be discusses in the next section.

After solving the BAMA's problems and disambiguating the data according to its context, the BAMA enhanced output along with the training data will be ready to be used in the next phase of analysis.

In the ICA, There are 5 tag sets categories of the stem which are divided into 26 tag types:

1. Verbal category: it contains 5 tag types; Command Verb, Imperfect Verb, Imperfect Passive Verb, Past Verb and Past Passive Verb.
2. Nominal category: it contains 9 tag types; Adjective, Noun, Adverb of Manner, Adverb of Place, Adverb of Time, Verbal Noun, Proper Noun, Proper Noun (Adverb of Time) and Proper Noun (Interjection).
3. Pronouns category: it contains 3 tag types; Demonstrative Pronoun, Pronoun and Relative Pronoun.
4. Particles category: it contains 7 tags; Focus Particle, Future Particle, Interrogative Particle, Negative Particle, Particle, Verbal Particle and Exception Particle.
5. Conjunctions category: it contains 2 tags; Conjunctions and Sub Conjunctions.

In addition, there are 2 tags that are not divided into any types; Preposition and Interjection tags.

Some words were found to have no solution for one of three reasons. First, some words are not analyzed altogether by BAMA; second, some words are analyzed, but none of the provided solutions is suitable to their contexts in the text; third, some words are wrongly segmented by BAMA. Consequently, 15,605 words have been analyzed manually in the same manner they would have been analyzed automatically.

3.1 Bibliotheca Alexandrina Morphological Analysis Enhancer (BAMAE)

It is a system that has been built to morphologically analyze and disambiguate the Arabic texts depending on BAMA's enhanced output of the ICA. It was preferred to use BAMA's enhanced output of the ICA since it contains more information than any other system of BAMA's output. This is the reason that made the members of the ICA team aim to build their own morphological disambiguator (BAMAE).

In order to reach the best solution for the input word, BAMAE preforms automatic disambiguation process carried on three levels that depends primarily on the basic POS information (Prefix(s), Stem, Tag and Suffixes) that is obtained from the enhanced BAMA's output. (Alansary, 2012):

- Word level which avoids or eliminates the impossible solutions that Buckwalter provides due to the wrong concatenations of prefix(s), stem and suffix(s).
- Context level where some linguistic rules have been extracted from the training data to help in disambiguating words depending on their context.
- Memory based level which is not applicable in all cases; it is only applicable when all the previous levels fail to decide the best solution for the Arabic input word.

Figure 3 shows BAMAE architecture starting from the input text and the numerous solutions for each word in order to predict the best POS solution for each word.

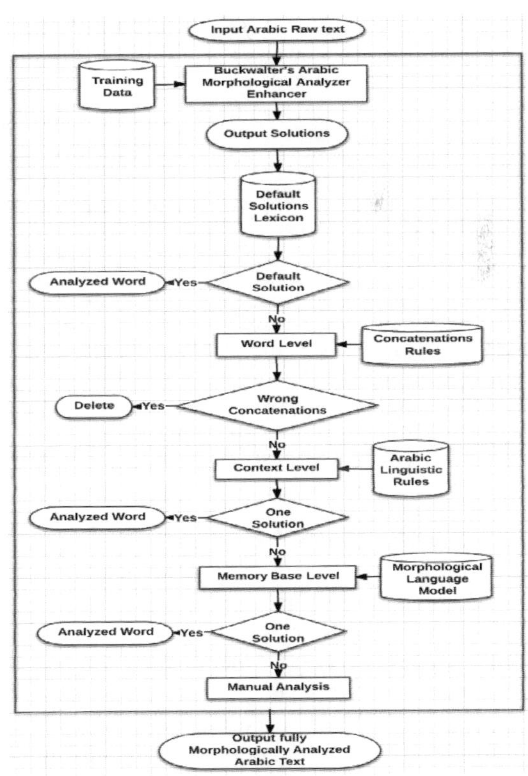

"Figure 3: BAMAE Architecture."

After selecting the best POS solution for each word, BAMAE detects the rest of information accordingly. It detects the lemmas, roots (depending primarily on the lemmas), stem patterns (depending on stems, roots and lemmas), number (depending on basic POS and stem patterns), gender (depending also on basic POS, stem patterns and sometimes depending on number), definiteness (depending on POS or their sequences), case (depending on definiteness and sequences of POS) and finally it detects the vocalization of each word.

3.2 ICA Analysis Evaluation

The testing data has been evaluated based on the rules extracted from the manually disambiguated training data in order to determine the strengths and weaknesses of the enhancer module in reaching the best solution. The testing data set will contain 1,000,000 representative words that were manually analyzed specially for the testing stage. Precision and Recall are the evaluation measures used to evaluate the BAMAE system. Precision is a measure of the ability of a system to present only relevant results. Recall is a measure of the ability of a system to present all relevant results. The evaluation has been conducted on two levels; the first level includes the precision, recall and accuracy for each qualifier separately as shown in table 5. The second level includes the basic POS in addition to adding a new qualifier each time to investigative how it would affect the accuracy as shown in table 6.

Qualifier	Precision	Recall	Accuracy
Lemma	95%	94%	89.1
Pr1	98.50%	96.40%	95.1
Pr2	98.70%	98%	96.7
Pr3	100%	100%	100
Stems	95.20%	95%	90
Tags	93.20%	93%	86.2
Suf1	92%	88.80%	81.1
Suf2	95.10%	93.50%	88.7
Gender	93.60%	92.60%	85.2
Number	99.40%	97.40%	96.8
Definiteness	97%	80.10%	77.7
Arabic Stem	97.20%	97.10%	94.4
Root	98.70%	94.10%	92.9
Stem Pattern	96%	90.60%	87

"Table 5: Precision, Recall and Accuracy for each qualifier"

Qualifiers Sequences Evaluation	Precision	Recall
Pr1 + Pr2 + Pr3 + Stems + Tags + Suf1 + Suf2	95.8	92%
Pr1 + Pr2 + Pr3 + Stems + Tags + Suf1 + Suf2 + Lemma	95.1	91.5%
Pr1 + Pr2 + Pr3 + Stems + Tags + Suf1 + Suf2 + Lemma +Root	94.9	89.8%
Pr1 + Pr2 + Pr3 + Stems + Tags + Suf1 + Suf2 + Lemma +Root + Number	94.8	88.9%
Pr1 + Pr2 + Pr3 + Stems + Tags + Suf1 + Suf2 + Lemma +Root + Number + Gender	93.8	87%
Pr1 + Pr2 + Pr3 + Stems + Tags + Suf1 + Suf2 + Lemma +Root + Number + Gender + Definiteness	93.4	86.1%
Pr1 + Pr2 + Pr3 + Stems + Tags + Suf1 + Suf2 + Lemma +Root + Number + Gender + Definiteness + Arabic Stem	92.9	86%
Pr1 + Pr2 + Pr3 + Stems + Tags + Suf1 + Suf2 + Lemma +Root + Number + Gender + Definiteness + Arabic Stem + Stem Pattern	92.3	85%

"Table 6: Accuracy decreasing as a result of adding new qualifier each time to the main POS Tag"

3.3 Comparing BAMAE with MADA

MADA (Morphological Analysis and Disambiguation for Arabic) is selected to be compared with BAMAE since both of them uses Buckwalter's output analyses to help in disambiguating the Arabic texts. The primary purpose of MADA 3.2 is to extract linguistic information as much as possible about each word in the text, from given raw Arabic text, in order to reduce or eliminate any ambiguity concerning the word. MADA does this by using ALMORGEANA[14] (an Arabic lexeme-based morphology analyzer) to generate every possible interpretation of each input word. Then, MADA applies a number of language models to determine which analysis is the most probable for each word, given the word's context.

MADA makes use of up to 19 orthogonal features to select, for each word, a proper analysis from a list of potential analyses that are provided

14 http://clipdemos.umiacs.umd.edu/ALMORGEANA/

by the Buckwalter Arabic Morphological Analyzer (BAMA; Buckwalter 2004). The BAMA analysis that most closely matches the collection of weighted, predicted features, is chosen. The 19 features include 14 morphological features that MADA predicts using 14 distinct Support Vector Machines (SVMs) trained on the PATB. In addition, MADA uses five features that capture information such as spelling variations and n-gram statistics.

Since MADA selects a complete analysis from BAMA, all decisions regarding morphological ambiguity, lexical ambiguity, tokenization, diacritization and POS tagging in any possible POS tag set are made in one fell swoop (Habash and Rambow, 2005; Habash and Rambow 2007; Roth et al, 2008). The choices are ranked in terms of their score. MADA has over 96% accuracy on basic morphological choice (including tokenization but excluding case, mood, and nunation) and on lemmatization. MADA has over 86% accuracy in predicting full diacritization (including case and mood). Detailed comparative evaluations are provided in the following publications: (Habash and Rambow, 2005; Habash and Rambow 2007; Roth et al, 2008).

In order to compare between BAMAE and MADA, the selected text, to be run on both systems, was selected from the ICA training data to facilitate the comparing process. To make the comparing process more accurate, some justifications were needed in MADA to be compatible with BAMAE format. For example, in number qualifier the feature of singular (s) was handled to be (SG), in case qualifier the feature of nominative (u) was handled to be (NOM), in tags qualifier the verbs were handled with relation to aspect and stem category. The comparing process will be done in terms of some qualifiers; diacritization, tags, stems, number, gender and definiteness including Arabic words only as shown in Table 7:

Qualifier	BAMAE	MADA
Diacritization	89.61%	78.78%
Tags	93.94%	85.28%
Stems	96.97%	91.34%
Number	96.10%	64.93%
Gender	96.53%	66.67%
Definiteness	96.53%	60.61%

"Table 7: Comparing between MADA and BAMAE."

There are some notes that must be taken into consideration:

- The problems of detecting the diacritization in BAMAE are related to either predicting the case ending wrongly or predicting the whole solution wrongly.
- The problems of detecting the diacritization in MADA are related to predicting the case ending wrongly, predicting the whole solution wrongly, missing some diacritics in some words, or missing all diacritics in some words.
- The problems of detecting the tags in MADA are related to either predicting the tags wrongly or the differences in some tags from those of BAMAE. For example the adverbs of time or place in BAMAE are assigned with 'NOUN (ADV_T)' or 'NOUN (ADV_P)' in BAMAE while they are assigned with 'NOUN', sub conjunction 'SUB_CONJ', and preposition 'PREP'. This happens as a result of using BAMA's output without enhancing such tags. In addition the wrong concatenations of BAMA's output cause problems in detecting some tags.
- The problems of detecting stems in both BAMAE and MADA are related to predicting the solution wrongly.
- The problem of detecting number, gender and definiteness in MADA are related to using BAMA's output without regarding morphosyntactic properties.
- The comparison between cases in BAMAE and MADA can't be done since MADA assigns case without regarding the diacritics of this case. For example, it assigns the accusative case 'ACC' for both 'a/ACC' and 'i/ACC' in BAMAE.
- There are some qualifiers in BAMAE which are not found in MADA; Root and Stem Pattern. The root qualifier has been assigned with accuracy 99.45% while the stem pattern qualifier has been assigned with accuracy 94.34%.
- The lemma qualifier has been assigned in BAMAE with accuracy 96.54%, while it is does not existed in MADA.

4. ICA Website[15]

It is an interface that allows users to interact with the corpus data in a number of ways. The interface provides four options of searching the corpus content; namely, Exact Match Search, Lemma Based Search, Root Based Search and Stem Based Search.

More search options are available; namely, Word Class and Sub Class, Stem Pattern, Num-

[15]http://www.bibalex.org/ica/en/

ber, Definiteness, Gender, Country (Advanced search). Moreover, the scope of search may include the whole corpus, Source(s), Sub-Source(s), Genre(s), Sub-Sub-Genre(s) or Sub-Genre(s).

Figure 4 presents an example of a query of the analyzed data that states: when the word 'وعد' is searched for using a Lemma-Based search option, the system will highlight all possible lemmas that the word may have, since Arabic is orthographically ambiguous. In this example, the system will highlight several possible lemmas; 'waʕada' 'to promise', 'waʕd' 'Promise' and 'ʕaada' 'return'. If the lemma 'waʕd' 'Promise' is chosen the output search in this case will include all words that have this lemma such as 'وعود' 'Promises', 'alwaʕd'...etc. with all possible word forms together with concordance lines.

"Figure 4: The lemma 'waʕd' 'Promise' output search."

In the search output information about the number of search result, country, source, genre, sentence and context are also available. This is phase one of ICA website and more enhancements are expected in later phases. The current phase of ICA application does not represent the final release as we are still receiving users comments and reports till all of them are implemented. However, The official phase of ICA application will give the opportunity for the researchers to save their query results.

5. Conclusion

The International Corpus of Arabic (ICA) is built, about 80 million words have been collected, covering all of the Arab world. About 2 million words have been disambiguated manually as a training data. About 50 million words have been disambiguated using (BAMAE). The evaluation has been done using precision and recall measurements for 1,000,000 words. At this point, Precision measurement ranges from 95%-92% while recall measurement was 92%-89%. The percentages are expected to rise by implementing the improvements while working on larger amounts of data. ICA website plays a role in overcoming the lack of Arabic resources. It is the 1st online freely available easy access query on 100,000,000 words which reflect the richness and variation of the ICA analyzed corpus to help the NLP community in specific and other researchers in general.

References

Ahmed Abdelali, James Cowie&Hamdy S. Soliman. 2005, *Building a modern standard Arabic corpus*. In Proceedings of workshop on computational modeling of lexical acquisition. The split meeting. Croatia, (25-28 July).

CaminoR. Rizzo. 2010, *Getting on with corpus compilation: From theory to practice*. In ESP World Journal, Issue 1 (27), Volume 9.

Charles F. Meyer. 2002, *English Corpus Linguistics: An Introduction*, Cambridge University Press.

Hajic J., Smrz O., Zemánek P., Šnaidauf J., &Beška E. (2004, September), Prague Arabic Dependency Treebank: Development in Data and Tools. InProc. of the NEMLAR Intern. Conf. on Arabic Language Resources and Tools (pp. 110-117).

Jan Hajic J., OtkarSmrz O., Petr Zemánek P., Jan Šnaidauf J., &Emanuel Beška E. 2004, *(2004, September), Prague Arabic Dependency Treebank: Development in Data and Tools*. In Proceedings of the NEMLAR Intern. Conf. on Arabic Language Resources and Tools (pp. 110-117). (2004, September).

Jan Hajic, OtakarSmrz, Tim Buckwalter ,& Hubert Jin. September. 2005, *Feature-based tagger of approximations of functional Arabic morphology*. In Proceedings of the Workshop on Treebanks and Linguistic Theories (TLT), Barcelona, Spain.

John Sinclair. 1991, *Corpus, Concordance and Collocation (Describing English Language)*. Oxford University Press.

Mahmoud El-Haj & Rim Koulali. 2013, *KALIMAT a Multipurpose Arabic Corpus*. In Proceedings of the

2nd Workshop on Arabic Corpus Linguistics (WACL-2) .

Mohamed Maamouri, Ann Bies, Tim Buckwalter &WegdanMekki. 2004, *The Penn Arabic Treebank: Building a Large-Scale Annotated Arabic Corpus*, In Proceedings of NEMLAR conference on Arabic language resources and tools (pp. 102-109).

Muhammad Atiyya, Khalid Choukri& Mustafa Yaseen. (2005), *Specifcations of the Arabic Written Corpus*. NEMLAR Project. September 29th 2005.

Nizar Habash , Owen Rambow, & Ryan Roth. 2009, *MADA+ TOKAN: A Toolkit for Arabic Tokenization, Diacritization, Morphological Disambiguation, POS Tagging, Stemming and Lemmatization*. In Proceedings of the 2nd International Conference on Arabic Language Resources and Tools (MEDAR), Cairo, Egypt.

Nizar Habash and Owen Rambow. 2005, *Arabic Tokenization, Part-Of-Speech Tagging and Morphological Disambiguation in One Fell Swoop*. In Proceedings of ACL'05, Ann Arbor, MI, USA.

Petter Zemanek. 2001, *CLARA (Corpus Linguae Arabica): An Overview*. In Proceedings of ACL/EACL Workshop on Arabic Language.

Piotr Pęzik. 2010, *New Ways to Language*. Chapter 21 (pp. 433-46), WydawnictwoUniwersytetuŁódzkiego.

Ryan Roth, Owen Rambow, Nizar Habash, Mona Diab, and Cynthia Rudin. 2008, *Arabic Morphological Tagging, Diacritization, and Lemmatization Using Lexeme Models and Feature Ranking*. In Proceedings of ACL-08: HLT, Short Papers (Companion Volume), pages (117–120), Columbus, Ohio, USA, June 2008.

Sameh Alansary, Magdy Nagi & Noha Adly. 2008, *Towards Analysing the International Corpus of Arabic (ICA): Progress of Morphological Stage*. In Proceedings of 8th International Conference on Language Engineering, Egypt.

Sameh Alansary. 2012, *BAMAE: Buckwalter Arabic Morphological Analyser Enhancer*. in Proceedings of 4th international conference on Arabic language processing, Mohamed Vth University Souissi, Rebate, Morocco, May 2-3 2012.

Sue Atkins S., Jeremy Clear J.& Nicholas Ostler N. (1992), *Corpus Design Criteria*, Literary and linguistic computing, 7(1), 1-16.

Tim Buckwalter. 2004, *Buckwalter Arabic Morphological Analyzer Version 2.0*. Linguistic Data Consortium (LDC) catalogue number LDC2004L02, ISBN 1-58563-324-0.

WajdiZaghouani. 2014, *Critical Survey of the Freely Available Arabic Corpora*. In Proceedings of Workshop on Free/Open-Source Arabic Corpora and Corpora Processing Tools.

Building a Corpus for Palestinian Arabic: a Preliminary Study

Mustafa Jarrar, *Nizar Habash, Diyam Akra, Nasser Zalmout

Birzeit University, West Bank, Palestine
{mjarrar,nzalmout}@birzeit.edu, diyam@student.birzeit.edu

*New York University Abu Dhabi, United Arab Emirates
nizar.habash@nyu.edu

Abstract

This paper presents preliminary results in building an annotated corpus of the Palestinian Arabic dialect. The corpus consists of about 43K words, stemming from diverse resources. The paper discusses some linguistic facts about the Palestinian dialect, compared with the Modern Standard Arabic, especially in terms of morphological, orthographic, and lexical variations, and suggests some directions to resolve the challenges these differences pose to the annotation goal. Furthermore, we present two pilot studies that investigate whether existing tools for processing Modern Standard Arabic and Egyptian Arabic can be used to speed up the annotation process of our Palestinian Arabic corpus.

1. Introduction and Motivation

This paper presents preliminary results towards building a high-coverage well-annotated corpus of the Palestinian Arabic dialect (henceforth PAL), which is part of an ongoing project called *Curras*. Building such a PAL corpus is a first important step towards developing natural language processing (NLP) applications, for searching, retrieving, machine-translating, spell-checking PAL text, etc. The importance of processing and understanding such text is increasing due to the exponential growth of socially generated dialectal content at recent Social Media and Web 2.0 breakthroughs.

Most Arabic NLP tools and resources were developed to serve Modern Standard Arabic (MSA), which is the official written language in the Arab World. Using such tools to understand and process Arabic dialects (DAs) is a challenging task because of the phonological and morphological differences between DAs and MSA. In addition, there is no standard orthography for DAs. Moreover, DAs have limited standardized written resources, since most of the written dialectal content is the result of ad hoc and unstructured social conversations or commentary, in comparison to MSA's vast body of literary works.

The rest of this paper is structured as follows: We present important linguistic background in Section 2, followed by a survey of related work in Section 3. We then present the process of collecting the Curras Corpus (Section 4) and the challenges of annotating it (Section 5).

2. Linguistic Background

In this section we summarize some important linguistic facts about PAL that influence the decisions we made in this project. For more information on PAL and Levantine Arabic in general, see (Rice and Sa'id, 1960; Cowell, 1964; Bateson, 1967; Brustad, 2000; Halloun, 2000; Holes, 2004; Elihai, 2004). For a discussion of differences between Levantine and Egyptian Arabic (EGY), see Omar (1976).

2.1 Arabic and its dialects

The Arabic language is a collection of variants among which a standard variety (MSA) has a special status, while the rest are considered colloquial dialects (Bateson, 1967, Holes, 2004; Habash, 2010). MSA is the official written language of government, media and education in the Arab World, but it is not anyone's native language; the spoken dialects vary widely across the Arab World and are the true native varieties

Proceedings of the EMNLP 2014 Workshop on Arabic Natural Langauge Processing (ANLP), pages 18–27,
October 25, 2014, Doha, Qatar.

of Arabic, yet they have no standard orthography and are not taught in schools (Habash et al., 2012, Zribi et al., 2014).

PAL is the dialect spoken by Arabic speakers who live in or originate from the area of Historical Palestine. PAL is part of the South Levantine Arabic dialect subgroup (of which Jordanian Arabic is another dialect). PAL is historically the result of interaction between Syriac and Arabic and has been influenced by many other regional language such as Turkish, Persian, English and most recently Hebrew. The Palestinian refugee problem has led to additional mixing among different PAL sub-dialects as well as borrowing from other Arabic dialects. We discuss next some of the important distinguishing features of PAL in comparison to MSA as well as other Arabic dialects. We consider the following dimensions: phonology, morphology, and lexicon. Like other Arabic dialects, PAL has no standard orthography.

2.2 Phonology

PAL consists of several sub-dialects that generally vary in terms of phonology and lexicon preferences. Commonly identified sub-dialects include urban (which itself varies mostly phonologically among the major cities such as Jerusalem, Jaffa, Gaza, Nazareth, Nablus and Hebron), rural, and Bedouin. The Druze community has also some distinctive phonological features that set it apart. The variations are a miniature version of the variations in Levantine Arabic in general. Perhaps the most salient variation is the pronunciation of the /q/ phoneme (corresponding to MSA ق *q*[1]), which realizes as /'/ in most urban dialects, /k/ in rural dialects, and /g/ in Bedouin dialects. The Druze dialect retains the /q/ pronunciation. Another example is the /k/ phoneme (corresponding to MSA ك k), which realizes as /tš/ in rural dialects. These difference cause the word for قلب *qlb* 'heart' to be pronounced as /qalb/, /'alb/, /kalb/ and /galb/ and to be ambiguous out of context with the word كلب *klb* 'dog' /kalb/ and /tšalb/. And similarly to EGY (but unlike Tunisian Arabic), the MSA phoneme /θ/ (ث *θ*) becomes /s/ or /t/, and the MSA phoneme /ð/ (ذ *ð*) becomes /z/ or /d/ in different lexical contexts, e.g., MSA كذب *kðb* /kaðib/ 'lying' is pronounced /kizib/ in PAL and /kidb/ in EGY.

Similar to many other dialects, e.g. EGY and Tunisian (Habash et al., 2012; Zribi et al., 2014), the glottal stop phoneme that appears in many MSA words has disappeared in PAL: compare MSA رأس *rÂs* /ra's/ 'head' and بئر *bŷr* /bi'r/ 'well' with their Palestinian urban versions: /rās/ and /bīr/. Also, the MSA diphthongs /ay/ and /aw/ generally become /ē/ and /ō/; this transformation happens in EGY but not in other Levantine dialects such as Lebanese, e.g., MSA بيت *byt* /bayt/ 'house' becomes PAL /bēt/.

PAL also elides many short vowels that appear in the MSA cognates leading to heavier syllabic structure, e.g. MSA جبال /jibāl/ 'mountains' (and EGY /gibāl/) becomes PAL /jbāl/. Additionally long vowels in unstressed positions in some PAL sub-dialects shorten, a phenomenon shared with EGY but not MSA: e.g., compare /zāru/ (زاروا zAr+uwA) 'they visited' with /zarū/ (زاروه zAr+uw+h) 'they visited him'. Finally, PAL has commonly inserted epenthetic vowels (Herzallah, 1990), which are optional in some cases leading to multiple pronunciations of the same word, e.g., /kalb/ and /kalib/ (كلب *klb* 'dog'). This multiplicity is not shared with MSA, which has a simpler syllabic structure and more limited epenthesis than PAL.

2.3 Morphology

PAL, like MSA and its dialects and other Semitic languages, makes extensive use of templatic morphology in addition to a large set of affixations and clitics. There are however some important differences between MSA and PAL in terms of morphology. First, like many other dialects, PAL lost nominal case and verbal mood, which remain in MSA. Additionally, PAL in most of its sub-dialects collapses the feminine and masculine plurals and duals in verbs and

---

[1] Arabic orthographic transliterations are provided in the Habash-Soudi-Buckwalter (HSB) scheme (Habash et al., 2007), *except where indicated.* HSB extends Buckwalter's transliteration scheme (Buckwalter, 2004) to increase its readability while maintaining the 1-to-1 correspondence with Arabic orthography as represented in standard encodings of Arabic, i.e., Unicode, etc. The following are the only differences from Buckwalter's scheme (indicated in parentheses): Ā آ (|), Â أ (>), ŵ ؤ (&), Ǎ إ (<), ŷ ئ (}), ħ ة (p), θ ث (v), ð ذ (*), š ش ($), Ď ظ (Z), ς ع (E), γ غ (g), ý ى (Y), ã ً (F), ũ ٌ (N), ĩ ٍ (K). Orthographic transliterations are presented in italics. For phonological transcriptions, we follow the common practice of using '/…/' to represent phonological sequences and we use HSB choices with some extensions instead of the International Phonetic Alphabet (IPA) to minimize the number of representations used, as was done by Habash (2010).

most nouns. Some specific inflections are ambiguous in PAL but not MSA, e.g., حبيت *Hbyt* /Habbēt/ 'I (or you [m.s.]) loved'.

Second, some specific morphemes are slightly or quite different in PAL from their MSA forms, e.g., the future marker is /sa/ in MSA but /Ha/ or /raH/ in PAL. Another prominent example is the feminine singular suffix morpheme (Ta Marbuta), which in MSA is pronounced as /at/ except at utterance final positions (where it is /a/). In some PAL urban sub dialects, it has multiple allomorphs that are phonologically and syntactically conditioned: /a/ (after non-front and emphatic consonants), /e/ (after front non-emphatic consonants), /it/ (nouns in construct state such as before possessive pronouns) and /ā/ (in deverbals before direct objects): e.g. بطة *bTħ* /baTT+a/ 'duck', حبة *Hbħ* /Habb+e/ 'pill', بطتنا *bTnA* /baTT+it+na/ 'our duck' and /mdars+ā +hum/ 'she taught them'.

Third, PAL has many clitics that do not exist in MSA, e.g., the progressive particle /b+/ (as in /b+tuktub/ 'she writes'), the demonstrative particle /ha+/ (as in /ha+l+bēt/ 'this house'), the negation cirmcumclitic /ma+ +š/ (as in /ma+katab+š/ 'he did not write') and the indirect object clitic (as in /ma+katab+l+ō+š/ 'he did not write to him'). All of these examples except for the demonstrative particle are used in EGY.

2.4 Lexicon

The PAL lexicon is primarily Arabic with numerous borrowings from many different languages. MSA cognates generally appear with some minor phonological changes as discussed above; a few cases include more complex changes, e.g. /biddi/ 'I want' is from MSA /bi+widd+i/ 'in my desire' or /illi/ 'relative pronoun which/who/that' which corresponds to a set of MSA forms that inflect for gender and number (الذي *Alðy*, التي *Alty*, etc.). Some common PAL words are portmanteaus of MSA words, e.g., /lēš / 'why?' corresponds to MSA /li+'ayy+i šay'/ 'for what thing?'. Examples of common words that are borrowed from other languages include the following:

- روزنامه /roznama/ 'calendar' (Persian)
- كندرة /kundara/ 'shoe' (Turkish)
- بندورة /banadora/ 'tomato' (Italian)
- بريك /brēk/ 'brake (car)' (English)
- تليفيزيون /talifizyon/ 'television' (French)
- محسوم /maHsūm/ 'checkpoint' (Hebrew)

3. Related Work

3.1 Corpus Collection and Annotation

There have been many contributions aiming to develop annotated Arabic language corpora, with the main objective of facilitating Arabic NLP applications. Notable contributions targeting MSA include the work of Maamouri and Cieri, (2002), Maamouri et al. (2004), Smrž and Hajič (2006), and Habash and Roth (2009). These efforts developed annotation guidelines for written MSA content producing large-scale Arabic Treebanks.

Contributions that are specific to DA include the development of a pilot Levantine Arabic Treebank (LATB) of Jordanian Arabic, which contained morphological and syntactic annotations of about 26,000 words (Maamouri et al., 2006). To speed up the process of creating the LATB, Maamouri et al. (2006) adapted MSA Treebank guidelines to DA and experimented with extensions to the Buckwalter Arabic Morphological Analyzers (Buckwalter, 2004). The LATB was used in the Johns Hopkins workshop on Parsing Arabic Dialect (Rambow et al., 2005; Chiang et al., 2006), which supplemented the LATB effort with an experimental Levantine-MSA dictionary. The LATB effort differs from the work presented here in two respects. First, the LATB corpus consists of conversational telephone speech transcripts, which eliminated the orthographic variations issues that we face in this paper. Secondly, when the LATB was created, there were no robust tools for morphological analysis of any dialects; this is not the case any more. We plan to exploit existing tools for EGY to help the annotation effort.

Other DA contributions include the Egyptian Colloquial Arabic Lexicon (ECAL) (Kilany, et al., 2002), which was developed as part of the CALLHOME Egyptian Arabic (CHE) corpus (Gadalla, et al., 1997). In addition to YADAC (Al-Sabbagh and Girju, 2012), which was based on dialectal content identification and web harvesting of blogs, micro blogs, and forums of EGY content. Similarly, the COLABA project (Diab et al., 2010) developed annotated dialectal content resources for Egyptian, Iraqi, Levantine, and Moroccan dialects, from online weblogs.

3.2 Dialectal Orthography

Due to the lack of standardized orthography guidelines for DA, along with the phonological differences in comparison to MSA, and dialectal variations within the dialects themselves, there are many orthographic variations for written DA content. Writers in DA, regardless of the context, are often inconsistent with others and even with themselves when it comes to the written form of a dialect; writing with MSA driven orthography, or writing words phonologically sometimes. These orthography variations make it difficult for computational models to properly identify and reason about the words of a given dialect (Habash et al, 2012a), hence, a conventional form for the orthographic notations is important. Within this scope, we can view this problem for Levantine dialects as an extension of the work of Habash et al. (2012a) who proposed the so-called CODA (Conventional Orthography for Dialectal Arabic). CODA is designed for the purpose of developing conventional computational models of Arabic dialects in general. Habash et al. (2012a) provides a detailed description of CODA guidelines as applied to EGY. Eskander et al. (2013) identify five goals for CODA: (i) CODA is an internally consistent and coherent convention for writing DA; (ii) CODA is created for computational purposes; (iii) CODA uses the Arabic script; (iv) CODA is intended as a unified framework for writing all DAs; and (v) CODA aims to strike an optimal balance between maintaining a level of dialectal uniqueness and establishing conventions based on MSA-DA similarities. CODA guidelines will be extended to cover PAL in this paper, as discussed in Section 5.3.

3.3 Dialectal Morphological Annotation

Most of the work that explored morphology in Arabic focused on MSA (Al-Sughaiyer and Al-Kharashi, 2004; Buckwalter, 2004; Habash and Rambow, 2005; Graff et al., 2009; Habash, 2010). The contributions for DA morphology analysis, however, are relatively scarce and are usually based on either extending available MSA tools to tackle DA specificities, as in the work of (Abo Bakr et al., 2008; Salloum and Habash, 2011), or modeling DAs directly, without relying on existing MSA contributions (Habash and Rambow, 2006). Due to the variations between MSA and DAs, available MSA tools and resources cannot be easily extended or transferred to work properly for DA (Maamouri, et al., 2006; Habash, et al., 2012b). Therefore, it is important to develop annotated and morpheme-segmented resources, along with morphological analysis tools, that are specific and tailored for DAs. One of the notable recent contributions for EGY morphological analysis was CALIMA (Habash et al., 2012b). The CALIMA analyzer for EGY and the commonly used SAMA analyzer for MSA (Graff et al., 2009) are central in the functioning of the EGY morphological tagger MADA-ARZ (Habash et al., 2013), and its successor MADAMIRA (Pasha et al., 2014), which supports both MSA and EGY.

The work we present in this paper builds on the shoulders of these previous efforts from the development of guidelines for orthography and morphology (in MSA and EGY) to the use of existing tools (specifically MADAMIRA MSA and EGY) to speed up the annotation process.

4. Corpus Collection

Written dialects in general tend to have scarce resources in terms of written literature; written materials usually involve informal conversations or traditional folk literature (stories, songs, etc.). It is therefore often difficult to find resources for written dialectal content. In addition, resources of dialectal content are prone to significant noise and inconsistency because they tend to lack standard orthographies and rely on ad hoc transcriptions and orthographic borrowing from the standard variety. In the case of Arabic, unlike MSA that dominates the formal and written content outlets, as in the press, scientific articles, books, and historical narration, DAs are more naturally used in traditional and informal contexts, such as conversations in TV series, movies, or on social media platforms, providing socially powered commentary on different domains and topics. And given the lack of standard orthography, there is common mixing of phonetic spelling and MSA-cognate-based spelling in addition to the so-called Arabizi spelling – writing DAs in Roman script, rather than Arabic script (Darwish, 2014 and Al-Badrashiny et al., 2014). Such noise imposes many challenges regarding the collection of high-coverage high-accuracy DA corpora. It is therefore important to remark that although *bigger is better* when it comes to corpus size, we focus more in this first iteration of our PAL corpus on precision and variety rather than mere size. That is, we tried not only to manually select and review the content of the corpus, but also to assure that we covered a variety of topics and contexts, localities and sub-dialects, including the social class and gender of the speakers and writers. This is because such aspects help us discover new language phenomena in the dialect as will be discussed in the next section.

Table 1 presents the resources that we manually collected to build the PAL Curras corpus. There are 133 social media threads (about 16k words) from blogs (e.g., مدونة عبد الحميد العاطي Abdelhameed Alaaty's blog), forums (e.g., شبكة الحوار الفلسطيني The Palestinian dialogue network), Twitter, and Facebook. The collection was done by reading many discussion threads and selecting the relevant ones to assure diversity and PAL representative content. Content that is heavily written in a mix of languages, or a mix of other dialects was excluded. In the same way, we also manually collected some PAL stories, and a list of PAL terms and their meanings, which reflect additional diversity of topics, contexts, and social classes. About half of our corpus comes from 41 episode scripts from the Palestinian TV show وطن ع وتر "Watan Aa Watar". Each episode discusses and provides satirical critiques regarding different topics of relevance to the Palestinian viewers about daily life issues. The show's importance stems from the fact that the actors use a variety of Palestinian local dialects, hence enriching the coverage of the corpus.

Table 1. The Curras Corpus Statistics

Document Type	Word Tokens	Word Types	Documents
Facebook	3,120	1,985	35 threads
Twitter	3,541	2,133	38 threads
Blogs	8,748	4,454	37 threads
Forums	1,092	798	33 threads
Palestinian Stories	2,407	1,422	6 stories
Palestinian Terms	759	556	1 doc
TV Show: وطن ع وتر *Watan Aa Watar*	23,423	8,459	41 episodes
Curras Total	**43,090**	**19,807**	**191**

5. Corpus Annotation Challenges

This section presents our approach to annotating the Curras corpus. We start with a specification of our annotation goals, followed by a discussion of our general approach. We then discuss in more details two important challenges that need to be addressed for annotation of a new dialectal corpus: orthography and morphology.

5.1 Annotation Specification

The words are annotated in context. As such, the same word may receive different annotations in different contexts. We define the annotation of a word as a tuple $<w, w_B, c, c_B, l, p_B, g, i>$ described as follow. (Examples of such annotations are illustrated in Table 5.):

- ***w*: Raw (Unicode)** The raw input word defined as a string of letters delimited by white space and punctuation. The word is represented in Arabic script (Unicode).
- **w_B: Raw (Buckwalter)** The same raw input word in the commonly used Buckwalter transliteration (Buckwalter, 2004).
- ***c*: CODA (Unicode)** The Conventional Orthography (Habash et al., 2012) version of the input word.
- **c_B: CODA (Buckwalter)** The Buckwalter transliteration of the CODA form.
- ***l*: Lemma** The lemma of the word in Buckwalter transliteration. The lemma is the citation form or dictionary entry that abstracts over all inflectional morphology (but not derivational morphology). The lemma is fully diacritized. We follow the definition of lemma used in BAMA (Buckwalter, 2004) and CALIMA-ARZ (Habash et al., 2012b).
- **p_B: Buckwalter POS** The Buckwalter full POS tag, which identifies all clitics and affixes and the stem and assigns each a sub-tag. This representation treats clitics as separate tokens and abstracts the orthographic rewrites they undergo when cliticized. See the handling of the l/PREP+Al/DET in word #6 in Table 5. This representation is used by the LDC in the Penn Arabic Treebank (PATB) (Maamouri et al., 2004) and tools such as MADAMIRA (Pasha et al., 2014). It is a high granularity representation that allows researchers to easily go to coarser granularity POS (Diab 2007; Habash, 2010; Alkuhlani et al., 2013). The Buckwalter POS tag can be fully diacritized or undiacritized. Given the added complexity of producing diacritized text manually by annotators, we opted at this stage to only use undiacritized forms.

- ***g*: Gloss** The English gloss, an informal semantic denotation of the lemma. In Tables 3-5, we only use one English word for space limitations.
- ***i*: Analysis** A specification of the source of the annotation, e.g., ANNO is a human annotator, and MADA is the MADAMIRA system with some minor or no automatic post-processing. In Tables 3 and 4, which are produced automatically, the Analysis field is replaced with a status indicating how usable the automatic annotation is.

5.2 General Approach

To speed up the process of annotating our corpus, we made the following decisions. First, and quite obviously from the previous section, we made a conscious decision to follow on the footsteps of previous efforts for MSA and EGY annotation done at the Linguistic Data Consortium and Columbia's Arabic Modeling group in terms of guidelines for orthography conventionalization and morphological annotation. This allows us to exploit existing guidelines with only essential modification to accommodate PAL and produce annotations that are comparable to those done for MSA and EGY. This, we hope, will encourage research in dialectal adaptation techniques and will make our annotations more familiar and thus usable by the community.

Second, and closely related to the first point, we exploit existing tools to speed up the annotation process. In this paper, we specifically use the MADAMIRA tool (Pasha et al., 2014) for morphological analysis and disambiguation of MSA and EGY. Our choice of using this tool is motivated by the assumption that EGY/MSA and PAL share many orthographic and morphological features. This assumption was validated by pilot experiments, presented below, and which show most of the PAL annotations can be generated automatically. However, a manual step is then needed to verify every annotation, to correct errors and fill in gaps. The manual annotation has not been completed yet as of the writing of this paper submission.

Finally, we made one major simplification to the annotations to minimize the load on the human annotator: we do not produce diacritized morphological analyses in the Buckwalter POS tag. The reasons for this decision are the following: (i) full diacritization is a complex task that most Arabic speakers do not do and thus it requires a lot of training and precious attention to detail; (ii) MSA and EGY produce many morphemes and lexical items that are quite similar to PAL except in terms of the short vowels (compare the lemmas for word #5 in Tables 3, 4 and 5); (iii) PAL has many cases of multiple valid diacritizations as mentioned above. While we think a convention should be defined to explain the variation and model it, it is perhaps the topic of a future effort that is more focused on PAL phonology. We make an exception for the lemmas and diacritize them since lemmas are important in indicating the core meaning of the word. In case of different pronunciations of the lemma, we choose the shortest.

5.3 A Conventional Orthography for PAL

As explained in Section 2, PAL, like other Arabic dialects, does not have a standard orthography. Furthermore, there are numerous phonological, morphological and lexical differences between PAL and MSA that make the use of MSA spelling as is undesirable. PAL speakers who write in the dialect produce spontaneous inconsistent spellings that sometimes reflect the phonology of PAL, and other times the word's cognate relationship with MSA. For example, the word for 'heart' (MSA قلب qalb) has four spellings that correspond to four sub-dialectal pronunciations: قلب *qlb* /qalb/, ألب Âlb /'alb/, كلب *klb* /kalb/, and جلب *jlb* /galb/. Similarly, the common shortening of some long vowels (from MSA to PAL) leads to different orthographies as in قانون *qAnwn* 'law' (MSA /qānūn/), which can also be written with a shortened first vowel قنون *qnwn* /'anūn/ reflecting the PAL pronunciation. PAL also has some clitics that do not exist in MSA, which leads to different spellings, e.g. the PAL future particle ح *H* /Ha/ can be written attached to or separate from the verb that follows it. Even when a morpheme exists in MSA and PAL, it may have additional forms or pronunciations. One example is the definite article morpheme ال *Al* /il/ which has a non-MSA/non-EGY allomorph /li/ when attached to nominals with initial consonant clusters. As a result, a word like /li+blād/ 'the homeland/countries' can be spelled to reflect the morphology as البلاد *AlblAd* or the phonology لبلاد *lblAd*, with the latter being ambiguous with 'for countries' (in PAL /la+blād/). Finally, there are words in PAL that have no cognate in MSA and as such have no clear obvious spelling to go with, e.g., the word /barDo/ 'additionally' is spontaneously written as برضو *brDw*, برضه *brDh* and برضة *brDħ*.

This, of course, is not a unique PAL problem. Researchers working on NLP for EGY and Tunisian dialects developed CODA guidelines for them (Habash et al., 2012a; Zribi et al., 2014). These guidelines were by design intended to apply (or be easily extended) to all Arabic dialects, but were only demonstrated for two. Our challenge was to take these guidelines (specifically the EGY version) and extend them. There were three types of extensions. First, in terms of phonology-orthography, we added the letter ك k to the list of root letters to be spelled in the MSA cognate to cover the PAL rural sub-dialects that pronounces it as /tš/. Second, in terms of morphology, we added the non-EGY demonstrative proclitic ه *h+* and the conjunction proclitic ت *t+* 'so as to' to the list of clitics, e.g., بهالبيت *bhAlbyt* 'in this house' and تيشوف *tyšwf* 'so that he can see'. Finally, we extended the list of exceptional words to cover problematic PAL words. All of the basic CODA rules for EGY (and Tunisian) are kept the same.

Pilot Study (I): We conducted a small pilot study in annotating the CODA for PAL words. We considered 1,000 words from 77 tweets in Curras. The CODA version of each word was created in context. 15.9% of all words had a different CODA form from the input raw word form. 42% of these changes involve consonants (two-fifths of the cases), vowels (one-fifth of the cases) and the hamzated/bare forms of the letter Alif ا *A*. Examples of consonant change can be seen in Table 5 (words #4 and #10). An additional 29% word changes involve the spelling of specific morpheme. The most common change (over half of the time) was for the first person imperfect verbal prefix ا *A* when following the progressive particle ب *b*: بكتب *bktb* as opposed to باكتب *bAktb*. About 18% of the changed words experience a split or a merge (with splits happening five time more than merges). An example of a CODA split is seen in Table 5 (word #9). Finally, only about 8% of the changed words were PAL specific terms; and less than 7% involved a typo or speech effect elongation. These results are quite encouraging as they suggest the differences between CODA and spontaneously written PAL are not extensive. Further analysis is still needed of course.

In Tables 3 and 4 (column CODA), we show the results of using the MADAMIRA-MSA and MADAMIRA-EGY systems on a set of ten words, while Table 5 shows the manually selected or corrected CODA. MADAMIRA generates a CODA version (contextually) by default. We expect the EGY version to be more successful than the MSA version in producing the CODA for PAL given the shared presence of many morphemes in EGY and PAL. However, when we ran the same set of words through MADAMIRA-EGY, we encountered many errors in words, morphemes and spelling choices in PAL that are different from EGY, e.g., the raw word منحب *mnHb* 'we love' (CODA بنحب *bnHb*) is analyzed as the EGY ما نحب *mA nHb* 'we do not love'!

5.4 Morphological Annotation Process and Challenges

To study the value of using an existing morphological analyzer for MSA or EGY in creating PAL annotations, we conducted the following pilot study.

Pilot Study (II): We ran the words from a randomly selected episode of the PAL TV show "Watan Aa Watar" (460 words) through both MADAMIRA-MSA and MADAMIRA-EGY. We analyzed the output from both systems to determine its usability for PAL annotations. We consider all analyses that are correct for PAL annotation or usable via simple post processing (such as removing CASE endings on MSA words) to be correct (as in word #2 in Tables 3-5). Words that receive incorrect analyses or no analyses require manual modifications.

The results of this experiment are summarized in Table 2. Table 3 and 4 illustrate sample results for ten words and Table 5 includes the manually created results.[2]

Table 2. Accuracy of automatic annotation of PAL text

Statistics	MADAMIRA MSA	MADAMIRA EGY
No Analysis	17.78%	7.24%
Wrongly Analyzed	18.43%	14.75%
Correctly Analyzed	63.79%	78.01%

The No Analysis (NA) words in Tables 2, 3 and 4 refer to the words that the morphological analyzer couldn't recognize. This failure may be

[2] The examples in Tables 3-5 are presented in the Buckwalter transliteration (Buckwalter, 2004) to match the forms as they appear in the annotated corpus.

a result of missing lexical entry, specific PAL morphology or typos. As expected, MADAMIRA-MSA had 2.5 times the number of NA cases compared to MADAMIRA-EGY. Examples include dialectal lexical terms (word #7) or dialectal morphology (words # 1 and #9).

The wrongly analyzed words are words that were assigned incorrect POS tag *in context*. For example, word #3 in Tables 3 and 4 is the result of mis-analyzing the proclitic l- as the preposition 'for/to' as opposed to the non-CODA spelling of the definite article in PAL. The analysis provided by MADAMIRA-EGY is correct for other contexts than the one illustrated here. Another example is word #8, which is a Levantine specific term hardly used in EGY and not used at all in MSA. MADAMIRA-MSA has a higher proportion of wrongly analyzed words than MADAMIRA-EGY.

Overall MADAMIRA-EGY produced analyses that were either correct and ready to use for PAL or requiring some minor modifications such as adjusting the vowels on the lemmas (e.g., word #5) in one of every five words.

Table 3 Automatic annotations by the MADAMIRA-MSA system. Entries with Status NA had no analysis.

	Raw		CODA		Lemma	Buckwalter POS (Diacritized)	Gloss	Status
1	ابوكوا	AbwkwA						NA
2	الاكل	AlAkl	الأكل	Al>kl	>akol	Al/DET+>akol/NOUN+a/CASE_DEF_ACC	eating	Usable
3	لبنوك	lbnwk	لبنوك	lbnwk	banok	li/PREP+bunuwk/NOUN+K/CASE_INDEF_GEN	bank	Wrong
4	التاني	AltAny	التأني	Alt>ny	ta>an~iy	Al/DET+ta>an~iy/NOUN	prudence	Wrong
5	الحمار	AlHmAr	الحمار	AlHmAr	HimAr	Al/DET+HimAr/NOUN+u/CASE_DEF_NOM	donkey	Usable
6	للراتب	llrAtb	للراتب	llrAtb	rAtib	li/PREP+Al/DET+rAtib/NOUN+i/CASE_DEF_GEN	salary	Usable
7	ايوة	Aywp						NA
8	بدها	bdhA	بدها	bdhA	bud~	bud~/NOUN+i/CASE_DEF_GEN+hA/POSS_PRON_3FS	escape	Wrong
9	بنردلك	bnrdlk						NA
10	هدول	hdwl						NA

Table 4 Automatic annotations by the MADAMIRA-EGY system. Entries with Status NA had no analysis.

	Raw		CODA		Lemma	Buckwalter POS (Diacritized)	Gloss	Status
1	ابوكوا	AbwkwA	ابوكو	Abwkw	Abuw	Abuw/NOUN+kuw/POSS_PRON_3MS	father	Correct
2	الاكل	AlAkl	الأكل	Al>kl	>akl	Al/DET+>akol/NOUN	eating	Correct
3	لبنوك	lbnwk	لبنوك	lbnwk	bank	li/PREP+bunuwk/NOUN	bank	Wrong
4	التاني	AltAny	التاني	AltAny	tAniy	Al/DET+tAniy/ADJ_NUM	second	Usable
5	الحمار	AlHmAr	الحمار	AlHmAr	HumAr	Al/DET+HumAr/NOUN	donkey	Usable
6	للراتب	llrAtb	للراتب	llrAtb	rAtib	li/PREP+Al/DET+rAtib/NOUN	salary	Correct
7	ايوة	Aywp	أيوه	>ywh	>ayowah	>ayowah/INTERJ	yes	Correct
8	بدها	bdhA	بدها	bdhA	bud~	bud~/NOUN+hA/POSS_PRON_3FS	escape	Wrong
9	بنردلك	bnrdlk	بنرد_لك	bnrd_lk	rad~	bi/PROG_PART+nu/IV1P+rud~/IV+li/PREP+ak/PRON_2MS	answer	Usable
10	هدول	hdwl						NA

Table 5 Manual Annotations in Curras. Entries with Analysis MADA were automatically converted and validated by the annotator. Entries with Analysis ANNO required some modification of the MADAMIRA output or were created from scratch.

	Raw		CODA		Lemma	Buckwalter POS (Undiacritized)	Gloss	Analysis
1	ابوكوا	AbwkwA	ابوكو	Abwkw	Abuw	Abw/NOUN+kw/POSS_PRON_3MS	father	MADA
2	الاكل	AlAkl	الأكل	Al>kl	>akl	Al/DET+>kl/NOUN	eating	MADA
3	لبنوك	lbnwk	البنوك	Albnwk	bank	Al/DET+bnwk/NOUN	bank	ANNO
4	التاني	AltAny	الثاني	AlvAny	vAniy	Al/DET+vAny/ADJ_NUM	second	ANNO
5	الحمار	AlHmAr	الحمار	AlHmAr	HmAr	Al/DET+HmAr/NOUN	donkey	MADA
6	للراتب	llrAtb	للراتب	llrAtb	rAtib	l/PREP+Al/DET+rAtb/NOUN	salary	MADA
7	ايوة	Aywp	أيوه	>ywh	>ayowah	>ywh/INTERJ	yes	MADA
8	بدها	bdhA	بدها	bdhA	bid~	bd/NOUN+hA/POSS_PRON_3FS	want	ANNO
9	بنردلك	bnrdlk	بنرد_لك	bnrd_lk	rad~	b/PROG_PART+n/IV1P+rd/IV+l/PREP+k/PRON_2MS	answer	MADA
10	هدول	hdwl	هذول	h*wl	ha*A	h*wl/DEM_PRON	these	ANNO

5 Conclusion and Future Work

We presented our preliminary results towards building an annotated corpus of the Palestinian Arabic dialect. The challenges and linguistic variations of the Palestinian dialect, compared with Modern Standard Arabic, were discussed especially in terms of morphology, orthography, and lexicon. We also discussed and showed the potential, and limitations, of using existing resources, especially MADAMIRA-EGY, to semi-automate and speed up the annotation process.

The paper has also pointed out several issues that need to be considered and researched further, especially the development of Palestinian-specific morphological annotation and CODA guidelines, a Palestinian lexicon, and the extension of MADAMIRA to analyze Palestinian text. Our corpus will be further extended to include more text, and all lexical annotations (i.e., Lemmas) will be linked with existing Arabic ontology resources such as the Arabic WordNet (Black et al., 2006). The corpus will be publicly available for research purposes.

Acknowledgement

This work is part of the ongoing project *Curras*, funded by the Palestinian Ministry of Higher Education, Scientific Research Council. Nizar Habash performed most of his work on this paper while he was in the Center for Computational Learning Systems at Columbia University.

References

H. Abo Bakr, K. Shaalan, and I. Ziedan. A Hybrid Approach for Converting Written Egyptian Colloquial Dialect into Diacritized Arabic. In The 6th International Conference on Informatics and Systems, INFOS2008. Cairo University, 2008.

M. Al-Badrashiny, R. Eskander, N. Habash, and O. Rambow. Automatic Transliteration of Romanized Dialectal Arabic. CoNLL, 2014.

S. Alkuhlani, N. Habash and R. M. Roth. Automatic Morphological Enrichment of a Morphologically Underspecified Treebank. In Proc. of Conference of the North American Association for Computational Linguistics (NAACL), Atlanta, Georgia, 2013.

R. Al-Sabbagh and R. Girju. YADAC: Yet another dialectal Arabic corpus. In Proc. of the Language Resources and Evaluation Conference (LREC), pages 2882–2889, Istanbul, 2012.

M. C. Bateson. Arabic Language Handbook. Center for Applied Linguistics, Washington D.C., USA, 1967.

W. Black, Elkateb, S., & Vossen, P. (2006). Introducing the Arabic wordnet project. In In Proceedings of the third International WordNet Conference (GWC-06).

K. Brustad. The Syntax of Spoken Arabic: A Comparative Study of Moroccan, Egyptian, Syrian, and Kuwaiti Dialects. Georgetown University Press, 2000.

T. Buckwalter. Buckwalter Arabic morphological analyzer version 2.0. LDC catalog number LDC2004L02, ISBN 1-58563-324-0, 2004.

D. Chiang, M. Diab, N. Habash, O. Rambow, and S. Shareef. Parsing Arabic Dialects. In Proceedings of the European Chapter of ACL (EACL), 2006.

M. W. Cowell. A Reference Grammar of Syrian Arabic. Georgetown University Press, 1964.

Kareem Darwish. Arabizi Detection and Conversion to Arabic. In the Arabic Natural Language Processing Workshop, EMNLP, Doha, Qatar, 2014.

M. Diab. Towards an Optimal POS tag set for Modern Standard Arabic Processing. In Proc. of Recent Advances in Natural Language Processing (RANLP), Borovets, Bulgaria, 2007.

M. Diab, N. Habash, O. Rambow, M. Altantawy, and Y. Benajiba. COLABA: Arabic Dialect Annotation and Processing. LREC Workshop on Semitic Language Processing, Malta, 2010.

Y. Elihai. The olive tree dictionary: a transliterated dictionary of conversational Eastern Arabic (Palestinian). Washington DC: Kidron Pub, 2004.

R. Eskander, N. Habash, O. Rambow, and N. Tomeh. Processing Spontaneous Orthography. In Proceedings NAACL-HLT, Atlanta, GA, 2013.

H. Gadalla, H. Kilany, H. Arram, A. Yacoub, A. El-Habashi, A. Shalaby, K. Karins, E. Rowson, R. MacIntyre, P. Kingsbury, D. Graff, and C. McLemore. CALLHOME Egyptian Arabic Transcripts. Linguistic Data Consortium, Catalog No.: LDC97T19, 1997.

D. Graff, M. Maamouri, B. Bouziri, S. Krouna, S. Kulick, and T. Buckwalter. Standard Arabic Morphological Analyzer (SAMA) Version 3.1. Linguistic Data Consortium LDC2009E73, 2009.

N. Habash and O. Rambow. Arabic Tokenization, Part-of-Speech Tagging and Morphological Disambiguation in One Fell Swoop. In ACL, Ann Arbor, Michigan, 2005.

N. Habash, A. Soudi, and T. Buckwalter. On Arabic Transliteration. In A. van den Bosch and A. Soudi, editors, Arabic Computational Morphology: Knowledge-based and Empirical Methods. Springer, 2007.

N. Habash and R. Roth. CATiB: The Columbia Arabic Treebank. In ACL, 2009.

N. Habash. Introduction to Arabic natural language processing, volume 3. Morgan & Claypool Publishers, 2010.

N. Habash, M. Diab, and O. Rabmow. (2012a) Conventional Orthography for Dialectal Arabic. In Proc. of LREC, Istanbul, Turkey, 2012.

N. Habash, R. Eskander, and A. Hawwari. (2012b) A Morphological Analyzer for Egyptian Arabic. In Proc. of the Special Interest Group on Computational Morphology and Phonology, Montréal, Canada, 2012.

N. Habash, R. Roth, O. Rambow, R. Eskander, and N. Tomeh. Morphological Analysis and Disambiguation for Dialectal Arabic. In Proc. of NAACL, Atlanta, Georgia, 2013.

M. Halloun. A Practical Dictionary of the Standard Dialect Spoken in Palestine. Bethlehem University, 2000.

R. Herzallah. Aspects of Palestinian Arabic Phonology: A Nonlinear Approach. Ph.D. thesis, Cornell University. Distributed as Working Papers of the Cornell Phonetics Laboratory No. 4, 1990.

C. Holes. Modern Arabic: Structures, Functions, and Varieties. Georgetown Classics in Arabic Language and Linguistics. Georgetown University Press, 2004.

H. Kilany, H. Gadalla, H. Arram, A. Yacoub, A. El-Habashi, and C. McLemore. Egyptian Colloquial Arabic Lexicon. Linguistic Data Consortium, Catalog No.: LDC99L22, 1999.

M. Maamouri, A. Bies, T. Buckwalter, M. Diab, N. Habash, O. Rambow, and D. Tabessi. Developing and using a pilot dialectal Arabic treebank. In Proc. of LREC, Genoa, Italy, 2006.

M. Maamouri, A. Bies, T. Buckwalter, and W. Mekki. The Penn Arabic Treebank: Building a Large-Scale Annotated Arabic Corpus. In NEMLAR Conference on Arabic Language Resources and Tools, Cairo, Egypt, 2004.

M. Maamouri, A. Bies, S. Kulick, M. Ciul, N. Habash and R. Eskander. Developing an Egyptian Arabic Treebank: Impact of Dialectal Morphology on Annotation and Tool Development. In Proc. of LREC, Reykjavik, Iceland, 2014.

M. Maamouri, and C. Cieri. Resources for Arabic Natural Language Processing at the Linguistic Data Consortium. In Proc. of the International Symposium on Processing of Arabic. Faculté des Lettres, University of Manouba, Tunisia, 2002.

M. Omar. Levantine and Egyptian Arabic: Comparative Study. Foreign Service Institute. Basic Course Series, 1976.

A. Pasha, M. Al-Badrashiny, M. Diab, A. El Kholy, R. Eskander, N. Habash, M. Pooleery, O. Rambow and R. M. Roth. MADAMIRA: A Fast, Comprehensive Tool for Morphological Analysis and Disambiguation of Arabic. In Proc. of LREC, Reykjavik, Iceland, 2014.

O. Rambow, D. Chiang, M. Diab, N. Habash, R. Hwa, K. Sima'an, V. Lacey, R. Levy, C. Nichols, and S. Shareef. 2005. Parsing Arabic Dialects. Final Report, 2005 JHU Summer Workshop.

F. Rice and M. Sa'id. Eastern Arabic: an introduction to the spoken Arabic of Palestine, Syria and Lebanon. Beirut: Khayat's 1960.

W. Salloum and N. Habash. Dialectal to Standard Arabic Paraphrasing to Improve Arabic-English Statistical Machine Translation. In Proc. of the First Workshop on Algorithms and Resources for Modeling of Dialects and Language Varieties, Edinburgh, Scotland, 2011.

O. Smrž and J. Hajič. The Other Arabic Treebank: Prague Dependencies and Functions. In Ali Farghaly, editor, Arabic Computational Linguistics. CSLI Publications, 2006.

I. Zribi, R. Boujelbane, A. Masmoudi, M. Ellouze Khmekhem, L. Hadrich Belguith, and N. Habash. A Conventional Orthography for Tunisian Arabic. In Proc. of LREC, Reykjavik, Iceland, 2014.

Annotating corpus data for a quantitative, constructional analysis of motion verbs in Modern Standard Arabic

Dana Abdulrahim
University of Bahrain
darahim@uob.edu.bh

Abstract

This article proposes an annotation method of corpus data for the purposes of providing a constructionist account of lexical behavior. The lexical items in question are seven verbs of motion in Modern Standard Arabic that pertain to the events of COME (*atā*, *ǧā'a*, *ḥaḍara*, and *qadima*) and GO (*ḏahaba*, *maḍā*, and *rāḥa*). The tag set selected for the annotation of the COME and GO data frames consists of morphosyntactic tags that characterize verb usage as well as semantic tags that aim to highlight the semantic component of, for instance, adverbial and adpositional phrases that accompany the verb. I will briefly demonstrate the analytical potential of such data frame by discussing the various kinds of statistical tests such data frame is designed to undergo, as a means of better understanding lexical behavior in context, and, eventually, arriving at a better understanding of lexical and constructional choices made by native speakers of Arabic, as demonstrated in corpora.

1 Introduction

The core tenets of constructionist theories of language claim that the basic unit of linguistic organization is a construction. According to Croft and Cruse (2004:257), a construction "consist[s] of pairings of form and meaning that are at least partially arbitrary", where 'meaning' is referred to as the conventionalized function of a construction. This conventionalization of a construction's meaning/function includes not only the literal meaning of an utterance, but also the discourse situation of that utterance, as well as any pragmatic implication conveyed by that utterance (Croft and Cruse, 2004).

The concept of a 'construction' in cognitive approaches to grammar, therefore, relates to both the idiomatic portions of language, where the meaning of an utterance is not predictable from the component parts of which it consists (e.g. *raining cats and dogs*), as well as the co-occurrence of any two (free or bound) morphemes that reflect general morphosyntactic structures and where the meaning of an utterance is fully predictable from its component parts (e.g. *I need to sleep*). Such view of grammar postulates that "the interaction of syntax and lexicon is much wider and deeper than the associations of certain verbs with certain complements" (Bybee, 2010:77), and that a considerable part of our linguistic knowledge consists of conventionalized expressions, or constructions (Langacker, 1987).

In light of these constructionist assumptions, therefore, the behavior of a lexical item is best understood in its context of use and not in isolation, an idea that stretches back decades (cf. Firth, 1957). This includes not only lexical collocates, but also the entire morphosyntactic frame that hosts a lexical item. All these elements contribute to the composed or conventionalized meaning/function expressed by a particular linguistic item. In order to examine lexical behavior, therefore, we need to move beyond single semantic, morphological, or syntactic properties of a lexical item and scrutinize the entire lexico-syntactic frame in which it occurs. Increasingly, this is done through examination of corpus data. The availability of corpora facilitates and motivates such highly contextualized analytical approach, since corpora provide a large amount of naturally occurring, contextualized uses (as opposed to the reliance on introspective and elicited data that may not reflect actual language usage at all). Moreover, corpora provide large amounts of linguistic data, which allows the researcher to conduct extensive quantitative analyses of the phenomenon in question.

In Modern Standard Arabic, the existence of several verbs denoting the motion events COME (*atā*, *ǧā'a*, *ḥaḍara*, and *qadima*) and GO (*ḏahaba*, *maḍā*, and *rāḥa*) provides an excellent case study for a constructionist, corpus-based examination of the features that characterize the usage of supposedly near-synonymous lexical items. In Abdulrahim (2013) I have argued that the four COME verbs – as well as the three GO verbs – can be interchangeably used in contexts where the event depicts a strictly deictic and physical motion event, as in (1) and (2).

Proceedings of the EMNLP 2014 Workshop on Arabic Natural Langauge Processing (ANLP), pages 28–38,
October 25, 2014, Doha, Qatar.

(1) أتت / جاءت / حضرت / قدمت جدتي إلى المطار

atā / ǧā'a / ḥaḍara / qadima.PERF.3SG.F	grandmother.CL.1SG.GEN
came	my grandmother

ALL	ART=airport
to	the airport

'My grandmother came to the airport'

(2) ذهب \ مضى \ راح الأب إلى مركز الشرطة

ḏahaba / maḍā / rāḥa.PERF.3SG.M	ART=father-NOM	ALL
went	the father	to

station	ART=police
station	the police

'The father went to the police station'

However, these verbs diverge greatly in their metaphorical and idiomatic uses, in addition to showing idiosyncratic patterns of lexico-syntactic behavior. For instance, The sentence in (1) would not admit all four verbs when the aspect inflection on the verb is changed. To illustrate, in (3), if we hold all constructional features constant and change verb inflection from perfective to jussive, this results in a preference for *atā* and *ḥaḍara* by native speakers of Arabic over *ǧā'a* or *qadima*.

(3) لم تأت / ؟تجيء / تحضر / ؟تقدم جدتي إلى المطار

NEG	*atā / ǧā'a / ḥaḍara / qadima*.JUSS.3SG.F
did not	come

grandmother.CL.1SG.GEN	ALL	ART=airport
my grandmother	to	the airport

'My grandmother did not come to the airport'

The above example stresses the need to investigate features of the lexico-syntactic construction that each COME verb most typically associates with. For these purposes, I have adopted the methodological approach outlined in Gries (2006), Gries & Divjak (2009), and Gries & Otani (2010) for a constructionist description of the Behavioral Profile of a lexical item. I have also employed logistic regression – namely polytomous logistic regression, outlined in detail in Δrppe (2008) – as a statistical method that models lexical or constructional choices as a function of a wide range of contextual features.

The quantitative approach to lexical analysis presented in this paper involves constructing a data frame for every lexical item under study, in which numerous corpus concordance lines are individually marked-up for an extensive set of linguistic features (morphological, syntactic, and semantic). This includes, for examples, specific elements pertaining to verb morphology, phrase structure, as well as the different elements that co-occur with the verb in specific constructions. Such data frame can undergo numerous exploratory and multi-variate statistical tests as a means of zeroing in on the kinds of constructions associated with the verbs in question.

2 The corpus

In order to construct the multi-variate data frame for the analysis of motion verbs in Arabic, I chose ArabiCorpus (arabicorpus.byu.edu) as the source for data. ArabiCorpus is a free online corpus developed by Dilworth Parkinson at Brigham Young University. As of October 2012, the corpus contains around 146,000,000 word tokens from different written and spoken genres. At the time of data collection (Fall 2010) the corpus contained around 69,000,000 word tokens. Additional MSA as well as pre-modern texts have been added to the corpus since the beginning of 2011. Texts included in ArabiCorpus almost exclusively belong to the written genre, save for a small sub-corpus of spoken Egyptian Arabic. The written genres covered in ArabiCorpus vary from newspaper writing, pre-modern writing, modern literature, to nonfiction. These genres are represented in the corpus in varying proportions with newspaper writing accounting for over 90% of the total size of the entire corpus. News articles included in this sub-section of ArabiCorpus cover issues from 1996 to 2010 and are extracted from periodicals published in different parts of the Arab world (North Africa, Egypt, Arabian Gulf, the Levant, etc.). For this study, the MSA sub-corpora that were queried for COME and GO uses are related to newspaper, modern literature, and nonfiction writing. As expected, most examples returned from corpus queries were in fact drawn from the newspaper genre.

ArabiCorpus is not tagged for parts-of-speech (POS) which makes the search for particular grammatical categories a daunting task. Nevertheless, it can be easily queried using regular expressions. This study targeted very specific inflected forms of the MSA verb: perfective, imperfective, jussive, subjunctive, and imperative; and excluded participial forms (e.g. active participle) and nominal forms (e.g. verbal nouns). Relying on orthographic regular expressions, therefore, proved to be the most efficient method for querying these particular forms. What may complicate any search in an Arabic written corpus is the lack of short vowels which are indicated by certain diacritics written over or underneath a letter. Naturally, it was necessary to filter corpus returns manually to eliminate any irrelevant forms that may have been returned in the corpus search.

Despite the time-consuming nature of such corpus querying steps, ArabiCorpus proved to be a reliable and rich source for contextualized language uses. Add to that the fact that even though the online interface of ArabiCorpus only displays 10 words before and after the KWIC (key word in context), the researcher can still retrieve the entire text hosting that sentence. Therefore when the analysis or the annotation requires going beyond the 10 word window to examine the entire phrase structure, it is possible to retrieve such information from ArabiCorpus. Another added benefit of using the online interface of ArabiCorpus is the ease of downloading all returned hits of a certain lexical item or construction to be viewed in a spreadsheet, which was a major step in the collection of data for this research.

3 COME and GO data frames

In Abdulrahim (2013) I proposed a quantitative (as well as a qualitative) analysis based on the construction of a data frame for each one of the seven verbs of motion. Each individual data frame is typically composed of a large number of corpus concordance lines (500 concordance lines) involving the KWIC (i.e. verb under investigation) in its natural context of use. Every concordance line is thoroughly examined and tagged for a wide range of morphosyntactic and semantic features. These constructional features include the syntactic structure that hosts the verb, the patterns of verbal inflections for every instance of verb use (e.g. subject number, person, and gender, as well as other morphosyntactic aspects of the Arabic verb), the semantic properties of other components of the construction (e.g. semantic properties of the subject), as well as the inclusion or exclusion of phrases, lexical items, or clitics denoting a starting point of the event (SOURCE), a terminal point of the event (GOAL), etc.

Such a heavily annotated dataset has the potential of being explored statistically in multiple ways via simple frequency count methods as well as complex multi-variate statistical modeling. Such quantitative approach to analyzing corpus data aims to define the specific characteristics of the constructions associated with the various meanings and functions of each MSA COME and GO verb involved in this study. In the following section I will elaborate on the selection of these contextual features for the annotation of COME and GO data frames.

3.1 Selection of contextual features and the annotation of corpus data

The first step for creating a multi-variate data frame is to generate a list of features or variables which are relevant to the motion event schemas in questions and which reflect the morphosyntax of Modern Standard Arabic. Along the lines of Gries's study on the polysemy of the English verb *run* (2006), Gries and Divjak's (2006) investigation of Russian verbs of TRY, as well as Gries and Otani's (2010) analysis of the synonymy and polysemy of adjectives of size in English, I developed a large set of morphological, syntactic, and semantic features that reflect the usage of MSA motion verbs.

The variable set includes nominal variables (multiple levels) and binary variables (YES/NO values indicating absence or presence of feature). Table 1 shows the different categories of variables subsumed under morphological, syntactic, and semantic variables. In Appendix A, I provide examples and illustrations of the different annotations of levels within semantic variables taken from the actual data frame. [1]

Morphological variables	*Levels*
TENSE	PRESENT, PAST, FUTURE, IRREALIS (non-finite forms)
ASPECT	SIMPLE, HABITUAL, PROGRESSIVE, PERFECT, INCHOATIVE, NON-FIN (non-finite forms)
MORPHOLOGICAL ASPECT AND MOOD OF THE VERB	IMPERFECTIVE, PERFECTIVE, SUBJUNCTIVE, JUSSIVE, IMPERATIVE
SUBJECT PERSON	1ST, 2ND, 3RD
SUBJECT NUMBER	SINGULAR, DUAL, PLURAL
SUBJECT GENDER	FEMININE, MASCULINE, NIL (for 1st person inflections)

[1] The data frame was, in fact, coded for more variables than the set laid out in Table 4, such as the different morphosyntactic realizations of GOAL, SOURCE, MANNER, etc., as well as certain recurring lexical elements (e.g. adverbs, adverbial uses, and other lexical items). These additional variables did not form part of the quantitative analysis in Abdulrahim (2013). Nevertheless, they are of some interest and proved to be useful for a qualitative analysis of MSA motion verbs.

Syntactic variables	*Levels*
TRANSITIVITY	YES, NO
INTERROGATIVE	YES, NO
NEGATIVE	YES, NO
PREPOSITIONAL PHRASE	YES, NO
LOCATIVE ADVERB PHRASE	YES, NO
ADVERBIAL PHRASE	YES, NO
SERIAL VERB CONSTRUCTION	YES, NO
Semantic variables	***Levels***
SUBJECT CATEGORY	ACTIVITY, ANIMAL, ATTRIBUTE, BODY, COGNITION, COMMUNICATION, CONTENT (of a document/speech), DEMONSTRATIVE, DUMMY SUBJECT, EVENT, GROUP, HUMAN, LOCATION, NOTION, OBJECT/ARTIFACT, SENSE, STATE, SUBSTANCE, TIME
GOAL PHRASE	YES, NO
SOURCE PHRASE	YES, NO
MANNER PHRASE	YES, NO
SETTING PHRASE	YES, NO
PATH PHRASE	YES, NO
PURPOSIVE PHRASE	YES, NO
COMITATIVE PHRASE	YES, NO
TEMPORAL PHRASE	YES, NO
DEGREE PHRASE	YES, NO

Table 1. A selection of variables GO and COME corpus hits were coded for.

As mentioned earlier, the primary motivation for this set of 23 linguistic features/tags has been the lexico-syntactic properties of deictic motion event schemas in MSA. For instance, a deictic motion event is likely to include a phrase specifying a GOAL and/or a SOURCE of the motion event. In addition, it may include MANNER of motion and the inclusion of a COMITATIVE phrase (i.e. accompaniment by an object/individual in the GO or COME event). Each verb usage was also coded for the semantic category of the sentential subject or, conceptually speaking, the moving entity involved in the motion event. These categories include HUMAN, OBJECT or ARTIFACT, and also more abstract/non-physical entities such as EVENT, COMMUNICATION (e.g. a statement), COGNITION (e.g. an idea), etc. As for the morphosyntactic features selected for tagging motion verbs, these reflect the inflectional properties of the MSA verb (MORPHOLOGICAL ASPECT AND MOOD, NUMBER, PERSON, and GENDER) as well as TENSE and ASPECT. The variable labeled TRANSITIVITY, only pertains to certain uses of COME verbs in MSA where COME verbs can appear in transitive constructions in which the direct object is the GOAL of the motion event.

Text genre was not considered a variable since, as I mentioned earlier, the majority of the annotated 3,500 corpus hits belong to the genre of newspaper writing. Results obtained from examining this data frame should, therefore, be considered as mostly reflective of the usage of COME and GO verbs in newspaper writing. Sentence (4) is an example of a contextualized verb use annotated for the features listed above.

(4) وهي تمضي بسرعة في مؤامراتها

CONJ=PP	*maḍā*.IMPF.3SG.F	INST=speed
and she	goes	quickly

LOC	conspiracies-CL.3SG.F.GEN
in	her conspiracies

'And it's [i.e. Israel] quickly going ahead with its conspiracies'

VERB	*maḍā*	TENSE	PRESENT
ASPECT	SIMPLE	MORPH_ASP/ MOOD	IMPERFECTIVE
SUBJ_NUM	SINGULAR	SUBJ_PER	3RD
SUBJ_GEN	FEM	SUBJ_CAT	GROUP
INTEROG	NO	NEGATION	NO
SVC	NO	PP	YES
LOC_ADV	NO	ADVERBIAL	YES
GOAL	NO	SOURCE	NO
MANNER	YES	SETTING	YES
PATH	NO	PURPOSIVE	NO
COMITATIVE	NO	TEMPORAL	NO
DEGREE	NO		

4 Statistical analyses

A wide range of statistical tests can be applied in order to explore the data frames described above for various purposes.[2] For instance, we can simply run the COME and GO data frames through mono-variate exploratory tests such as chi-square tests as a means of zeroing in on the distribution of contextual elements per each GO and COME verb. This kind of analysis would constitute a first step towards identifying divergence in usage patterns associated with each MSA motion verb. This preliminary step further motivates and justifies the examination of interaction patterns among the contextual features, as

[2] See Hastie, T., et al (2009), and Agresti (2002) – among others – for comprehensive discussions on statistical tests that can be applied to multi-variate data frames.

well as the identification of clusters of features that are closely tied to certain verb uses. A multivariate analysis eventually facilitates the identification of prototypical uses of each verb as well as the less prototypical uses. In the following I will briefly discuss three types of statistical methods that can be applied to the MSA COME and GO data frames: (i) chi-square test; (ii) cluster analysis; and (iii) polytomous logistic regression analysis.[3]

4.1 Chi-square tests

The primary purpose of subjecting the COME and GO data frames to chi-square test of independence is to examine whether the distribution of the different levels of variables (tags) do not vary as a function of verb (null hypothesis), or, if they actually do vary as a function of verb (alternative hypothesis). For instance, if we examine the occurrence of a GOAL phrase per each GO verb, would the distribution of variables be the same or different across the three verbs. To test this hypothesis –where we have an independent variable (verb) and a dependent variable (GOAL) –we can run a chi-square test on variable distribution. Table 2 shows the observed frequencies for the occurrence/absence of a GOAL phrase per each GO verb, while Table 3 shows the expected frequencies calculated by the command chisq.test()$expected in R (www.r-project.org).

VERB	GOAL - YES OBS. FREQ.	GOAL - NO OBS. FREQ.
ḏahaba	298	202
maḍā	32	468
rāḥa	1	499

Table 2. Observed values for the variable GOAL by GO verb.

VERB	GOAL - YES EXP. FREQ.	GOAL - NO EXP. FREQ.
ḏahaba	110.3333	389.6667
maḍā	110.3333	389.6667
rāḥa	110.3333	389.6667

Table 3. Expected values for the variable GOAL by GO verb.

The calculated Pearson's *chi*-square test for the distribution given in Table 4 proved to be quite significant: $X^2 = 277.1034$, $df = 6$, *p-value* $< 2.2e\text{-}16$. This indicates that the distribution the variable GOAL for each GO verb deviates highly significantly from the expected distribution.

We can also examine the cell-wise divergences from a uniform distribution for this particular contingency table by conducting a standardized Pearson's residual (discussed in Agresti 2002: 81; Arppe, 2008: 83-84). These test statistics can either be retrieved in R by using the command chisq.test()$std or by running the function chisq.posthoc(), which is part of the statistical package {polytomous} developed by Antti Arppe (2012). Table 4 contains the calculated values, which indicate whether the observed co-occurrence frequency reported in each individual cell is significantly *more* or *less* than expected.[4] The chisq.posthoc()function presents an easier way to interpret these figures, in that it assigns +/–/0 values for each cell, which can be interpreted as insignificant (0), significantly more than expected (+), or significantly less than expected (–).

VERB	GOAL - YES	GOAL - NO
ḏahaba	24.78665 (+)	-24.78665 (–)
maḍā	-10.34611 (–)	10.34611 (+)
rāḥa	-14.44053 (–)	14.44053 (+)

TABLE 4. Standardized Pearson's residuals for the occurrence of GOAL by GO verb.

As discussed earlier, these exploratory tests constitute a first attempt at understanding the distributional patterns of selected variables among the different verbs. Such mono-variate methods undoubtedly set the stage for the more complex multi-variate analyses that will follow and to which I turn next.

4.2 Cluster analysis

Clustering methods can help us examine the joint effect on the overall verbal behavior for each verb in the GO and COME verb set. One such method is referred to as hierarchical agglomera-

[3] See Abdulrahim (2013) for further description of the properties and applications of these statistical analyses on the MSA COME and GO data frames.

[4] Typically, the standardized Pearson's residual value is significantly higher than what is expected when it is > 2.0, and significantly lower than expected when the value is < -2.0 (Arppe, 2008).

tive cluster analysis (explained more in detail in Gries, 2006; Diviaj and Gries, 2006; Gries and Otani, 2010, among others). Generally speaking, this clustering method groups together the lexical elements that are most similar to one another and, at the same time, the ones that are highly dissimilar to other elements in other clusters. Therefore, what we expect to see from this statistical method is a clustering dendrogram that shows us which COME or GO verbs overlap in their usage as opposed to the ones with which they hardly share any characteristics.

This method requires generating a table that lists relative frequencies (or proportions) of co-occurrence values of dependent variables per independent variable (the GO and COME verbs under study). A similarity/dissimilarity matrix is first computed, followed by computing a cluster structure based on a specific amalgamation rule.[5] The resulting cluster structure can then be visually represented in a dendrogram. The calculations involved in the different stages of hierarchical agglomerative cluster analysis have been made easier to conduct using BP 1.01 script, a program written by Stefan Gries (2009) for R. This R-based script uses a host of statistical methods required in the stages mentioned above. It initially generates a co-occurrence table of relative frequencies of the different levels (IDTAG-LEVELs) within variables (IDTAGs).[6] Table 5 shows a sample of such output table generated by BP 1.01 for the distribution of TENSE by COME verb.

IDTAG-LEVEL	*atā*	*ḥaḍara*	*ǧā'a*	*qadima*	
FUT	0.028	0.076	0	0.002	columns
IRR	0.188	0.126	0.022	0.022	sum
PAST	0.162	0.694	0.97	0.966	to
PRES	0.622	0.104	0.008	0.01	1.0

Table 5. Sample of a co-occurrence table generated by the BP 1.01 script for the variable (IDTAG) TENSE by COME verb.

The BP 1.01 script returns a comprehensive table with similar values for all dependent by independent variable co-occurrences that have been fed into the script. This particular table can be subjected to a number of tests including the hierarchical agglomerative cluster analysis. For this particular clustering technique I relied on the (dis)similarity metric 'Canberra', and 'Ward' as the amalgamation rule that computes a cluster structure.[7]

The dendrogram in Figure 1 shows two major divides between the four verbs that the hierarchical agglomerative cluster analysis deemed significant. The first cluster (on the left) formed in this analysis appears to group the verbs *atā* and *ǧā'a* together, while the other cluster groups *ḥaḍara* and *qadima* together. Here, we find that the AU *p*-value (Approximately Unbiased) – which is a probability measure computed through multi-scale bootstrap resampling – for the cluster containing *ḥaḍara* and *qadima* is calculated to approximate 87%, while the AU *p*-value for the cluster of *atā* and *ǧā'a* is 82%. Again, this does not necessarily imply that *ḥaḍara* and *qadima* are highly similar, but that they are very dissimilar from *atā* and *ǧa'a* in their usage. Indeed, subsequent mutli-variate as well as qualitative analyses showed that *atā* and *ǧā'a* shared more usage patterns than they did with the other COME verbs.

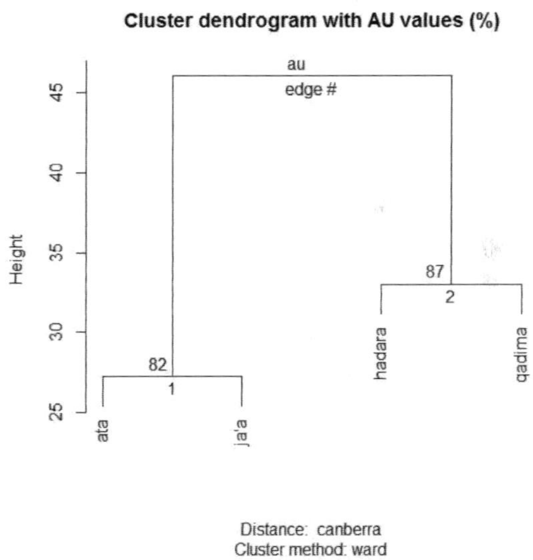

Figure 1. Dendrogram based on the COME multi-variate data frame.

4.3 Polytomous logistic regression

Another multi-variate analysis that can be applied to this kind of data frame for the purpose of examining patterns of variable interaction is logistic regression. Polytomous logistic regression analysis (explained in detail in Arppe,

[5] An amalgamation rule is what determines whether or not two items are sufficiently similar in order to be linked or clustered together.

[6] The idea of an ID tag was introduced by Atkins (1987) in her work on *danger*, where she examined collocates, colligations, POS, as well as other characteristics of the key word. An ID tag was therefore used to refer to the individual contextual features co-occurring with the keyword.

[7] For a detailed description of this clustering method see Gries (2009), pp 306-319.

2008), in particular, applies advanced algorithms in order to determine the relative effects of multiple predictor variables (the tags/contextual features) on the choice of more than two outcome variables (i.e. the four COME verbs and the three GO verbs). Generally speaking, logistic regression would estimate probabilities of the occurrence of each COME or GO verb given a particular context of use, and is therefore compatible with the view that linguistic choices are probabilistic rather than categorical (Bresnan, 2006; Arppe, 2007, 2008, 2009; among others). In a nutshell, polytomous logistic regression estimates variable parameters which can be interpreted "naturally" as *odds* (Harrell 2001). In other words, it determines the extent to which the existence of a variable (i.e. feature/tag) in the context increases (or decreases) the *chances* of a particular outcome (i.e. verb) to occur, with all the other explanatory variables being equal.

To illustrate, we can conduct such analysis on the annotated COME data frame. The first step is to select a set of variables to include in the model. Note, however, that the binary and nominal variables listed in Table 1 need to be converted into the form of logical variables in order to be included in the logistic regression model.[8] The selection of these variables relies, first of all, on a mono-variate analysis (such as the inspection of standardized Pearson's residuals) as a means of figuring out which variables seem to have explanatory potential as opposed to those that do not. A second criterion for variable selection relies on inspecting pair-wise association patterns between variables. That is to say, we need to examine the extent to which certain variables have a high rate of co-occurrence, as a means of reducing collinearity in the regression model. The model listed in (5) includes 30 logical variables as the independent variables and the COME verb as a dependent variable.

(5) **VERB** ~ TENSE.FUT + TENSE.PAST + TENSE.PRES + ASPECT.HAB + ASPECT.SIMPLE + MORPH_ASP.MOOD.SUBJN + TRANSITIVITY.YES + SUBJ_NUM.PL + SUBJ_PER.1ST + SUBJ_PER.3RD + SUBJ_GEN.FEM + SUBJ_CAT.ACTIVITY + SUBJ_CAT.COMMUNICATION + SUBJ_CAT.DEMONSTRATIVE + SUBJ_CAT.EVENT + SUBJ_CAT.GROUP + SUBJ_CAT.INDIVIDUAL + SUBJ_CAT.STATE + SUBJ_CAT.TIME + NEGATION.YES + PP.YES + LOC_ADV.YES + ADVERBIAL.YES + GOAL.YES + SOURCE.YES + MANNER.YES + SETTING.YES + PURPOSIVE.YES + COMITATIVE.YES + TEMPORAL.YES

The overall *accuracy* rate calculated for this model is 0.845. The *accuracy* measure (Menard, 1995: 28-30; Arppe, 2008: 129-132) corresponds to the number of times the model assigned the highest probability estimate to the actually observed verb in a given annotated context. We can also examine the individual accuracy rates per verb as a means of zeroing in on which particular verb(s) the model was more successful in predicting. We can now examine the probability estimates that the polytomous logistic regression analysis assigns to each of the COME verbs per annotated context (4 verbs * 2,000 sentences). These estimated probabilities range from very high values (approaching 1.00) to very low values (approaching 0.00) and any values in between, depending on the set of predictors (i.e. contextual features) present in a particular context of use. We can illustrate with sentences (6) and (7) which are extracted from the original data frame. In (6) the verb received an almost categorical probability estimate, while in (7) the verb received a less categorical probability estimate. It is also possible to examine the set of contextual features that each sentences was tagged for and which were used as predictor variables in the logistic regression model

(6)

atā = *0.022* *ḥaḍara* = *0.000* ***ğā'a* = *0.978*** **(observed)** *qadima* = *0.000*	**contextual features used (in the model):** TENSE.PAST + ASPECT.SIMPLE + SUBJ_PER.3RD + SUBJ_CAT.DEM + LOC_ADV.YES + SETTING.YES

جاء ذلك خلال تصريحات أدلى بها الوزير خورشيد

ğā'a.PERF.3SG.M DEM ADV
came that during

statements declare.PERF.3SG.M
statements declared

INST=CL.3SG.F ART=minister Khurshid
by it the minister Khurshid

'This came during statements that the minister Khurshid made'

[8] Every level of variable is turned into an individual (logical) variable with the levels TRUE/FALSE indicating whether this variable has or has not been observed in the context of use. For instance, the variable TENSE has four levels: PRESNT / PAST / FUTURE / NIL. When turned into logical variables, we end up with four different variables (TENSE_PRESENT, TENSE_PAST, TENSE_FUTURE and TENSE_NIL), the presence or absence of which is indicated by TRUE or FALSE.

(7)

atā = 0.199 ***ḥaḍara* = 0.137** **(observed)** *ǧā'a = 0.247* *qadima = 0.416*	**contextual features used (in the model):** TESNE.PAST + ASPECT.SIMPLE + SUBJ_PER.3RD + SUBJ_CAT.HUMAN + PP.YES + LOC.ADV.YES + MANNER.YES + COMITATIVE.YES

وقد حضر الأب علي الفور ومعه عددا من زملائه الأطباء

CONJ=DM	***ḥaḍara***.PERF.3SG.M	ART=father	LOC
and already	came	the father	on

ART=immediately	CONJ=COM-CL.3SG.M	number
the immediately	and with him	number

ABL	colleagues-CL.3SG.M.GEN	ART=doctors
of	his colleagues	the doctors

'And the father came immediately with a number of his physician colleagues'

The sentence in (6) can be considered as a prototypical use of the verb *ǧā'a*. In (7), however, note that the verb which received the highest probability estimate was not the actually observed verb in that context. Nevertheless, all four verbs were assigned more-or-less equal probability estimates. This may indicate that this is one context of use in which the four COME verbs can be used interchangeably. Relying on my native speaker intuition, substituting the observed verb with the other COME verbs in (7) does not raise any red flags, especially since this particular contexts of use indicates physical motion of a HUMAN agent, as I discussed earlier in this paper.

Of course, not all predictions made by the model were accurate. Among the sentences for which a single verb received a very high probability estimate, a number of instances in which the predicted verb was not the observed verb were found. Such sentences proved to be worthy of scrutiny due to the fact that some of these "mis-predictions" were associated with less typical uses of the verb that was actually observed in context. For instance, in (8), the verb *qadima* was the verb observed in context, yet the model chose *ḥaḍara* instead as the verb that was most fitting in that context.

(8)

atā = 0.022 ***ḥaḍara* = 0.962** **(predicted)** *ǧā'a = 0.005* ***qadima* = 0.011** **(observed)**	**contextual features used (in the model):** SUBJ_PER.3RD + SUBJ_CAT.HUMAN + ADVERBIAL.YES + GOAL.YES + MANNER.YES + TRANSITIVITY.YES

وكان علي بن عبد الله إذا قدم مكة حاجا أو معتمرا عطلت قريش مجالسها

wa=kāna	*'ali bin 'abdillah*	*iḏā*
CONJ=be.PERF.3SG.M	Ali Bin Abdullah	COND
and was	Ali Bin Abdullah	if

qadima	*makka-ta*	*ḥāǧǧan*	*aw*
qadima.PERF.3SG.M	Mecca-ACC	pilgrim	CONJ
he came	Mecca	pilgrim	or

mu'tamiran	*'aṭṭalat*
pilgrim	suspend.PERF.3SG.F
minor.pilgrim	suspended

qurayš	*maǧālisa-ha*
Quraysh	meetings-CL.3SG.F
Quraysh	its meetings

'When Ali bin Abdullah used to come to Mecca on a pilgrimage Quraysh would suspend its meetings'

Interestingly, this particular usage of *qadima* in (8) can be found in a specific genre, that of historical narrative. While *atā, ǧā'a*, and *ḥaḍara* may all appear in transitive constructions in MSA, *qadima* normally does not. It is, however, used in transitive constructions to signal a shift in register, as in the example in (8). Since such pattern of use occurs less frequently than the general overall usage of *qadima*, the model assigns *ḥaḍara* instead as the most plausible verb choice for such context. Careful inspection of "mis-predictions" such as the above is, therefore, an important step to identify the less typical uses of verbs, as well as to decide whether the variable set chosen for the model has or has not been effective in accounting for verb usage. The probability estimates calculated for the GO data frame did not yield such satisfying results, and did not necessarily agree with my native speaker's intuition. In Abdulrahim (2013: 101) I attributed such findings to the set of variables that GO verbs were coded for in the data frame (which, more or less, resembled the variable set COME verbs were coded for). More specifically I suggested that the data frame should include more lexical or collocational variables.

5 Conclusions

The methodological approach to lexical analysis, described here, represents a departure from traditional, compartmentalized treatments of the Arabic verb. In this paper, I have adopted a construction-based approach that considers various aspects of language (morphology, syntax, semantics, etc.) as equally responsible for defining the behavior of a linguistic item. The creation of a 500-row data frame per verb has allowed us to probe into the frequency and distribution facts regarding the usage of seven highly frequent motion verbs in MSA. Moreover, the annotation of each corpus return for a wide range of contextual and semantic features offered the possibility of foregrounding the most prototypical aspects of use for each verb, as well as highlighting shared patterns of usage among the near-synonymous verbs in a set. In this paper, I have argued that the value of constructing a data frame of this type lies in developing more sophisticated lexico-syntactic frames of linguistic items, in that it allows us to extract preferred profiles of the lexical or constructional items under study.

Thankfully, there is a wide range of statistical tests that have made the examination of and search for lexico-syntactic patterns in large data frames easier and more manageable. These statistical tests vary from simple, mono-variate exploratory test to complex and multi-variate predictive models. Each one of the three statistical analyses discussed in this paper serves to highlight a particular aspect of variable distribution and variable interaction and, thus, helps us understand the complexity of the relationship between the near-synonymous COME and GO verbs. Generally speaking, the application of such statistical tests to large, multi-variate data frames helps us examine the particular linguistic features that characterize lexical and constructional choices, which may have direct applications in natural language generation. In addition, the identification of prototypical and marginal uses of verbs – discussed particularly in 4.3 – can possibly contribute to developing readability assessment of texts for learners of MSA.[9]

Finally, lexicographic treatments of the highly frequent motion verbs discussed in this paper, as exhibited in bilingual and, mostly, monolingual dictionaries, range from almost adequate to completely mis-representative descriptions of the major and minor senses of these verbs (Abdulrahim, 2013). Many monolingual dictionaries follow a traditional and highly ideological system of lexical representation whereby archaic uses of a lexical item are foregrounded and little attention is paid to more contemporary uses. The quantitative (and qualitative) analysis of a data frame such as the ones described here can help tease apart the different idiosyncratic uses for each of the seven motion verbs as well as identify the most and the least prototypical uses. One of the practical applications of such a data frame, therefore, is to create extensive, usage-based dictionary entries that are more representative of contemporary language use and that would be useful for the native speaker of the language, the language learner, and the language researcher.[10]

Acknowledgments

I would like to thank Professors Antti Arppe, John Newman, and Sally Rice at the University of Alberta for their constant guidance and feedback throughout the various stages of the creation of this data frame, the application of statistical tests, and the linguistic analysis. I would also like to thank the ANLP 2014 reviewers of this paper for their encouraging feedback and insights.

References

Abdulrahim, Dana. 2013. A corpus study of basic motion events in Modern Standard Arabic. Unpublished doctoral dissertation. University of Alberta. Edmonton, Alberta. To be found on http://hdl.handle.net/10402/era.33921

Abdulrahim, Dana. (submitted). Quantitative approaches to analyzing COME constructions in Modern Standard Arabic. To appear in A. Hardie, A. T. McEnrey (eds.), *Arabic Corpus Linguistics*.

Agresti, Alan. 2002. *Categorical data analysis* (2nd ed.). Hoboken: John Wiley & Sons, Hoboken.

Arppe, Antti. 2007. Multi-variate methods in corpus-based lexicography: A study of synonymy in finnish. *Proceedings from the Corpus Linguistics Conference (CL2007),* Birmingham, United Kingdom.

[9] I would like to thank an anonymous reviewers of this paper for pointing out these particular applications of the statistical methods discussed here.

[10] See Abdulrahim for three samples of suggested usage-based dictionary entries for the COME verb *atā*: (1) a *corpus-illustrated* dictionary entry that elaborates on the existing (bilingual) dictionary entries of the verb by supplementing relevant corpus examples for each verb sub-sense or usage; (2) a minimalist sub-sense frequency-based dictionary entry that orders the verb entries according to the frequency of occurrence of the overall general usage (physical, metaphorical, etc); and (3) a *usage-based* dictionary entry for *atā* that is directly based on the quantitative and qualitative analyses conducted in her study (2013: 243-249)

Arppe, Antti. 2008. Univariate, bivariate and multivariate methods in corpus-based lexicography - a study of synonyms. (PhD, University of Helsinki). *Publications of the Department of General Linguistics,* 44.

Arppe, Antti. 2009. Linguistic choices vs. probabilities - how much and what can linguistic theory explain? In: Featherston, Sam & Winkler, Susanne (eds.) *The Fruits of Empirical Linguistics 1*, pp 1-24. Berlin: de Gruyter.

Atkins, Beryl. T. S. 1987. Semantic ID tags: Corpus evidence for dictionary senses. Proceedings of the Third Annual Conference of the UW Centre for the New Oxford English Dictionary, pp17–36.

Bresnan, Joan. 2006. Is syntactic knowledge probabilistic? Experiments with the English dative alternation. *Pre-Proceedings of the International Conference on Linguistic Evidence,* Tübingen, Germany. (pp. 2-4).

Bybee, Joan. 2010. *Language, usage and cognition*. Cambridge: Cambridge University Press.

Croft, William. & Allan. D. Cruse. 2004. *Cognitive linguistics*. Cambridge: Cambridge University Press.

Divjak, Dagmar. S., & Stefan T. Gries. 2006. Ways of trying in Russian: Clustering and comparing behavioral profiles. *Corpus Linguistics and Linguistic Theory, 2*(1), 23-60.

Firth, John. R. 1957. A synopsis of linguistic theory, 1930-1955. In J. R. Firth. 1968. *Selected Papers of J. R. Firth 1952-1959* (pp. 168-205). London: Longman.

Gries, Stefan Th. 2006. Corpus-based methods and cognitive semantics: The many meanings of *to run*. In S. Th. Gries, & A. Stefanowitsch (Eds.), *Corpora in cognitive linguistics: Corpus-based approaches to syntax and lexis,*pp 57-99. Berlin/New York: Mouton de Gruyter.

Gries, Stefan Th. 2009. *Statistics for linguistics with R: A practical introduction*. Berlin: De Gruyter Mouton.

Gries, Stefan Th. & Dagmar S. Divjak. 2009. Behavioral profiles: A corpus-based approach towards cognitive semantic analysis. In Vyvyan Evans, & S. S. Pourcel (Eds.), *New directions in cognitive linguistics*, pp 57-75. Amsterdam/Philadelphia: John Benjamins.

Gries, Stefan. Th. & Naoki Otani. 2010. Behavioral profiles: A corpus-based perspective on synonymy and antonymy. *ICAME Journal, 34*, pp 121-150

Harrell, Frank E. 2001. *Regression modeling strategies: With applications to linear models, logistic regression and survival analysis*. New York: Springer-Verlag.

Hastie, Trevor, Robert Tibshirani, & Jerome Friedman. 2009. *The elements of statistical learning: Data mining, inference, and prediction*. New York: Springer.

Langacker, Ronald. 1987. *Foundations of cognitive grammar, vol. I: Theoretical prerequisites*. Stanford, Calif.: Stanford University Press.

Menard, Scott. 1995. *Applied logistic regression analysis*. Thousand Oaks: Sage Publications.

Data sets and R scripts

Abdulrahim, Dana. (forthcoming). Arabic come and go. A micro-corpus of 3500 occurrences of seven motion verbs in MSA (*atā*, *ǧā'a*, *ḥaḍara*, *qadima*, *ḏahaba*, *maḍā*, and *rāḥa*), annotated for a wide range of morphological, syntactic, and semantic variables

Arppe, Antti. 2012. polytomous: Polytomous Logistic Regression for fixed and mixed effects. R package version 0.1.4.

Gries, Stefan. Th. (2009). BehavioralProfiles 1.01. A program for R 2.7.1 and higher.

Appendix A. Examples for annotation for semantic variables

variable	**sample of annotation**
SUBJECT CATEGORY:	
ACTIVITY	هجوم 'attack', عمليات 'operations', تصويت 'voting'
ANIMAL	جواد 'horse', كلب 'dog'
ATTRIBUTE	كرم 'generosity', شهرة 'fame'
BODY	عيون 'eyes', قدم 'foot'
COGNITION	تفكير 'thought', خيال 'imagination'
COMMUNICATION	سؤال 'question', تقرير 'report'
CONTENT (of a document/speech)	جاء في البيان *ǧā'a*.PERF.3SG.M LOC ART=statement 'came in the statement…', جاء في الرسالة *ǧā'a*.PERF.3SG.M LOC ART=letter 'came in the statement…',

DEMONSTRA-TIVE	جاء ذلك *ǧā'a*.PERF.3SG.M LOC DEM 'that came…', جاء هذا *ǧā'a*.PERF.3SG.M LOC DEM 'this came…', etc.
EVENT	إجتماع 'meeting', ندوة 'sympo-sium', قمة 'summit'
GROUP (repre-senting humans collectively)	اليابان 'Japan', المنتخب 'varsity', الحكومة 'the government'
HUMAN	الأولاد 'the boys', البابا 'the Pope'
LOCATION	موقع 'location', المدن 'the cities'
NOTION	الأذية 'harm', مصدر 'source'
PHYSICAL OB-JECT/ARTIFACT	منح 'grants', القمح 'wheat'
SENSE	صوت 'voice/sound'
STATE	الموت 'the death', مرحلة 'phase'
SUBSTANCE	حرائق 'fires', مطر 'rain'
TIME	موسم'season', الغد 'tomorrow'
GOAL PHRASE: YES	مساعداتنا تذهب **إلى الشيشان** aid.CL.1PL.GEN *ḏahaba*.IMPF.3SG.F **ALL** **ART=Chechnya** 'Our aid goes to Chechnya'
SOURCE PHRASE: YES	الهجرات الجنوبية التي قدمت **من الهند** ART=immigrations ART=southern RP *qadima*.PERF.3SG.F **ABL** **ART=India** 'The southern immigrations that came from India…'
MANNER PHRASE: YES	هذه الجهود لم تذهب **هدرا** DEM ART=efforts NEG *ḏahaba*.JUSS.3SG.F **vain.ADV** 'These efforts weren't in vain'
SETTING PHRASE: YES	بل تأتي **في اطار مخطط شامل** CONJ *atā*.IMPF.3SG.F **LOC frame** **plan comprehensive** 'It, however, comes as part of a comprehensive plan'
PATH PHRASE: YES	خسارة أتت **على رأسمال البنك** deficit *atā*.PERF.3SG.F **LOC capi-tal ART=bank** 'A deficit that destroyed the bank's capital'
PURPOSIVE PHRASE: YES	ذهبت **لزيارته** وسألته *ḏahaba*.PERF.1SG **PURP=visit.CL.3SG.M.ACC** CONJ=ask.CL.3SG.M.ACC 'I went to visit him and asked him'
COMITATIVE PHRASE: YES	برنامجكم لم يأت **بجديد** show.CL.3PL.M.GEN NEG *atā*.PERF.3SG.M **COM=new** 'Your show did not come up with anything new'
TEMPORAL PHRASE: YES	أذهب لتناول أيس كريم **في أي وقت** *ḏahaba*.IMPF.1SG PURP=have.VN ice cream **LOC any time** 'I go to have ice cream at any time'

DEGREE PHRASE: YES	تأتي **دائما** عبر عمليات السطو المنتظم *atā*.IMPF.3SG.F **ADV** LOC opera-tions burglary ART=organized 'Comes always through opera-tions of organized burglary'

The First QALB Shared Task on Automatic Text Correction for Arabic

Behrang Mohit[1*], **Alla Rozovskaya**[2*], **Nizar Habash**[3], **Wajdi Zaghouani**[1], **Ossama Obeid**[1]

[1]Carnegie Mellon University in Qatar
[2]Center for Computational Learning Systems, Columbia University
[3]New York University Abu Dhabi

behrang@cmu.edu, alla@ccls.columbia.edu, nizar.habash@nyu.edu
wajdiz@qatar.cmu.edu, owo@qatar.cmu.edu

Abstract

We present a summary of the first shared task on automatic text correction for Arabic text. The shared task received 18 systems submissions from nine teams in six countries and represented a diversity of approaches. Our report includes an overview of the QALB corpus which was the source of the datasets used for training and evaluation, an overview of participating systems, results of the competition and an analysis of the results and systems.

1 Introduction

The task of text correction has recently gained a lot of attention in the Natural Language Processing (NLP) community. Most of the effort in this area concentrated on English, especially on errors made by learners of English as a Second Language. Four competitions devoted to error correction for non-native English writers took place recently: HOO (Dale and Kilgarriff, 2011; Dale et al., 2012) and CoNLL (Ng et al., 2013; Ng et al., 2014). Shared tasks of this kind are extremely important, as they bring together researchers who focus on this problem and promote development and dissemination of key resources, such as benchmark datasets.

Recently, there have been several efforts aimed at creating data resources related to the correction of Arabic text. Those include human annotated corpora (Zaghouani et al., 2014; Alfaifi and Atwell, 2012), spell-checking lexicon (Attia et al., 2012) and unannotated language learner corpora (Farwaneh and Tamimi, 2012). A natural extension to these resource production efforts is the creation of robust automatic systems for error correction.

* These authors contributed equally to this work.

In this paper, we present a summary of the QALB shared task on automatic text correction for Arabic. The Qatar Arabic Language Bank (QALB) project[1] is one of the first large scale data and system development efforts for automatic correction of Arabic which has resulted in annotation of the QALB corpus. In conjunction with the EMNLP Arabic NLP workshop, the QALB shared task is the first community effort for construction and evaluation of automatic correction systems for Arabic.

The results of the competition indicate that the shared task attracted a lot of interest and generated a diverse set of approaches from the participating teams.

In the next section, we present the shared task framework. This is followed by an overview of the QALB corpus (Section 3). Section 4 describes the shared task data, and Section 5 presents the approaches adopted by the participating teams. Section 6 discusses the results of the competition. Finally, in Section 7, we offer a brief analysis and present preliminary experiments on system combination.

2 Task Description

The QALB shared task was created as a forum for competition and collaboration on automatic error correction in Modern Standard Arabic. The shared task makes use of the QALB corpus (Zaghouani et al., 2014), which is a manually-corrected collection of Arabic texts. The shared task participants were provided with training and development data to build their systems, but were also free to make use of additional resources, including corpora, linguistic resources, and software, as long as these were publicly available.

For evaluation, a standard framework devel-

[1]http://nlp.qatar.cmu.edu/qalb/

Proceedings of the EMNLP 2014 Workshop on Arabic Natural Langauge Processing (ANLP), pages 39–47,
October 25, 2014, Doha, Qatar.

Original	Corrected
لا تتصوروا مدي سعادتي عند قرائة هذة التحليلات الرائعة و المحترمة لأني شاب و كنت بتمني من اللّه ان أؤدي العمرة مرورا بالمسجد الاقصي و كان يبدوا ان هذا بعيد المنال فكل ما في حد يسمع الامنية كان بيقول انك ممكن تتمني ان أحفاد أحفادك يحققوهالأن امنيتك مستحيلة.	لا تتصوروا مدى سعادتي عند قراءة هذه التحليلات الرائعة والمحترمة. لأنني شاب وكنت أتمنى من اللّه أن أؤدي العمرة مرورا بالمسجد الأقصى، وكان يبدو أن هذا بعيد المنال، فكل واحد يسمع الأمنية كان يقول أنك ممكن أن تتمنى أن أحفاد أحفادك يحققوها لأن أمنيتك مستحيلة.
lA ttSwrwA mdy[1] sςAdty ςnd qrAŷ¯ħ hð¯ħ AltHlylAt AlrAŷς¯hw AlmHtrmħ[4] lÂAny[6] šAb w knt[7] btmny[8] mn Allh An[9] Âŵdy Alςmr¯hmr-wrA bAlmsjd AlAqSy[10] w kAn[12] ybdwA[13] An[14] hðA bςyd AlmnAl fkl mA[16] fy[17] Hd[18] ysmς AlAmny¯ħ[9] kAn byqwl[20] Ank[21] mmkn ttmny[23] An[24] ÂHfAd ÂHfAdk yHqqwhAlÂn[25] Amnytk[26] mstHyl¯h	lA ttSwrwA mdý[1] sςAdty ςnd qrA'¯ħ hðh[3] AltHlylAt AlrAŷς¯hwAlmHtrm¯ħ.[5] lÂnny[6] šAb wknt[7] Âtmný[8] mn Allh Ân[9] Âŵdy Alςmr¯h mrwrA bAlmsjd AlÂqSý[10],[11] wkAn[12] ybdw[13] Ân[14] hðA bςyd AlmnAl,[15] fkl wAHd[18] ysmς AlÂmny¯ħ[9] kAn yqwl[20] Ânk[21] mmkn Ân[22] ttmný[23] Ân[24] ÂHfAd ÂHfAdk yHqqwhA lÂn[25] Âmnytk[26] mstHyl¯h

Translation

You cannot imagine the extent of my happiness when I read these wonderful and respectful analyses because I am a young man and I wish from God to perform Umrah passing through the Al-Aqsa Mosque; and it seemed that this was elusive that when anyone heard the wish, he would say that you can wish that your great grandchildren may achieve it because your wish is impossible.

Table 1: A sample of an original (erroneous) text along with its manual correction and English translation. The indices in the table are linked with those in Table 2 and the Appendix.

#	Error	Correction	Error Type	Correction Action
#1	mdy مدي	mdý مدى	Ya/Alif-Maqsura Spelling	Edit
#9	An ان	Ân أن	Alif-Hamza Spelling	Edit
#11	*Missing Comma*	،	Punctuation	Add_before
#12	w kAn و كان	wkAn وكان	Extra Space	Merge
#13	ybdwA يبدوا	ybdw يبدو	Morphology	Edit
#20	byqwl بيقول	yqwl يقول	Dialectal	Edit
#25	yHqqwhAlÂn يحققوهالأن	yHqqwhA lÂn يحققوها لأن	Missing Space	Split

Table 2: Error type and correction action for a few examples extracted from the sentence pair in Table 1. The indices are linked to those in Table 1 and the Appendix.

oped for similar error correction competitions is adopted: system outputs are compared against gold annotations using *Precision*, *Recall* and F_1. Systems are ranked based on the F_1 scores obtained on the test set.

After the initial registration, the participants were provided with training and development sets and evaluation scripts. During the test period, the teams were given test data on which they needed to run their systems. Following the announcement of system results, the answer key to the test set was released. Participants authored description papers which will be presented in the Arabic NLP workshop.

3 The QALB Corpus

One of the goals of the QALB project is to create a large manually corrected corpus of errors for a variety of Arabic texts, including user comments on news web sites, native and non-native speaker essays, and machine translation output. Within the framework of this project, comprehensive annotation guidelines and a specialized web-based annotation interface have been developed (Zaghouani et al., 2014; Obeid et al., 2013).

The annotation process includes an initial automatic pre-processing step followed by an automatic correction of common spelling errors by the morphological analysis and disambiguation system MADA (v3.2) (Habash and Rambow, 2005; Habash et al., 2009). The pre-processed files are then assigned to a team of expert (human) annotators.

For a given sentence, the annotators were instructed to correct all errors; these include spelling, punctuation, word choice, morphology, syntax, and dialectal usage. It should be noted that the error classification was only used for guiding the annotation process; the annotators were not instructed to mark the type of error but only needed to specify an appropriate correction.

Once the annotation was complete, the corrections were automatically grouped into the following seven *action categories* based on the *action* required to correct the error: {*Edit, Add, Merge, Split, Delete, Move, Other*}.[2] Table 1 presents a sample erroneous Arabic news comment along with its manually corrected form, its romanized transliteration,[3] and the English translation. The errors in the original and the corrected forms are underlined and co-indexed. Table 2 presents a subset of the errors from the example shown in Table 1 along with the error types and annotation actions. The Appendix at the end of the paper lists **all** annotation actions for that example.

To ensure high annotation quality, the annotators went through multiple phases of training; the inter-annotator agreement was reviewed routinely. Zaghouani et al. (2014) report an average Word Error Rate (WER) of 3.8% for all words (excluding punctuation), which is quite high. When punctuation was included, the WER rose to 11.3%. The high level of agreement indicates that the annotations are reliable and the guidelines are useful in producing homogeneous and consistent data. Punctuation, however, remains a challenge.

4 Shared Task Data

The shared task data comes from the QALB corpus and consists of user comments from the Aljazeera News webpage written in Modern Standard Arabic.

Comments belonging to the same article were included only in one of the shared task subsets (i.e., training, development or test). Furthermore, we split the data by the annotation time. Consequently, the training data is comprised of comments annotated between June and December, 2013; the development data includes texts annotated in December 2013; the test data includes documents annotated in the Spring of 2014.

Statistics	Train.	Dev.	Test
Number of docs.	19,411	1,017	968
Number of words	1M	54K	51K
Number of errors	306K	16K	16K

Table 3: Statistics on the shared task data.

We refer to each comment in the shared task data as *document* and assign it a special ID that indicates the ID of the article to which the comment refers and the comment's number.

The data was made available to the participants in three versions: (1) plain text, one document per line; (2) text with annotations specifying errors and the corresponding corrections; (3) feature files specifying morphological information obtained by running MADAMIRA, a tool for morphological analysis and disambiguation of Modern Standard Arabic (Pasha et al., 2014). MADAMIRA performs morphological analysis and contextual disambiguation. Using the output of MADAMIRA, we generated for each word thirty-three features. The features specify various properties: the part-of-speech (POS), lemma, aspect, person, gender, number, and so on.

Among its features, MADAMIRA produces forms that correct a large subset of a special class of spelling mistakes in words containing the letters *Alif* and final *Ya*. These letters are a source of the most common spelling types of spelling errors in Arabic and involve *Hamzated Alifs* and *Alif-Maqsura/Ya* confusion (Habash, 2010; El Kholy and Habash, 2012). We refer to these errors as *Alif/Ya* errors (see also Section 6).

Table 3 presents statistics on the shared task data. The training data contains over one million words of text; the development and test data contain slightly over 50,000 words each. Table 4 shows the distribution of annotations by the action type. The majority of corrections (over 50%) belong to the type *Edit*. This is followed by mistakes that require several words to be merged together (about a third of all errors).

[2]In the shared task, we specified two *Add* categories: *addBefore* and *addAfter*. Most of the add errors fall into the first category, and we combine these here into a single *Add* category.

[3]Arabic transliteration is presented in the Habash-Soudi-Buckwalter scheme (Habash et al., 2007): (in alphabetical order) *AbtθjHxdðrzsšSDTĎςγfqklmnhwy* and the additional symbols: ' ء, Â أ, Ǎ إ, Ā آ, ŵ ؤ, ŷ ئ, ħ ة, ý ى.

Data	Error type (%)						
	Edit	Add	Merge	Split	Delete	Move	Other
Train.	55.34	32.36	5.95	3.48	2.21	0.14	0.50
Dev.	53.51	34.24	5.97	3.67	2.03	0.08	0.49
Test	51.94	34.73	5.89	3.48	3.32	0.15	0.49

Table 4: Distribution of annotations by type in the shared task data. Error types denotes the action required in order to correct the error.

Team Name		Affiliation
CLMB	(Rozovskaya et al., 2014)	Columbia University (USA)
CMUQ	(Jeblee et al., 2014)	Carnegie Mellon University in Qatar (Qatar)
CP13	(Tomeh et al., 2014)	Université Paris 13 (France)
CUFE	(Nawar and Ragheb, 2014)	Computer Engineering Department, Cairo University (Egypt)
GLTW	(Zerrouki et al., 2014)	Bouira University (Algeria), The National Computer Science Engineering School (Algeria), and Tabuk University (KSA)
GWU	(Attia et al., 2014)	George Washington University (USA)
QCRI	(Mubarak and Darwish, 2014)	Qatar Computing Research Institute (Qatar)
TECH	(Mostefa et al., 2014)	Techlimed.com (France)
YAM	(Hassan et al., 2014)	Faculty of Engineering, Cairo University (Egypt)

Table 5: List of the nine teams that participated in the shared task.

Team	Approach	External Resources
CLMB	Corrections proposed by MADAMIRA; a Maximum Likelihood model trained on the training data; regular expressions; a decision-tree classifier for punctuation errors trained on the training data; an SVM character-level error correction model; a Naïve Bayes classifier trained on the training data and the Arabic Gigaword corpus	Arabic Gigaword Fourth Edition (Parker et al., 2009)
CMUQ	A pipeline consisting of rules, corrections proposed by MADAMIRA, a language model for spelling mistakes, and a statistical machine-translation system	AraComLex dictionary (Attia et al., 2012)
CP13	A pipeline that consists of an error detection SVM classifier that uses MADAMIRA features and language model scores; a character-level back-off correction model implemented as a weighted finite-state transducer; a statistical machine-translation system; a discriminative re-ranker; a decision tree classifier for inserting missing punctuation	None
CUFE	Rules extracted from the Buckwalter morphological analyser; their probabilities are learned using the training data	Buckwalter morphological analyzer Version 2.0 (Buckwalter, 2004)
GLTW	Regular expressions and word lists	AraComLex dictionary (Attia et al., 2012); in-house resources; Ayaspell dictionary
GWU	A CRF model for punctuation errors; a dictionary and a language model for spelling errors; normalization rules	AraComLex Extended dictionary (Attia et al., 2012); Arabic Gigaword Fourth Edition (Parker et al., 2009)
QCRI	Word errors: a language model trained on Arabic Wikipedia and Aljazeera data; punctuation mistakes: a CRF model and a frequency-based model trained on the shared task data	Arabic Wikipedia; Aljazeera articles
TECH	Off-the-shelf spell checkers and a statistical machine-translation model	Newspaper articles from Open Source Arabic Corpora; other corpora collected online; Hunspell
YAM	*Edit* errors: a Naïve Bayes classifier that uses the following features: a character confusion matrix based on the training data; a collocation model that uses the target lemma and the surrounding POS tags; a co-occurrence model that uses lemmata of the surrounding words; *Split* and *Merge* errors: a language model trained on the training data; *Add* errors: a classifier	AraComLex dictionary (Attia et al., 2012); Buckwalter Analyzer Version 1.0 (Buckwalter, 2002); Arabic stoplists

Table 6: Approaches adopted by the participating teams.

5 Participants and Approaches

Nine teams from six countries participated in the shared task. Table 5 presents the list of participating institutions and their names in the shared task. Each team was allowed to submit up to three outputs. Overall, we received eighteen outputs. The submitted systems included a diverse set of approaches that incorporated rule-based frameworks, statistical machine translation and machine learning models, as well as hybrid systems. The teams that scored at the top employed a variety of techniques and attempted to classify the errors in some way using that classification in developing their systems: the CLMB system combined machine-learning modules with rules and MADAMIRA corrections; the CUFE system extracted rules from the morphological analyzer and learned their probabilities using the training data; and the CMUQ system combined statistical machine-translation with a language model, rules, and MADAMIRA corrections. Table 6 summarizes the approaches adopted by each team.

6 Results

In this section, we present the results of the competition. For evaluation, we adopted the standard Precision (P), Recall (R), and F_1 metric that was used in recent shared tasks on grammatical error correction in English: HOO competitions (Dale and Kilgarriff, 2011; Dale et al., 2012) and CoNLL (Ng et al., 2013). The results are computed using the M2 scorer (Dahlmeier and Ng, 2012) that was also used in the CoNLL shared tasks.

Table 7 presents the official results of the evaluation on the test set. The results are sorted according to the F_1 scores obtained by the systems. The range of the scores is quite wide – from 20 to 67 F_1 – but the the majority of the systems stay in the 50-60 range.

It is interesting to note that these results are considerably higher than those shown on the similar shared tasks on English non-native data. For instance, the highest performance in the CoNLL-2013 shared task that also used the same evaluation metric was 31.20 (Rozovskaya et al., 2013).[4] The highest score in the HOO-2011 shared task (Dale and Kilgarriff, 2011) that addressed all errors was 21.1 (Rozovskaya et al., 2011). Of course, the setting was different,as we are dealing with texts written by native speakers. But, in addition to that, we hypothesize that our data contains a set of language-specific errors that may be "easier", e.g Alif/Ya errors.

We also asked the participants for the outputs of their systems on the development set. We show the results in Table 8. While these results are not used for ranking, since the development set was used for tuning the parameters of the systems, it is interesting to see how much the performance differs from the results obtained on the test. In general, we do not observe substantial differences in the performance and the rankings, with a few exceptions. In particular, CP13 submissions did much better on the development set, as well as the CUFE system: the CUFE system suffers a major drop in precision on the test set, while the CP13 systems lose in recall. For more details, we refer the reader to the system description papers.

In addition to the official rankings, it is also interesting to analyze system performance for different types of mistakes. Note that here we are not interested in the annotation classification by action type. Instead, we automatically assign errors to one of the following categories: punctuation errors;errors involving *Alif* and *Ya*; and all other errors. Punctuation errors account for 39% of all errors in the data[5] . Table 7 shows the performance of the teams in three settings: with punctuation errors removed; with *Alif/Ya* errors removed; and when both punctuation and *Alif/Ya* errors are removed. Observe that when punctuation errors are not taken into account, the CUFE team gets the first ranking (for each the results of the best-performing system were chosen).

7 Analysis of System Output

We conducted a couple of experiments to analyze the task challenges and system errors.

The Most and Least Challenging Sentences We examined some of the most, and the least challenging parts of the test data for the shared task systems. To identify these subsets, we ranked all sentences using their average sentence-level F_1 score and selected the top and bottom 50 sentences. Our manual examination of these two

[4]This year CoNLL was an extension of the CoNLL-2013 competition for all errors but in its evaluation favored precision twice as much as recall, so we are not comparing to this setting.

[5]For example, there are a lot of missing periods at the end of a sentence that may be due to the fact that the data was collected online.

Rank	Team	P	R	F_1
1	CLMB-1	73.34	63.23	**67.91**
2	CLMB-2	70.86	62.21	66.25
3	CUFE-1	87.49	52.63	65.73
4	CMUQ-1	77.97	56.35	65.42
5	CLMB-3	71.45	60.00	65.22
6	QCRI-1	71.70	56.86	63.43
7	GWU-1	75.47	52.98	62.25
8	GWU-2	75.34	52.99	62.22
9	QCRI-2	62.86	60.32	61.57
10	YAM-1	63.52	57.61	60.42
11	QCRI-3	60.66	59.28	59.96
12	TECH-1	73.46	50.56	59.89
13	TECH-2	73.50	50.53	59.88
14	TECH-3	72.34	50.51	59.49
15	CP13-2	76.85	47.33	58.58
16	CP13-1	77.85	38.77	51.76
17	GLTW-1	75.15	23.15	35.40
18	GLTW-2	69.80	12.33	20.96

Table 7: Official results on the test set. Column 1 shows the system rank according to the F_1 score.

Rank (test)	Rank (dev)	Team	P	R	F_1
1	2	CLMB-1	72.22	62.79	67.18
2	3	CLMB-2	69.49	61.73	65.38
3	1	CUFE-1	94.11	53.74	**68.42**
4	4	CMUQ-1	76.17	56.59	64.94
5	5	CLMB-3	69.71	59.42	64.15
6	6	QCRI-1	70.83	57.34	63.38
7	9	GWU-1	73.15	53.18	61.59
8	10	GWU-2	73.01	53.13	61.50
9	8	QCRI-2	62.21	61.30	61.75
10	14	YAM-1	57.81	59.19	58.49
11	12	QCRI-3	60.47	60.65	60.56
12	13	TECH-1	70.86	50.04	58.66
13	15	TECH-2	70.66	49.65	58.32
14	16	TECH-3	70.65	48.83	57.75
15	7	CP13-2	74.85	54.15	62.84
16	11	CP13-1	75.73	51.33	61.19
17	17	GLTW-1	73.83	22.80	34.84
18	18	GLTW-2	67.85	11.09	19.06

Table 8: Results on the **development** set. Columns 1 and 2 show the rank of the system according to F_1 score obtained on the test set shown in Table 7 and the development set, respectively.

sets shows that the differences between them relate to both the density and the type of errors. The more challenging sentences (with the lowest system performance) contain more errors in general, and their errors tend to be complex and challenging, e.g., the correction of the erroneous two-token string أدت عت (Âdt ςt) requires a character deletion and a merge to produce أدعت (Adςt). In contrast the less challenging sentences tend to have fewer and simpler errors such as the common Alif/Ya errors.

System Combination We took the 18 systems' output and conducted two system combination experiments: (a) an oracle upper-bound estimation and (b) a simple majority vote system combination. For these experiments we isolated and evaluated each sentence output individually to form a new combined system output.

In the oracle experiment, we combined different systems by selecting the output of the best performing system for each individual sentence. For that, we evaluated sentences individually for each system and chose the system output with the highest F_1 score. The combined output holds the best output of all systems for the test set. This is an oracle system combination which allows us to estimate an upper-bound combination of all 18 systems.

In the majority vote experiment, we combined system output based on majority vote of various systems at sentence level. For every sentence, we choose the output that is agreed by most systems. If all systems have different output for a sentence, we back-off to the best performing system (CLMB-1).

Table 10 compares the results of these two experiments against the best performing system (CLMB-1). We observe a large boost of performance in the oracle experiment. This promising result reflects the complementary nature of the different methods that have been applied to the shared task, and it motivates further research on system combination. The result for the majority-vote system combination is very close to the CLMB-1's performance. This is not surprising; since, for 92% of sentences, there was no sentence-level agreement among systems. As a result, the combined system was very close to the back-off CLMB-1 system.

8 Conclusion

We have described the framework and results of the first shared task on automatic correction of Arabic, which used data from the QALB corpus. The shared task received 18 systems submissions

Team	No punc. errors			No Alif/Ya errors			No punc. No Alif/Ya errors		
	P	**R**	**F_1**	**P**	**R**	**F_1**	**P**	**R**	**F_1**
CLMB-1	82.63	72.50	77.24	64.05	50.86	**56.70**	76.99	49.91	60.56
CMUQ-1	82.89	68.69	75.12	68.32	40.51	50.86	74.25	41.46	53.21
CP13-2	80.51	59.97	68.74	65.09	28.00	39.16	68.67	25.34	37.02
CUFE-1	85.22	78.79	**81.88**	83.34	36.21	50.48	80.63	63.25	**70.89**
GLTW-1	65.18	34.84	45.41	48.52	15.29	23.26	49.25	26.78	34.70
GWU-1	76.28	64.17	69.70	64.67	39.61	49.13	59.07	41.48	48.74
QCRI-1	76.74	74.93	75.82	59.66	41.90	49.23	63.22	55.10	58.88
TECH-1	81.23	62.99	70.95	59.39	34.59	43.72	64.93	35.69	46.06
YAM-1	77.38	63.99	70.05	50.77	43.43	46.81	64.63	34.71	45.17

Table 9: Results on the test set in different settings: with punctuation errors removed from evaluation; normalization errors removed; and when both punctuation and normalization errors are removed. Only the best output from each team is shown.

System	Precision	Recall	F_1
Oracle	83.25	68.72	75.29
Majority-Vote	73.96	62.88	67.97
CLMB-1	73.34	63.23	67.91

Table 10: Comparing the best performing system with two experimental hybrid systems.

from nine teams in six countries. We are pleased with the extent of participation, the quality of results and the diversity of approaches. We plan to release the output of all systems. Such dataset and all the methods used in this shared task are expected to introduce new directions in automatic correction of Arabic. We feel motivated to extend the shared task's framework and text domain to conduct new research competitions in the near future.

9 Acknowledgments

We would like to thank the organizing committee of EMNLP-2014 and its Arabic NLP workshop and also the shared task participants for their ideas and support. We thank Al Jazeera News (and especially, Khalid Judia) for providing the user comments portion of the QALB corpus. We also thank the QALB project annotators: Hoda Fathy, Dhoha Abid, Mariem Fekih, Anissa Jrad, Hoda Ibrahim, Noor Alzeer, Samah Lakhal, Jihene Wefi, Elsherif Mahmoud and Hossam El-Husseini. This publication was made possible by grants NPRP-4-1058-1-168 and YSREP-1-018-1-004 from the Qatar National Research Fund (a member of the Qatar Foundation). The statements made herein are solely the responsibility of the authors. Nizar Habash performed most of his contribution to this paper while he was at the Center for Computational Learning Systems at Columbia University.

References

A. Alfaifi and E. Atwell. 2012. Arabic Learner Corpora (ALC): A Taxonomy of Coding Errors. In *The 8th International Computing Conference in Arabic*.

M. Attia, P. Pecina, Y. Samih, K. Shaalan, and J. van Genabith. 2012. Improved Spelling Error Detection and Correction for Arabic. In *Proceedings of COLING*.

M. Attia, M. Al-Badrashiny, and M. Diab. 2014. GWU-HASP: Hybrid Arabic Spelling and Punctuation Corrector. In *Proceedings of EMNLP Workshop on Arabic Natural Language Processing: QALB Shared Task*.

T. Buckwalter. 2002. Buckwalter Arabic Morphological Analyzer Version 1.0.

T. Buckwalter. 2004. Buckwalter Arabic Morphological Analyzer Version 2.0.

D. Dahlmeier and H. T. Ng. 2012. Better Evaluation for Grammatical Error Correction. In *Proceedings of NAACL*.

R. Dale and A. Kilgarriff. 2011. Helping Our Own: The HOO 2011 Pilot Shared Task. In *Proceedings of the 13th European Workshop on Natural Language Generation*.

R. Dale, I. Anisimoff, and G. Narroway. 2012. A Report on the Preposition and Determiner Error Correction Shared Task. In *Proceedings of the NAACL Workshop on Innovative Use of NLP for Building Educational Applications*.

A. El Kholy and N. Habash. 2012. Orthographic and morphological processing for English–Arabic statistical machine translation. *Machine Translation*, 26(1-2).

S. Farwaneh and M. Tamimi. 2012. Arabic Learners Written Corpus: A Resource for Research and Learning. *The Center for Educational Resources in Culture, Language and Literacy.*

N. Habash and O. Rambow. 2005. Arabic Tokenization, Part-of-Speech Tagging and Morphological Disambiguation in One Fell Swoop. In *Proceedings of ACL.*

N. Habash, A. Soudi, and T. Buckwalter. 2007. On Arabic Transliteration. In A. van den Bosch and A. Soudi, editors, *Arabic Computational Morphology: Knowledge-based and Empirical Methods*. Springer.

N. Habash, O. Rambow, and R. Roth. 2009. MADA+TOKAN: A Toolkit for Arabic Tokenization, Diacritization, Morphological Disambiguation, POS Tagging, Stemming and Lemmatization. In *Proceedings of the Second International Conference on Arabic Language Resources and Tools.*

N. Habash. 2010. *Introduction to Arabic Natural Language Processing*. Morgan & Claypool Publishers.

Y. Hassan, M. Aly, and A. Atiya. 2014. Arabic Spelling Correction using Supervised Learning. In *Proceedings of EMNLP Workshop on Arabic Natural Language Processing: QALB Shared Task.*

S. Jeblee, H. Bouamor, W. Zaghouani, and K. Oflazer. 2014. CMUQ@QALB-2014: An SMT-based System for Automatic Arabic Error Correction. In *Proceedings of EMNLP Workshop on Arabic Natural Language Processing: QALB Shared Task.*

D. Mostefa, O. Asbayou, and R. Abbes. 2014. TECHLIMED System Description for the Shared Task on Automatic Arabic Error Correction. In *Proceedings of EMNLP Workshop on Arabic Natural Language Processing: QALB Shared Task.*

H. Mubarak and K. Darwish. 2014. Automatic Correction of Arabic Text: a Cascaded Approach. In *Proceedings of EMNLP Workshop on Arabic Natural Language Processing: QALB Shared Task.*

M. Nawar and M. Ragheb. 2014. Fast and Robust Arabic Error Correction System. In *Proceedings of EMNLP Workshop on Arabic Natural Language Processing: QALB Shared Task.*

H. T. Ng, S. M. Wu, Y. Wu, Ch. Hadiwinoto, and J. Tetreault. 2013. The CoNLL-2013 Shared Task on Grammatical Error Correction. In *Proceedings of CoNLL: Shared Task.*

H. T. Ng, S. M. Wu, T. Briscoe, C. Hadiwinoto, R. H. Susanto, and C. Bryant. 2014. The CoNLL-2014 Shared Task on Grammatical Error Correction. In *Proceedings of CoNLL: Shared Task.*

O. Obeid, W. Zaghouani, B. Mohit, N. Habash, K. Oflazer, and N. Tomeh. 2013. A Web-based Annotation Framework For Large-Scale Text Correction. In *The Companion Volume of the Proceedings of IJCNLP 2013: System Demonstrations*. Asian Federation of Natural Language Processing.

R. Parker, D. Graff, K. Chen, J. Kong, and K. Maeda. 2009. Arabic Gigaword Fourth Edition. LDC Catalog No.: LDC2009T30, ISBN: 1-58563-532-4.

A. Pasha, M. Al-Badrashiny, M. Diab, A. El Kholy, R. Eskander, N. Habash, M. Pooleery, O. Rambow, and R. Roth. 2014. MADAMIRA: A Fast, Comprehensive Tool for Morphological Analysis and Disambiguation of Arabic. In *Proceedings of the Ninth International Conference on Language Resources and Evaluation (LREC).*

A. Rozovskaya, M. Sammons, J. Gioja, and D. Roth. 2011. University of Illinois System in HOO Text Correction Shared Task. In *Proceedings of the European Workshop on Natural Language Generation (ENLG).*

A. Rozovskaya, K.-W. Chang, M. Sammons, and D. Roth. 2013. The University of Illinois System in the CoNLL-2013 Shared Task. In *Proceedings of CoNLL Shared Task.*

A. Rozovskaya, N. Habash, R. Eskander, N. Farra, and W. Salloum. 2014. The Columbia System in the QALB-2014 Shared Task on Arabic Error Correction. In *Proceedings of EMNLP Workshop on Arabic Natural Language Processing: QALB Shared Task.*

N. Tomeh, N. Habash, R. Eskander, and J. Le Roux. 2014. A Pipeline Approach to Supervised Error Correction for the QALB-2014 Shared Task. In *Proceedings of EMNLP Workshop on Arabic Natural Language Processing: QALB Shared Task.*

W. Zaghouani, B. Mohit, N. Habash, O. Obeid, N. Tomeh, A. Rozovskaya, N. Farra, S. Alkuhlani, and K. Oflazer. 2014. Large Scale Arabic Error Annotation: Guidelines and Framework. In *Proceedings of the Ninth International Conference on Language Resources and Evaluation (LREC)*. European Language Resources Association (ELRA).

T. Zerrouki, K. Alhawiti, and A. Balla. 2014. Autocorrection Of Arabic Common Errors For Large Text Corpus. In *Proceedings of EMNLP Workshop on Arabic Natural Language Processing: QALB Shared Task.*

Appendix A: Sample annotation file

Below is the complete list of correction actions for the example in Table 1 as they appear in the training and evaluation data. The first two columns are the error index linking to Table 1 and the original word, respectively. Only the column titled Correction Action is in the training and evaluation data. The two numbers following the `A` specify the start and end positions of the sentence token string to change. Following that (and delimited by `|||`) are the action type and the correction string. The last three fields are irrelevant to this discussion.

<table>
<tr><th>Error Index</th><th>Original Word</th><th>Correction Action</th></tr>
<tr><td>#1</td><td>مدي</td><td>A 2 3|||Edit|||مدى|||REQUIRED|||-NONE-|||0</td></tr>
<tr><td>#2</td><td>قرائة</td><td>A 5 6|||Edit|||قراءة|||REQUIRED|||-NONE-|||0</td></tr>
<tr><td>#3</td><td>هذة</td><td>A 6 7|||Edit|||هذه|||REQUIRED|||-NONE-|||0</td></tr>
<tr><td>#4</td><td>و المحترمة</td><td>A 9 11|||Merge|||والمحترمة|||REQUIRED|||-NONE-|||0</td></tr>
<tr><td>#5</td><td></td><td>A 11 11|||Add_before|||.|||REQUIRED|||-NONE-|||0</td></tr>
<tr><td>#6</td><td>لأاني</td><td>A 11 12|||Edit|||لأنني|||REQUIRED|||-NONE-|||0</td></tr>
<tr><td>#7</td><td>و كنت</td><td>A 13 15|||Merge|||وكنت|||REQUIRED|||-NONE-|||0</td></tr>
<tr><td>#8</td><td>بتمني</td><td>A 15 16|||Edit|||أتمنى|||REQUIRED|||-NONE-|||0</td></tr>
<tr><td>#9</td><td>ان</td><td>A 18 19|||Edit|||أن|||REQUIRED|||-NONE-|||0</td></tr>
<tr><td>#10</td><td>الاقصي</td><td>A 23 24|||Edit|||الأقصى|||REQUIRED|||-NONE-|||0</td></tr>
<tr><td>#11</td><td></td><td>A 24 24|||Add_before|||،|||REQUIRED|||-NONE-|||0</td></tr>
<tr><td>#12</td><td>و كان</td><td>A 24 26|||Merge|||وكان|||REQUIRED|||-NONE-|||0</td></tr>
<tr><td>#13</td><td>يبدوا</td><td>A 26 27|||Edit|||يبدو|||REQUIRED|||-NONE-|||0</td></tr>
<tr><td>#14</td><td>ان</td><td>A 27 28|||Edit|||أن|||REQUIRED|||-NONE-|||0</td></tr>
<tr><td>#15</td><td></td><td>A 31 31|||Add_before|||،|||REQUIRED|||-NONE-|||0</td></tr>
<tr><td>#16</td><td>ما</td><td>A 32 33|||Delete||||||REQUIRED|||-NONE-|||0</td></tr>
<tr><td>#17</td><td>في</td><td>A 33 34|||Delete||||||REQUIRED|||-NONE-|||0</td></tr>
<tr><td>#18</td><td>حد</td><td>A 34 35|||Edit|||واحد|||REQUIRED|||-NONE-|||0</td></tr>
<tr><td>#19</td><td>الامنية</td><td>A 36 37|||Edit|||الأمنية|||REQUIRED|||-NONE-|||0</td></tr>
<tr><td>#20</td><td>بيقول</td><td>A 38 39|||Edit|||يقول|||REQUIRED|||-NONE-|||0</td></tr>
<tr><td>#21</td><td>انك</td><td>A 39 40|||Edit|||أنك|||REQUIRED|||-NONE-|||0</td></tr>
<tr><td>#22</td><td></td><td>A 41 41|||Add_before|||أن|||REQUIRED|||-NONE-|||0</td></tr>
<tr><td>#23</td><td>تتمني</td><td>A 41 42|||Edit|||تتمنى|||REQUIRED|||-NONE-|||0</td></tr>
<tr><td>#24</td><td>ان</td><td>A 42 43|||Edit|||أن|||REQUIRED|||-NONE-|||0</td></tr>
<tr><td>#25</td><td>يحققوهالأن</td><td>A 45 46|||Split|||يحققوها لأن|||REQUIRED|||-NONE-|||0</td></tr>
<tr><td>#26</td><td>امنيتك</td><td>A 46 47|||Edit|||أمنيتك|||REQUIRED|||-NONE-|||0</td></tr>
</table>

A Framework for the Classification and Annotation of Multiword Expressions in Dialectal Arabic

Abdelati Hawwari, Mohammed Attia, Mona Diab
Department of Computer Science
The George Washington University
{Abhawwari,mohattia,mtdiab}@gwu.edu

Abstract

In this paper we describe a framework for classifying and annotating Egyptian Arabic Multiword Expressions (EMWE) in a specialized computational lexical resource. The framework intends to encompass comprehensive linguistic information for each MWE including: a. phonological and orthographic information; b. POS tags; c. structural information for the phrase structure of the expression; d. lexicographic classification; e. semantic classification covering semantic fields and semantic relations; f. degree of idiomaticity where we adopt a three-level rating scale; g. pragmatic information in the form of usage labels; h. Modern Standard Arabic equivalents and English translations, thereby rendering our resource a three-way – Egyptian Arabic, Modern Standard Arabic and English – repository for MWEs.

1 Introduction

Multiword expressions (MWEs) comprise a wide range of diverse, arbitrary and yet linguistically related phenomena that share the characteristic of crossing word boundaries (Sag et al., 2002). MWEs are computationally challenging because the exact interpretation of an MWE is not directly obtained from its component parts. MWEs are intrinsically single units on the deep conceptual and semantic levels, but on the surface (lexical and syntactic) levels they are expressed as multiple units. MWEs vary in their syntactic category, morphological behavior, and degree of semantic opaqueness. MWEs are pervasively present in natural texts, which makes it imperative to tackle them explicitly if we aspire to make large-scale, linguistically-motivated, and precise processing of a human language.

Integrating MWEs in NLP applications has evidently and consistently shown to improve the performance in tasks such as Information Retrieval (Acosta et al. 2011; da Silva and Souza, 2012), Text Mining (SanJuan and Ibekwe-SanJuan, 2006), Syntactic Parsing (Eryiğit et al., 2011; Nivre and Nilsson, 2004; Attia, 2006; Korkontzelos and Manandhar, 2010), Machine Translation (Deksne, 2008; Carpuat and Diab, 2010; Ghoneim and Diab 2013; Bouamor et al., 2011), Question Answering, and Named-Entity extraction (Bu et al., 2011).

In the current work, we propose guidelines for detailed linguistic annotation of an MWE lexicon for dialectal (Egyptian) Arabic that covers, among other types, expressions that are traditionally classified as idioms (e.g. على الريق EalaY Alriyq[1] 'on an empty stomach'), prepositional verbs (e.g. توكل على tawak~al EalaY 'rely on'), compound nouns (e.g. إشارة مرور <i$Arap muruwr 'traffic light'), and collocations (e.g. أخد دش >axad du$~ 'to take a shower').

Creating a repository of annotated MWEs that is focused on dialects is essential for computational linguistics research as it provides a crucial resource that is conducive to better analysis and understanding of the user-generated content rife in the social media (such as Facebook, Twitter, blogs, and forums). Moreover, it helps in understanding he correspondences between different languages and their representation of the semantic space. We hope that the multilingual data in this repository will lead to a significant enhancement in the processing of comparable and parallel corpora. We believe that our proposed framework will contribute to the sustainability of

[1] In this paper, we use the Buckwalter Transliteration Scheme for rendering Romanized Arabic as described in www.qamus.com.

Proceedings of the EMNLP 2014 Workshop on Arabic Natural Langauge Processing (ANLP), pages 48–56,
October 25, 2014, Doha, Qatar.

MWE research in general, and provide a blue print for research on MWEs in dialects, informal vernaculars, as well as morphologically rich languages.

MWE are not only interesting from an NLP perspective but also from a linguistic perspective, as MWE can help in understanding the link between lexicon, syntax and semantics. Until now, this is hampered by the lack of comprehensive resources for MWEs with fine-grained classification on different dimensions related to semantic roles and syntactic functions. Arabic comprises numerous divergent dialects, and having an annotated MWE lexical resource in dialects and Modern Standard Arabic (MSA) will allow for studying transformation, change and development in this language.

From a theoretical linguistic point of view, our work will be interesting particularly in studies related to Diglossia. Diglossia (Walters, 1996) is where two languages or dialects exist side by side within a community, where typically one is used in formal contexts while the other is used in informal communications and interactions. Studying the MWE space for dialects and MSA as a continuum will lead to deeper insights into variations as we note intersection and overlap between the two. In many instances, we see that MSA MWEs and their dialectal equivalents are not necessarily shared as they occupy complementary linguistic spaces. However, the nature of this complementarity and its cultural and social implications will need more exploration and investigation, which will be possible once a complete resource becomes available.

In the current work, we give detailed description of our methodology and guidelines for annotating phonological, morphological, syntactic, semantic and pragmatic information of an Egyptian Multiword Expressions (EMWE) lexical resource. Our annotation scheme covers the following areas.

a) Phonological and orthographic information;

b) POS tag, based on the observation of how an MWE functions as a whole lexical unit;

c) Syntactic variability and structural composition;

d) Lexicographic types, which includes the classifications followed in the dictionary-writing domain (idioms, support verbs, compound nouns, etc.);

e) Semantic information, where we cover semantic fields and relations;

f) Idiomaticity Degree; we adopt a three level rating scale (Mel'čuk, 1998) to measure the degree of semantic opaqueness;

g) Degree of morphological, lexical and syntactic flexibility (Sag et al., 2002);

h) Pragmatic information, which includes adding usage labels to MWEs where applicable;

i) Translation, which includes the MSA and English equivalents, either as an MWE in MSA and English if available or as a paraphrase otherwise.

2 Previous Work

There are four main areas of research on MWEs: extraction from structured and unstructured data, construction of lexicons for specific languages, integration in NLP applications, and the construction of guidelines and best practices. A significant amount of research has focused on the identification and extraction of MWEs (Ramisch et al., 2010; Dubremetz and Nivre, 2014; Attia et al., 2010; Weller and Heid, 2010; Schneider et al., 2014). Description and specifications of MWE lexical resources have been presented for Japanese (Shudo et al. 2011), Italian (Zaninello and Nissim, 2010), Dutch (Grégoire, 2010; Odijk, 2013), and Modern Standard Arabic (Hawwari et al., 2012). Moreover, Calzolari et al. (2002) presented a project that attempted to introduce best practice recommendations for the treatment of MWE in mono- and multi-lingual computational lexicons that incorporate both syntactic and semantic information, but the limitation of their work is that they focus on only two types of MWEs, namely, support verbs and noun compounds.

Apart from Schneider et al. (2014), who focused on the language of the social web, none of these projects dealt with informal or dialectal languages, which are rampant in user-generated content (UGC). With the explosion of social media, the language of Web 2.0 is undergoing fundamental changes: English is no longer dominating the web, and UGC is outpacing professionally edited content.

UGC is re-shaping the way people are consuming and dealing with information, as the user is no longer a passive recipient, but has now turned into an active participant, and in many instances, a source or producer of information. Social media have empowered users to be more creative and interactive, and allowed them to voice their opinions on events and products and exert powerful influence on the behavior and opinion of others. Yet, the current overflow of UGC poses significant challenges in data gathering, annotation and presentation.

3 MWE Taxonomy

Although the importance of the MWEs has been acknowledged by many researchers in the field of NLP as evident by the large number of research papers and dedicated workshops in the past decade, the theory of MWEs is still underdeveloped (Sag et al., 2002). There is critical need for studying MWEs both from the theoretical and practical point of views. MWEs have diverse categories, varying degrees of idiomaticity, different syntactic compositions, and different morphological, lexical and syntactic behavior, and dealing with them is complicated even further by the fact that there is no "watertight criteria" for distinguishing them them (Atkins and Rundell, 2008).

Moreover, there is no universally-agreed taxonomy of MWEs (Ramisch, 2012), and different researchers proposed different typology for this phenomena. Fillmore et al. (1988) proposed three types based on lexical and syntactic familiarity: a) unfamiliar pieces familiarly combined, b) familiar pieces unfamiliarly combined, and c) familiar pieces familiarly combined. Mel'čuk (1989), on the other hand, introduced three different classes: a) complete phraseme, b) semi-phraseme, c) and quasi-phraseme. Sag et al. introduced two classes: institutionalized phrases and lexicalized phrases, with lexicalized phrases subdivided into fixed, semi-fixed and syntactically flexible expressions. Ramisch (2012) introduced yet another set of classes: nominal, verbal and adverbial expressions.

From the lexicographic point of view, the legacy three-way division of MWEs proved to be too coarse-grained to cater for the needs of lexicographers who need to identify the large array of sub-types that fall under the umbrella of 'MWEs'. Atkins and Rundell (2008) emphasized the need for lexicographers to be able to recognize MWE types such as fixed phrases, transparent collocations, similes, catch phrases, proverbs, quotations, greetings, phatic expressions, compounds, phrasal verbs, and support verbs.

When we look deeply into the different classifications, we notice that each approach has looked at the phenomenon from a different angle, either focusing on its syntactic regularity, semantic and pragmatic properties, meaning compositionality, surface flexibility, POS (part of speech) category, or lexicographic relevance. What we propose is that it is not possible to come up with a hard and fast classification that cuts through all levels of representation. All afore-mentioned classifications are valid and can work parallel to each other, instead of substituting for each other. The assumption that we follow in this paper is that MWEs have different classifications at different levels of representation from the very deep level of semantics and pragmatics to the very shallow level of morphology and phonetics. The details of our annotation scheme are explained in the following section.

It is worth noting that in our current work, we move the focus away from edited text to the challenging and creative language found in UGC and by trying to close the language resource gap between edited and unedited text. We handle this gap by focusing on dialects, the language used in informal communications such as emails, chat rooms, and in social media in general. We cover the full range of MWEs (nominal, verbal, adverbial, adjectival and prepositional expressions) in Egyptian Arabic, covering 7,331 MWEs (collected from corpora and paper dictionaries).

4 Annotation of Linguistic Features in MWE

In this section, we provide a comprehensive specification of MWE types and the detailed linguistic information, including the phonological, orthographical, syntactic, semantic and pragmatic features.

4.1 Phonological

Each MWE is provided in full diacritization to indicate its common pronunciation in Cairene Arabic accent, such as عَلَى كَفّ عَفْرِيت *EalaY kaf~ Eaforiyt* 'at high risk', 'lit. on the palm of a demon'. We also list other phonological variants when available.

4.2 Orthography

Since dialects do not have a standard orthography, we follow the CODA style (Habash et al., 2012), which is a devised standard for conventionalizing the orthography of dialectal Arabic. CODA takes canonical forms and etymological facts into consideration. For example, the Egyptian expression أخد باله >axad bAluh ‘to pay attention’ is rendered in CODA as أخذ باله >axa* bAluh.

4.3 POS

At this level of annotation we consider the POS of the entire MWE when regarded as one unit from a functional perspective. We annotate each MWE with a POS tag from a predefined tagset. We define the POS tag based on the headword POS in the MWE. Our POS tagset includes verb, noun, adjective, adverb, interjection, proper noun, and preposition. The list of POS tags used along with examples is shown in Table 1.

	POS	Example
1	verb	جَرّ على الحِساب jar~ EalaY AlHisAb ‘pay later’
2	noun	أَكْل الْعِيْش >akol AlEay$ ‘making ends meet’ [lit. eating bread]
3	adjective	أشكال وألوان >a$okAl wa->alowAn ‘various shapes and colors’
4	adverb	أخرة المتمة >axorip Al-matam~ap ‘at the end’
5	interjection	يا ناس ياهوه yA nAs yAhuwh ‘anybody there’
6	proper nouns	شجرة الدر $ajarip Aldur~ ‘Shajar al-Durr’
7	preposition	بغض النظر عن bi-gaD~ AlnaZar Eano ‘irrespective of’

Table 1: MWE Examples with their POS Tags

4.4 Syntactic Annotation

A syntactic variable is a slot that intervenes between the component parts of an MWE, without being itself a part of it, but fills a syntactic gap. Syntactic variables are added, when needed, to MWEs to represent the syntactic behavior of an MWE and they exemplify how the MWE interacts with other elements within its scope. We create a tagset of syntactic variables reflecting the argument structure of an MWE. Examples are shown in Table 2.

No	Syntactic Variable	Example
1	فلانٌ somebody (masc_ nominative)	جسّ (فلانٌ) النبض jas~ (fulAn) AlnaboD ‘ (somebody) tested the waters’
2	فلانةً somebody (fem_ accusative)	أكل (فلانة) بعينيه >akal (fulAnap) bi-Eaynayh ‘he devoured (some woman/girl) with his eyes’
3	القومِ people (genitive)	دق بين (القوم) إسفين daq~ bayn (Alqawom) <isofiyn ‘he drove a wedge between (some people)’
4	الأمرَ some matter (accusative)	حط (الأمر) في حسابه Hat~ (Al>amora) fiy HisAbihi ‘he took (some matter) into consideration’
5	الشيءُ something (nominative)	(الشيء) متفصل عليه (Al$ayo') mitofaS~al Ealayh ‘(something) fits him perfectly’

Table 2: Syntactic variables and example usages

4.5 Lexicographic Annotation

In the dictionary market there are specialized dictionaries for idioms, phrasal verbs, proverbs and quotations. However, general domain dictionaries try to avoid the use of too technical terms in the description of MWEs and use for the sake of simplicity a general term like ‘phrase’ to denote them to users. Yet, in the meta language of the dictionary compiling profession, lexicographers make a more fine-grained distinction between the various types of MWEs. Our lexicographic classification of MWEs is adapted from Atkins and Rundell (2008) and includes the following tags. Examples are listed in Table 3.

1. Idiom: An idiom is an MWE whose meaning is fully or partially unpredictable from the meanings of its components (Nunberg et al., 1994);
2. Support verb, or ‘light verbs’, may be defined as semantically empty verbs, which share their arguments with a noun (Meyers et al., 2004);

3. Prepositional verb: These are verbs followed by prepositions with impact on the meaning;
4. Compound noun: A compound noun is a lexeme that consists of more than one noun;
5. Compound term: This is a technical compound noun used in a specific technical field;
6. Compound named entity: This is a multi-word proper name;
7. Phatic expression: an expression that is intended for performing a social function (such as greeting or well-wishing) rather than conveying information;
8. Proverb: We consider proverbs as multi-word expression if they are used as lexical units;
9. Quotation: We list only quotations that have gained currency in the language and have become familiar to the majority of the community.

	Classification	Example
1	Idiom	بيعمل من الحبة قبة biyiEomil min AlHab~ap qub~ap 'to make a mountain out of a molehill'
2	Support verb	أخَد تار >axad tAr 'to take revenge'
3	Prepositional verb	ضحك عليه DiHik Ealayh 'to play a joke on' [lit. laugh on him]'
4	Compound noun	أبو قردان >abuw qirodAn 'Cattle egret'
5	Compound term	عرق النسا Eiroq AlnisA 'Sciatica'
6	Compound named entity	أبُو الهول >abuw Alhuwl 'the Sphinx'
7	Phatic expression	أشوف وشك بخير >a$uwf wu$~ak bi-xayr 'see you later'
8	Quotation	يا مولاي كما خلقتني yA mawolAyA kamA xalaqotiniy 'penniless'
9	Proverb	العقل زينة AlEaqol ziynap 'wisdom is a blessing'

Table 3: Examples of Lexical Types

4.6 Structural Classification

We provide the syntactic phrase structure composition of the expressions, giving the MWE pattern or the POS of its component elements. The purpose is to show the normal productive syntactic patterns underlying the expressions. Table 4 shows the list of possible structural pattern in Egyptian MWEs.

	Structure	Example
1	adjective + conjunction + adjective	رَايق وَفايق rayiq wa-fayiq 'happy and relaxed'
2	adjective + noun	تنابلة السلطان tanaboliq Al-sulotAn 'couch potatoes' [lit. Sultan dependents]'
3	noun + noun	كِلْمِة حَق kilomiq Haq~ 'word of truth'
4	adjective + preposition + noun	غرقان لشوشته garoqAn li-uwotuh 'up to his ears'
5	adverb + noun	بين نارين bayn nArayn 'confused' [lit. between two fires]
6	adverb + verb	حَسْبَمَا اتَّفَقَ HasobamA Ait~afaq 'haphazardly' [lit. as happens]
7	noun + adjective	نفخة كدابه nafoxap kad~Abap 'false pride/arrogance' [lit. false blow]
8	verb + conjunction + verb	بِيَلِتّْ وَيَعْجِنُ yilit~ wa-yiEojin 'to babble' [lit. knead and fold]
9	verb + verb	امشى انجرّ Aimo$iy Ainojar~ 'get moving/get out' [lit. walk and drag]
10	verb + preposition + noun	تَوكّل عَلَى الله tawak~al EalaY Allah 'rely on Allah/go away'
11	preposition + noun	على الطبطاب EalaY AlTaboTAb 'effortlessly' [lit. on ease]
12	verb + noun	نفش ريشه nafa$ riy$uh 'show pride' [lit. stretched his feathers]
13	noun + verb	الله يرحمه! Allah yiroHamuh 'Allah have mercy on him'

Table 4: Examples Syntactic Classification

4.7 Semantic Fields

The entries in the current lexical resource are classified into semantic fields based on their semantic contents. The objective is to assign one semantic field tag for each MWE in the lexicon. Organizing Lexical data in semantic field format brings many theoretical and practical benefits, one of those is to allow the current lexical resource to function both as a lexicon and a thesaurus. In Table 5 we show a sample of our semantic field classification.

	Semantic Field	Example
1	Social Relation	سمن على عسل samon EalaY Easal 'getting on well' [lit. ghee on honey]
2	Oath and Emphasis	والله العظيم wa-Allah AlEaZiym 'I swear by Allah'
3	Occasions	يتربى في عزك yitrab~aY fiyEiz~ak 'congratulations on the new baby' [lit. may he grow up in your wealth]
4	Death	ربنا افتكره rab~inA Aifotakaruh 'he died' [lit. the Lord remembered him]
5	wishing and cursing	بَعْد الشَّر baEod Al$ar~ 'God forbid' [lit. may the evil be far away]
6	trickery	لبّسه العمة lab~isuh AlEim~ap 'to hoodwink' [lit. put the turban on him]
7	Occultism	ضرب الرمل Darab Alramol 'to practice divination' [lit. to strike the sand]'

Table 5: Semantic fields

4.8 Semantic Relations

Aiming at presenting detailed lexical semantic information, we further classify our entries based on semantic relations like synonymy, antonymy and polysemy.

- Synonymy: MWE synonyms are grouped together; as the following expressions which all mean 'to practice divination' قرا الفنجان qarA AlfinojAn [lit. read the cup], ضرب الودع Darab AlwadaE [lit. hit the shells], قَرَا الكف qarA Alkaf~ [lit. read the hand palm].
- Antonymy: MWE antonyms are two MWE having the opposite meaning to each other. For examples, إيده ناشفة <iyduh nA$ofap 'avaricious' [lit. his hand is dry] is the antonym of إيده مخرومة <iyduh maxoruwmap 'wasteful' [lit. his hand has a hole in it].
- Polysemy. This is when an MWE has more than one meaning. For example, إيده طويلة <iyduh Tawiylap [lit. his hand is long] can mean either a 'powerful person' or a 'thief'.

4.9 Idiomaticity Degree

Mel'čuk (1998) classified MWEs with regards to idiomaticity into three types: full phrasemes, quasi-phrasemes and semi-phrasemes.

- **Full phrasemes** are when the meaning of the expression does not match the meaning of the component words, such as وهلم جرا Wa-halum~ jar~A 'and so on'.
- **Quasi-phrasemes** are when the meaning of the expression matches the meaning of the component words in addition to an extra piece of meaning that is not directly derived from either components, such as مجلس الشعب majolis Al$aEob 'people's assembly'.
- **Semi-phrasemes** are when the meaning of the MWE is partially directly derived from one component and partially indirectly indicated by the other component, such as دراسات عليا dirAsAt EuloyA 'higher studies'.

4.10 Morpho-lexico-grammatical flexibility

A scale of three levels is used to measure the degree of morphological, lexical and grammatical flexibility of a MWE, adopted from Sag et al. (2002). The three levels are as follows:

- **Fixed MWE:** An MWE is considered as a fixed expression if it does not have any degree of syntactic, morphological or lexical flexibility, and its meaning cannot be predicted from its component elements, for example, سداح مداح sadAH madAH 'slapdash'.
- **Semi-Fixed MWE:** Semi-fixed expressions allow for a certain degree of morphological and lexical variation, but they are fixed in terms of the syntactic word order, for example, ماشية\ماشيين على حل شعرها\شعرهم mA$oyap/mA$oyiyn EalaY Hal~ $aEorahA/$aEoruhum [lit. living by letting down her/their hair] 'whore/whores' or 'loose women'.
- **Syntactically flexible MWE:** A syntactically flexible MWE is a frequent combination of two words or more, characterized by high degree of morphological and syntactic flexibility. Example, إدى (فلان) دش <id~aY

(fulAn) du$~ 'to scold someone harshly' [lit. give someone a shower].

4.11 Pragmatic Annotation (Usage Labels)

The reason we provide usage labels is inspired by the CALLHOME Egyptian Arabic corpus (Gadalla et al., 1997)), which is a collection of data gathered from spoken colloquial language. The usage labels present specifications on *who* uses an MWE and *how* it is used. The usage label tagset in our lexicon includes labels such *vulgar, youth, aggressive or taboo*, as exemplified in Table 6.

Who or how	Example
youth	يسوق الهبل فِي الجبل yisuwq Alhabal fiy Aljabal 'to act foolishly' [lit. to act madly in the mountain]'
women / girls	الشاطرة تغزل برجل حمار Al$ATrap tigozil birijol HumAr 'make do with what you have' [lit. a clever girl will knit with a donkey's leg]'
Aggressive	أديك في وشك >ad~iyk fiy wi$~ak 'I shall slap you in the face'

Table 6: Pragmatic annotation

5 Status of the current resource

The Egyptian MWE lexical resource at the current stage contains 7,331 entries, and work is still on going in the linguistic annotation of the dictionary. Table 7 presents the current annotation progress statistics regarding the various classifications and features.

	Feature	Completion
1	Diacritization	34.10%
2	Syntactic Variables	25.92%
3	MSA Equivalent	27.28%
4	POS	34.10%
5	Syntactic Classification	23.58%
6	English Equivalent	27.28%
7	Lexical Type	98.94%
8	Pragmatics Usage	4.09%
9	Synonymous	0.14%
10	Idiomaticity Degree	12.82%
11	Semantic-Field	2.29%

Table 7: Annotation work progress

6 Conclusion

We have described the annotation guidelines for a lexical database of MWE for dialectal Arabic. We provide descriptive specifications of MWE at the phonological, orthographical, syntactic and semantic levels. The main contribution of this paper is that it is the first description of a classification and annotation scheme of a lexical database for dialects, which can be extended for informal languages and with direct applicability on user-generated content.

Acknowledgement

This work was supported by the Defense Advanced Research Projects Agency (DARPA) Contract No. HR0011-12-C-0014, BOLT program with subcontract from Raytheon BBN.

References

Acosta, Otavio Costa, Aline Villavicencio, Viviane P. Moreira. (2011) Identification and Treatment of Multiword Expressions applied to Information Retrieval. Proceedings of the Workshop on Multiword Expressions: from Parsing and Generation to the Real World (MWE 2011), pages 101–109, Portland, Oregon, USA, 23 June 2011.

Atkins, B. T. S. and M. Rundell. 2008. *The Oxford Guide to Practical Lexicography.* Oxford University Press.

Attia, Mohammed, Antonio Toral, Lamia Tounsi, Pavel Pecina and Josef van Genabith. 2010. Automatic Extraction of Arabic Multiword Expressions. COLING 2010 Workshop on Multiword Expressions: from Theory to Applications. Beijing, China

Attia, Mohammed. (2006) Accommodating Multiword Expressions in an Arabic LFG Grammar. In T. Salakoski et al. (Eds.): Advances in Natural Language Processing. FinTAL 2006, *Lecture Notes in Computer Science*. Vol. 4139, pp. 87 - 98, 2006. Springer-Verlag Berlin Heidelberg.

Baldwin, T. (2005a). The deep lexical acquisition of English verb-particles. *Computer Speech and Language, Special Issue on Multiword Expressions* 19 (4), 398–414.

Baldwin, T. (2005b). Looking for prepositional verbs in corpus data. In Proceedings of the 2nd ACL-SIGSEM Workshop on the Linguistic Dimensions of Prepositions and their Use in Computational Linguistics Formalisms and Applications, Colchester, UK, pp. 115–126.

Baldwin, Timothy and Su Nam Kim. 2009. Multiword expressions. In Nitin Indurkhya and Fred J. Damerau, editors, Handbook of Natural Language

Processing, pages 267–292. CRC Press, Boca Raton, USA, 2nd edition.

Bannard, C. 2007. A Measure of Syntactic Flexibility for Automatically Identifying Multi Word Expressions in Corpora. Proceedings of A Broader Perspective on Multiword Expressions, Workshop at the ACL 2007 Conference: 1–8.

Benson, M. 1990. Collocations and general-purpose dictionaries. *International Journal of Lexicography*, 3(1):23--35.

Bouamor, Dhouha, Nasredine Semmar and Pierre Zweigenbaum. (2011) Improved Statistical Machine Translation Using MultiWord Expressions. International Workshop on Using Linguistic Information for Hybrid Machine Translation LIHMT. Barcelona, November 2011

Bu, Fan, Xiao-Yan Zhu, and Ming Li. (2011) A New Multiword Expression Metric and Its Applications. In *Journal of Computer Science and Technology*. 26(1): 3-13, Jan. 2011.

Calzolari, Nicoletta, Charles J. Fillmore, Ralph Grishman, Nancy Ide, Alessandro Lenci, Catherine MacLeod, Antonio Zampolli. (2002) Towards Best Practice for Multiword Expressions in Computational Lexicons. In Proceedings of the Third International Conference on Language Resources and Evaluation (LREC 2002), Las Palmas, Canary Islands, pp. 1934-1940

Carpuat, Marine and Mona Diab. (2010) Task-based evaluation of multiword expressions: a pilot study in statistical machine translation. Human Language Technologies: The 2010 Annual Conference of the North American Chapter of the Association for Computational Linguistics. Los Angeles, CA. Pp. 242-245.

Chafe, Wallace1968. Idiomaticity as an Anomaly in the Chomskyan Paradigm. *Foundations of Language* 4.109-127.

da Silva, Edson Marchetti and Renato Rocha Souza. (2012) Information retrieval system using Multiwords Expressions (MWE) as descriptors. JISTEM - *Journal of Information Systems and Technology Management*. Vol.9 no.2 São Paulo May/Aug. 2012.

Deksne, Daiga, Raivis Skadiņš, and Inguna Skadiņa. a. 2008. Dictionary of Multiword Expressions for Translation into Highly Infliected Languages. In the 6th International Conference on Language Resources and Evaluation (LREC 2008), Marrakech, Morocco.

Dubremetz, Marie and Joakim Nivre. (2014) Extraction of Nominal Multiword Expressions in French. In proceedings of the 10thWorkshop on Multiword Expressions (MWE 2014), the 14th Conference of the European Chapter of the Association for Computational Linguistics. 26-27 April 2014. Gothenburg, Sweden

Eryiğit, Gülşen, Tugay 'Ilbay Ozan and Arkan Can. (2011) Multiword Expressions in Statistical Dependency Parsing. Proceedings of the Second Workshop on Statistical Parsing of Morphologically Rich Languages.

Fillmore, C.J., P. Kay, M. O'Connor. (1988) Regularity and idiomaticity in grammatical constructions: the case of let alone. *Language*, 64, 3, 501–538.

Gadalla, Hassan, Hanaa Kilany, Howaida Arram, Ashraf Yacoub, Alaa El-Habashi, Amr Shalaby, Krisjanis Karins, Everett Rowson, Robert MacIntyre, Paul Kingsbury, David Graff, Cynthia McLemore. (1997) CALLHOME Egyptian Arabic Transcripts. LDC catalog number LDC97T19, ISBN 1-58563-115-9.

Ghoneim, Mahmoud and Mona Diab. (2013) Multiword Expressions in the context of Statistical Machine Translation. In the Proceedings of IJCNLP 2013, October, Nagoya, Japan.

Gibbs, R. W. (1980). Spilling the beans on understanding and memory for idioms. *Memory & Cognition*, 8, 449–456.

Grégoire, Nicole. (2010) DuELME: a Dutch electronic lexicon of multiword expressions. In *Language Resources and Evaluation*, 44(1-2):23-39 (2010)

Gross, Maurice, 1986. Lexicon-Grammar. The Representation of Compound Words. In COLING-1986 Proceedings, Bonn, pp. 1-6.

Habash, Nizar, Mona Diab, Owen Rambow (2012). CODA: A Conventional Orthography for Dialectal Arabic. Proceedings of LREC, Istanbul Turkey, May 2012.

Hawwari, Abdelati, Kfir Bar, and Mona Diab (2012). Building an Arabic Multiword Expressions Repository. Proceedings of the NAACL-HLT 2012 Workshop on Computational Linguistics for Literature, Montreal, Canada, June 2012.

Jackendoff, R. (1973). The base rules for prepositional phrases. In A *Festschrift for Morris Halle*, pp. 345–356. New York, USA: Rinehart and Winston.

Korkontzelos, Ioannis, and Suresh Manandhar. (2010) Can Recognising Multiword Expressions Improve Shallow Parsing? In proceedings of Human Language Technologies: The 2010 Annual Conference of the North American Chapter of the ACL, pages 636–644, Los Angeles, California, June 2010.

Mel'čuk, I. (1998) Collocations and Lexical Functions. In A.P. Cowie (ed.): *Phraseology. Theory, Analysis, and Applications*, Oxford: Clarendon Press, 23-53.

Mel'čuk, Igor (2004) Verbes supports sans peine. *Lingvisticæ Investigationes* 27: 2, 203-217.

Nivre, Joakim and Jens Nilsson. 2004. Multiword Units in Syntactic Parsing. InWorkshop on Methodologies and Evaluation of Multiword Units in Real-World Applications, the 4th International Conference on Language Resources and Evaluation (LREC 2004), pp. 39-46. Lisbon, Portugal.

Odijk, Jan. (2013) Identification and Lexical Representation of Multiword Expressions. In P. Spyns and J. Odijk (eds.), *Essential Speech and Language Technology for Dutch*, Theory and Applications of Natural Language Processing

Palmer, Martha, Dan Gildea, Paul Kingsbury. (2005) The Proposition Bank: An Annotated Corpus of Semantic Roles. *Computational Linguistics*, 31:1., pp. 71-105.

Ramisch, Carlos, Aline Villavicencio, Christian Boitet, "mwetoolkit: a Framework for Multiword Expression Identification", Proceedings of the Seventh International Conference on Language Resources and Evaluation (LREC 2010), Valetta, Malta, May, 2010.

Sag, I. A., Baldwin, T., Bond, F., Copestake, A., and Flickinger, D. 2002. Multiword Expressions: A Pain in the Neck for NLP. Proceedings of the 3rd International Conference on Intelligent Text Processing and Computational Linguistics, CICLING2002: 1–15.

SanJuan, Eric and Fidelia Ibekwe-SanJuan. 2006. Text mining without document context. In *Information Processing and Management*. Volume 42, Issue 6, pp. 1532-1552.

Schneider, Nathan, Spencer Onuffer, Nora Kazour, Emily Danchik, Michael T. Mordowanec, Henrietta Conrad, and Noah A. Smith. (2014) Comprehensive Annotation of Multiword Expressions in a Social Web Corpus. In Proceedings of the Language Resources and Evaluation Conference (LREC 2014), Reykjavik, Iceland, May 2014.

Shudo, Kosho, Akira Kurahone, and Toshifumi Tanabe. (2011) A Comprehensive Dictionary of Multiword Expressions. Proceedings of HLT '11 Proceedings of the 49th Annual Meeting of the Association for Computational Linguistics: Human Language Technologies, Portland, Oregon. Volume 1, pp. 161-170

Walters, Keith. Diglossia, linguistic variation, and language change in Arabic. 1996. In Eid, Mushira, *Perspectives on Arabic Linguistics VIII*. John Benjamins. 1996

Weller, Marion, Ulrich Heid. (2010) Extraction of German Multiword Expressions from Parsed Corpora Using Context Features. In proceedings of the seventh international conference on Language Resources and Evaluation (LREC), Val-letta, Malta.

Zaninello, Andrea, Malvina Nissim. (2010) Creation of lexical resources for a characterisation of multiword expressions in Italian. In proceedings of the seventh international conference on Language Resources and Evaluation (LREC), Valletta, Malta

Al-Bayan: An Arabic Question Answering System for the Holy Quran

Heba Abdelnasser
heba.abdelnasser@alex.edu.eg
Reham Mohamed
reham.mohmd@alex.edu.eg
Maha Ragab
maha.ragab@alex.edu.eg
Alaa Mohamed
alaa.mohmd@alex.edu.eg
Bassant Farouk
bassant.farouk@alex.edu.eg
Nagwa El-Makky
nagwa.elmakky@alex.edu.eg
Marwan Torki
marwan.torki@alex.edu.eg

Computer and Systems Engineering Department
Alexandria University, Egypt

Abstract

Recently, Question Answering (QA) has been one of the main focus of natural language processing research. However, Arabic Question Answering is still not in the mainstream. The challenges of the Arabic language and the lack of resources have made it difficult to provide Arabic QA systems with high accuracy. While low accuracies may be accepted for general purpose systems, it is critical in some fields such as religious affairs. Therefore, there is a need for specialized accurate systems that target these critical fields. In this paper, we propose Al-Bayan, a new Arabic QA system specialized for the Holy Quran. The system accepts an Arabic question about the Quran, retrieves the most relevant Quran verses, then extracts the passage that contains the answer from the Quran and its interpretation books *(Tafseer)*. Evaluation results on a collected dataset show that the overall system can achieve 85% accuracy using the top-3 results.

1 Introduction

Nowadays, the Web has become the main source of information where lots of terabytes of data are added every day in all fields. With this increase of data on the Web, there is a critical need for advanced search facilities that satisfy users' demands with high accuracy. This leads to several problems: the first problem is that most of the available search engines provide users with documents that are relevant to their demands; however, the users should take the trouble of searching for the answers inside each document. This increased the need for Question Answering (QA) systems that provide the users with direct answers to their questions. While great efforts have been made to provide reliable QA systems for different languages, very few attempts have been made to investigate QA for the Arabic language.

The second problem is the quality of the data. The development of social networks made the users not only encouraged to search on the Web but also to post their opinions and knowledge. Although this is an advantage for sharing knowledge in different fields and massively increasing the data on the Web, it is critical for religious affairs where users may post untrusted or false information. Observing the Arabic Web, we found that this problem is very common for the Holy Quran, where large amount of incorrect data is published on different sites which may provide a spurious view of the Islamic religion.

The third problem is the challenges of the Arabic language. **Arabic is highly inflectional and derivational**, which makes its morphological analysis a complex task. Derivational: where all the Arabic words have a three or four characters root verbs. Inflectional: where each word consists of a root and zero or more affixes (prefix, infix, suffix). **Arabic is characterized by diacritical marks (short vowels)**, the same word with different diacritics can express different meanings. Diacritics are usually omitted which causes ambiguity. **Absence of capital letters in Arabic** is an obstacle against accurate named entities recognition. Finally, **the lack of Arabic resources**, such as corpora, makes Arabic NLP research more challenging.

In this paper, we propose our solutions to these problems. We introduce Al-Bayan: a new Ara-

Proceedings of the EMNLP 2014 Workshop on Arabic Natural Langauge Processing (ANLP), pages 57–64,
October 25, 2014, Doha, Qatar.

bic QA system specialized for the Quran. Al-Bayan aims at understanding the semantics of the Quran and answering users questions using reliable Quranic resources. Mainly, we use the Quran and its interpretation books *(Tafseer)* of trusted Quranic scholars as our sources of information. Our main contribution can be summarized in the following points:

1. Building a Semantic Information Retrieval module that retrieves the semantically related verses to user's questions.

2. Increasing the accuracy of question analysis by applying a highly accurate Arabic tool for morphological analysis and disambiguation and by using a state of the art classifier, i.e. Support Vector Machine (SVM) to classify questions.

3. Extracting the ranked answers to the input questions from the retrieved verses and their interpretation with high accuracy.

The rest of the paper is organized as follows: Section 2 shows some of the work related to our system. Section 3 shows the details of the system model. Section 4 shows the datasets that we used to build the system. In Section 5, we show some of the initial results. Finally, we conclude the paper and give directions to future work in Section 6.

2 Related Work

Our work is related to prior work in both Quranic research and Question Answering systems.

(a) Quranic Research: Several studies have been made to understand the Quranic text and extract knowledge from it using computational linguistics. Saad et al. (2009) proposed a simple methodology for automatic extraction of concepts based on the Quran in order to build an ontology. In (Saad et al., 2010), they developed a framework for automated generation of Islamic knowledge concrete concepts that exist in the holy Quran. Qurany (Abbas, 2009) builds a Quran corpus augmented with a conceptual ontology, taken from a recognized expert source 'Mushaf Al Tajweed'. Quranic Arabic Corpus (Atwell et al., 2011) also builds a Quranic ontology of concepts based on the knowledge contained in traditional sources of Quranic analysis, including the sayings of the prophet Muhammad (PBUH), and the *Tafseer* books. Khan et al. (2013) developed a simple ontology for the Quran based on living creatures including animals and birds that are mentioned in the Quran in order to provide Quranic semantic search. AlMaayah et al. (2014) proposed to develop a WordNet for the Quran by building semantic connections between words in order to achieve a better understanding of the meanings of the Quranic words using traditional Arabic dictionaries and a Quran ontology.

Other attempts for text-mining the Quran were proposed such as: QurAna (Sharaf and Atwell, 2012) which is a corpus of the Quran annotated with pronominal anaphora and QurSim (Sharaf and Atwell, 2012) which is another corpus for extracting the relations between Quran verses.

b) Question Answering (QA) Systems: Although a large number of QA systems were proposed for the English language such as the work proposed by Fleischman et al. (2003), Ittycheriah and Roukos (2006), Kaisser (2012), the Arabic QA research is still limited in terms of accuracy. Some Arabic systems have been proposed such as: QARAB (Hammo et al., 2002) which is a QA system that takes factoid Arabic questions and attempts to provide short answers. ArabiQA (Benajiba et al., 2007) which is fully oriented to the modern Arabic language. It also answers factoid questions using Named Entity Recognition. However, this system is not completed yet. DefArabicQA (Trigui et al., 2010) presents a definitional QA system for the Arabic language. Arabic QA4MRE (Trigui et al., 2012) introduced the Arabic language for the first time at CLEF. This system proposed a new approach which can answer questions with multiple answer choices from short Arabic texts. However, its overall accuracy is 0.19. Also, all these systems target the modern standard Arabic. To the best of our knowledge, no previous research was proposed for the Quranic classical Arabic question answering.

3 System Model

Al-Bayan system architecture is shown in Figure 1. The input question passes mainly through three stages. The first stage is Question Analysis, where the input question is preprocessed and classified to get the expected answer type. The preprocessed question then enters the second stage, Information Retrieval. In this stage, the semantically relevant verses are retrieved using offline preprocessed Quranic data. Finally, the expected answer type and the retrieved verses are fed to the Answer Ex-

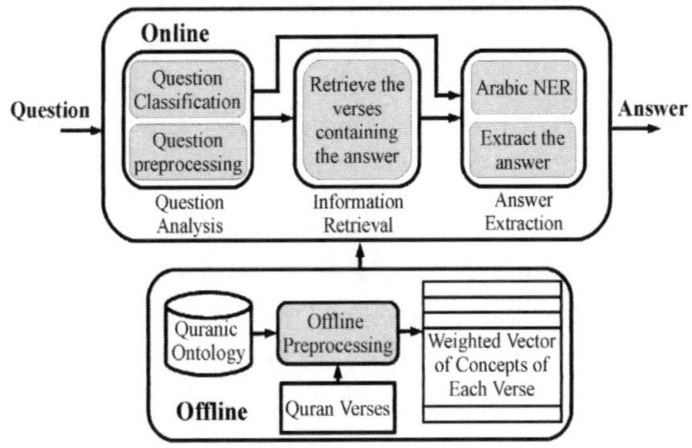

Figure 1: System Architecture

traction module which extracts the answer from the obtained verses and their *Tafseer* using a set of features. We first present the preprocessing operations that are used in online and offline phases. Then, we present the different modules of the system.

3.1 Preprocessing Operations

Text preprocessing is done by applying morphological analysis to identify the structure of text such as: morphemes, roots, affixes, stems, part of speech (POS) tags, etc. The Arabic language is, morphologically, one of the most complex and rich languages. Moreover, the Quranic Arabic is morphologically more complex, since each word may have more that one meaning and a word may have more than one POS tag. Also, the Arabic text of the Quran is fully diacritized, while most of the questions are written without diacritics. For preprocessing, we used MADA (Morphological Analysis and Disambiguation for Arabic) (Habash et al., 2009) which is one of the most accurate Arabic preprocessing toolkits. MADA can derive extensive morphological and contextual information from raw Arabic text, and then use this information for high-accuracy part-of-speech tagging, diacritization, lemmatization, disambiguation, stemming, and glossing in one step. Each term in the input text will be represented by its stem and POS tag, in the following format (stem:POS) using Buckwalter transliteration (Buckwalter, 2002). We remove pronouns, prepositions, conjunctions and other POS types, since these words are stopwords and must not affect the information retrieval indexing. In our system, we apply MADA preprocessing in two different phases: on the Quran and its *Tafseer* in the offline phase, and on the input question in the online phase.

3.2 Question Analysis

The system first takes the Arabic question which is preprocessed to extract the query that will be used in the Information Retrieval module. The question is also classified to get the type of the question, and consequently the type of its expected answer, which will then be used in the Answer Extraction module.

3.2.1 Question Preprocessing

The preprocessing operations discussed in Section 3.1 are applied to the input question. The preprocessed question is represented by a vector of terms where each term consists of a stem and a POS tag.

3.2.2 Question Classification

We classify the question to the anticipated type of the answer. This information would narrow down the search space to identify the correct answer. The most straight forward question classification is the Rule-based approach; where a set of rules is used to derive the answer type (for example: the answer of Who/Whom is of type person). The derivation of expected answer types is often carried out by means of machine learning approaches, such as the work of Li and Roth (2002). This task relies on three parts: taxonomy of answer types into which questions are to be classified, a corpus of questions prepared with the correct answer type classification, and an algorithm that learns to make the actual predictions given this corpus. We use an SVM classifier for this purpose and construct its training data. We also introduce a new taxonomy built specially for our system. More details about our dataset and taxonomy are mentioned in Section 4.

Unlike Rule-based classifies, our SVM classifier can classify questions in which the question word is omitted. For example the two questions: (Where did Allah talk to Moses?) and (What is the name of the mountain at which Allah talked to Moses?), both have the same answer type (Location). However, the Rule-based classifier cannot determine the correct answer type of the second question since the question word (Where) is omitted. Our SVM classifier, on the other hand, learns that a mountain name is of type location, therefore it correctly classifies the two questions.

3.3 Information Retrieval (IR)

The preprocessed question is now fed to the Information Retrieval module that retrieves the most semantically related verses from the Quran and its interpretation books *(Tafseer)*. Our approach is based on the explicit semantic analysis approach (Gabrilovich and Markovitch, 2007) that augments keyword-based text representation with concept-based features, automatically extracted from massive human knowledge repositories such as Wikipedia. However, instead of using Wikipedia as ontology, we build our Quranic ontology of concepts which classifies the Quran verses according to their topics. Details of building our Quranic ontology are shown in Section 4. We use machine-learning techniques to build a Semantic Interpreter as in (Gabrilovich and Markovitch, 2007) that maps fragments of natural language text into a weighted vector of Quranic concepts. Each leaf concept in the ontology has a list of verses, which are related to this concept. For each leaf concept C_i, a document D_i is constructed, where D_i is a document of verses and their *Tafseer* that belong to C_i. Then preprocessing on D_i is applied and finally an index on D_i is created using Lucene Indexer[1]. Each Quranic concept will be represented by a vector of terms that occur in the corresponding document. Entries of this vector are assigned weights using the TFIDF scheme. These weights quantify the strength of association between terms and concepts. To speed semantic interpretation, we build an inverted index which maps each term into a list of concepts in which it appears. Using the Semantic Interpreter in a way similar to that in (Gabrilovich and Markovitch, 2007), a weighted vector of concepts is generated for each verse in the Quran and stored in our database. This is done in the offline phase. Similarly, the vector of the input query is calculated in the online phase. To select the top-scoring verses that are semantically related to the user question we compute the cosine similarity between the concept vector of the input query and the concept vector of each verse in the Quran.

3.4 Answer Extraction

After the relevant verses are retrieved, these verses, their *Tafseer* and the expected answer type are fed into the Answer Extraction stage to extract the final answer to the input question. We define the answer as the phrase which contains the expected answer type (a named entity or a description of a named entity). The Answer extraction stage consists of the following steps: First, the named entities in the input question are identified. Then, several features are extracted which are used to rank each candidate answer.

3.4.1 Arabic Named Entity Recognition

Named Entity Recognition (NER) is a subtask of information extraction, where each proper name in the input passage - such as persons, locations and numbers - is assigned a named entity tag. We build the training data as shown in Section 4, then use it to feed LingPipe tool[2] which constructs the NER model. The NER model is then used in the online phase to tag the input text.

3.4.2 Feature Extraction

Once we have the preprocessed question Q tagged with named entities, we divide the relevant verses and their *Tafseer* into passages such that each passage is a candidate answer. For each candidate answer A, we get the probability of correctness C given the question Q and the candidate answer A. Then, the few candidate answers that have the highest probability of correctness are returned. A set of features are used to calculate the probability of correctness as mentioned by (Wang, 2006), such as:

(a) Maximum number of matched words between the input question and the candidate answer.

(b) The type of the question's expected answer if it matches with the extracted named entity in the answer passage in case of factoid questions.

(c) Is-A relationship in case of definitional questions, in the form: 'NE' is a 'description'.

(d) The maximum count of named entity types that occurred in the question occurring in the candidate answer.

(e) The minimum distance between matched terms in the passage.

4 Datasets

In this section, we describe the datasets that we used in different modules of the system.

[1] http://lucene.apache.org/

[2] http://alias-i.com/lingpipe/

Quranic Ontology and *Tafseer* Books:
We integrated the Quranic Corpus Ontology (Atwell et al., 2011) and the Qurany Ontology (Abbas, 2009), to form the Quranic conceptual ontology that we use in our system. The **Quranic Corpus Ontology** uses knowledge representation to define the key concepts in the Quran, and shows the relationships between these concepts using predicate logic. The **Qurany Ontology** is a tree of concepts that includes all the abstract concepts covered in the Quran. It is imported from 'Mushaf Al Tajweed' list of topics. This integration was difficult since we had to resolve the overlapping between the two ontologies. There were also some mistakes in the Qurany Concept Tree. So, we had to manually revise the 1200 concepts and their verses.
The Holy Quran consists of 6236 verses. In our Quranic ontology, each verse must be classified to one or more concepts depending on the semantics of this verse. After adding Quranic Corpus ontology, there were 621 verses without concepts, so we added them under their most suitable concepts to complete the ontology using a similarity measure module. This module measures the similarity between classified and unclassified verses to determine the concepts of unclassified verses. Now, our final ontology contains 1217 leaf concepts and all verses of the Quran. Under each concept in our ontology, we save the related verses with their *Tafseer*, that is used to build the inverted index. We use two *Tafseer* books: (Ibn-Kathir, 1370) and (Al-Jaza'iri, 1986), which are two of the most traditional books used by Islamic scholars. It is possible to add other books to enrich our corpus data. We also use the *Tafseer* books to extract the candidate answer passages.

NER Data:
To train our NER module, we need a new annotated corpus specialized for the Quran. Fortunately, Quranic Arabic corpus provides NE annotations for the Quran. This corpus is a hierarchical concept tree that has about 14 main classes. We mapped these classes to 5 categories and also manually added a new class for Numbers. We used a book called 'Numbers and Ratios in Quran' (Ali, 2008) to tag the numbers in the Quran. Table 1 shows the final classes and their members.

```
El O
Abogado B-PER
General I-PER
del I-PER
Estado I-PER
, O
Daryl B-PER
Williams I-PER
, O
```

(a) CoNLL 2002

```
وإذ 0
واعدنا 0
موسى B-creation
أربعين B-number
ليلة 0
ثم 0
اتخذتم 0
العجل B-entity
```

(b) Al-Bayan

Figure 2: Format of the NER training file. Each named entity is tagged with its beginning or continuing token picked out with tags B-class and I-class respectively. If the word is not named entity it is tagged with 0.

Our training data was annotated to have the same format of CoNLL 2002 corpora[3] as shown in Figure 2.

Question Classification Data:
We built a new taxonomy for Question Classification based on the NE categories discussed above. We also had to construct the training and test data suitable for this taxonomy. Our data consists of 230 classified questions collected randomly from forums or some common Quranic questions, divided into 180 questions used for training and 50 questions used for testing. The questions are classified according to their answer types into: (Creation, Entity, Physical, Location, Number, Description), where the first 5 classes are the named entities detected by the NER module, and the last class discriminates the definitional questions. The distribution of the questions among these classes is shown in Table 2

5 Evaluation

We evaluated the different modules of our system as well as the overall system accuracy.

5.1 NER Module

We evaluated this module using LingPipe evaluator. The training data is divided into 3 folds and the overall Precision, Recall and F-measure are calculated. Results are shown in Figure 3.

[3]http://www.cnts.ua.ac.be/conll2002/ner/

Al-Bayan NER classes	Members
Creation	Human - Angels - jinn. E.g. Muhammed, Jibreel and Satan
Location	After life locations - Geographical locations - Worship locations. For example, the heaven, Mosque, and Church
Entity	Events - Holy books - Languages - Religions - False deity - Organics. For example, Day of Resurrection, Quran, Injeel, Arabic, Islam, Christianity and Idol and (Bone)
Physical Entity	Astronomical Body - Artifact - Weather Phenomena - Physical Substance. For example, the Sun, Earth, (Boat), Rain, and Dust
Numbers	One, Two,...

Table 1: NER classes

Class	Creation	Entity	Physical	Location	Number	Description
Questions	90	40	17	22	14	45

Table 2: Distribution of the question classification data.

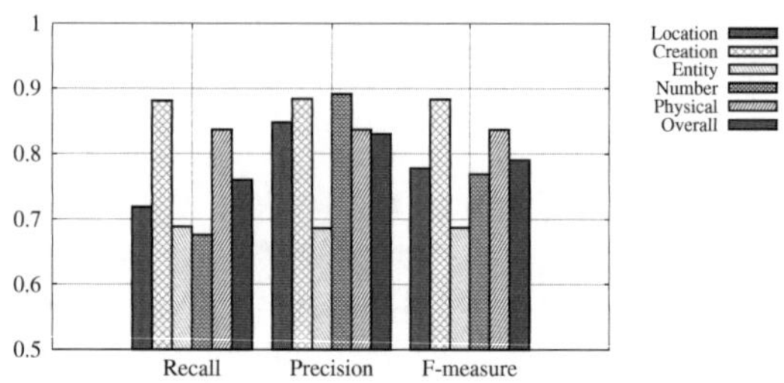

Figure 3: Quranic Arabic NER results

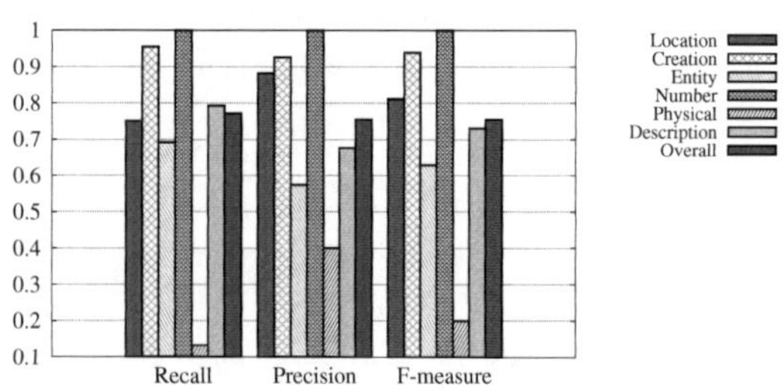

Figure 4: Question classifier results.

5.2 Question Classification Module

We evaluated the classifier based on our proposed taxonomy using 230 Arabic questions. We used 180 questions for training. The overall accuracy of the classifier using 3-folds cross-validation is 77.2%. The precision, recall and F-measure of the 6 classes is shown in Figure 4. We also evaluated the classifier using an independent set of 50 questions. The accuracy of the classifier on this set is 86%.

5.3 Overall System Evaluation

Evaluating our overall system is not an easy task, since we do not have a gold-standard for the Quran questions to compare with our results. Humans have the ability to judge the semantic relatedness of texts. Human judgments can be considered a gold standard against which computer algorithms are evaluated. Therefore, we asked some experts in Quran to judge our system accuracy. The system was evaluated by 5 Quran experts, using 59 questions. The output of our system for each question was the top-3 answers and the top-5 related verses. Each expert marked each verse or answer as right or wrong.

Figure 5 shows some examples of the evaluation questions with the answers retrieved by Al-Bayan system. For the first question (Who is the Queen of Sheba?), although the answer (Bilkis) is not explicitly mentioned in the Quran, the system was able to extract the correct answer from the Tafseer of the related verses. For the second question (How many months is the period of waiting of widows?), the system elegantly extracts the complete answer which includes different conditions of the pregnant and non-pregnant widows. The third and fourth questions are examples of definitional questions.

We used the TopN accuracy (Manning et al., 2008) to evaluate the overall system. TopN accuracy of correct answers is calculated as the number of questions in which at least one of the top N answer candidates is correct, divided by the total number of questions. We also calculate the preci-

	IR Module
Top-1	0.692
Top-5	0.847
Precision	0.57

(a)

	Overall System
Top-1	0.650
Top-3	0.854
Precision	0.73

(b)

Table 3: Experts Evaluation Results

sion when the system outputs 5 related verses and 3 answer passages. Table 3a shows the results of the verses retrieved from the IR module and Table 3b shows the results of the overall system. We notice that the Top-3 results of the overall system is better than Top-1 results, that is why we return Top-3 answers to the user to increase the probability of correct answers. We also noticed that the results of the overall system is better than information retrieval results, which shows that answer extraction module improves the accuracy of the overall system.

6 Conclusion and Future Work

In this paper, we proposed a novel Question Answering system for the Quran, that takes an Arabic question as an input and retrieves semantically relevant verses as candidate passages. Then an answer extraction module extracts the answer from the retrieved verses accompanied by their Tafseer. We also proposed a new taxonomy for Quranic Named Entities and constructed an Arabic Question Classifier based on state-of-the-art techniques. Our initial results evaluated by Quranic experts show the feasibility of constructing an accurate QA system specialized for the Quran.

In the future, we plan to explore more complex questions such as: list-type questions. In order to improve the accuracy of the system, we plan to use active learning techniques which are appropriate when the gold-standard is scarce or expensive to obtain. Thus, Quran experts can give their feedback about the answers and the system would learn from this feedback and improve its results. Finally, we plan to make the proposed system publicly available to the research community.

Acknowledgments

We would like to thank Dr. Noorhan Hassan Abbas and Prof. Dr. Eric Atwell from University of Leeds for providing us with the Qurany Ontology files.

References

Abdul-Baquee M. Sharaf and Eric Atwell. 2012. *QurAna: Corpus of the Quran annotated with Pronominal Anaphora*. LREC.

Abdul-Baquee M. Sharaf and Eric Atwell. 2012. *QurSim: A corpus for evaluation of relatedness in short texts*. LREC.

Abraham Ittycheriah and Salim Roukos. 2006. *IBM's statistical question answering system-TREC-11*. Technical report, DTIC Document.

Abu Bakr Al-Jaza'iri. 1986. *Aysar al-Tafasir li Kalaam il 'Aliyy il Kabir*.

Abu Islam Ahmed bin Ali. 2008. *Numbers and Ratios in the Quran*.

Bassam Hammo, Hani Abu-Salem and Steven Lytinen. 2002. *QARAB: a question answering system to support the Arabic language*. Proceedings of the ACL-02 workshop on Computational approaches to semitic languages.

Christopher D Manning, Prabhakar Raghavan and Hinrich Schütze. 2008. *Introduction to information retrieval*, volume 1. Cambridge university press Cambridge.

Eric Atwell, Claire Brierley, Kais Dukes, Majdi Sawalha and Abdul-Baquee Sharaf. 2011. *A An Artificial Intelligence Approach to Arabic and Islamic Content on the Internet*. Proceedings of NITS 3rd National Information Technology Symposium.

Evgeniy Gabrilovich and Shaul Markovitch. 2007. *Computing Semantic Relatedness Using Wikipedia-based Explicit Semantic Analysis*, volume 7. Proceedings of the 20th international joint conference on artificial intelligence.

Hikmat Ullah Khan and Syed Muhammad Saqlain and Muhammad Shoaib and Muhammad Sher. 2013. *Ontology Based Semantic Search in Holy Quran.*, volume 2. International Journal of Future Computer and Communication, 570-575.

Ismail Ibn-Kathir. 1370. *Tafsir al-Qur'an al-Azim*.

Manal AlMaayah, Majdi Sawalha, and Mohammad AM Abushariah. 2014. *A Proposed Model for Quranic Arabic WordNet*. LRE-REL2, 9.

Mengqiu Wang. 2006. *A Survey of Answer Extraction Techniques in Factoid Question Answering*, volume 1. Association for Computational Linguistics.

Michael Fleischman, Eduard Hovy and Abdessamad Echihabi. 2003. *Offline strategies for online question answering: answering questions before they are asked*, volume 1. Proceedings of the 41st Annual Meeting on Association for Computational Linguistics.

من هي ملكة سبأ ؟
فَكَتَبَ سُليمانُ كِتَاباً إِلى بلْقِيسَ مَلِكَةِ سَبَأ، وأمَرَ الهُدْهُدَ بحَمْلِهِ إليها، وبإلْقَائِه بينَ يَدَيْها، ثُمَّ أَمَرَهُ بالتَّنَحي عنهُمْ جَانِباً لِيُلاحِظَ ما ستفْعَلُهُ بالكتابِ، وماذا يكونُ رَدُّهَا عليهِ، فحمَلَ الهُدْهُدْ الكِتَابَ إليْها، وألقاهُ بينَ يدَيْها
كم شهر عدة الأرامل ؟
يَأمُرُ اللهُ تَعَالَى النِسَاءَ اللَّواتِي يُتَوفَّى عَنْهُنَّ أزْوَاجُهُنَّ بِأَنْ يَعْتَدِدْنَ أرْبَعَةَ أشْهُرٍ وَعَشْرَ لَيَالٍ (وَالحُكْمُ يَشْمَلُ الزَّوْجَاتِ المَدْخُولَ بِهِنَّ وَغَيْرَ المَدْخُولِ بِهِنَّ)، وَلا يَشُذُّ عَنْ هَذِهِ الحَالَةِ إلا المُتَوَفَّى عَنْهَا زَوْجُها وَهِيَ حَامِلٌ، فَإِنَّ عِدَّتَهَا تَكُونُ بِوَضْعِ حَمْلِها
ما هي عقوبة السارق؟
يَأمُرُ اللهُ تَعَالَى بِقَطْعِ يَدِ السَّارِقِ وَالسَّارِقَةِ، وَكَانَ القَطْعُ مَعْمَولاً بِهِ فِي الجَاهِلِيَّةِ، فَقَرَّرَهُ الإسْلامُ، وَجُعِلَتْ لَهُ شُرُوطٌ
ما معنى الجاثية ؟
جَاثِيةً بَارِكَةً عَلَى الرُّكَبِ، لِشِدَّةِ الهَوْلِ

Figure 5: Examples of the evaluation questions with the answers retrieved by Al-Bayan system.

Michael Kaisser. 2012. *Answer sentence retrieval by matching dependency paths acquired from question/answer sentence pairs*. Proceedings of the 13th Conference of the European Chapter of the Association for Computational Linguistics.

Nizar Habash, Owen Rambow and Ryan Roth. 2009. *MADA+ TOKAN: A toolkit for Arabic tokenization, diacritization, morphological disambiguation, POS tagging, stemming and lemmatization*. Proceedings of the 2nd International Conference on Arabic Language Resources and Tools (MEDAR), Cairo, Egypt.

Noorhan Hassan Abbas. 2009. *Quran'search for a Concept'Tool and Website*. M. Sc. thesis, University of Leeds (School of Computing).

Omar Trigui, Lamia Hadrich Belguith and Paolo Rosso. 2010. *DefArabicQA: Arabic Definition Question Answering System*. Workshop on Language Resources and Human Language Technologies for Semitic Languages, 7th LREC, Valletta, Malta.

Omar Trigui, Lamia Hadrich Belguith, Paolo Rosso, Hichem Ben Amor and Bilel Gafsaoui. 2012. *Arabic QA4MRE at CLEF 2012: Arabic Question Answering for Machine Reading Evaluation*. CLEF (Online Working Notes/Labs/Workshop).

Saidah Saad, Naomie Salim, and Hakim Zainal. 2009. *Pattern extraction for Islamic concept.*, volume 2. Electrical Engineering and Informatics, ICEEI.

Saidah Saad, Naomie Salim, Hakim Zainal and S. Azman M. Noah. 2010. *A framework for Islamic knowledge via ontology representation.*. Information Retrieval & Knowledge Management, (CAMP).

Tim Buckwalter. 2002. *Arabic transliteration*. URL http://www.qamus.org/transliteration.htm.

Xin Li and Dan Roth. 2002. *Learning question classifiers*, volume 1. Proceedings of the 19th international conference on Computational linguistics.

Yassine Benajiba, Paolo Rosso and Abdelouahid Lyhyaoui. 2007. *Implementation of the ArabiQA Question Answering System's components*. Proc. Workshop on Arabic Natural Language Processing, 2nd Information Communication Technologies Int. Symposium, ICTIS-2007, Fez, Morroco.

Automatic Arabic diacritics restoration based on deep nets

Mohsen A. A. Rashwan
ELC Dept., Cairo University,
mohsen_rashwan@rdi-eg.com

Ahmad A. Al Sallab
ELC Dept., Cairo University
ahmad.elsallab@gmail.com

Hazem M. Raafat
Computer Science Dept., Kuwait University
hazem@cs.ku.edu.kw

Ahmed Rafea
Computer Science Dept., American University in Cairo
Rafea@aucegypt.edu

Abstract

In this paper, Arabic diacritics restoration problem is tackled under the deep learning framework presenting Confused Subset Resolution (CSR) method to improve the classification accuracy, in addition to Arabic Part-of-Speech (PoS) tagging framework using deep neural nets. Special focus is given to syntactic diacritization, which still suffer low accuracy as indicated by related works. Evaluation is done versus state-of-the-art systems reported in literature, with quite challenging datasets, collected from different domains. Standard datasets like LDC Arabic Tree Bank is used in addition to custom ones available online for results replication. Results show significant improvement of the proposed techniques over other approaches, reducing the syntactic classification error to 9.9% and morphological classification error to 3% compared to 12.7% and 3.8% of the best reported results in literature, improving the error by 22% over the best reported systems

1 Introduction

Arabic is a wide spread language spoken by over 350 million people on the planet. Arabic alphabet and vocabulary are very rich, with the same word morphology being a candidate of different meanings and pronunciations. For example the word عمر might bear the meaning of the person name "Omar" عُمَر or the meaning of "age" عُمْر. What distinguish them is the diacritization signs assigned to each character of the word.

Diacritics are marks added on the character to reflect its correct pronunciation, according to grammatical, syntactical and morphological rules of the language.

Nowadays, Modern Standard Arabic (MSA) transcripts are written without diacritics, left to the ability of the reader to restore them from the context and knowledge. Diacritics restoration is not an easy task even for knowledgeable, native Arabic speakers. On the other hand, there are many machine learning tasks, like Text-To-Speech (TTS), translation, spelling correction, word sense disambiguation,...etc, that require diacritizing the script as a pre-processing step before applying the core application technique.

In its basic form, the problem can be reduced to a pattern classification problem, with seven diacritics classes being the targets. In addition, the diacritics classification can be divided into syntactical diacritization, caring about case-ending and morphological diacritization, caring about the rest of the word diacritics. So far, morphological part of the problem is almost solved, leaving a marginal error of around 3-4%, Rashwan et al. (2009, 2011). On the other hand, syntactical diacritization errors are still high, hitting a ceiling that is claimed to be asymptotic and cannot be squeezed any further, Rashwan et al. (2009, 2011). For this reason, we focus our effort to squeeze this error beyond the least 12.5% error obtained in Rashwan et al. (2009, 2011).

Recently, a significant advancement in the area of deep learning has been witnessed, with the development of a generative model; Deep Belief Nets (DBN), with a fast algorithm for inference of the model parameters. Deep Neural Networks (DNN) shall be the basic machine learning classifier used in this work, employing the latest results reached in the deep learning field. An efficient features' vector is designed under the umbrella of deep learning to distinguish different words diacritics. Features that are tested in the current work are: PoS, morphological quadruple of lexemes, last character and word identity. In addition, context features are essential to the diacritization problem. Context features include, the

Proceedings of the EMNLP 2014 Workshop on Arabic Natural Langauge Processing (ANLP), pages 65–72,
October 25, 2014, Doha, Qatar.

previous word features, as well as the previous word diacritic.

Part-of-Speech (PoS) features are critical to syntactic diacritization, which is the focus of this work. For some datasets PoS tags are manually annotated by professional linguistics, while for the real case and most datasets, they are not available. For this reason, standalone PoS taggers are built under the deep learning framework, which can reused in Arabic PoS tagging systems, needed for many other applications, not only for Arabic diacritization.

The deep learning model often hit a performance barrier which cannot be crossed. Hence, error analysis and diagnosis is run on the confusion matrix results, proposing the Confused Subset Resolution (CSR) method to train sub-classifiers to resolve the identified confusions and automatically generate a deep network-of-networks composed of the main classifier and the sub-classifiers working together to offer improved accuracy system purified of the identified confusions, offering around 2% error enhancement.

Evaluation of the proposed techniques is done on two datasets; the first is a custom one collected from many different sources, which is available online at (http://www.RDI-eg.com/RDI/TrainingData is where to download TRN_DB_II). Manually extracted PoS and morphological quadruples are available for only a part of this dataset. The PoS tags of this part of the dataset were used to build the DNN PoS taggers to tag the rest of the dataset. The corresponding test set is available online at (http://www.RDI-eg.com/RDI/TestData is where to download TST_DB), which is quite challenging and collected from different sources than training ones. The second dataset is the standard LDC Arabic Tree Bank dataset LDC Arabic Tree Bank Part 3, (http://www.ldc.upenn.edu/Catalog/catalogEntry.jsp?catalogId=LDC2005T20) used to bench mark the system against state-of-the art systems in Arabic diacritization area.

The rest of the paper is organized as follows: first the related works in literature are surveyed, followed by a formulation of the CSR method. The next section is dedicated to describing the features used in the system, and how they are encoded and represented in the features' vector followed by the details of building the DNN PoS tagger for Arabic. The datasets used for evaluation are then described. The next section describes the system evaluation experiments. Experimental results include an error analysis study of the effect of each feature and method on the system performance, in addition to benchmarking against state-of-the art systems in literature, evaluated on standard datasets. Finally, the paper is concluded with the main results and conclusion.

2 Related work

There have been many attempts to approach the Arabic diacritization problem by different techniques. Focus will be around three works strongly related to what is proposed here, and having the best results in literature. Zitouni et al. (2006) apply Maximum Entropy classification to the problem taking the advantage of the MaxEnt framework to combine different features together, like lexical, segment-based, and PoS features. Segmentation involves getting the prefix, suffix, and stem of the word. PoS features are also generated under the MaxEnt framework. Habash and Rambow (2007) perform Morphological Analysis and Disambiguation of Arabic (MADA) system, and then apply SVM classification. Last, Rashwan et al. (2009 and 2011) propose a hybrid approach composed of two stages: first, maximum marginal probability via A* lattice search and n-grams probability estimation. When full-form words are OOV, the system switches to the second mode which factorizes each Arabic word into all its possible morphological constituents, then uses also the same techniques used by the first mode to get the most likely sequence of morphemes, hence the most likely diacritization. The latter system shall be our baseline, since it gives the best results in literature so far, and the dataset used to evaluate it is available at our hand, and hence fair comparison is possible. Also, comparison to the three systems is made on the LDC Arabic Tree Bank data set.

3 System architecture

In this section the overall system is presented. The raw text input is fed to the system word by word. According to the configured context depth, a number of succeeding and preceding words are stored in a context memory. In our system the context is experimentally taken as three preceding words and one succeeding word (N=3, M=1), which is found to give the best accuracy results versus other tunings: (N=1, M=1), (N=2, M=2), (N=3, M=2), (N=1, M=3) and (N=1, M=3). If the word is the first or last one in a sentence, the preceding or succeeding context is zero padded. Word context serves in case of syntactic diacritization, while for morphological case, characters context is also needed, which is directly present in the character sequence of the single input word itself.

Features extraction procedure depends on the feature itself. For PoS tags, a special DNN is trained for that purpose, which also makes use of the context of the word. For other features, like sequence of characters forming the word, the last character of the word and the morphological quadruples are directly extracted from the single word.

The framework in Figure 2 is employed. Three layers network architecture is used for each features extraction subnet or classification network. For the classification network a 20-20-20 architecture was used, while for PoS-tagging networks a 60-60-60 is used. The network architecture is determined empirically. By experiments it was found that the best architecture is the symmetric one, with the same width for all layers. The best width is found to be the same as the average number of ones in the training set features vectors.

The neural network training undergoes DBN pre training as in Hinton et al. (2006) for 20 epochs per layer, with batch size of 1000 examples each without mini batches. Momentum is used initially with 0.5 for the first 5 epochs and then raised to 0.9 for the next epochs. The discriminative fine tuning is performed using conjugate gradient minimization for 30 epochs. For the first 6 epochs, only the upper layer is adjusted, then the rest of the layers are trained for the next epochs.

Once the features are ready of a certain raw word it is fed to the DNN classifier. The resulting confusion matrix from the training phase is then fed to the CSR method to generate the tree structure that improves the system accuracy. During testing phase, the raw input features are fed to the DNN classifier to obtain an initial guess of the target diacritic. This guess is then improved in the next CSR stage to obtain the final diacritic decision.

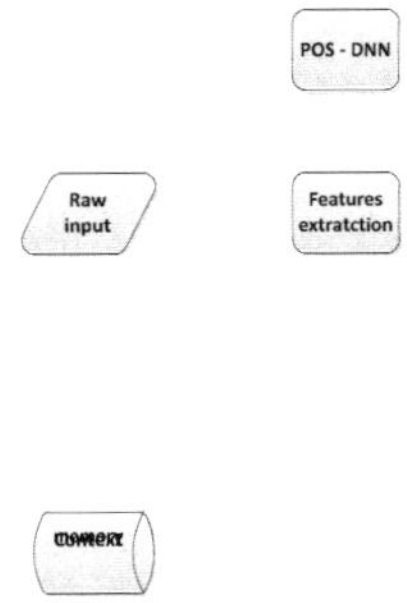

This enables building a standalone system that operates on the raw text only.

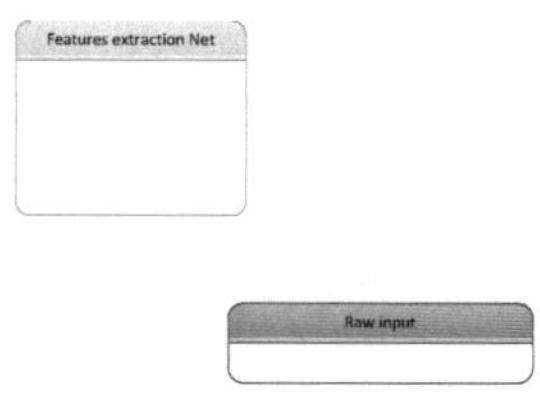

TABLE II CONFUSION MATRIX RESULTS FOR DNN CLASSIFIER ON SYNTACTIC DIACRITIZATION

	Fathten	Dammeten	Kasreten	Fatha	Damma	Kasra	Shadda	Sukkun
Fathten	4762	2179	2455	336	389	197	0	120
Dammeten	2647	6976	2720	660	1144	408	0	231
Kasreten	4560	3378	32588	801	303	**4868**	0	951
Fatha	438	475	1458	92755	11671	8340	0	1980
Damma	262	727	579	5858	72994	14995	0	952
Kasra	59	184	**3275**	2682	3657	220357	0	1970
Shadda	2	78	86	51	75	0	416	4
Sukkun	3	128	271	1150	630	1565	0	73983

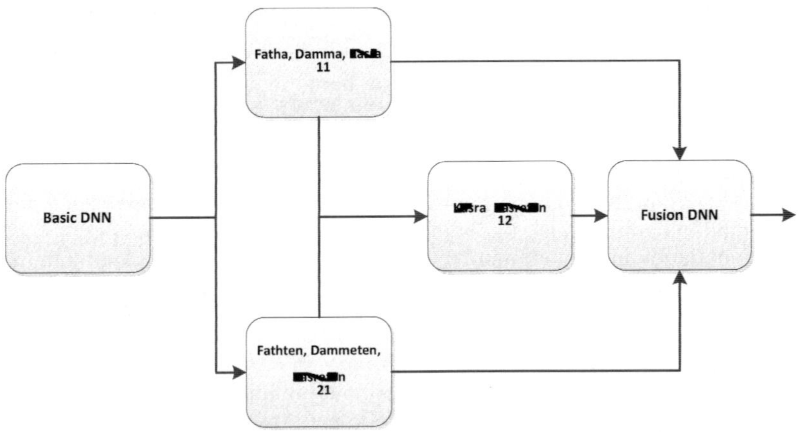

Figure 4 CSR model for syntactic Arabic diacritization task

6 Features

The input to text processing tasks is a transcript or document containing raw text. For Arabic diacritization task specifically, a set of features have proved good performance in literature, such as morphological lexemes, PoS, word identity,…etc see Rashwan et al. (2009, 2011), Zitouni et al. (2006) and Habash and Rambow (2007). In this section the features employed in our features vector are described.

Last character identity: case-ending diacritization is about adding diacritics on the last character of the word. Arabic language prohibits some diacritics from being placed over some characters. For example fatha on"و" is phonetically forbidden. Also, it favors some diacritics over some character like fatheten on "ا". A rule based system would have set a rule for that, however, in DNN framework, the system is left to learn such rules. Hence, the last character identity is an effective feature for syntactic diacritization task.

The raw word identity: is another type of possible features. The system proposed by Rasshwan et al. (2009, 2011) uses this feature. There are two possibilities of encoding such feature, the first would be to use a raw index representing the word index from a vocabulary vector built from training set. However, this could lead to many out of vocabulary (OOV) cases, in addition to long vector. On the other hand, a word can be encoded as sequence of the identities of its composing characters, which is more efficient under the DNN framework to avoid OOV, because even if a word is not encountered during training, at least a similar one with a character less or more was encountered during training, generating nearly similar activation of the stochastic binary units and leading to similar result as the original word. The same exact word need not be present during training phase, instead only a similar word is enough so that the word is not considered OOV. This is a direct result of encoding words as sequence of their constituting characters.

Context features: Considering the features vector of the preceding and/or succeeding words or characters can improve significantly the classification accuracy. This is what we refer to as context features. Context features are essential to syntactic and morphological diacritization tasks. For morphological diacritization context is just the surrounding characters, while for syntactic diacritization context is represented by the surrounding words. We denote the depth of the preceding context by N and the succeeding context elements by M.

Context class labels: The context does not only include the features' vectors of inputs, it can also include the context of class labels. For example, the decision of the classifier for the previous diacritic can be re-considered as an input feature for the current diacritic classification. This results in something like an auto-regressive model, where the previous decisions affect the next one recursively

Part-of-Speech tags: are essential features to discriminate syntactic diacritics cases, where syntactic diacritics restoration is strongly related to grammatically parsing and analyzing the sentence into its syntactic language units or PoS. There are many models for Arabic PoS tags. In this work we adopt the one in Rashwan et al. (2011), which sets 62 context-free atomic units to represent all possible Arabic language PoS tags. A very rich dataset of Arabic words, extracted from different sources, is used to train the system (available on http://www.RDI-eg.com/RDI/TrainingData is where to download TRN_DB_II). PoS tags are manually annotated for this dataset by expert Arabic linguistics. A DNN is trained on this dataset to identify different PoS tags.

7 Datasets

In all the coming experiments one of the following datasets is used:

- ***TRN_DB_I:*** This is a 750,000 words dataset, collected from different sources and manually annotated by expert linguistics with every word PoS and Morphological quadruples.
- ***TRN_DB_II:*** This is 2500,000 words train set.
- ***TST_DB:*** This is 11,000 words test data set. For more information refer to Rashwan et al. (2009, 2011).
- ***ATB:*** LDC Arabic Tree Bank.

For TRN_DB_I, PoS tags are available as ready features added manually. When the manually PoS tags are used as input features, the dataset is referred to as TRN_DB_I – Ready PoS. While, when our PoS-DNN nets are used, a derivative dataset with only raw text is referred as TRN_DB_I – Raw text.

8 System evaluation

8.1 Effect of CSR method

The objective of this experiment is to show the effect of CSR method. The test set is TST_DB. Results in TABLE III show improvement around 2% in all tested datasets. This represents 17.09% improvement of error.

TABLE III EFFECT OF CSR

Dataset	Accuracy with CSR (%)	Accuracy without CSR (%)
TRN_DB_I – Ready PoS	90.2	88.2
TRN_DB_I – Raw text	88.2	86.2

8.2 Effect of class context learning

The objective of this experiment is to evaluate the effect of employing sequential class labels model. Test set is TST_DB. The results in TABLE IV show that employing this feature offers 1% to 2% improvement of accuracy over basic DBN model alone. This represents 15.625% improvement of error.

TABLE IV EFFECT OF CLASS LABELS CONTEXT ON SYNTACTIC DIACRITIZATION

Dataset	Accuracy with class labels context (%)	Accuracy without class labels context (%)
TRN_DB_I – Ready PoS	88.3	87.2
TRN_DB_I – Raw text	86.7	85.1
TRN_DB_I + TRN_DB_II / TST_DB	86.3	84.3

8.3 Effect of last character feature for syntactic case

The identity of the last character of a word is a critical feature for syntactic diacritization task. The dataset used for training is TRN_DB_I and for testing TST_DB. TABLE V shows the effect of utilizing this feature. A significant error improvement of about 4% is witnessed with this new feature.

TABLE V EFFECT OF LAST CHARACTER FEATURE ON SYNTACTIC DIACRITIZATION

	Accuracy (%)
With last character	88.2
Without last character	84.5

Justification to this strong improvement is that; Arabic language prohibits some diacritics from being placed over some characters. For example fatha on"ﻭ" is prohibited phonetically. Also, it favors some diacritics over some character like fatheten on "ا". A rule based system would have set a rule for that, however, in DNN framework, the system is left to learn such rules.

8.4 Effect of character level encoding of the word

The word identity is an important feature for diacritization task. The dataset used for training is TRN_DB_I and for testing TST_DB. TABLE VI shows the effect of utilizing this feature. A significant error improvement of about 2% is witnessed with this feature.

TABLE VI EFFECT OF CHARACTER LEVEL WORD ENCODING ON SYNTACTIC DIACRITIZATION

Encoding	Accuracy (%)
Word level	88.2
Character level	86.3

"Word level" could lead to many out of vocabulary (OOV) cases, in addition to long vector. On the other hand, "Character level" is more efficient under the DNN framework to avoid OOV suffered in Rashwan et al. (2009, 2011), because even if a word is not encountered during training, but a similar one with a character less or more was encountered, then a nearly similar activation of the stochastic binary units would be generated, leading to similar result to the most similar word existing in training data set.

8.5 Comparison to other systems

The objective of this experiment is to evaluate the performance of the proposed system for Arabic diacritization versus the architecture in Rashwan et al. (2009, 2011)., the MaxEnt model proposed in Zitouni et al. (2006) and the MADA system Habash and Rambow (2007). These systems represent the state of the art Arabic diacritization systems, with the best reported accuracy in literature. The evaluation was done on all the datasets as explained in Rashwan et al. (2011). The PoS features are extracted using the DNN-PoS tagger, since TRN_DB_II / TST_DB dataset contains only raw text without ready PoS features.

Results in TABLE VIII show that the proposed system achieves improved performance by around 1.2% over the system in 0Rashwan et al. (2011), which represents 9.23% of the error, evaluated on the (TRN_DB_I + TRN_DB_II / TST_DB) dataset. Also, on ATB standard dataset, the proposed system achieves 0.9% improvement over the best result in literature using the same training and testing data same as evaluation in Rashwan et al. (2011) was done.

Another comparison is done when the dataset TRN_DB_I is used with ready PoS features. Results in show that the proposed system achieves better performance by 3.2% over the system in Rashwan et al. (2011), which represents 24.6% of the error. The importance of this experiment is to isolate the automatic PoS tagging errors from the evaluation.

TABLE VII COMPARISON TO HYBRID ARCHITECTURE WITH READY PoS FEATURES

System	Syntactical accuracy (%)
Deep network + CSR	90.2
Hybrid Architecture 0Rashwan et al. (2011)	88.3

TABLE VIII COMPARISON TO OTHER SYSTEMS

System	Dataset	Case-ending accuracy (%)	Morphological accuracy (%)
Deep network + CSR (This paper)	TRN_DB_I + TRN_DB_II / TST_DB	**88.2**	**97**
	ATB	**88.4**	**97**
Hybrid Architecture – Rashwan et al. (2009, 2011)	TRN_DB_I + TRN_DB_II / TST_DB	87	96.4
	ATB	87.5	96.2
MaxEnt - Zitouni et al. (2006)	ATB	82	94.5
MADA - Habash and Rambow (2007)	ATB	85.1	95.2

9 Conclusion

In this paper the problem of Arabic diacritization restoration is tackled under the deep learning framework taking advantage of DBN model training. As part of the proposed deep system, a PoS tagger for Arabic transcript is proposed as well using deep networks. The first contribution is the introduction of the Confused Sub-set Resolution (CSR) architecture to enhance the accuracy.

Design of features vector played a key role in error improvement. Specifically, using features like last character identity had valuable contribution to error improvement by about 4%. Including class labels context features in auto-regressive fashion has also good impact of 1.1% on error improvement. Finally, encoding of word as sequence of characters enables to reduce OOV cases and enhance the accuracy.

CSR enables to purify the cross confusions between diacritics. A network-of-network architecture formed of group of classifiers, each working to resolve a set of confusions, is directly generated to enhance the overall accuracy by about 2%. The identified confusions and the architecture go smoothly with the grammatical and syntactical rules of the Arabic language.

Evaluation of the proposed system is made on two different datasets; custom and standard, both available online to enable replicating the experiments. Details of features vectors formatting and the used features are presented to facilitate results re-generation. The standard LDC Arabic Tree Bank dataset is used to bench mark the system against the best three systems in literature, showing that our system outperforms all previously published baselines. The effect of each proposed method is presented separately. Results show improvements ranging from 1.2% to 2.8% over the best reported results representing 22% improvement of the error.

Reference

Rashwan, Mohsen A A; Attia, Mohamed; Abdou, Sherif M.; Abdou, S.; Rafea, Ahmed A. 2009. "A Hybrid System for Automatic Arabic Diacritization", International Conference on Natural Language Processing and Knowledge Engineering, pp 1-8, 24-27.

Rashwan, Mohsen A A , Al-Badrashiny, Mohamed A S A A; Attia, Mohamed; Abdou, Sherif M.; Rafea, Ahmed A. 2011. "A Stochastic Arabic Diacritizer Based on a Hybrid of Factorized and Unfactorized Textual Features", IEEE Transactions on Audio, Speech, and Language Processing, vol. 19, issue 1, pp 166-175.

I. Zitouni; J. S. Sorensen; R. Sarikaya, 2006. "Maximum Entropy Based Restoration of Arabic Diacritics", Proceedings of the 21st International Conference on Computational Linguistics and 44th Annual Meeting of the Association for Computational Linguistics (ACL); Workshop on Computational Approaches to Semitic Languages; Sydney-Australia

N. Habash; O. Rambo. 2007. "Arabic Diacritization through Full Morphological Tagging", Proceedings of the 8th Meeting of the North American Chapter of the Association for Computational Linguistics (ACL); Human Language Technologies Conference (HLT-NAACL).

G. E. Hinton; S. Osindero; Y. Teh, "A fast learning algorithm for deep belief nets" Neural Computation, vol. 18, pp. 1527–1554, 2006.

Ruslan Salakhutdinov. 2009."Learning Deep Generative Models" PhD thesis, Graduate Department of Computer Science, University of Toronto,

Raafat, H.; Rashwan, M.A.A. 1993. "A tree structured neural network, Proceedings of the Second International Conference on Document Analysis and Recognition" , pp. 939 – 941, ISBN: 0-8186-4960-7

Hai-Son Le ; Oparin, I. ; Allauzen, A. ; Gauvain, J., 2011. "Structured Output Layer neural network language model" 2011 IEEE International Conference on Acoustics, Speech and Signal Processing (ICASSP), pp. 5524 - 5527, ISBN: 978-1-4577-0537-3

http://www.RDI-eg.com/RDI/TrainingData is where to download TRN_DB_II.

http://www.RDI-eg.com/RDI/TestData is where to download TST_DB

LDC Arabic Tree Bank Part 3, http://www.ldc.upenn.edu/Catalog/catalogEntry.jsp?catalogId=LDC2005T20

Combining strategies for tagging and parsing Arabic

Maytham Alabbas
Department of Computer Science
University of Basrah
Basrah, Iraq
maytham.alabbas@gmail.com

Allan Ramsay
School of Computer Science
University of Manchester
Manchester M13 9PL, UK
Allan.Ramsay@manchester.ac.uk

We describe a simple method for combining taggers which produces substantially better performance than any of the contributing tools. The method is very simple, but it leads to considerable improvements in performance: given three taggers for Arabic whose individual accuracies range from 0.956 to 0.967, the combined tagger scores 0.995–a sevenfold reduction in the error rate when compared to the best of the contributing tools.

Given the effectiveness of this approach to combining taggers, we have investigated its applicability to parsing. For parsing, it seems better to take pairs of similar parsers and back off to a third if they disagree.

1 Introduction

If you have several systems that perform the same task, it seems reasonable to suppose that you can obtain better performance by using some judicious combination of them than can be obtained by any of them in isolation. A large number of combining strategies have been proposed, with majority voting being particularly popular (Stefano et al., 2002). We have investigated a range of such strategies for combining taggers and parsers for Arabic: the best strategy we have found for tagging involves asking each of the contributing taggers how confident it is, and accepting the answer given by the most confident one. We hypothesise that the reason for the effectiveness of this strategy for tagging arises from the fact that the contributing taggers work in essentially different ways (different training data, different underlying algorithms), and hence if they make systematic mistakes these will tend to be different. This means, in turn, that the places where they *don't* make mistakes will be different.

This strategy is less effective for parsing. We have tried combining two members of the MALTParser family (Nivre et al., 2006; Nivre et al., 2007; Nivre et al., 2010) with MSTParser (McDonald et al., 2006a; McDonald et al., 2006b). The best strategy here seems to be to accept the output of the two versions of MALTParser when they agree, but to switch to MSTParser if the MALTParser versions disagree. It may be that this is because the MALTParser versions are very similar, so that when they disagree this suggests that there is something anomalous about the input text, and that neither of them can be trusted at this point.

2 Tagging

We present a very simple strategy for combining part-of-speech (POS) taggers which leads to substantial improvements in accuracy. A number of combination strategies have been proposed in the literature (Zeman and Žabokrtský, 2005). In experiments with combining three Arabic taggers (AMIRA (Diab, 2009), MADA (Habash et al., 2009) and a simple affix-based maximum-likelihood Arabic tagger (MXL) (Ramsay and Sabtan, 2009)) the current strategy significantly outperformed voting-based strategies.

We used the Penn Arabic Treebank (PATB) Part 1 v3.0 as a resource for our experiments. The words in the PATB are already tagged, which thus provides us with a widely-accepted Gold standard. Even PATB tagging is not guaranteed to be 100% accurate, but it nonetheless provides as good a reference set as can be found.[1]

The PATB uses the tags provided by the Buckwalter morphological analyser (Buckwalter, 2004; Buckwalter, 2007), which carry a great deal

[1]The PATB is the largest easily available tagged Arabic corpus, with about 165K words in the section we are using. Thus for each fold of our 10-fold testing regime we are training on 150K words and testing on 15K, which should be enough to provide robust results.

Proceedings of the EMNLP 2014 Workshop on Arabic Natural Langauge Processing (ANLP), pages 73–77,
October 25, 2014, Doha, Qatar.

of syntactically relevant information (particularly case-marking). This tagset contains 305 tags, with for instance 47 tags for different kinds of verb and 44 for different kinds of noun. The very fine distinctions between different kinds of nouns and verbs (e.g. between subject and object case nouns) in the absence of visible markers make this an extremely difficult tagset to work with. It is in general virtually impossible to decide the case of an Arabic noun until its overall syntactic role is determined, and it is similarly difficult to decide the form of a verb until the overall syntactic structure of the sentence is determined. For this reason taggers often work with a coarser set of tags, of which the 'Bies tagset' (Maamouri and Bies, 2004) is widely used (see for instance the Stanford Arabic parser (Green and Manning, 2010)). We carried out our experiments with a variant of the original fine-grained tagset, and also with a variant of the coarser-grained Bies set obtained by deleting details such as case- and agreement-markers. We carried out two sets of experiments, with a coarse-grained set of tags (a superset of the Bies tagset with 39 tags, shown in Figure 1) and the original fine-grained one with 305 tags.

ABBREV	EXCEPT_PART	PART
ADJ	FOCUS_PART	POSS_PRON
ADV	FUT+IV	PREP
CONJ	INTERJ	PRON
CV	INTERROG_PART	PUNC
CVSUFF_DO	IV	PV
DEM_PRON	IVSUFF_DO	PVSUFF_DO
DET	LATIN	RC_PART
DET+ADJ	NEG_PART	REL_ADV
DET+NOUN	NOUN	REL_PRON
DET+NOUN_PROP	NOUN_PROP	SUB
DET+NUM	NO_FUNC	SUB_CONJ
EMPH_PART	NUM	VERB_PART

Table 1: Coarse-grained tagset

The accuracy of a tagger clearly depends on the granularity of the tagset: the contributing taggers produced scores from 0.955 to 0.967 on the coarse-grained tagset, and from 0.888 to 0.936 on the fine-grained one. We applied transformation-based retagging (TBR) (Brill, 1995; Lager, 1999) to the output of the basic taggers, which produced a small improvement in the results for MADA and MXL and a more substantial improvement for AMIRA. Table 2 shows the performance of the three taggers using the two tagsets with and without TBR. The improvement obtained by using

POS	TBR	AMIRA	MXL	MADA
Coarse	×	0.896	0.952	0.941
	√	0.953	0.956	**0.967**
Fine	×	0.843	0.897	0.917
	√	0.888	0.912	**0.936**

Table 2: Tagger accuracies in isolation, with and without TBR

TBR for AMIRA arises largely from the fact that in some cases AMIRA uses tags similar to those used in the English Penn Treebank rather than the ones in the the tags in the PATB, e.g. `JJ` for adjectives where the PATB uses `ADJ`. TBR provides a simple and reliable mechanism for discovering and patching systematic renamings of this kind, and hence is extremely useful when working with different tagsets. A significant component of the remaining errors produced by AMIRA arise because AMIRA has a much coarser classification of particles than the classification provided by the Buckwalter tagset. Since AMIRA assigns the same tag to a variety of different particles, TBR cannot easily recover the correct fine-grained tags, and hence AMIRA makes a substantial number of errors on these items.

The key to the proposed combining strategy is that each of the contributing taggers is likely to make systematic mistakes; and that if they are based on different principles they are likely to make *different* systematic mistakes. If we classify the mistakes that a tagger makes, we should be able to avoid believing it in cases where it is likely to be wrong. So long as the taggers are based on sufficiently different principles, they should be wrong in different places.

We therefore collected confusion matrices for each of the individual taggers showing how likely they were to be right for each category of item–how likely, for instance, was MADA to be right when it proposed to tag some item as a noun (very likely–accuracy of MADA when it proposes NN is 0.98), how likely was AMIRA to be right when it proposed the tag RP (very unlikely–accuracy of 0.08 in this case)? Given these tables, we simply took the tagger whose prediction was most likely to be right.[2]

Table 3 shows an excerpt from the output of the

[2]All the tagging results reported below were obtained by using 10-fold cross validation, i.e. carrying out 10 experiments each of which involved removing 10% of the data for testing and training on the remaining 90%.

Word	Gold standard	MADA	MXL	AMIRA	TAG
...	...	...	...	...	...
gyr	NEG_PART	NOUN (0.979)	NEG_PART (0.982)	RP (0.081)	NEG_PART
<lA	EXCEPT_PART	EXCEPT_PART (1.00)	SUB_CONJ (0.965)	RP (0.790)	EXCEPT_PART
...	...	...	...	...	...

Table 3: Confidence levels for individual tags

three individual taggers looking at a string containing the two words *gyr* and *<lA*, with the tags annotated with the accuracy of each tagger on the given tag, e.g. in this sequence MADA has tagged *gyr* as a noun, and MXL has tagged it as a negative particle and AMIRA has tagged it as RP; and when MADA suggests NOUN as the tag it is right 97.9% of the time, whereas when MXL suggests NEG_PART it is right 98.2% of the time and AMIRA is right just 8.1% of the time when it suggests RP. It is important to note that the tags are assigned to words in context, but the confidence levels are calculated across the entire training data. The fact that MADA is right 97.9% of the time when it assigns the tag NOUN is not restricted to the word *gyr*, and certainly not to this occurrence of this word.

We compared the results of this simple strategy, which is similar to a strategy proposed for image classification by Woods at el. (1997), with a strategy proposed by (2005), in which you accept the majority view if at least two of the taggers agree, and you back off to one of them if they all disagree, and with a variation on that where you accept the majority view if two agree and back off to the most confident if they all disagree. The results are given in Table 4.

All four strategies produce an improvement over the individual taggers. The fact that majority voting works better when backing off to MXL than to MADA, despite the fact that MADA works better in isolation, is thought-provoking. It seems likely to be that this arises from the fact that MADA and AMIRA are based on similar principles, and hence are likely to agree *even when they are wrong*. This hypothesis suggested that looking at the likely accuracy of each tagger on each case might be a good backoff strategy. It turns out that it is not just a good backoff strategy, as shown in the third column of Table 4: it is even better when used as the main strategy (column 5). The differences between columns 4 and 5 are not huge,[3] but that should not be too surprising, since these two strategies will agree in every case where all three of the contributing taggers agree, so the only place where these two will disagree is when one of the taggers disagrees with the others *and* the isolated tagger is more confident than either of the others.

The idea reported here is very simple, but it is also very effective. We have reduced the error in tagging with fairly coarse-grained tags to 0.05%, and we have also produced a substantial improvement for the fine grained tags, from 0.936 for the best of the individual taggers to 0.96 for the combination.

3 Parsing

Given the success of the approach outlined above for tagging, it seemed worth investigating whether the same idea could be applied to parsing. We therefore tried using it with a combination of dependency parsers, for which we used MSTParser (McDonald et al., 2006a; McDonald et al., 2006b) and two variants from the MALTParser family (Nivre et al., 2006; Nivre et al., 2007; Nivre et al., 2010), namely Nivre arc-eager, which we will refer to as MALTParser$_1$, and stack-eager, which we will refer to as MALTParser$_2$. The results in Table 5 include (i) the three parsers in isolation; (ii) a strategy in which we select a pair and trust their proposals wherever they agree, and back-off

[3] In terms of error rate the difference looks more substantial, since the error rate, 0.005, for column 5 for the fine-grained set is 62.5% of that for column 4, 0.008; and for the coarse-grained set the error rate for column 5, 0.04, is 73% of that for column 4, 0.055

Tagset	Majority voting (back off to MXL)	Majority voting (back off to MADA)	Majority voting (back off to AMIRA)	Majority voting (most confident)	Just most confident
Coarse-grained	0.982	0.979	0.975	0.992	**0.995**
Fine-grained	0.918	0.915	0.906	0.945	**0.96**

Table 4: Modified majority voting vs proposed strategy

	Parser	LA
(i)	MSTParser	0.816
	$MALTParser_1$	0.797
	$MALTParser_2$	0.796
(ii)	Use MSTParser & $MALTParser_1$ if they agree, backoff to $MALTParser_2$	0.838
	Use MSTParser & $MALTParser_2$ if they agree, backoff to $MALTParser_2$	0.837
	Use $MALTParser_1$ & $MALTParser_2$ if they agree, backoff to MSTParser	**0.848**
(iii)	Use MSTParse & $MALTParser_1$ if they agree, backoff to most confident	0.801
	Use MSTParser & $MALTParser_2$ if they agree, backoff to most confident	0.799
	Use $MALTParser_1$& $MALTParser_2$ if they agree, backoff to most confident	0.814
(iv)	If at least two agree use their proposal, backoff to most confident	0.819
	If all three agree use their proposal, backoff to most confident	0.797
	Most confident parser only	0.789

Table 5: Labelled accuracy (LA) for various combinations of MSTParser, $MALTParser_1$ and $MALTParser_2$ five fold cross-validation with 4000 training sentences and 1000 testing

to the other one when they do not; (iii) a strategy in which we select a pair and trust them whenever they agree and backoff to the parser which is most confident (which may be one of these or may be the other one) when they do not; (iv) strategies where we either just use the most confident one, or where we take either a unanimous vote or a majority vote and backoff to the most confident one if this is inconclusive. All these experiments were carried using fivefold cross-validation over a set of 5000 sentences from the PATB (i.e. each fold has 4000 sentences for training and 1000 for testing).

These results indicate that for parsing, simply relying on the parser which is most likely to be right when choosing the head for a specific dependent in isolation does not produce the best overall result, and indeed does not even surpass the individual parsers in isolation. For these experiments, the best results were obtained by asking a predefined pair of parsers whether they agree on the head for a given item, and backing off to the other one when they do not. This fits with Henderson and Brill (2000)'s observations about a similar strategy for dependency parsing for English. It seems likely that the problem with relying on the most confident parser for each individual daughter-head relation is that this will tend to ignore the big picture, so that a collection of relations that are individually plausible, but which do not add up to a coherent overall analysis, will be picked.

4 Conclusions

It seems that the success of the proposed method for tagging depends crucially on having taggers that exploit different principles, since under those circumstances the *systematic* errors that the different taggers make will be different; and on the fact that POS tags can be assigned largely independently (though of course each of the individual taggers makes use of information about the local context, and in particular about the tags that have been assigned to neighbouring items). The reason why simply taking the most likely proposals in isolation is ineffective when parsing may be that global constraints such as Henderson and Brill's 'no crossing brackets' requirement are likely to be violated. Interestingly, the most effective of our strategies for combining parsers takes two that use the same learning algorithm and same feature sets but different parsing strategies ($MALTParser_1$ and $MALTParser_2$), and relies on them when they agree; and backs off to MSTParser, which exploits fundamentally different machinery, when these two disagree. In other words, it makes use of two parsers that depend on very similar underlying principles, and hence are likely to make the same systematic errors, and backs off to one that exploits different principles when they disagree.

We have not carried out a parallel set of experiments on taggers for languages other than Arabic because we do not have access to taggers where we have reason to believe that the underlying principles are different for anything other than Arabic. In situations where three (or more) distinct approaches to a problem of this kind are available, it seems at least worthwhile investigating whether the proposed method of combination will work.

Acknowledgements

Maytham Alabbas owes his deepest gratitude to Iraqi Ministry of Higher Education and Scientific Research for financial support in his PhD study. Allan Ramsay's contribution to this work was partially supported by the Qatar National Research Fund (grant NPRP 09-046-6-001).

References

E Brill. 1995. Transformation-based error-driven learning and natural language processing: a case study in part of speech tagging. *Computational Linguistics*, 23(4):543–565.

T Buckwalter. 2004. Buckwalter Arabic morphological analyzer version 2.0. Linguistic Data Consortium.

T Buckwalter. 2007. Issues in Arabic morphological analysis. *ARabic computational morphology*, pages 23–41.

M. Diab. 2009. Second Generation Tools (AMIRA 2.0): Fast and Robust Tokenization, POS Tagging, and Base Phrase Chunking. In *Proceedings of the Second International Conference on Arabic Language Resources and Tools*, pages 285–288, Cairo, Eygpt, April. The MEDAR Consortium.

S Green and C D Manning. 2010. Better arabic parsing: Baselines, evaluations, and analysis. In *Proceedings of the 23rd International Conference on Computational Linguistics*, COLING '10, pages 394–402, Stroudsburg, PA, USA. Association for Computational Linguistics.

N. Habash, O. Rambow, and R. Roth. 2009. MADA+TOKAN: A Toolkit for Arabic Tokenization, Diacritization, Morphological Disambiguation, POS Tagging, Stemming and Lemmatization. In *Proceedings of the Second International Conference on Arabic Language Resources and Tools*, Cairo. The MEDAR Consortium.

J C Henderson and E Brill. 2000. Exploiting diversity in natural language processing: Combining parsers. *CoRR*, cs.CL/0006003.

T Lager. 1999. μ-tbl lite: a small, extendible transformation-based learner. In *Proceedings of the 9th European Conference on Computational Linguistics (EACL-99)*, pages 279–280, Bergen. Association for Computational Linguistics.

M Maamouri and A Bies. 2004. Developing an Arabic treebank: methods, guidelines, procedures, and tools. In *Proceedings of the Workshop on Computational Approaches to Arabic Script-based Languages*, pages 2–9, Geneva.

R McDonald, K Lerman, and F Pereira. 2006a. Multilingual dependency parsing with a two-stage discriminative parser. In *Tenth Conference on Computational Natural Language Learning (CoNLL-X)*, New York.

R McDonald, K Lerman, and F Pereira. 2006b. Multilingual dependency parsing with a two-stage discriminative parser. In *Tenth Conference on Computational Natural Language Learning (CoNLL-X)*, New York.

J. Nivre, J. Hall, and J. Nilsson. 2006. MaltParser: A data-driven parser-generator for dependency parsing. In *Proceedings of the International Conference on Language Resources and Evaluation (LREC)*, volume 6, pages 2216–2219.

J. Nivre, J. Hall, J. Nilsson, A. Chanev, G. Eryigit, S. Kübler, S. Marinov, and E. Marsi. 2007. MaltParser: A language-independent system for data-driven dependency parsing. *Natural Language Engineering*, 13(02):95–135.

J Nivre, L Rimell, R McDonald, and C Gómez-Rodríguez. 2010. Evaluation of dependency parsers on unbounded dependencies. In *Proceedings of the 23rd International Conference on Computational Linguistics*, COLING '10, pages 833–841, Beijing.

A. Ramsay and Y. Sabtan. 2009. Bootstrapping a lexicon-free tagger for Arabic. In *Proceedings of the 9th Conference on Language Engineering*, pages 202–215, Cairo, Egypt, December.

Claudio De Stefano, Antonio Della Cioppa, and Angelo Marcelli. 2002. An adaptive weighted majority vote rule for combining multiple classifiers. In *ICPR (2)*, pages 192–195.

Kevin Woods, W. Philip Kegelmeyer, Jr., and Kevin Bowyer. 1997. Combination of multiple classifiers using local accuracy estimates. *IEEE Trans. Pattern Anal. Mach. Intell.*, 19(4):405–410, April.

D. Zeman and Z. Žabokrtský. 2005. Improving parsing accuracy by combining diverse dependency parsers. In *Proceedings of the Ninth International Workshop on Parsing Technology*, pages 171–178. Association for Computational Linguistics.

Named Entity Recognition for Dialectal Arabic

Ayah Zirikly
Department of Computer Science
The George Washington University
Washington DC, USA
ayaz@gwu.edu

Mona Diab
Department of Computer Science
The George Washington University
Washington DC, USA
mtdiab@gwu.edu

Abstract

To date, majority of research for Arabic Named Entity Recognition (NER) addresses the task for Modern Standard Arabic (MSA) and mainly focuses on the newswire genre. Despite some common characteristics between MSA and Dialectal Arabic (DA), the significant differences between the two language varieties hinder such MSA specific systems from solving NER for Dialectal Arabic. In this paper, we present an NER system for DA specifically focusing on the Egyptian Dialect (EGY). Our system delivers $\approx$ 16% improvement in F1-score over state-of-the-art features.

1 Introduction

Named Entity Recognition (NER) aims to identify predefined set of named entities types (e.g. Location, Person) in open-domain text (Nadeau and Sekine, 2007). NER has proven to be an essential component in many Natural Language Processing (NLP) and Information Retrieval tasks. In (Thompson and Dozier, 1997), the authors show the significant impact NER imposes on the retrieval performance, given the fact that names occur with high frequency in text. Moreover, in Question Answering, (Ferrndez et al., 2007) report that Questions on average contain $\approx$ 85% Named Entities.

Although NER has been well studied in the literature, but the majority of the work primarily focuses on English in the newswire genre, with near-human performance (f-score$\approx$ 93% in MUC-7). Arabic NER has gained significant attention in the NLP community with the increased availability of annotated datasets. However, due to the rich morphological and highly inflected nature of Arabic language (Ryding, 2005), Arabic NER faces many challenges (Abdul-Hamid and Darwish, 2010), that manifest in:

- Lack of capitalization: Unlike English (and other Latin-based languages), proper nouns are not capitalized, which renders the identification of NER more complicated;
- Proper nouns can also represent regular words (e.g. *jamilah, gmylp* [1]" which means 'beautiful' and can be a proper noun or an adjective;
- Agglutination: Since Arabic exhibits concatenate morphology, we note the pervasive presence of affixes agglutinating to proper nouns as prefixes and suffixes (Shaalan, 2014). For instance: Determiners appear as prefixes as in *Al* (*AlqAhrp* 'Cairo'), likewise with affixival prepositions such as *l* meaning 'for' (*ldm$q* -'to/from Damascus'-), as well as prefixed conjunctions such as *w* meaning 'and' (*wAlqds* -'and Jerusalem'-);
- Absence of Short Vowels (Diacritics): Written MSA, even in newswire, is undiacritized; resulting in ambiguity that can only be resolved using contextual information (Benajiba et al., 2009). Instances of such phenomena: *mSr*, which is underspecified for short vowels, can refer to *miSor* 'Egypt' or *muSir* 'insistent'; *qTr* may be 'Qatar' if *qaTar*, 'sugar syrup' if *qaTor*, 'diameter' if *quTor*.

Previously proposed Arabic NER systems (Benajiba et al., 2007) and (Abdallah et al., 2012) were developed exclusively for MSA and primarily address the problem in the newswire genre. Nevertheless, with the extensive use of social networking and web blogs, DA NLP is gaining more

[1]The second form of the name is written in Buckwalter encoding http://www.qamus.org/transliteration.htm

Proceedings of the EMNLP 2014 Workshop on Arabic Natural Langauge Processing (ANLP), pages 78–86,
October 25, 2014, Doha, Qatar.

attention, yielding a more urgent need for DA NER systems. Furthermore, applying NLP tools, such as NER, that are designed for MSA on DA results in considerably low performance, thus the need to build resources and tools that specifically target DA (Habash et al., 2012).
In addition to the afore mentioned challenges for Arabic NER in general compared to Latin based languages, DA NER faces additional issues:

- Lack of annotated data for supervised NER;
- Lack of standard orthographies or language academics (Habash et al., 2013): Unlike MSA, the same word in DA can be rewritten in so many forms, e.g. *mAtEyT$, mtEyt$, mA tEyT$* 'do not cry' are all acceptable variants since there is no one standard;
- Lack of comprehensive enough Gazetteers: this is a problem facing all NER systems for all languages addressing NER in social media text, since by definition such media has a ubiquitous presence of highly productive names exemplified by the usage of nick names, hence the PERSON class in social media NER will always have a coverage problem.

In this paper, we propose a DA NER system – using Egyptian Arabic (EGY) as an example dialect. Our contributions are as follows:

- Provide an annotated dataset for EGY NER;
- To the best of our knowledge, our system is one of the few systems that specifically targets DA.

2 Related Work

Significant amount of work in the area of NER has taken place. In (Nadeau and Sekine, 2007), the authors survey the literature of NER and report on the different set of used features such as contextual and morphological. Although more research has been employed in the area of English NER, Arabic NER has been gaining more attention recently. Similar to other languages, several approaches have been used for Arabic NER: Rule-based methods, Statistical Learning methods, and a hybrid of both.

In (Shaalan and Raza, 2009), the authors present rule-based NER system for MSA that comprises gazetteers, local grammars in the form of regular expressions, and a filtering mechanism that mainly focuses on rejecting incorrect NEs based on a blacklist. Their system yields a performance of 87.7% F1 measure for PER, 85.9% for LOC, and 83.15% for ORG when evaluated on corpora built by the authors. (Elsebai et al., 2009) proposed a rule-based system that is targeted for personal NEs in MSA and utilizes the Buckwalter Arabic Morphological Analyser (BAMA) and a set of keywords used to introduce a PER NE. The proposed system yields an F-score of 89% when tested on a dataset of 700 news articles extracted from Aljazeera television website. Although this approach proved to be successful, but most of the recent research focuses on Statistical Learning techniques for NER (Nadeau and Sekine, 2007).
In the area of Statistical Learning for NER, numerous research studies have been published. (Benajiba et al., 2007) proposes a system (ANERsys) based on n-grams and maximum entropy. The authors also introduce ANERCorp corpora and ANERGazet gazetteers. (Benajiba and Rosso, 2008) presents NER system (ANERsys) for MSA based on CRF sequence labeling, where the system uses language independent features: POS tags, Base Phrase Chunking (BPC), gazetteers, and nationality information. The latter feature is included based on the observation that personal NEs come after mentioning the nationality, in particular in newswire data. In (Benajiba et al., 2008), a different classifier is built for each NE type. The authors study the effect of features on each NE type, then the overall NER system is a combination of the different classifiers that target each NE class label independently. The set of features used are a combination of general features as listed in (Benajiba and Rosso, 2008) and Arabic-dependent (morphological) features. Their system's best performance was 83.5% for ACE 2003, 76.7% for ACE 2004, and 81.31% for ACE 2005, respectively. (Benajiba et al., 2010) presents an Arabic NER system that incorporates lexical, syntactic, and morphological features and augmenting the model with syntactic features derived from noisy data as projected from Arabic-English parallel corpora. The system F-score performance is 81.73%, 75.67%, 58.11% on ACE2005 Broadcast News, Newswire, and Web blogs respectively. The authors in (Abdul-Hamid and Darwish, 2010) suggest a number of features, that we incorporate a subset of in our DA NER

system, namely, the head and trailing bigrams (L2), trigrams (L3), and 4-grams (L4) characters. (Shaalan and Oudah, 2014) presents a hybrid approach that targets MSA and produces state-of-the-art results. However, due to the lack of availability of the used rules, it is hard to replicate their results. The rule-based component is identical to their previous proposed rule-based system in (Shaalan and Raza, 2009). The features used are a combination of the rule-based features in addition to morphological, capitalization, POS tag, word length, and dot (has an adjacent dot) features. We reimplement their Machine Learning component and present it as one of our baselines (BAS2). (Abdul-Hamid and Darwish, 2010) produce near state-of-the-art results with the use of generic and language independent features that we use to generate baseline results (BAS1). The proposed system does not rely on any external resources and the system outperforms (Benajiba and Rosso, 2008) performance with an F-score of 81% on ANERCorp vs. the latter's performance of 72.68% F-score. All the work mentioned has focused on MSA, albeit with variations in genres to the extent exemplified by the ACE data and author generated data. However unlike the work mentioned above, (Darwish and Gao, 2014) proposed an NER system that specifically targets microblogs as a genre, as opposed to newswire data. Their proposed language-independent system relies on set of features that are similar to (Abdul-Hamid and Darwish, 2010). Their dataset contains dialectal data, since it is collected from Twitter. However, the dataset contains English and Arabic; in this work we only target Dialectal Arabic. Their overall performance, on their proposed data, is 65.2% (LOC 76.7%, 55.6% ORG, 55.8% PER).

3 Approach

In this paper, we use a supervised machine learning approach since it has been shown in the literature that supervised typically outperform unsupervised approaches for the NER task (Nadeau et al., 2006). We use Conditional Random Field (CRF) sequence labeling as described in (Lafferty et al., 2001). Moreover, (Benajiba and Rosso, 2008) demonstrates that CRF yields better results over other supervised machine learning techniques.

3.1 Baseline

In this paper, we introduce two baselines to compare our work against. The first baseline (BAS1) is based on work reported in (Abdul-Hamid and Darwish, 2010). We adopt their approach since it produces near state-of-the-art results. Additionally, the features proposed are applicable to DA as they do not rely on the availability of morphological or syntactical analyzers. We reimplement their listed features that yield the highest performance and report those results as our BAS1 system. The list of features used are: previous and next word, in addition to the leading and trailing character bigrams, trigrams, and 4-grams.

The second baseline (BAS2) adopted is the work proposed in (Shaalan and Oudah, 2014). The authors present state-of-the-art results when evaluated on ANERcorp (Benajiba and Rosso, 2008) using the following features: Rule-based features, Morphological features generated by MADAMIRA (Pasha et al., 2014) presented in Table 1, targeted word POS tag, word length flag which is a binary feature that is true if the word length is ≥ 3, a binary feature to represent whether the word has an adjacent dot, capitalization binary feature which is dependent on the English gloss generated by MADAMIRA, nominal binary feature that is set to true if the POS tag is noun or proper noun, and binary features to represent whether the current, previous, or next word belong to the gazetteers. We omit Rule-based features in our baseline since we do not have access to the exact rules used and their rules specifically targeted MSA, hence would not be directly applicable to DA.

3.2 NER Features

In our approach, we propose the following NER features:

- **Lexical Features**: Similar to BAS1 (Darwish and Gao, 2014) character n-gram features, the head and trailing bigrams (L2), trigrams (L3), and 4-grams (L4) characters;
- **Contextual Features** (CTX): The surrounding undiacritized lemmas and words of a context window $= \pm 1$; (LEM-1, LEM0, LEM1) and (W-1,W0,W1)
- **Gazetteers** (GAZ): We use two sets of gazetteers. The first set (ANERGaz) proposed by (Benajiba and Rosso, 2008), which

Feature	Feature Values
Aspect	Verb aspect: Command, Imperfective, Perfective, Not applicable
Case	Grammatical case: Nominative, Accusative, Genitive, Not applicable, Undefined
Gender	Nominal Gender: Feminine, Masculine, Not applicable
Mood	Grammatical mood: Indicative, Jussive, Subjunctive, Not applicable, Undefined
Number	Grammatical number: Singular, Plural, Dual, Not applicable, Undefined
Person	Person Information: 1st, 2nd, 3rd, Not applicable
State	Grammatical state: Indefinite, Definite, Construct/Poss/Idafa, Not applicable, Undefined
Voice	Verb voice: Active, Passive, Not applicable, Undefined
Proclitic3	Question proclitic: No proclitic, Not applicable, Interrogative particle
Proclitic2	Conjunction proclitic: No proclitic, Not applicable, Conjunction *fa*, Connective particle *fa*, Response conditional *fa*, Subordinating conjunction *fa*, Conjunction *wa*, Particle *wa*, Subordinating conjunction *wa*
Proclitic1	Preposition proclitic: No proclitic, Not applicable, Interrogative *i$*, Particle *bi*, Preposition *bi*, Progressive verb particle *bi*, Preposition *Ea*, Preposition *EalaY*, Preposition *fy*, Demonstrative *hA*, Future marker *Ha*, Preposition *ka*, Emphatic particle *la*, Preposition *la*, Preposition *li* + preposition *bi*, Emphatic *la* + future marker *Ha*, Response conditional *la* + future marker *Ha*, Jussive *li*, Preposition *li*, Preposition *min*, Future marker *sa*, Preposition *ta*, Particle *wa*, Preposition *wa*, Vocative *wA*, vocative *yA*
Proclitic	Article proclitic: No proclitic, Not applicable, Demonstrative particle *Aa*, Determiner, Determiner *Al* + negative particle *mA*, Negative particle *lA*, Negative particle *mA*, Negative particle *mA*, Particle *mA*, relative pronoun *mA*
Enclitics	Pronominals: No enclitic, Not applicable, 1st person plural/singular, 2nd person dual/plural, 2nd person feminine plural/singular, 2nd person masculine plural/singular, 3rd person dual/plural, 3rd person feminine plural/singular, 3rd person masculine plural/singular, Vocative particle, Negative particle *lA*, Interrogative pronoun *mA*, Interrogative pronoun *mA*, Interrogative pronoun *man*, Relative pronoun *man, ma, mA*, Subordinating conjunction *ma, mA*.

Table 1: Morphological Features

contains a total of 4893 names between Person (PER), Location (LOC), and Organization (ORG). The second gazetteer is a large Wikipedia gazetteer (WikiGaz) from (Darwish and Gao, 2014); 50141 locations, 17092 organizations, 65557 persons. which represents a significantly more extensive and comprehensive list. We introduce three methods for exploiting GAZ:

- Exact match (EM-GAZ): For more efficient search, we use Aho-Corasick Algorithm that has linear running time in terms of the input length plus the number of matching entries in a gazetteer. When a word sequence matches an entry in the gazetteer, EM-GAZ for the first word will take the value "B-<NE class>" where <NE class>is one of the previously discussed classes (PER, LOC, ORG), whereas the following words will be assigned I-<NE class>, where <NE class>will be assigned the same value of the matched sequence's head;

- Partial match(PM-GAZ): This feature is created to handle the case of compound gazetteer entries. If the token is part of the compound name then this feature is set to true. For example, if we have in the gazetteer the compound name *yAsr ErfAt* 'Yasser Arafat' and the input text is *yAsr BarakAt* then PM-GAZ for the token *yAsr* will be set to true. This is particularly useful in the case of PER as it recovers a large list of first names in compounds;

- Levenshtein match (LVM-GAZ): Due to the non-standard spelling of words in dialectal Arabic, we use Levenshtein distance (Levenshtein, 1966) to compare the similarity between the input and a gazetteer entry;

• **Morphological Features**: The morphological features that we employ in our feature set are generated by MADAMIRA (Pasha et al., 2014):

  - Gender (GEN): Since Arabic nouns are either masculine or feminine, we believe that this information should help NER. Moreover, instances of the same name will share the same gender. MADAMIRA generates three values for this feature: Feminine, Masculine, or Not Applicable (such as the case for prepositions, for instance);

- Capitalization (CAPS): In order to circumvent the lack of capitalization in Arabic, we check the capitalization of the translated NE which could indicate that a word is an NE (Benajiba et al., 2008). This feature is dependent on the English gloss that is generated by MADAMIRA;

- Part of Speech (POS) tags: We use POS tags generated from MADAMIRA, where the POS tagger has a reported accuracy of 92.4% for DA;

- **Distance from specific keywords** within a window (KEY): This feature captures certain patterns in person names that are more commonly used in DA (e.g. using the nickname pattern of *Abw* + proper noun instead of an actual name). In this feature, if the distance is set to one, the feature will be true if the previous token equals an entry in a keywords list, otherwise false. Examples of keywords: *Abw* 'father of', *yA* invocation particle, typically used before names to call a person, terms of address, or honorifics, such as *dktwr/dktwrp* 'doctor -masculine and feminine-', and *AstA*/AstA*p* 'Mr/Mrs/Ms/teacher -masculine and feminine-';

- **Brown Clustering** (BC): Brown clustering as introduced in (Brown et al., 1992) is a hierarchical clustering approach that maximizes the mutual information of word bigrams. Word representations, especially Brown Clustering, have been demonstrated to improve the performance of NER system when added as a feature (Turian et al., 2010). In this work, we use Brown Clustering IDs of variable prefixes length (4,7,10,13) as features resulting in the following set of features BC4, BC7, BC10, BC13. For example if *AmrykA* 'America' has the brown cluster ID 11110010 then BC4 = 1111, BC7=1111001, whereas BC10 and BC13 are empty strings. This feature is based on the observation that semantically similar words will be grouped together in the same cluster and will have a common prefix.

4 Experiments & Discussion

4.1 Datasets and Tools

Evaluation Data Due to the very limited resources in DA for NER, we manually annotate a portion of the DA data collected and provided by the LDC from web blogs.[2] The annotated data was chosen from a set of web blogs that are manually identified by LDC as Egyptian dialect and contains nearly 40k tokens. The data was annotated by one native Arabic speaker annotator who followed the Linguistics Data Consortium (LDC) guidelines for NE tagging. Our dataset is relatively small and contains 285 PER, 153 LOC, and 10 ORG instances.

Brown Clustering Data In our work, we run Brown Clustering on BOLT Phase1 Egyptian Arabic Treebank (ARZ)[3], where the chosen number of clusters is 500.

Parametric features values We use the following values for the parametric features:

- CTX features: we set context window = ± 1 for lemmas and tokens;
- Keyword distance: we set the distance from the token to a keyword to 1 and 2, namely, KEY1 and KEY2, respectively;
- LM-GAZ: The threshold of the number of deletion, insertion, or modification ≤ 2;
- BC: the length of the prefixes of the Brown Clusters ID is set to 4,7,10,13;

Tools In this work, we used the following tools:

1. MADAMIRA (Pasha et al., 2014): For tokenization and other features such as lemmas, gender and Part of Speech (POS) tags, and other morphological features;
2. CRFSuite implementation (Okazaki, 2007).

4.2 Evaluation Metrics

We choose precision (PREC), recall (REC), and harmonic F-measure (F1) metrics to evaluate the performance of our NER system over accuracy. This decision is based on the observation that the baseline accuracy on the token level in NER is not

[2]GALE Arabic-Dialect/English Parallel Text LDC2012T09

[3]LDC2012E98

a fair assessment, since NER accuracy is always high as the majority of the tokens in free text are not named entities.

4.3 Results & Discussion

In our NER system, we solely identify PER and LOC NE classes and omit the ORG class. This is due to the small frequency ($\leq 0.05\%$) of ORG instances in our annotated data, which does not represent a fair training data to the system. The reported results are the average of 5-fold cross validation on the blog post level. Also, it is worth mentioning that we use IOB tagging scheme; Inside *I* NE, Outside *O*, and Beginning *B* of NE. Table 2 depicts the two baselines discussed in 3.1. BAS1 yields a weighted macro-average F-score=54.762% using near state-of-the-art features on our annotated data. On the other hand, BAS2 F-score is 31%. Although BAS2 presents state-of-the-art results, it actually produces lower performance than BAS1. It should be noted that our implementation of BAS2 does not incorporate rule-based features (Shaalan and Oudah, 2014). However, by extrapolation using their performance improvement of $\approx 6\%$ attributed to rule-based features alone, such a relative gain in performance for BAS2 in our setting would still be outperformed by both BAS1 and our current system.

In Table 3, we show our NER system performance using different permutations of features proposed in Section 3.2. Additionally, in Table 3, we use the weighted macro-average (Overall) in order to assess the system's overall performance. We use the following abbreviation annotation:

- FEA1: includes n-gram characters and CTX on the word and lemma level features;
- FEA2: includes FEA1 in addition to KEY features with distance 1&2;
- FEA3: includes FEA2 in addition to the morphological features (MORPH) and it is subcategorized as follow: FEA3-GEN takes into account the gender feature only, FEA3-POS takes into account POS tag (FEA2+POS), whereas FEA3-CAPS takes into account the use of CAPS with FEA2;
- FEA4: shows the impact of adding EM-GAZ features (FEA3+EM-GAZ);
- FEA5: shows the impact of adding PM-GAZ features (FEA4+PM-GAZ);
- FEA6: shows the impact of adding LVM-GAZ features (FEA5+LM-GAZ);
- FEA7: shows the impact of adding Brown Clustering (BC) features on the performance;

The best results for precision, recall and F1-score are bolded in Table 3. FEA6 delivers the best NER performance of F1-score=70.305%

Baseline		PREC	REC	F1
BAS1	*LOC*	80	72.727	76.191
	PER	56.25	23.684	33.333
	AVG	68.125	48.201	**54.762**
BAS2	*LOC*	47.368	52.941	50
	PER	8.571	20	12
	AVG	27.97	36.471	31

Table 2: Baseline NER performance

In comparing FEA1, FEA2 results, we note that KEY features increase the F1-score by 2% absolute. This improvement mirrors the fact that *Abw*+name, for example, is very commonly used in dialects, where it represents $\approx 46\%$ of PER names. The morphological features (GEN, POS, CAPS), produce the most significant improvement $\approx +9\%$ absolute. Although the gazetteers help NER performance overall, the boost is not as significant as with using the MORPH features. Likewise, we note that LVM-GAZ using Levenshtein distance addresses the spelling variation challenge that DA pose and yields the best performance (F1-score=70.305%) when combining all features except the Brown clustering. Unlike the BC effect noted in English NER case studies, BC degrades the performance of our DA NER system. We further analyze this result by closely examining the clustering quality obtained on the dataset. For example, the following instances of the LOC class from our dataset: *mSr* 'Egypt', *AmrykA* 'America', and *qtr* 'Qatar'; the cluster IDs assigned by the Brown Clustering algorithm are 111101110, 11110010, 00111000, respectively. The common prefix among the three instances is very short (1111 in case of Egypt and America and none with Qatar), thus leading to poorer performance.
Overall, we note more stable performance for LOC class in comparison to PER. This is mainly due to the high PER singleton instances frequencies which results in high unseen vocabulary in

Features	LOC			PER			Overall		
	PREC	*REC*	*F1*	*PREC*	*REC*	*F1*	*PREC*	*REC*	*F1*
FEA1={L2,L3,L4,W-1,W0,W1,LEM-1,LEM0,LEM1}	93.333	77.778	84.849	54.546	14.286	22.642	73.94	46.032	53.746
FEA2={FEA1, KEY1, KEY2}	93.75	83.333	88.235	60	14.286	23.077	76.875	48.81	55.656
FEA3-GEN={FEA2, GEN}	93.75	83.333	88.235	63.636	16.667	26.415	78.693	50	57.325
FEA3-POS={FEA2, POS}	93.333	77.778	84.849	78.571	26.191	39.286	85.952	51.985	62.068
FEA3-CAPS={FEA2, CAPS}	93.333	77.778	84.849	78.571	26.191	39.286	85.952	51.985	62.068
FEA3={FEA2, MORPH}	94.118	88.889	91.429	83.333	23.81	37.037	88.7255	56.3495	64.233
FEA4={FEA3, EM-GAZ}	94.118	88.889	91.429	72.222	30.952	43.333	83.17	59.9205	67.381
FEA5={FEA4, PM-GAZ}	94.118	88.889	91.429	73.684	33.333	45.902	83.901	61.111	68.666
FEA6={FEA5, LVM-GAZ}	94.118	88.889	**91.429**	78.947	35.714	**49.18**	86.533	62.302	**70.305**
FEA7={FEA6, BC}	93.333	77.778	84.849	77.778	33.333	46.667	85.556	55.556	65.758

Table 3: Dialectal Arabic NER

the test data. In addition, LOC members, unlike PER, convey tag consistency, where most of the time it will be tagged as NE. For instance, *mSr* 'Egypt' occurred in the data 35 times and in all of which it was assigned a LOC tag, unlike *EAdl* that appears as an adjective 'fair/rightful' and proper name 'Adel' in the same dataset. The former reason explains why the GAZ helps PER class performance but does not affect LOC performance.

If we discuss in more detail the MORPH feature set, we notice that CAPS and POS produce identical results in terms of PREC, REC, and F-1 score on each of the NE classes. However, CAPS and POS help in PER class, whereas GEN helps in the LOC class. For example in LOC class, the number of false negatives, when POS is employed, is higher as opposed to GEN.

As mentioned earlier, LVM-GAZ produces the best F-score. However, LVM main contribution is on the PER class which is caused by the nature of Arabic names' different spelling variations, especially the last name (e.g. with or without Al).

5 Conclusion & Future Work

In this paper we present Dialectal Arabic NER system using state-of-the-art features in addition to proposing new features that improve the performance. We show that our proposed system improves over state-of-the-art features performance. Our contribution is not solely limited to the NER system, but further includes, our manually annotated data.[4] In future work, we would like to annotate more data in more variable genre and with more dialects including code switched data.

6 Acknowledgment

This work was supported by the Defense Advanced Research Projects Agency (DARPA) Contract No. HR0011-12-C-0014, the BOLT program with subcontract from Raytheon BBN.

[4]Please contact the authors for access to the annotated data.

References

Sherief Abdallah, Khaled Shaalan, and Muhammad Shoaib. 2012. Integrating rule-based system with classification for arabic named entity recognition. In *Computational Linguistics and Intelligent Text Processing*, pages 311–322. Springer.

Ahmed Abdul-Hamid and Kareem Darwish. 2010. Simplified feature set for arabic named entity recognition. In *Proceedings of the 2010 Named Entities Workshop*, NEWS '10, pages 110–115, Stroudsburg, PA, USA. Association for Computational Linguistics.

Yassine Benajiba and Paolo Rosso. 2008. Arabic named entity recognition using conditional random fields. In *Proc. of Workshop on HLT & NLP within the Arabic World, LREC*, volume 8, pages 143–153. Citeseer.

Yassine Benajiba, Paolo Rosso, and José-Miguel Benedí. 2007. Anersys: An arabic named entity recognition system based on maximum entropy. In *CICLing*, pages 143–153.

Yassine Benajiba, Mona Diab, and Paolo Rosso. 2008. Arabic named entity recognition using optimized feature sets. In *Proceedings of the Conference on Empirical Methods in Natural Language Processing*, pages 284–293. Association for Computational Linguistics.

Yassine Benajiba, Mona Diab, and Paolo Rosso. 2009. Arabic named entity recognition: A feature-driven study. *Audio, Speech, and Language Processing, IEEE Transactions on*, 17(5):926–934.

Yassine Benajiba, Imed Zitouni, Mona Diab, and Paolo Rosso. 2010. Arabic named entity recognition: Using features extracted from noisy data. In *Proceedings of the ACL 2010 Conference Short Papers*, ACLShort '10, pages 281–285, Stroudsburg, PA, USA. Association for Computational Linguistics.

Peter F Brown, Peter V Desouza, Robert L Mercer, Vincent J Della Pietra, and Jenifer C Lai. 1992. Class-based n-gram models of natural language. *Computational linguistics*, 18(4):467–479.

Kareem Darwish and Wei Gao. 2014. Simple effective microblog named entity recognition: Arabic as an example. In *Proceedings of the Ninth International Conference on Language Resources and Evaluation (LREC-2014), Reykjavik, Iceland, May 26-31, 2014.*, pages 2513–2517.

Ali Elsebai, Farid Meziane, and Fatma Zohra Belkredim. 2009. A rule based persons names arabic extraction system. *Communications of the IBIMA*, 11(6):53–59.

Sergio Ferrndez, Antonio Toral, scar Ferrndez, Antonio Ferrndez, and Rafael Muoz. 2007. Applying wikipedias multilingual knowledge to cross-lingual question answering. In *In Zoubida Kedad, Nadira Lammari, Elisabeth Mtais, Farid Meziane, and Yacine Rezgui, editors, NLDB, volume 4592 of Lecture Notes in Computer Science*. Springer.

Nizar Habash, Mona T Diab, and Owen Rambow. 2012. Conventional orthography for dialectal arabic. In *LREC*, pages 711–718.

Nizar Habash, Ryan Roth, Owen Rambow, Ramy Eskander, and Nadi Tomeh. 2013. Morphological analysis and disambiguation for dialectal arabic. In *Human Language Technologies: Conference of the North American Chapter of the Association of Computational Linguistics, Proceedings, June 9-14, 2013, Westin Peachtree Plaza Hotel, Atlanta, Georgia, USA*, pages 426–432.

John Lafferty, Andrew McCallum, and Fernando CN Pereira. 2001. Conditional random fields: Probabilistic models for segmenting and labeling sequence data.

Vladimir I Levenshtein. 1966. Binary codes capable of correcting deletions, insertions and reversals. In *Soviet physics doklady*, volume 10, page 707.

David Nadeau and Satoshi Sekine. 2007. A survey of named entity recognition and classification. *Lingvisticae Investigationes*, 30(1):3–26.

David Nadeau, Peter Turney, and Stan Matwin. 2006. Unsupervised named-entity recognition: Generating gazetteers and resolving ambiguity.

Naoaki Okazaki. 2007. Crfsuite: A fast implementation of conditional random fields (crfs).

Arfath Pasha, Mohamed Al-Badrashiny, Ahmed El Kholy, Ramy Eskander, Mona Diab, Nizar Habash, Manoj Pooleery, Owen Rambow, and Ryan Roth. 2014. Madamira: A fast, comprehensive tool for morphological analysis and disambiguation of arabic. In *In Proceedings of the 9th International Conference on Language Resources and Evaluation, Reykjavik, Iceland.*

Karin C Ryding. 2005. *A Reference Grammar of Modern Standard Arabic*. Cambridge University Press.

Khaled Shaalan and Mai Oudah. 2014. A hybrid approach to arabic named entity recognition. *Journal of Information Science*, 40(1):67–87.

Khaled Shaalan and Hafsa Raza. 2009. Nera: Named entity recognition for arabic. *Journal of the American Society for Information Science and Technology*, 60(8):1652–1663.

Khaled Shaalan. 2014. A survey of arabic named entity recognition and classification. *Comput. Linguist.*, 40(2):469–510, June.

Paul Thompson and Christopher C. Dozier. 1997. Name searching and information retrieval. In *In Proceedings of Second Conference on Empirical Methods in Natural Language Processing*, pages 134–140.

Joseph Turian, Lev Ratinov, and Yoshua Bengio. 2010. Word representations: A simple and general method for semi-supervised learning. In *Proceedings of the 48th Annual Meeting of the Association for Computational Linguistics*, pages 384–394. Association for Computational Linguistics.

Semantic Query Expansion for Arabic Information Retrieval

Ashraf Y. Mahgoub
Computer Engineering Department, Cairo University, Egypt

ashraf.thunderstorme@gmail.com

Mohsen A. Rashwan
Electronics and Communications Engineering Department, Cairo University, Egypt
mrashwan@rdi-eg.com

Hazem Raafat
Computer Science Department, Kuwait University, Kuwait City, Kuwait
hazem@cs.ku.edu.kw

Mohamed A. Zahran
Computer Engineering Department, Cairo University, Egypt
moh.a.zahran@eng.cu.edu.eg

Magda B. Fayek
Computer Engineering Department, Cairo University, Egypt

magdafayek@ieee.org

Abstract

Traditional keyword based search is found to have some limitations. Such as word sense ambiguity, and the query intent ambiguity which can hurt the precision. Semantic search uses the contextual meaning of terms in addition to the semantic matching techniques in order to overcome these limitations. This paper introduces a query expansion approach using an ontology built from Wikipedia pages in addition to other thesaurus to improve search accuracy for Arabic language. Our approach outperformed the traditional keyword based approach in terms of both F-score and NDCG measures.

1 Introduction

As traditional keyword based search techniques are known to have some limitations, many researchers are concerned with overcoming these limitations by developing semantic information retrieval techniques. These techniques are concerned with the meaning the user seeks rather than the exact words of the user's query. We consider four main features that make users prefer semantic based search systems over keyword-based: Handling Generalizations, Handling Morphological Variants, Handling Concept matches, and Handling synonyms with the correct sense (Word Sense Disambiguation).

2 Semantic-based Search Features

In this section we will discuss the main features of semantic search that makes it more tempting choice over the traditional keyword based techniques.

2.1 Handling Generalization

Handling generalizations allows the system to provide the user with pages that contains material relevant to sub-concepts of the user's query. Consider the following example in Table 1 where a query contains a general term or concept "عنف"(Violence).

User's Query In Arabic	Equivalent Query In English
"اعمال عنف فى افريقيا"	"Violence in Africa"

Table1: Example Query 1

Semantic-based search engines should be able to recognise pages with sub-concepts like: "ابادة"(extermination),"قمع" (suppression),"تعذيب" (torture) as relevant to user's query.

2.2 Handling Morphological Variations

Handling morphological variations allows the system to provide the user with pages that contain words derived from the same root as those in user's query. Consider the following example in Table 2.

User's Query In Arabic	Equivalent Query In English
"التطور فى الشرق الاوسط"	"Development in the Middle East"

Table2: Example Query 2

Pages that contain morphological variants of the word "التطور" (Development) such as "تَطوُّر", "تَطوير", and "تَطوُّرات" should also be considered relevant to user's query.

2.3 Handling Concept Matches

The system should also be aware of concepts or named entities that may be addressed with different words. Consider the following example in Table 3.

User's Query In Arabic	Equivalent Query In English
"مصر"	"Egypt"

Table3: Example Query 3

The term "مصر" has other equivalent expressions like ["جمهورية مصر العربية", "أرض الكنانة", "أم الدنيا"]. So documents that contain any of these expressions should be considered relevant.

2.4 Handling Synonyms With Correct Sense

Although the meaning of many Arabic words depends on the word's diacritics, most Arabic text is un-vowelized. For example, Table 4 shows the word "شعب" has more than a single meaning depending on its diacritization. System should be aware which meaning to consider for expansion.

Arabic vowelized word	English equivalent	Arabic synonyms
شَعْب	People, nation	مواطنين,أمم
شُعَب	Branches	فروع

Table4: Different senses for word "شعب"

3 Related Work

Query expansion techniques have been considered by many researchers. The most successful query expansion techniques depend on automatic relevance feedback with no consideration of semantic relations.

(Jinxi Xu and Ralph, 2001) used the highest TF-IDF 50 terms extracted from the top 10 retrieved documents from AFP (i.e. the TREC2001 corpus). These 50 terms where weighted due to their TF-IDF scores and added to the original query -with addition to terms from other thesaurus-with the following formula:

$$weight(t) = oldWeight(t) + 0.4 \times \sum_{\forall t,D} TFIDF(t, D)$$

Where D is the top retrieved documents and t is the original term. Larkey and Connell (2001) used a similar technique, but with a different scoring method.

Wikipedia has been considered as an ontology source by many researchers. This is due to its large coverage, up-to-date, and domain independency. As in (Alkhalifa and Rodrguez, 2008), they proposed an automatic technique for extending Named Entities of Arabic WordNet using Wikipedia. They depended mainly on Wikipedia's "redirect" pages and Cross-Lingual links. Also a large scale taxonomy from Wikipedia deriving technique was proposed by (Pozetto and Strube, 2007).

(Abouenour et al., 2010) proposed a system that uses Arabic WordNet to enhance Arabic question/answering. Synonyms from WordNet are used to expand the question in order to extract the most semantically relevant passages to the question.

(Milne et al., 2007) proposed a system called "KORU" for query expansion using Wikipedia's most relevant articles to user's query. The system allows the user to refine the set of Wikipedia pages to be used for expansion. KORU used "Redirect" pages for expansion; "Hyper Links" and "Disambiguation Pages" to disambiguate unrestricted text.

Our proposed system differs from KORU in several points:

(1) Adding "Subcategories" to handle generalization.
(2) Adding Wikipedia "Gloss" – First phrase of the article – when there is no "Redirect" pages available.
(3) Allowing the user to either expand all terms in a single query, or expand each term separately producing multiple queries. The result lists of these multiple queries are then combined into a single result list.
(4) Adding terms from another two supportive thesaurus, namely "Al Raed" dictionary and our constructed "Google_WordNet" dictionary.

4 Proposed System

4.1 Arabic Resources

We depend in our query expansion mechanism on three Arabic resources: (1) Arabic Wikipedia Dump, (2) "Al Raed" Dictionary. (2) "Google_WordNet" Dictionary.

4.1.1 Arabic Wikipedia

Our system depends mainly on Arabic Wikipedia as the main semantic information source. According to Wikipedia, the Arabic Wikipedia is currently the 23rd largest edition of Wikipedia by article count, and is the first Semitic language to exceed 100,000 articles.

We were able to extract 397,552 Arabic Semantic set, with 690,236 collocations. The term "Semantic Set" stands for a set of expressions that refer to the same Meaning or Entity. For example, the following set of concepts forms a semantic set for "بريطانيا" (Britain): [‘المملكة المتحدة لبريطانيا’, ‘أنكلترة’, ‘المملكة المتحدة لبريطانيا العظمى وآيرلندا’, ‘بريطانيا العظمي’].

To extract the semantic sets, we depend on the "redirect" pages in addition to the article gloss that may contain a semantic match. This match appears in the first paragraph of the article in a bold font. The categorization system of Wikipedia is very useful in the task of expanding generic queries in a more specified form. This is done by adding "subcategories" of the original term to the expanded terms.

4.1.2 The Al Raed Monolingual Dictionary:

The "Al Raed" Dictionary is a monolingual dictionary for modern words [1]. The dictionary contains 204303 modern Arabic expressions.

4.1.3 The Google_WordNet Dictionary

We collected all the words in WordNet, and translated them to Arabic using Google Translate. For each English word, Google Translate provides different Arabic translations for the English word each corresponds to a different sense, each sense has a list of different possible English synonyms. Using this useful information we were able to extend WordNet Synset entries into a bilingual Arabic-English dictionary that maps a set of Arabic synonyms to its equivalent set of English synonyms. The basic idea is that, two sets of English synonyms (each allegedly belongs to a different sense) can be fused together into one sense if the number of overlapping words between the two sets is two or more. Fusing two English sets together will fuse also their Arabic translations into one set, thus forming a list of Arabic synonyms matched to a list of English synonyms. Table 5 shows a sample of Google Translate for the word "tough". We can fuse the first and the fourth sense together because they have two words in common namely "strong" and "robust". The same applies to the second and the third senses with "strict" and "tough" in common.

[1] Available at http://www.almaany.com/appendix.php?language=arabic&category=الرائد&lang_name=عربي

Thus forming two new mappings as shown in Table 6.

متين	solid, **strong**, **robust**, firm, durable
صارم	strict, rigorous, tough, rigid, firm, stringent
قاسي	tough, harsh, rough, severe, strict, stern
قوي	**strong**, powerful, sturdy, **robust**, vigorous

Table 5: A sample of Google Translate result for the word "tough"

قوي, متين	solid, strong, robust, firm, durable, powerful, sturdy, vigorous
قاسي, صارم	strict, rigorous, tough, rigid, firm, stringent, harsh, rough, severe, stern

Table 6: Mapping between a set of Arabic synonyms to a set of English synonyms.

Finally, we use words of the same Arabic set as an expansion to each other in queries.

4.2 Indexing and Retrieval

Our system depends on "LUCENE", which is free open source information retrieval library released under the Apache Software License. LUCENE was originally written in Java, but it has ported to other programming languages as well. We use the ".Net" version of LUCENE.

LUCENE depends on the Vector Space Model (VSM) of information retrieval, and the Boolean model to determine how relevant a given Document is to a User's query. LUCENE has very useful set of features, as the "OR" and "AND" operators that we depend on for our expanded queries. Documents are analyzed before adding to the index on two steps: diacritics and stop-words Removal, and text Normalization. A list of 75 words (Contains: Pronouns, Prepositions…etc.) has been used as stop-words.

4.2.1 Normalization

Three normalization rules were used:

- Replace "إ" with "ي".
- Replace "ا", "آ", "أ" with "ا"
- Replace "ه" with "ة"

4.2.2 Stemming

We implemented Light-10 stemmer developed by Larkey (2007), as it showed superior performance over other stemming approaches.

Instead of stemming the whole corpus before indexing, we grouped set of words with the same stem and found in the same document into a dictionary, and then use this dictionary in expansion. This reduces the probability of matching between two words sharing the same stem but with different senses, as they must be found in the same document in corpus to be used in expansion.

Consider the following example in table 7:

Arabic Word	Stem	English Equivalent
الطاعة	طَاعَ	Obedience
الطاعون	طَاع	Plague

Table 7: Example of two words sharing the same stem but have different senses.

We see that both words share the same stem "طاع", yet we don't expand the word "طاعة" with the word "الطاعون" as there is no document in the corpus that contains both words.

4.3 Query Expansion

To expand a query, we first locate named entities or concepts that appear in the query in Wikipedia. If a named entity or a concept has been located, we add title of "redirect" pages that leads to the same concept in addition to its subcategories from Wikipedia's categorization system. If not, we depend on the other two dictionaries –Al Raed and Google_WordNet- for expansion.

We investigated two methodologies for query expansion; the first is the most common query expansion methodology which is to produce a single expanded query that contains all expanded terms. The second methodology we introduced is to expand each term one at a time producing multiple queries, and then combine the results of these queries into a single result list. The second methodology was found less sensitive to noise because for each expanded query, there is only one source of noise which is the term being expanded, while other terms are left without expansion. It also allows the system to boost documents from one expanded query over other documents according to the relevancy score of the expanded term.

The following example explains this intuition:
For the query "أحكام الأضاحي"
Single Expanded Query:

(أحكام OR احكام OR حكم) (الأضاحي OR الاضاحي OR إضحية OR أضاحي OR ليلة إضحية مضيئة OR ضحو OR شاة يضحى بها)

Multiple Expanded Queries:

1-(أحكام OR احكام OR حكم) الأضاحي
2- أحكام (الأضاحي OR الاضاحي OR إضحية OR أضاحي OR ليلة إضحية مضيئة OR ضحو OR شاة يضحى بها)

We see that the term "أحكام" gets fewer expansions than the term "الأضاحي"; this is because the term "الأضاحي" is less frequent in the corpus thus it needs more expansions. We then combine the results of the two queries by the following algorithm:

1- Foreach expanded query Q_i
   a. Foreach retrieved document DQ_i for Q_i
   b. If the final list contains DQ_i increment the score of DQ_i by $RF[tQ_i] \times Score(Q_i, DQ_i)$
   c. Else add DQ_i to final list

Where RF is a list of relevancy factors calculated for each term in the original query. This factor depends on the term frequency in corpus. RF is calculated according to the following formula:

$$RF[t] = \frac{1}{\log(frequency[t] + 0.5 \times \log(frequency[stemmed_t])}$$

Where t is the term we need to calculate its relevancy score, $frequency[t]$ is the numbers of times the term t appeared in the corpus, and $frequency[stemmed\_t]$ is the number of times words that share the same stem of the term appeared in the corpus. Then we sort the final list in ascending order according to their scores.

Note that the multiple expanded queries methodology consumes more time over the single expanded query. This is because each expanded query is sent to LUCENE separately. Then we combine the returned documents lists of the queries into a final documents list.

We also limit the maximum number of added terms for each term in order to reduce the noise effect of query expansion step; this maximum number also depends on the term's relevancy factor. We set the maximum number of added terms to a single query to 50. Each term gets expanded with number of terms proportional to its relevancy score. This also increases the recall as less frequent terms gets expanded more times than most frequent terms, allowing LUCENE to find more relevant pages for infrequent terms.

5 Experiments

For testing our system, we used a data set constructed from "Zad Al Ma'ad" book written by the Islamic scholar "Ibn Al-Qyyim". The data set contains 25 queries and 2730 documents. Titles of the book chapters are used as "Queries" and sections of each chapter are used as set of relevant documents for that query. Each query is tested against the whole sections.

The following tables show the values of precision, recall, f-score, and NDCG (Normalize Discounted Cumulative Gain) of three runs.
R1: No expansion is used (base line).
R2: Single expanded query.
R3: Multiple expanded queries methodology.

	R1	R2	R3
Precision @1	0.68	0.6	**0.72**
Precision @5	0.504	**0.576**	0.568
Precision @10	0.38	0.436	**0.444**
Precision @20	0.268	0.3	**0.326**
Precision @30	0.2038	0.232	**0.2546**

Table 8: Levels of Precision

	R1	R2	R3
Recall @1	0.1346	0.1067	**0.1361**
Recall @5	0.3258	**0.35721**	0.3465
Recall @10	0.3908	0.4292	**0.4390**
Recall @20	0.4804	**0.5487**	0.5393
Recall @30	0.5089	0.5806	**0.5944**

Table 9: Levels of Recall

	R1	R2	R3
F-score @1	0.1919	0.1535	**0.1948**
F-score @5	0.3249	**0.3635**	0.3528
F-score @10	0.3067	0.3466	**0.3516**
F-score @20	0.2701	0.3122	**0.3243**
F-score @30	0.2334	0.2697	**0.2868**

Table 10: Levels of F-Score

	R1	R2	R3
NDCG @1	0.68	0.6	**0.72**
NDCG @5	0.8053	**0.8496**	0.8349
NDCG @10	0.7659	0.8304	**0.8316**
NDCG @20	0.7392	0.7993	**0.8186**
NDCG @30	0.7323	0.7944	**0.8001**

Table 11: Levels of NDCG

6 Conclusion

In this paper we introduced a new technique for semantic query expansion using a domain independent semantic ontology constructed from Arabic Wikipedia. We focused on four features for semantic search: (1) Handling Generalizations. (2) Handling Morphological Variants. (3) Handling Concept Matches. (4) Handling Synonyms with correct senses. We compared both single expanded query and multiple expanded queries approaches against the traditional keyword based search. Both techniques showed better results than the base line. While the Multiple Expanded Queries approach performed better than Single Expanded Query in most levels.

7 ACKNOWLEDGMENT

The authors wish to thank the anonymous reviewers for their constructive comments and suggestions. This work was supported by RDI© (http://www.rdi-eg.com/)

8 References

David Milne Ian H. Witten David M. Nichols. 2007. A knowledge-based search engine powered by Wikipedia. Conference on Information and Knowledge Management (CIKM).

Jinxi Xu, Alexander Fraser and Ralph Weischedel. 2001. Cross-lingual Retrieval at BBN. TREC10 Proceedings.

Lahsen Abouenour, Karim Bouzouba, and Paolo Rosso. 2010. An evaluated semantic query expansion and structure-based approach for enhancing Arabic question/answering. International Journal on Information and Communication Technologies.

Leah S. Larkey and Margaret E. Connell. 2001. Arabic Information Retrieval at UMass. TREC10 Proceedings.

Leah S. Larkey and Lisa Ballesteros and Margaret E. Connell. 2007. Arabic Computational Morphology Text, Speech and Language Technology.

Musa Alkhalifa and Horacio Rodrguez. 2008. Automatically Extending Named Entities coverage of Arabic WordNet using Wikipedia. International Journal on Information and Communication Technologies.

Simone Paolo Ponzetto and Michael Strube. 2007. Deriving a large scale taxonomy from Wikipedia. AAAI'07 Proceedings of the 22nd national conference on Artificial intelligence.

Transliteration of Arabizi into Arabic Orthography: Developing a Parallel Annotated Arabizi-Arabic Script SMS/Chat Corpus

Ann Bies, Zhiyi Song, Mohamed Maamouri, Stephen Grimes, Haejoong Lee, Jonathan Wright, Stephanie Strassel, Nizar Habash†, Ramy Eskander‡, Owen Rambow‡
Linguistic Data Consortium, University of Pennsylvania
{bies,zhiyi,maamouri,sgrimes,haejoong,
jdwright,strassel}@ldc.upenn.edu
†Computer Science Department, New York University Abu Dhabi
†nizar.habash@nyu.edu
‡Center for Computational Learning Systems, Columbia University
‡{reskander,rambow}@ccls.columbia.edu

Abstract

This paper describes the process of creating a novel resource, a parallel Arabizi-Arabic script corpus of SMS/Chat data. The language used in social media expresses many differences from other written genres: its vocabulary is informal with intentional deviations from standard orthography such as repeated letters for emphasis; typos and non-standard abbreviations are common; and non-linguistic content is written out, such as laughter, sound representations, and emoticons. This situation is exacerbated in the case of Arabic social media for two reasons. First, Arabic dialects, commonly used in social media, are quite different from Modern Standard Arabic phonologically, morphologically and lexically, and most importantly, they lack standard orthographies. Second, Arabic speakers in social media as well as discussion forums, SMS messaging and online chat often use a non-standard romanization called Arabizi. In the context of natural language processing of social media Arabic, transliterating from Arabizi of various dialects to Arabic script is a necessary step, since many of the existing state-of-the-art resources for Arabic dialect processing expect Arabic script input. The corpus described in this paper is expected to support Arabic NLP by providing this resource.

1 Introduction

The language used in social media expresses many differences from other written genres: its vocabulary is informal with intentional deviations from standard orthography such as repeated letters for emphasis; typos and non-standard abbreviations are common; and non-linguistic content is written out, such as laughter, sound representations, and emoticons.

This situation is exacerbated in the case of Arabic social media for two reasons. First, Arabic dialects, commonly used in social media, are quite different from Modern Standard Arabic (MSA) phonologically, morphologically and lexically, and most importantly, they lack standard orthographies (Maamouri et.al. 2014). Second, Arabic speakers in social media as well as discussion forums, Short Messaging System (SMS) text messaging and online chat often use a non-standard romanization called "Arabizi" (Darwish, 2013). Social media communication in Arabic takes place using a variety of orthographies and writing systems, including Arabic script, Arabizi, and a mixture of the two. Although not all social media communication uses Arabizi, the use of Arabizi is prevalent enough to pose a challenge for Arabic NLP research.

In the context of natural language processing of social media Arabic, transliterating from Arabizi of various dialects to Arabic script is a necessary step, since many of the existing state-of-the-art resources for Arabic dialect processing and annotation expect Arabic script input (e.g., Salloum and Habash, 2011; Habash et al. 2012c; Pasha et al., 2014).

To our knowledge, there are no naturally occurring parallel texts of Arabizi and Arabic script. In this paper, we describe the process of creating such a novel resource at the Linguistic Data Consortium (LDC). We believe this corpus will be essential for developing robust tools for converting Arabizi into Arabic script.

Proceedings of the EMNLP 2014 Workshop on Arabic Natural Langauge Processing (ANLP), pages 93–103,
October 25, 2014, Doha, Qatar.

The rest of this paper describes the collection of Egyptian SMS and Chat data and the creation of a parallel text corpus of Arabizi and Arabic script for the DARPA BOLT program.[1] After reviewing the history and features in Arabizi (Section 2) and related work on Arabizi (Section 3), in Section 4, we describe our approach to collecting the Egyptian SMS and Chat data and the annotation and transliteration methodology of the Arabizi SMS and Chat into Arabic script, while in Section 5, we discuss the annotation results, along with issues and challenges we encountered in annotation.

2 Arabizi and Egyptian Arabic Dialect

2.1 What is Arabizi?

Arabizi is a non-standard romanization of Arabic script that is widely adopted for communication over the Internet (World Wide Web, email) or for sending messages (instant messaging and mobile phone text messaging) when the actual Arabic script alphabet is either unavailable for technical reasons or otherwise more difficult to use. The use of Arabizi is attributed to different reasons, from lack of good input methods on some mobile devices to writers' unfamiliarity with Arabic keyboard. In some cases, writing in Arabizi makes it easier to code switch to English or French, which is something educated Arabic speakers often do. Arabizi is used by speakers of a variety of Arabic dialects.

Because of the informal nature of this system, there is no single "correct" encoding, so some character usage overlaps. Most of the encoding in the system makes use of the Latin character (as used in English and French) that best approximates phonetically the Arabic letter that one wants to express (for example, either *b* or *p* corresponds to ب). This may sometimes vary due to regional variations in the pronunciation of the Arabic letter (e.g., *j* is used to represent ج in the Levantine dialect, while in Egyptian dialect *g* is used) or due to differences in the most common non-Arabic second language (e.g., *sh* corresponds to ش in the previously English dominated Middle East Arab countries, while *ch* shows a predominantly French influence as found in North Africa and Lebanon). Those letters that do not have a close phonetic approximate in the Latin script are often expressed using numerals or other characters, so that the numeral graphically approximates the Arabic letter that one wants to express (e.g., the numeral *3* represents ع because it looks like a mirror reflection of the letter).

Due to the use of Latin characters and also frequent code switching in social media Arabizi, it can be difficult to distinguish between Arabic words written in Arabizi and entirely unrelated foreign language words (Darwish 2013). For example, *mesh* can be the English word, or Arabizi for مش "not". However, in context these cases can be clearly labeled as either Arabic or a foreign word. An additional complication is that many words of foreign origin have become Arabic words ("borrowings"). Examples include *banadoora* بندورة "tomato" and *mobile* موبايل "mobile phone". It is a well-known practical and theoretical problem to distinguish borrowings (foreign words that have become part of a language and are incorporated fully into the morphological and syntactic system of the host language) from actual code switching (a bilingual writer switches entirely to a different language, even if for only a single word). Code switching is easy to identify if we find an extended passage in the foreign language which respects that language's syntax and morphology, such as *Bas eh ra2yak I have the mask*. The problem arises when single foreign words appear without Arabic morphological marking: it is unclear if the writer switched to the foreign language for one word or whether he or she simply is using an Arabic word of foreign origin. In the case of *banadoora* بندورة "tomato", there is little doubt that this has become a fully Arabic word and the writer is not code switching into Italian; this is also signaled by the fact that a likely Arabizi spelling (such as *banadoora*) is not in fact the Italian orthography (*pomodoro*). However, the case is less clear cut with *mobile* موبايل "mobile phone": even if it is a borrowing (clearly much more recent than *banadoora* بندورة "tomato"), a writer will likely spell the word with the English orthography as *mobile* rather than write, say, *mubail*. More research is needed on this issue. However, because of the difficulty of establishing the difference between code switching and borrowing, we do not attempt to make this distinction in this annotation scheme.

2.2 Egyptian Arabic Dialect

Arabizi is used to write in multiple dialects of Arabic, and differences between the dialects themselves have an effect on the spellings chosen by individual writers using Arabizi. Because Egyptian Arabic is the dialect of the corpus cre-

[1] http://www.darpa.mil/Our_Work/I2O/Programs/Broad_Operational_Language_Translation_%28BOLT%29.aspx

ated for this project, we will briefly discuss some of the most relevant features of Egyptian Arabic with respect to Arabizi transliteration. For a more extended discussion of the differences between MSA and Egyptian Arabic, see Habash et al. (2012a) and Maamouri et al. (2014).

Phonologically, Egyptian Arabic is characterized by the following features, compared with MSA:

(a) The loss of the interdentals /ð/ and /θ/ which are replaced by /d/ or /z/ and /t/ or /s/ respectively, thus giving those two original consonants a heavier load. Examples include ذكر /zakar/ "to mention", ذبح /dabaħ/ "to slaughter", ثلج /talg/ "ice", ثمن /taman/ "price", and ثبت /sibit/ "to stay in place, become immobile".

(b) The exclusion of /q/ and /ǰ/ from the consonantal system, being replaced by the /ʔ/ and /g/, e.g., قطن /ʔuṭn/ "cotton", and جمل /gamal/ "camel".

At the level of morphology and syntax, the structures of Egyptian Arabic closely resemble the overall structures of MSA with relatively minor differences to speak of. Finally, the Egyptian Arabic lexicon shows some significant elements of semantic differentiation.

The most important morphological difference between Egyptian Arabic and MSA is in the use of some Egyptian clitics and affixes that do not exist in MSA. For instance, Egyptian Arabic has the future proclitics h+ and ħ+ as opposed to the standard equivalent s+.

Lexically, there are lexical differences between Egyptian Arabic and MSA where no etymological connection or no cognate spelling is available. For example, the Egyptian Arabic بص /buṣṣ/ "look" is أنظر /'unZur/ in MSA.

3 Related Work

Arabizi-Arabic Script Transliteration Previous efforts on automatic transliterations from Arabizi to Arabic script include work by Chalabi and Gerges (2012), Darwish (2013) and Al-Badrashiny et al. (2014). All of these approaches rely on a model for character-to-character mapping that is used to generate a lattice of multiple alternative words which are then selected among using a language model. The training data used by Darwish (2013) is publicly available but it is quite limited (2,200 word pairs). The work we are describing here can help substantially improve the quality of such system. We use the system of Al-Badrashiny et al. (2014) in this paper as part of the automatic transliteration step because they target the same conventional orthography of dialectal Arabic (CODA) (Habash et al., 2012a, 2012b), which we also target. There are several commercial products that convert Arabizi to Arabic script, namely: Microsoft Maren,[2] Google Ta3reeb,[3] Basis Arabic chat translator[4] and Yamli.[5] Since these products are for commercial purposes, there is little information available about their approaches, and whatever resources they use are not publicly available for research purposes. Furthermore, as Al-Badrashiny et al. (2014) point out, Maren, Ta3reeb and Yamli are primarily intended as input method support, not full text transliteration. As a result, their users' goal is to produce Arabic script text not Arabizi text, which affects the form of the romanization they utilize as an intermediate step. The differences between such "functional romanization" and real Arabizi include that the users of these systems will use less or no code switching to English, and may employ character sequences that help them arrive at the target Arabic script form faster, which otherwise they would not write if they were targeting Arabizi (Al-Badrashiny et al., 2014).

Name Transliteration There has been some work on machine transliteration by Knight and Graehl (1997). Al-Onaizan and Knight (2002) introduced an approach for machine transliteration of Arabic names. Freeman et al. (2006) also introduced a system for name matching between English and Arabic. Although the general goal of transliterating from one script to another is shared between these efforts and ours, we are considering a more general form of the problem in that we do not restrict ourselves to names.

Code Switching There is some work on code switching between Modern Standard Arabic (MSA) and dialectal Arabic (DA). Zaidan and Callison-Burch (2011) were interested in this problem at the inter-sentence level. They crawled a large dataset of MSA-DA news commentaries, and used Amazon Mechanical Turk to annotate the dataset at the sentence level. Elfardy et al. (2013) presented a system, AIDA, that tags each word in a sentence as either DA or MSA based on the context. Lui et al. (2014) proposed a system for language identification in

[2] http://www.getmaren.com

[3] http://www.google.com/ta3reeb

[4] http://www.basistech.com/arabic-chat-translator-transforms-social-media-analysis/

[5] http://www.yamli.com/

multilingual documents using a generative mixture model that is based on supervised topic modeling algorithms. Darwish (2013) and Voss et al. (2014) deal with exactly the problem of classifying tokens in Arabizi as Arabic or not. More specifically, Voss et al. (2014) deal with Moroccan Arabic, and with both French and English, meaning they do a three-way classification. Darwish (2013)'s data is more focused on Egyptian and Levantine Arabic and code switching with English.

Processing Social Media Text Finally, while English NLP for social media has attracted considerable attention recently (Clark and Araki, 2011; Gimpel et al., 2011; Gouws et al., 2011; Ritter et al., 2011; Derczynski et al., 2013), there has not been much work on Arabic yet. Darwish et al. (2012) discuss NLP problems in retrieving Arabic microblogs (tweets). They discuss many of the same issues we do, notably the problems arising from the use of dialectal Arabic such as the lack of a standard orthography. Eskander et al. (2013) described a method for normalizing spontaneous orthography into CODA.

4 Corpus Creation

This work was prepared as part of the DARPA Broad Operational Language Translation (BOLT) program which aims at developing technology that enables English speakers to retrieve and understand information from informal foreign language sources including chat, text messaging and spoken conversations. LDC collects and annotates informal linguistic data of English, Chinese and Arabic, with Egyptian Arabic being the representative of the Arabic language family. Egyptian Arabic has the advantage over all other dialects of Arabic of being the language of the largest linguistic community in the Arab region, and also of having a rich level of internet communication.

4.1 SMS and Chat Collection

In BOLT Phase 2, LDC collected large volumes of naturally occurring informal text (SMS) and chat messages from individual users in English, Chinese and Egyptian Arabic (Song et al., 2014). Altogether we recruited 46 Egyptian Arabic participants, and of those 26 contributed data. To protect privacy, participation was completely anonymous, and demographic information was not collected. Participants completed a brief language test to verify that they were native Egyptian Arabic speakers. On average, each participant contributed 48K words. The Egyptian Arabic SMS and Chat collection consisted of 2,140 conversations in a total of 475K words after manual auditing by native speakers of Egyptian Arabic to exclude inappropriate messages and messages that were not Egyptian Arabic. 96% of the collection came from the personal SMS or Chat archives of participants, while 4% was collected through LDC's platform, which paired participants and captured their live text messaging (Song et al., 2014). A subset of the collection was then partitioned into training and eval datasets.

Table 1 shows the distribution of Arabic script vs. Arabizi in the training dataset. The conversations that contain Arabizi were then further annotated and transliterated to create the Arabizi-Arabic script parallel corpus, which consists of 1270 conversations.[6] All conversations in the training dataset were also translated into English to provide Arabic-English parallel training data.

	Total	Arabic script only	Arabizi only	Mix of Arabizi and Arabic script	
				Arabizi	Arabic script
Conversations	1,503	233	987	283	
Messages	101,292	18,757	74,820	3,237	4,478
Sentence units	94,010	17,448	69,639	3,017	3,906
Words	408,485	80,785	293,900	10,244	23,556

Table 1. Arabic SMS and Chat Training Dataset

Not surprisingly, most Egyptian conversations in our collection contain at least some Arabizi;

[6] In order to form single, coherent units (Sentence units) of an appropriate size for downstream annotation tasks using this data, messages that were split mid-sentence (often mid-word) due to SMS messaging character limits were rejoined, and very long messages (especially common in chat) were split into two or more units, usually no longer than 3-4 sentences.

only 15% of conversations are entirely written in Arabic script, while 66% are entirely Arabizi. The remaining 19% contain a mixture of the two at the conversation level. Most of the mixed conversations were mixed in the sense that one side of the conversation was in Arabizi and the other side was in Arabic script, or in the sense that at least one of the sides switched between the two forms in mid-conversation. Only rarely are individual messages in mixed scripts. The annotation for this project was performed on the Arabizi tokens only. Arabic script tokens were not touched and were kept in their original forms.

The use of Arabizi is predominant in the SMS and Chat Egyptian collection, in addition to the presence of other typical cross-linguistic text effects in social media data. For example, the use of emoticons and emoji is frequent. We also observed the frequent use of written out representations of speech effects, including representations of laughter (e.g., *hahaha*), filled pauses (e.g., *um*), and other sounds (e.g., *hmmm*). When these representations are written in Arabizi, many of them are indistinguishable from the same representations in English SMS data. Neologisms are also frequently part of SMS/Chat in Egyptian Arabic, as they are in other languages. English words use Arabic morphology or determiners, as in *el anniversary* "the anniversary". Sometimes English words are spelled in a way that is closer phonetically to the way an Egyptian speaker would pronounce them, for example *lozar* for "loser", or *beace* for "peace".

The adoption of Arabizi for SMS and online chat may also go some way to explaining the high frequency of code mixing in the Egyptian Arabic collection. While the auditing process eliminated messages that were entirely in a non-target language, many of the acceptable messages contain a mixture of Egyptian Arabic and English.

4.2 Annotation Methodology

All of the Arabizi conversations, including the conversations containing mixtures of Arabizi and Arabic script were then annotated and transliterated:

1. Annotation on the Arabizi source text to flag certain features
2. Correction and normalization of the transliteration according to CODA conventions

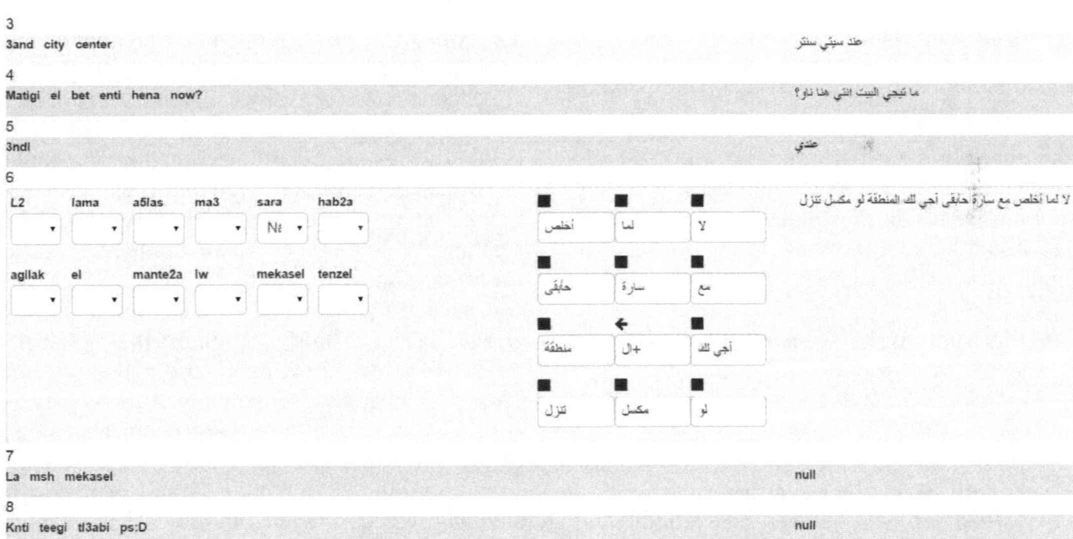

Figure 1. Arabizi Annotation and Transliteration Tool

The annotators were presented with the source conversations in their original Arabizi form as well as the transliteration output from an automatic Arabization system, and used a web-based tool developed by LDC (see Figure 1) to perform the two annotation tasks, which allowed annotators perform both annotation and transliteration token by token, sentence by sentence and review the corrected transliteration in full context. The GUI shows the full conversation in both the original Arabizi and the resulting Arabic script transliteration for each sentence. Annotators must annotate each sentence in order, and the annotation is displayed in three columns. The first column shows the annotation of flag features on the source tokens, the second column is the working panel where annotators correct the automatic transliteration and retokenize, and the third column displays the final corrected and retokenized result.

Annotation was performed according to annotation guidelines developed at the Linguistic Data Consortium specifically for this task (LDC, 2014).

4.3 Automatic Transliteration

To speed up the annotation process, we utilized an automatic Arabizi-to-Arabic script transliteration system (Al-Badrashiny et al., 2014) which was developed using a small vocabulary of 2,200 words from Darwish (2013) and an additional 6,300 Arabic-English proper name pairs (Buckwalter, 2004). The system has an accuracy of 69.4%. We estimate that using this still allowed us to cut down the amount of time needed to type in the Arabic script version of the Arabizi by two-thirds. This system did not identify Foreign words or Names and transliterated all of the words. In one quarter of the errors, the provided answer was plausible but not CODA-compliant (Al-Badrashiny et al., 2014).

4.4 Annotation on Arabizi Source Text to Flag Features

This annotation was performed only on sentences containing Arabizi words, with the goal of tagging any words in the source Arabizi sentences that would be kept the same in the output of an English translation with the following flags:

- **Punctuation** (not including emoticons)
  - *Eh ?!//Punct*
  - *Ma32ula ?!//Punct*
  - *Ebsty ?//Punct*

- **Sound effects**, such as laughs ('haha' or variations), filled pauses, and other sounds ('mmmm' or 'shh' or 'um' etc.)
  - *hahhhahhah//Sound akeed 3arfa :p da enty t3rafy ablia :pp*
  - *Hahahahaahha//Sound Tb ana ta7t fel ahwaa*
  - *Wala Ana haha//Sound*
  - *Mmmm//Sound okay*

- **Foreign language** words and numbers. All cases of code switching and all cases of borrowings which are rendered in Arabizi using standard English orthography are marked as "Foreign".
  - *ana kont mt25er fe t2demm l projects//Foreign*
  - *oltilik okay//Foreign ya Babyy//Foreign balashhabal!!!!*
  - *zakrty ll sat//Foreign*
  - *Bat3at el whatsapp//Foreign*
  - *La la la merci//Foreign gedan bs la2*
  - *We 9//Foreign galaeeb dandash lel banat*

- **Names**, mainly person names
  - *Youmna//Name 7atigi??*

4.5 Correction and Normalization of the Transliteration According to CODA Conventions

The goal of this task was to correct all spelling in the Arabic script transliteration to CODA standards (Habash et al., 2012a, 2012b). This meant that annotators were required to confirm both (1) that the word was transliterated into Arabic script correctly and also (2) that the transliterated word conformed to CODA standards. The automatic transliteration was provided to the annotators, and manually corrected by annotators as needed.

Correcting spelling to a single standard (CODA), however, necessarily included some degree of normalization of the orthography, as the annotators had to correct from a variety of dialect spellings to a single CODA-compliant spelling for each word. Because the goal was to reach a consistent representation of each word, orthographic normalization was almost the inevitable effect of correcting the automatic transliteration. This consistent representation will allow downstream annotation tasks to take better advantage of the SMS/Chat data. For example, more consistent spelling of Egyptian Arabic words will lead to better coverage from the CALIMA morphological analyzer and therefore improve the manual annotation task for morphological annotation, as in Maamouri et al. (2014).

Modern Standard Arabic (MSA) cognates and Egyptian Arabic sound changes

Annotators were instructed to use MSA orthography if the word was a cognate of an MSA root, including for those consonants that have undergone sound changes in Egyptian Arabic.[7]

- use mqfwl مقفول and not ma>fwl مأفول for "locked"
- use HAfZ حافظ and not HAfz حافز for the name (a proper noun)

Long vowels

Annotators were instructed to reinstate missing long vowels, even when they were written as short vowels in the Arabizi source, and to correct long vowels if they were included incorrectly.

- use sAEap ساعة and not saEap سعة for "hour"
- use qAlt قالت and not qlt قلت for "(she) said"

Consonantal ambiguities

Many consonants are ambiguous when written in Arabizi, and many of the same consonants are also difficult for the automatic transliteration script. Annotators were instructed to correct any errors of this type.

- S vs. s/ ص vs. س
  - use SAyg صايغ and not sAyg سايغ for "jeweler"
- D vs. Z/ ض vs. ظ
  - use DAbT ضابط and not ZAbT ظابط for "officer"
  - use Zlmp ظلمة and not Dlmp ضلمة for "darkness"
- Dotted ya vs. Alif Maqsura/ ي vs. ى. Although the dotted ya/ ي and Alif Maqsura/ ى are often used interchangeably in Egyptian Arabic writing conventions, it was necessary to make the distinction between the two for this task.
  - use Ely علي and not ElY على for "Ali" (the proper name)
- Taa marbouta. In Arabizi and so also in the Arabic script transliteration, the taa marbouta/ ة may be written for both nominal final -h/ ه and verbal final -t/ ت, but for different reasons.
  - mdrsp Ely مدرسة علي "Ali's school"
  - mdrsth مدرسته "his school"

Morphological ambiguities

Spelling variation and informal usage can combine to create morphological ambiguities as well. For example, the third person masculine singular pronoun and the third person plural verbal suffix can be ambiguous in informal texts. For example:

- use byHbwA bED بيحبوا بعض and not byHbh bED بيحبه بعض for "(They) loved each other"
- use byEmlwA بيعملوا and not byEmlh بيعمله for "(They) did" or "(They) worked"

In addition, because final -h is sometimes replaced in speech by final /-uw/, it was occasionally necessary to correct cases of overuse of the third person plural verbal suffix (-wA) to the pronoun -h as well.

Merging and splitting tokens written with incorrect word boundaries

Annotators were instructed to correct any word that was incorrectly segmented. The annotation tool allowed both the merging and splitting of tokens.

Clitics were corrected to be attached when necessary according to (MSA) standard writing conventions. These include single letter proclitics (both verbal and nominal) and the negation suffix -$, as well as pronominal clitics such as possessive pronouns and direct object pronouns. For example,

- use fAlbyt فالبيت and not fAl byt فال بيت or flbyt فلبيت for "in the house"
- use EAlsTH عالسطح and not EAl sTH عال سطح or ElsTH علسطح for "on the roof"

The conjunction w- / -و is always attached to its following word.

- use wkAn وكان and not w kAn و كان for "and was"
- use wrAHt وراحت and not w rAHt و راحت for "and (she) left"

Words that were incorrectly segmented in the Arabizi source were also merged. For example,

- use msHwrp مسحورة and not ms Hwrp مس حورة for "bewitched (fem.sing.)"
- use $ErhA شعرها and not $Er hA شعر ها for "her hair"

Particles that are not attached in standard MSA written forms were corrected as necessary by the splitting function of the tool. For example,

- use yA Emry يا عمري and not yAEmry ياعمري for "Hey, dear!"
- use lA trwH لا تروح and not lAtrwH لاتروح for "Do not go"

[7] Both Arabic script and the Buckwalter transliteration (http://www.qamus.org/transliteration.htm) are shown for the transliterated examples in this paper.

Abbreviations in Arabizi

Three abbreviations in Arabizi received special treatment: msa, isa, 7ma. These three abbreviations only were expanded out to their full form using Arabic words in the corrected Arabic script transliteration.

- msa: use mA $A' All~h ما شاء الله for "As God wills"
- isa: use <n $A' All~h إن شاء الله for "God willing"
- 7ma: use AlHmd ll~h for الحمد لله "Thank God, Praised be the Lord"

All other Arabic abbreviations were not expanded, and were transliterated simply letter for letter. When the abbreviation was in English or another foreign language, it was kept as is in the transliteration, using both consonants and semi-vowels to represent it.

- use Awkyh اكيه for "OK" (note that this is an abbreviation in English, but not in Egyptian Arabic)

Correcting Arabic typos

Annotators were instructed to correct typos in the transliterated Arabic words, including typos in proper names. However, typos and non-standard spellings in the transliteration of a foreign words were kept as is and not corrected.

- Ramafan رمفان should be corrected to rmDAn رمضان for "Ramadan"
- babyy بيبي since it is the English word "baby" it should not be corrected

Flagged tokens in the correction task

Tokens flagged during task 1 as Sound and Foreign were transliterated into Arabic script but were not corrected during task 2. Note that even when a whole phrase or sentence appeared in English, the transliteration was not corrected.

- ks كس for "kiss"
- Dd yA hAf fAn ضد يا هاف فان for "did you have fun"

The transliteration of proper names was corrected in the same way as all other words.

Emoticons and emoji were replaced in the transliteration with #. Emoticons refer to a set of numbers or letters or punctuation marks used to express feelings or mood. Emoji refers to a special set of images used in messages. Both Emoticons and Emoji are frequent in SMS/Chat data.

5 Discussion

Annotation and transliteration were performed on all sentence units that contain Arabizi. Sentence units that contain only Arabic script were ignored and untouched during annotation. In total, we reviewed 1270 conversations, among which over 42.6K sentence units (more than 300K words) were deemed to be containing Arabizi and hence annotated and transliterated.

The corpus files are in xml format. All conversations have six layers: source, annotation on the source Arabizi tokens, automatic transliteration via 3ARRIB, manual correction of the automatic transliteration, re-tokenized corrected transliteration, and human translation. See Appendix A for examples of the file format.

Each conversation was annotated by one annotator, with 10 percent of the data being reviewed by a second annotator as a QC procedure. Twenty six conversations (roughly 3400 words) were also annotated dually by blind assignment to gauge inter-annotator agreement.

As we noted earlier, code switching is frequent in the SMS and Chat Arabizi data. There were about 23K words flagged as foreign words. Written out speech effects in this type of data are also prevalent, and 6610 tokens were flagged as Sounds (laughter, filled pause, etc.). Annotators most often agreed with each other in the detection and flagging of tokens as Foreign, Name, Sound or Punctuation, with over 98% agreement for all flags.

The transliteration annotation was more difficult than the flagging annotation, because applying CODA requires linguistic knowledge of Arabic. Annotators went through several rounds of training and practice and only those who passed a test were allowed to work on the task. In an analysis of inter-annotator agreement in the dually annotated files, the overall agreement between the two annotators was 86.4%. We analyzed all the disagreements and classified them in four high level categories:

- **CODA** 60% of the disagreements were related to CODA decisions that did not carefully follow the guidelines. Two-fifths of these cases were related to Alif/Ya spelling (mostly Alif Hamzation, rules of hamza support) and about one-fifth involved the spelling of common dialectal words. An additional one-third were due to non-CODA root, pattern or affix spelling. Only one-tenth of the cases were because of split or merge decisions. These issues suggest that additional training may be needed. Additionally, since some of the CODA errors may be easy to detect and correct using available tools for morphological analysis of Egyptian Arabic (such as the CALIMA-ARZ analyzer), we will consider integrating such support in the annotation interface in the future.

• **Task** In 23% of the overall disagreements, the annotators did not follow the task guidelines for handling punctuation, sounds, emoticons, names or foreign words. Examples include disagreement on whether a question mark should be split or kept attached, or whether a non-Arabic word should be corrected or not. Many of these cases can also be caught as part of the interface; we will consider the necessary extensions in the future.

• **Ambiguity** In 12% of the cases, the annotators' disagreement reflected a different reading of the Arabizi resulting in a different lemma or inflectional feature. These differences are unavoidable and reflect the natural ambiguity in the task.

• **Typos** Finally, in less than 5% of the cases, the disagreement was a result of a typographical error unrelated to any of the above issues.

Among the cases that were easy to adjudicate, one of the two annotators was correct 60% more than the other. This is consistent with the observation that more training may be needed to fill in some of the knowledge gaps or increase the annotator's attention to detail.

6 Conclusion

This is the first Arabizi-Arabic script parallel corpus that supports research on transliteration from Arabizi to Arabic script. We expect to make this corpus available through the Linguistic Data Consortium in the near future.

This work focuses on the novel challenges of developing a corpus like this, and points out the close interaction between the orthographic form of written informal genres of Arabic and the specific features of individual Arabic dialects. The use of Arabizi and the use of Egyptian Arabic in this corpus come together to present a host of spelling ambiguities and multiplied forms that were resolved in this corpus by the use of CODA for Egyptian Arabic. Developing a similar corpus and transliteration for other Arabic dialects would be a rich area for future work.

We believe this corpus will be essential for NLP work on Arabic dialects and informal genres. In fact, this corpus has recently been used in development by Eskander et al. (2014).

Acknowledgements

This material is based upon work supported by the Defense Advanced Research Projects Agency (DARPA) under Contract No. HR0011-11-C-0145. The content does not necessarily reflect the position or the policy of the Government, and no official endorsement should be inferred.

Nizar Habash performed most of his contribution to this paper while he was at the Center for Computational Learning Systems at Columbia University.

References

Mohamed Al-Badrashiny, Ramy Eskander, Nizar Habash, and Owen Rambow. 2014. Automatic Transliteration of Romanized Dialectal Arabic. In *Proceedings of the Conference on Computational Natural Language Learning (CONLL)*, Baltimore, Maryland, 2014.

Tim Buckwalter. 2004. *Buckwalter Arabic Morphological Analyzer Version 2.0*. LDC catalog number LDC2004L02, ISBN 1-58563-324-0.

Achraf Chalabi and Hany Gerges. 2012. Romanized Arabic Transliteration. In *Proceedings of the Second Workshop on Advances in Text Input Methods (WTIM 2012)*.

Eleanor Clark and Kenji Araki. 2011. Text normalization in social media: Progress, problems and applications for a pre-processing system of casual English. *Procedia - Social and Behavioral Sciences*, 27(0):2 – 11.

Kareem Darwish, Walid Magdy, and Ahmed Mourad. 2012. Language processing for arabic microblog re- trieval. In *Proceedings of the 21st ACM International Conference on Information and Knowledge Management, CIKM '12*, pages 2427–2430, New York, NY, USA. ACM.

Kareem Darwish. 2013. Arabizi Detection and Conversion to Arabic. *CoRR*, arXiv:1306.6755 [cs.CL].

Leon Derczynski, Alan Ritter, Sam Clark, and Kalina Bontcheva. 2013. Twitter part-of-speech tagging for all: Overcoming sparse and noisy data. In *Proceedings of the International Conference Recent Advances in Natural Language Processing RANLP 2013*, pages 198–206, Hissar, Bulgaria, September. INCOMA Ltd. Shoumen, Bulgaria.

Heba Elfardy, Mohamed Al-Badrashiny, and Mona Diab. 2013. Code Switch Point Detection in Arabic. In *Proceedings of the 18th International Conference on Application of Natural Language to Information Systems (NLDB2013)*, MediaCity, UK, June.

Ramy Eskander, Mohamed Al-Badrashiny, Nizar Habash and Owen Rambow. 2014. Foreign Words and the Automatic Processing of Arabic Social Media Text Written in Roman Script. In *Arabic Natural Language Processing Workshop, EMNLP*, Doha, Qatar.

Ramy Eskander, Nizar Habash, Owen Rambow, and Nadi Tomeh. 2013. Processing Spontaneous Orthography. In *Proceedings of the 2013 Conference of the North American Chapter of the Association for Computational Linguistics: Human Language Technologies (NAACL-HLT)*, Atlanta, GA.

Andrew T. Freeman, Sherri L. Condon and Christopher M. Ackerman. 2006. Cross Linguistic Name Matching in English and Arabic: A "One to Many Mapping" Extension of the Levenshtein Edit Distance Algorithm. In *Proceedings of HLT-NAACL*, New York, NY.

Kevin Gimpel, Nathan Schneider, Brendan O'Connor, Dipanjan Das, Daniel Mills, Jacob Eisenstein, Michael Heilman, Dani Yogatama, Jeffrey Flanigan, and Noah A. Smith. 2011. Part-of-speech tagging for twitter: Annotation, features, and experiments. In *Proceedings of ACL-HLT '11*.

Stephan Gouws, Donald Metzler, Congxing Cai, and Eduard Hovy. 2011. Contextual bearing on linguistic variation in social media. In *Proceedings of the Workshop on Languages in Social Media, LSM '11*, pages 20–29, Stroudsburg, PA, USA. Association for Computational Linguistics.

Nizar Habash, Mona Diab, and Owen Rambow (2012a).Conventional Orthography for Dialectal Arabic: Principles and Guidelines – Egyptian Arabic. Technical Report CCLS-12-02, Columbia University Center for Computational Learning Systems.

Nizar Habash, Mona Diab, and Owen Rabmow. 2012b. Conventional Orthography for Dialectal Arabic. In *Proceedings of the Language Resources and Evaluation Conference (LREC)*, Istanbul.

Nizar Habash, Ramy Eskander, and Abdelati Hawwari. 2012c. A Morphological Analyzer for Egyptian Arabic. In *Proceedings of the Twelfth Meeting of the Special Interest Group on Computational Morphology and Phonology*, pages 1–9, Montréal, Canada.

Kevin Knight and Jonathan Graehl. 1997. Machine Transliteration. In *Proceedings of the Conference of the Association for Computational Linguistics (ACL)*.

Linguistic Data Consortium. 2014. *BOLT Program: Romanized Arabic (Arabizi) to Arabic Transliteration and Normalization Guidelines, Version 3.1*. Linguistic Data Consortium, April 21, 2014.

Marco Lui, Jey Han Lau, and Timothy Baldwin. 2014. Automatic detection and language identification of multilingual documents. In *Proceedings of the Language Resources and Evaluation Conference (LREC)*, Reykjavik, Iceland.

Mohamed Maamouri, Ann Bies, Seth Kulick, Michael Ciul, Nizar Habash and Ramy Eskander. 2014. Developing a dialectal Egyptian Arabic Treebank: Impact of Morphology and Syntax on Annotation and Tool Development. In *Proceedings of the Language Resources and Evaluation Conference (LREC)*, Reykjavik, Iceland.

Yaser Al-Onaizan and Kevin Knight. 2002. Machine Transliteration of Names in Arabic Text. In *Proceedings of ACL Workshop on Computational Approaches to Semitic Languages*.

Arfath Pasha, Mohamed Al-Badrashiny, Mona Diab, Ahmed El Kholy, Ramy Eskander, Nizar Habash, Manoj Pooleery, Owen Rambow, and Ryan M. Roth. 2014. MADAMIRA: A Fast, Comprehensive Tool for Morphological Analysis and Disambiguation of Arabic. In *Proceedings of the Language Resources and Evaluation Conference (LREC)*, Reykjavik, Iceland.

Alan Ritter, Sam Clark, Mausam, and Oren Etzioni. 2011. Named entity recognition in tweets: An experimental study. In *Proceedings of the Conference on Empirical Methods in Natural Language Processing, EMNLP '11*.

Wael Salloum and Nizar Habash. 2011. Dialectal to Standard Arabic Paraphrasing to Improve Arabic-English Statistical Machine Translation. In *Proceedings of the First Workshop on Algorithms and Resources for Modelling of Dialects and Language Varieties*, pages 10–21, Edinburgh, Scotland.

Zhiyi Song, Stephanie Strassel, Haejoong Lee, Kevin Walker, Jonathan Wright, Jennifer Garland, Dana Fore, Brian Gainor, Preston Cabe, Thomas Thomas, Brendan Callahan, Ann Sawyer. Collecting Natural SMS and Chat Conversations in Multiple Languages: The BOLT Phase 2 Corpus. In *Proceedings of the Language Resources and Evaluation Conference (LREC) 2014*, Reykjavik, Iceland.

Clare Voss, Stephen Tratz, Jamal Laoudi, and Douglas Briesch. 2014. Finding romanized Arabic dialect in code-mixed tweets. In *Proceedings of the Ninth International Conference on Language Resources and Evaluation (LREC'14)*, Reykjavik, Iceland.

Omar F Zaidan and Chris Callison-Burch. 2011. The arabic online commentary dataset: an annotated dataset of informal arabic with high dialectal content. In *Proceedings of ACL*, pages 37–41.

Appendix A: File Format Examples

Example 1:

```
<su id="s1582">
    <source>marwan ? ana walahi knt gaya today :/</source>
    <annotated_arabizi>
        <token id="t0" tag="name">marwan</token>
        <token id="t1" tag="punctuation">?</token>
        <token id="t2">ana</token>
        <token id="t3">walahi</token>
        <token id="t4">knt</token>
        <token id="t5">gaya</token>
        <token id="t6" tag="foreign">today</token>
        <token id="t7">:/</token>
        </annotated_arabizi>
    <auto_transliteration> مروان ؟ انا والله كنت جاية تودي :/ </auto_transliteration>
<corrected_transliteration> مروان ؟ انا والله كنت جاية  تودي # </corrected_transliteration>
<retokenized_transliteration> مروان ؟ انا والله كنت جاية تودي # </retokenized_transliteration>
    <translation lang="eng">Marwan? I swear I was coming today :/</translation>
    <messages>
<message id="m2377" time="2013-10-01 22:03:34 UTC" participant="139360">marwan ? ana
walahi knt gaya today :/</message>
    </messages>
 </su>
```

Example 2:

```
<su id="s3">
<source>W sha3rak ma2sersh:D haha</source>
<annotated_arabizi>
<token id="t0">W</token>
<token id="t1">sha3rak</token>
<token id="t2">ma2sersh:D</token>
<token id="t3" tag="sound">haha</token>
</annotated_arabizi>
<auto_transliteration> و[+] شعرك مقصرش[-] # هه </auto_transliteration>
<corrected_transliteration> و[+] شعرك ما[-]قصرش[-]# هه </corrected_transliteration>
<retokenized_transliteration> وشعرك ما قصرش # هه </retokenized_transliteration>
<translation lang="eng">And your hair did not become short? :D Haha</translation>
<messages>
<message id="m0004" medium="IM" time="2012-12-22 15:36:31 UTC" participant="138112">W
sha3rak ma2sersh:D haha</message>
</messages>
</su>
```

Tunisian dialect Wordnet creation and enrichment using web resources and other Wordnets

Rihab Bouchlaghem
LARODEC, ISG de Tunis
2000 Le Bardo, Tunisie
rihab.bouchlaghem@isg.rnu.tn

Aymen Elkhlifi
Paris-Sorbonne University,
28 Rue Serpente, Paris, France
Aymen.Elkhlifi@paris.sorbonne.fr

Rim Faiz
LARODEC, IHEC de Carthage,
2016 Carthage Présidence, Tunisie
Rim.Faiz@ihec.rnu.tn

Abstract

In this paper, we propose TunDiaWN (Tunisian dialect Wordnet) a lexical resource for the dialect language spoken in Tunisia. Our TunDiaWN construction approach is founded, in one hand, on a corpus based method to analyze and extract Tunisian dialect words. A clustering technique is adapted and applied to mine the possible relations existing between the Tunisian dialect extracted words and to group them into meaningful groups. All these suggestions are then evaluated and validated by the experts to perform the resource enrichment task. We reuse other Wordnet versions, mainly for English and Arabic language to propose a new database structure enriched by innovative features and entities.

1 Introduction

The Arabic Dialects have become increasingly used in social networks and web 2.0 (blogs, forums, newspaper, newsgroups, etc.) instead of Standard Arabic (SA).
Consequently, new kinds of texts appeared being mainly dialect-written or having a mixture between Arabic Dialects and Standard Arabic. Thus, innovative opportunities and challenges arise when we try to deal with the automatic processing of such data in order to seek out useful information and take advantages of their growing availability and popularity. The NLP approaches generally applied lexical resources for the target language. Such resources are useful in several tasks which involve a language meaning understanding like: opinion mining (Kim et al., 2004; Bouchlaghem et al. 2010), information retrieval (Valeras et al., 2005; Rosso et al., 2004), query expansion (Parapar et al., 2005), text categorization (Rosso et al., 2004; Ramakrishnan et al., 2003), and many other applications.
However, this situation poses significant difficulties in the context of dialectal data because of the huge lack of Dialect-Standard Arabic lexical resources. Building similar ones is a big challenge since spoken dialects are not officially written, don't have a standard orthography and are considered as under-resourced languages, unlike standard languages.
In this paper, we address the problem of creating a linguistic resource for an Arabic dialect. We describe our approach towards building a Wordnet for Tunisian dialect (TD). We proceed, firstly, to construct a TD corpus by collecting data from various resources (social networks, websites, TD dictionaries, etc.). We develop a clustering based method that aims to organize the TD corpus words by grouping them into clusters. The suggested organization possibilities are, then, analyzed and validated by the TD experts during the TunDiaWN enrichment process. Our proposed database structure is designed to be able to highlight the specificities of the TD lexicon. It also takes advantage of Arabic Wordnet (AWN) (Elkateb et al., 2006), the Arabic version of the widely used lexico-semantic resource Princeton WordNet (PWN) (Fellbaum, 1998). This can be justified by the assumption that Tunisian Arabic has a great resemblance with Standard Arabic.
The rest of the paper is organized as follows: we begin by presenting works related to existing wordnets and approaches focused on the auto-

Proceedings of the EMNLP 2014 Workshop on Arabic Natural Langauge Processing (ANLP), pages 104–113,
October 25, 2014, Doha, Qatar. ©2014 Association for Computational Linguistics

matic processing of the Tunisian dialect. We then introduce the posed challenges and the hypothesis we have assumed in building the TunDiaWN. In the next section, we proceed to explain and justify the proposed approach for developing the initial version of the Tunisian Arabic lexical resource. Firstly, we detail the TD data collect process and the MultiTD corpus construction. Secondly, we present the method developed to suggest possible organizations of TD words extracted from the corpus. Then, we describe the proposed structure of TunDiaWN, especially the new added features and entities as well as the validation task performed by the TD experts. In the following section, we perform a linguistic analysis by reporting significant observations related to TD-SA discovered during the enrichment process. Conclusion and future works are presented in section 5.

2 Related works

The first version of wordnet (Fellbaum, 1998) was developed for English at Princeton University. It's a large lexical database where words having the same part of speech (Nouns, verbs, adjectives, adverbs) are gathered in sets of cognitive synonyms (synsets), each one expressing a distinct concept. Each word can belong to one or more synsets. The resulting synsets are connected by means of conceptual-semantic and lexical relations well labeled such as hyponymy and antonymy.

The success of the Princeton WordNet has motivated the development of similar resources for other languages, such as EuroWordNet, EWN (Vossen, 1998) interlinking wordnets of several European languages (Dutch, Italian, Spanish, German, French, Czech and Estonian); Balkanet (Tufis, 2004) comprising wordnets of the Balkan languages; and recently Arabic Wordnet (AWN) (Elkateb et al., 2006).

AWN was released following methods developed for EuroWordNet. These methods revolve about the manual encoding of a set of Common Base Concepts (CBC), the most important concepts from the 12 languages in EWN and BalkaNet. Other language-specific concepts are added and translated manually to the closest synset(s) in Arabic. Such resource aims to link arabic words and synsets to english ones.

AWN is related to the Classical Arabic (or Literal Arabic) which refers to the official standard form of the Arabic language used in Arab world. Other variants of Arabic are dialects which are spoken and informal. They are the primary form of Arabic Language.

The Tunisian dialect (cf. Table 1) or 'Darija' is one of the Maghreb Dialects and is mainly spoken by Tunisian people (Baccouche, 1994).

Tunisian dialect words	Transliteration	Meaning
فْلُوسْ	foluws	money
بَرْشَا	baro$aA	many
مَالَّة	maAlah	then

Table 1. Examples of popular TD words

Most of the works that dealt with the automatic processing of Tunisian dialect are based on spoken dialogue corpus. To mention, Graja et al. (2011) performed a lexical study of manual transcription of conversations recorded in the railway station for understanding speech. The application is domain dependant and, thus, the vocabulary is limited. Moreover, Zribi et al. (2013) introduced a lexicon for the Tunisian dialect in order to adapt an existing morphological analyzer initially designed for Standard Arabic. Although the method shows good results, the proposed lexicon is far to be complete. Boujelbane et al. (2013) presented a method that aims to construct bilingual dictionary using explicit knowledge about the relation between Tunisian dialect and Standard Arabic. This approach was limited to the verbs.

3 Challenges

In the last years, Tunisian dialect is widely used in new written media and web 2.0, especially in social networks, blogs, forums, weblogs, etc., in addition to conversational media (Diab et al., 2007).

Thinking about building a wordnet for Tunisian dialect is a big challenge. In fact, like most of dialects around the world, Tunisian Arabic is considered as spoken language with no conventional written form. Moreover, there is a lack of Tunisian dialect-Standard Arabic resources and tools.

Recently, Cavalli-Sforza et al. (2013) proposed a process for creating a basic Iraqi Dialect WordNet. This work is based on other languages wordnets as well as a bidirectional English-Iraqi Arabic dictionary. To our knowledge, no other open source Wordnet for the Standard Arabic or Arabic Dialect has been developed to date.

To deal with these difficulties, we decide to produce a TD corpus gathering texts from multiple

sources. This corpus provides a useful starting point for building a wordnet for Tunisian dialect.
We assume that Arabic Dialects can be presumed to be similar to Standard Arabic, particularly in their conceptual organization. Indeed, the Tunisian dialect has a sophisticated form which combines Standard Arabic and Tunisian dialect specific forms. It has a great resemblance to the SA and adds some variances such as foreign words borrowed from other languages. Thus, given the similarities between the TD and the SA, the resources available to SA, such as AWN, can be favorably used for creating Tunisian dialectal resources.

4 Proposed approach for TunDiaWN construction

The classical building WordNets methodologies start from the CBC, and then make changes according to the concerned language.
We propose a new corpus-based approach to create WordNet resource for Tunisian dialect, which deviates from the strategies commonly adopted.
As shows Figure 1, our approach is performed in four steps:

a. *Tunisian dialect textual data collect:* it consists in producing our **MultiTD** corpus (***Multi-source Tunisian dialect** corpus*) which gathers TD texts from many sources: social networks (Twitter, Facebook, etc.), written pieces of theater, dictionaries, transcriptions of spontaneous speech, etc.

b. *TD words extraction:* is to preprocess the produced corpus in order to preserve useful data and extract TD words.

c. *TD words clustering*: we propose here a clustering based method that aims to group the extracted TD words into meaningful clusters, which represent great suggestions for possible enrichments of TunDiaWN.

d. *TunDiaWN enrichment*: this step is performed by the TD experts. It includes the manual validation of the suggestions proposed by the previous step. We propose, in this stage, a new database structure for TunDiaWN. The experts have to add the necessary features values, particularly the TD specific attributes (details in section 4.4).

4.1 TD data collection and *MultiTD* corpus presentation

We set out to collect data for Tunisian dialect in order to address the general lack of resources, on the one hand, and to produce a multi source corpus, on the other.
We created the **MultiTD** corpus by gathering TD data from diverse sources.
The most practical source of TD texts is online data, which is more individual-driven and less formal, and consequently more likely to comprise dialectal contents.

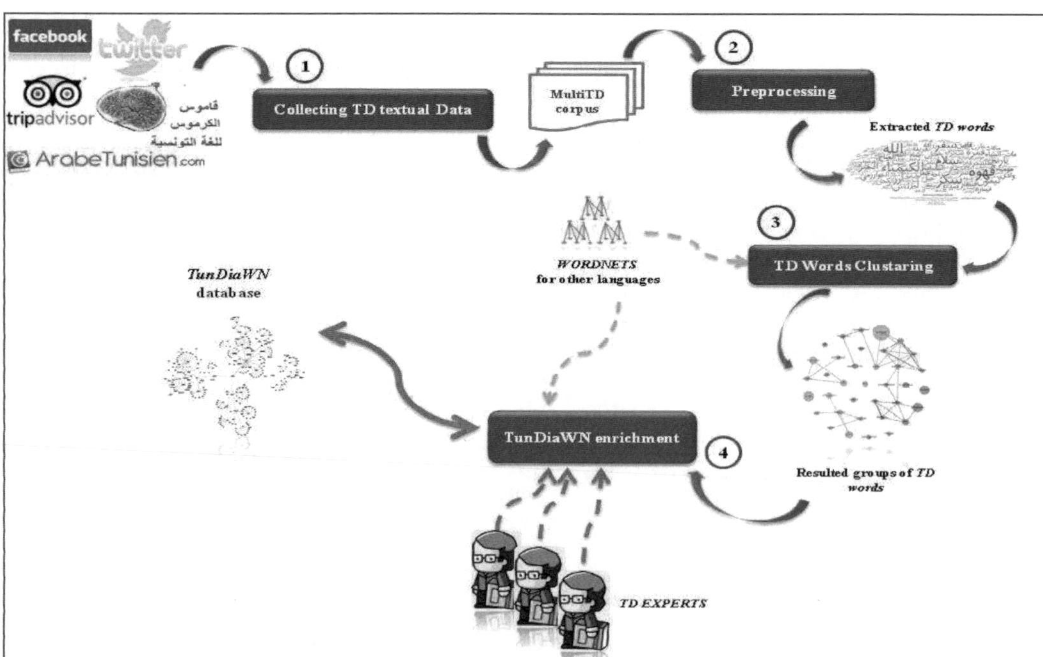

Figure 1. Proposed approach of *TunDiaWN* building

We automatically collected a great amount of TD texts from user's comments and status from *Twitter*, *Facebook* and *TripAdviser*.

We have implemented three specific modules:

- TwtterCollecter based on *Twitter4j java* api,
- FacebookAspirator using a *PHP* script and a Facebook account developer,
- TripadvisorScreen a java module to analyze Tripadvisor web pages and extract comments forms.

Manual transcriptions of TD recorded spontaneous speech are also added to the *MultiTD* corpus. Such data allows highlighting the Tunisian accent in the dialogue and, therefore, enriching the corpus by new varieties of the TD lexicon.
Other online available TD resources are used to enrich the *MultiTD* corpus. We cite notably, the *Karmous* dictionary for Tunisian Arabic[1] which comprises more than 3,800 TD words and several Tunisian proverbs and expressions organized by themes.
We use also an online TD dictionary [2] consisting of over 4,000 words and expressions; and many short TD texts[3] related to various areas: songs, theater, newspaper articles, etc.

4.2 TD words extraction

To successfully extract all TD words, the input texts must be preprocessed. In our study, the preprocessing consists, firstly, to clean the input files so as to identify the textual content. The cleaned texts are then segmented in order to extract all existing TD words.
Cleaning a raw textual source is necessary in our approach because the documents are collected from the Web. All non-textual data such as images, advertisements, scripts, etc. have to be eliminated. For this purpose, we have developed a module that removes all unwanted parts from the input documents.

The cleaned texts are then segmented into elementary textual units and the obtained TD words are extracted and stored in CSV files.

The Table 2 gives statistics about the TD words composing the *MultiTD* corpus.

		TD words count
Social netwoks	Twitter	10249
	Facebook	7470
	Tripadvisor	3258
TD transcripts texts		2351
Other sources (pieces of theatre, dictionaries, etc.)		9520
TOTAL		32848

Table 2. Distribution of TD words in *MultiTD* corpus, according to sources

4.3 TD words clustering using k-modes algorithm

The TunDiaWN construction is based on a semi-automatic process in which the validation tasks performed by experts are crucial.
As Table 2 Shows, the MultiTD corpus includes a huge number of TD words. The manual analysis and organization of such large data looks wasteful and time consuming.
In order to support experts in the organization and validation tasks and guide them during the construction process, we propose a clustering-based method to automatically arrange the TD words set into groups. The method aims to suggest possible organizations of the given TD words by gathering them into meaningful clusters.
To enhance similarities and meanings into the produced groups, we propose to cluster the TD words according to their TD roots. We rely here on the derivational morphology that characterizes the Tunisian dialect as well as the Standard Arabic.
In fact, many SA words having a common root [4] can be derived from a base verbal form and have related meanings. An example of such a field for the root درس, 'to study,' is shown in Table 3.

Arabic words	Part of speach	Meaning
دَرَسَ	verb	study
دَرَّسَ	verb	teach
تَدْرِيس	noun	teaching

Table 3. Some derivatives of Arabic root "درس" (Elkateb et al., 2006)

In the same context, the TD morphology is derivational too (cf. Table 4).

Taking advantage of this central characteristic, the set of TD words can be organized into distinct semantic groups according to the TD roots from which they are derived. The list of TD roots

[1] The dictionary can be obtained from : *http://www.fichier pdf.fr/2010/08/31/m14401m/dico-karmous.pdf*
[2] Link : *http://www.arabetunisien.com/*
[3] Download link: *http://www.langue-arabe.fr/spip.php? article25*

[4] جَذر *in Arabic:* a sequence of typically three consonants.

we have used was obtained by translating the SA roots provided by AWN.

TD words	Transliteration	Part of speach	Meaning
قرى	qoraY	verb	study
قرّى	qar~aY	verb	teach
قرَايَة	qoraAyap	noun	teaching

Table 4. Some derivatives of TD root " قرى"

We don't search here to automatically enrich the TunDiaWN structure by attaching new TD words, but we rather suggest new attachments and enrichment possibilities which can help the experts.

Our aim at this step is to group words having the same root. To do this task, we apply and adapt the K-modes clustering algorithm (Huang, 1997). The K-modes algorithm extends K-means (Forgy, 1965; MacQueen, 1967) paradigm to cluster categorical data by removing the numeric data limitation. Indeed, the K-modes algorithm introduces a new simple matching dissimilarity measure for categorical data objects. The algorithm replaces means of clusters with modes, and uses a frequency based method to update modes in the clustering process.

The choice of K-modes clustering algorithm is mainly motivated because of its widely use in real world applications due to its efficiency in dealing with large categorical database (He et al., 2011). K-modes algorithm is also faster than other clustering algorithms (mainly k-means) since it needs less iteration to produce a stable distribution. .

The K-modes algorithm requires a similarity measurement to be used between the objects. In our case, we propose to use the N-Gram similarity measurement between words. N-Gram is language independent in nature and doesn't require specific resources to be applied. Therefore, N-gram model seems suitable for dealing with a Tunisian dialect context. We applied the N-Gram distance proposed by Kondrak (2005) and we used the implementation provided by Apache Lucene spellchecking API[5].

The K-modes algorithm consists of the following steps:

a) Select K initial modes, one for each of the cluster.

b) Allocate data object to the cluster whose mode is nearest to it, according to the simple matching dissimilarity

c) Compute new modes of all clusters.

d) Repeat step b to c until no data object has changed cluster membership.

The classical K-modes algorithm assumes that the number of clusters, K, is known in advance and the clusters' modes are randomly initialized. The K-modes algorithm is very sensitive to these choices and an improper choice may then yield highly undesirable cluster structures. (Khan et al., 2013).

In order to deal with these drawbacks and, thereafter, maximize the performance of the algorithm, we propose a new initialization strategy for the k-modes algorithm.

Indeed, since our goal is to cluster words according to their roots, the TD roots are assigned to clusters modes in the initialization step instead of random initialization. The number of clusters (K) will, thus, take the cardinality of the target TD roots set. Therefore, the K-modes algorithm starts with k clusters each having as mode one root among the TD roots list initially translated.

We have also adopted a new strategy based on the N-Gram similarity measurement to update clusters' modes. The modes update is performed at the end of each iteration. For each cluster, the item qualified as new cluster mode must maximize the similarity sum with the rest of cluster objects.

The K-modes algorithm adapted for our purpose performs as following:

a. Initialization
   $K = |\text{set of } TD\ roots|$
   Initial modes = *TD roots*, one for each of the cluster.

b. Allocate each word (itm_i) of TD words set to the cluster $Cluster_s$ whose mode $ModeCL_s$ is nearest to it according to the equation (1) ·

$$ModeCL_s = \underset{j}{\overset{k}{argmin}}\ (1 - simNGram(itm_i, ModeCL_s)) \quad (1)$$

c. Update modes of all clusters :

$$\forall Cluster_s, s = 1 \rightarrow K$$

c.1. Similarity computing

$$\forall itm_i \in Cluster_s, i = 1 \rightarrow | Cluster_s |$$

[5] The project can be freely obtained from: http://lucene.apache.org/core/

$$ModeSim(itm_i, Cluster_s) = \sum_{j=1}^{|Cluster\ s|} simNGram(itm_i, itm_j) \quad (2)$$

c.2. Modes selection

$$\forall ModeCL_s, s = 1 \rightarrow K$$

$$ModeCL_s = \underset{i}{\overset{n}{argmax}} \ (ModeSim(itm_i, Cluster_s)) \quad (3)$$

d. Repeat step (b) to (c) until no TD words has changed cluster membership.

After performing the new proposed version of the k mode algorithm, the obtained results are suggested to be validated by the TD experts in order to enrich TunDiaWN structure, which will be presented in the next section.

4.4 TD groups' validation and TunDiaWN enrichment

In this section, we begin by describing the proposed structure of TunDiaWN. After that, we detail the enrichment task performed by the TD experts. Then, we present a linguistic study performed during the enrichment process.

TunDiaWN structure

As our target language is an Arabic Dialect and therefore likely to share many of the Standard Arabic concepts, we decide to preserve the AWN design. However, the AWN current structure is unable to support the specificities of the Tunisian dialect lexicon. The proposed TunDiaWN structure is then enriched by new features, entities and relations. Moreover, we aim to create a parallel resource which maintains the linkage between Tunisian dialectal, Arabic as well as English synsets and words. That's why AWN and PWN contents are preserved rather than the structures. Thus, the proposed database is designed to be able to support English, Tunisian and Standard Arabic content and correspondence.
In this section, we detail the structure of the proposed TunDiaWN database and we focus on the new features we added to keep up the TD vocabulary particularities, compared to the SA and English ones.

TWN entity types

The database structure incorporates mainly the following entity types: *synset, word, form, synset relations, words relations, annotator:*

***Synset*:** includes English and Arabic synsets. A synset has descriptive information such as Name, POS (Part Of Speech), root (Boolean feature indicating if the target synset is a root or not).

Word: comprises words from different languages. In addition to the unique identifier, every word is described by his value, and a Boolean "valid" attribute which indicates if one word is already validated by experts or not yet.

Form: includes mainly the root of Arabic as well as Tunisian dialect words.

Synsets relations: includes links relating two synsets, like "*has_instance*", "*equivalent*", "*similar*", etc. We preserve here all sunsets' links without adding new ones.

Words relations: two English words can be linked by "*pertainym*" or "*antonym*" relations. There are no added Arabic words relations.

Annotator: is used to indicate who has validated each word. The attribute "*region*" helps to classify words by region and identify where words come from. We assume here that the annotator will do his job according to the background of his native region.

TunDiaWN new features

Since the Tunisian dialect is not a standard language, new features are required to be added to the TunDiaWN resource in order to preserve the TD specificities. We describe below the most important TD characteristics integrated in the proposed resource:

SMS language

In the context of Tunisian dialect, the SMS language is a written form which combines Latin script and some numbers in order to express dialectal words.
The SMS language is widely used especially in social networks and blogs.
Table 5 gives examples of the most used numbers which aim to replace specific Arabic letters. TD words are illustrated with Latin Script (Latin), Arabic Letters (Ar-L) and using transliteration[6].

[6] Throughout this paper we use the Buckwalter transliteration : http://www.qamus.org/transliteration.htm

Numbers	Arabic replaced letters	Dialectal words			Part of speech	Arabic translation	English translation
		Latin Scrip	Arabic letters	Transliteration			
3	العَيْن ع	3ayyet	عَيِّط	Eay~iT	verb	صَاحَ	To cry
5	الخَاء خ	5allé	خَلّى	xal~aY	verb	تَرَكَ	To leave
7	الحاء ح	7outa	حُوتَة	Huwtap	noun	سَمَكَة	A fish
9	القَاف ق	9ale9	قَالِقْ	qaAliq	adjec-tive	ضَجِرٌ	bored

Table 5. TD words written using the SMS language

Foreign words

The use of foreign words is a prominent feature in the Tunisian community due to historical reasons. Foreign words are used in almost everyday conversation.

The following table (table 6) illustrates the use of foreign words next to Tunisian dialect ones in the same sentence.

Tunisian dialect (Latin)	**En tout cas**, n7eb n9ollek **merci** 3alli 3maltou m3aya. Net9ablou mba3ed, **à toute**.
Tunisian dialect (Ar-L)	**أُنْتُوكَا**، نْحِبّ نْقُلّكْ **مِيرْسِي** عَلِّي عْمَلْتُو مْعَايَا. نِتْقَابْلُو مْبَاعِدْ، **آتُوتْ**
French Translation	**En tout cas**, je veux te dire **merci** pour tout ce que t'as fais pour moi. on se voit après, **à toute**.
English Translation	Anyway, I want to say thank you for everything you've done for me. See you later.

Table 6. Examples of French words widely used in TD communications

A TD corpus study found that pure French origin words are ubiquitous and represent 11.81% of the dialogue corpus (Graja et al, 2010).
Tunisian dialect can also borrow and adapt words from other languages in order to make them sound and behave like TD words.
As an illustration, the TD word " تْنَرْفِيزْ/ tonarofiyzo" is derived from the French word "nervosité" and is synonym to the English word "anger".

As can be seen, the foreign words are part of the Tunisian dialect vocabulary. Such words must not be neglected. They must be added to any dictionary of Tunisian dialect lexicon (Graja et al. 2010).
The foreign words used with their original forms are added to the TunDiaWN database.
Concerning the TD words having foreign origins, they are firstly distinguished from other TD words. The second step consists in finding the origin words in other languages, saving them and linking them to the concerned TD words. Consequently, the borrowed TD words are easily identified. Their basic language and words are straightforwardly found and browsed.

Morphology

Since the Tunisian dialect has no standard orthography, one word can be written in many forms using Arabic letters or Latin script. For example, the word "will" can be expressed in different ways: "bech"/ "بَاشْ", "bich" /"بِشْ", "mich"/"مِشْ".
To deal with this situation, our database structure is enriched by a new entity named "morphology" which allows storing all versions of a given TD word.

Sub-dialect group

There are many varieties of Tunisian dialect taking into account the lexical variation depending on Tunisian regions. We can distinguish mainly three sub-dialects in the dialect of each region: *the townspeople*, *peasants/farmers*, *Be-Douin*. This is mainly due to the difference in cultures which adds several different words from different backgrounds having the same meaning. (Graja et al, 2010). The feature "sub-dialect" as well as the "Region" of the annotator are used to give further information about the origin of the target word.
The TD words: "$aAf/شَافْ", "roEaY/رْعَى", "$obaH/شْبَحْ", "gozar/غْزَرْ ", are used in different Tunisian regions and are synonyms< to the English word "to look".

TunDiaWN enrichment task

One of our strategic goals is to provide a parallel resource which deal with the lack of parallel TD-SA dictionaries and corpus. Therefore, we proceed by gathering Tunisian dialect and Standard Arabic in one unique structure and maintain the link with the Standard English too.
The starting point of the TunDiaWN enrichment step is the groups of TD words, resulted of per-

forming our clustering based method. The TD roots presumed to be the center of groups are obtained by translating the SA roots available in AWN.

For each TD root, the SA words related to the equivalent SA root are extracted. Two lists of words derived from equivalent roots are available: one is related to a SA root, and the other is from a TD one. The concerned SA synsets are also available.

After that, the TD experts analyze and confront the lists in order to find new synsets enrichment opportunities. The TD words qualified to be retained are those maximizing the synset harmony. The TD experts must also fill in the necessary attributes related to the added words and manually make the necessary changes and enrichments.

In fact, the added words have to be described according to the new features added to the TunDiaWN database, so as to bring different knowledge of different vocabularies and give all useful details related to the target word.

Linguistic study of the enriched TunDiaWN

The linguistic study of the enrichment possibilities validated by the TD experts shows many important lexical trends in the TD lexicon comparing to the SA vocabulary.

A great part of Arabic synsets is enriched by words that conserve the same SA roots and derivation patterns but appear with small changes in vowels (cf. table 7).

Arabic	Tunisian dialect			Translation
	Ar-L	SMS langage	Transliteration	
قَرَّرَ	قَرِّرْ	9arrer	qar~ir	to decide
زَلَقَ	زْلُقْ	zlo9	zoluq	to slide

Table 7. Example of TD words having SA roots and derivation patterns

We distinguish also words derived from SA roots via the application of specific derivation patterns of TD (cf. table 8). Those words are omnipresent in the TD lexicon.

Moreover, some TD words has identical morphologies comparing to other SA words, but the meaning is far to be similar (cf. table 9).

SA	SA→English translation	TD	TD→English translation
تَعَرَّضَ	To be exposed to	تْعَرِّضْ	to disagree

Table 9. Examples of TD words having similar SA morphologies and different meanings

There is another category of TD words which are very similar to SA words, but use a different preposition.

For example, the SA word "تَسَبَّبَ ب/ttasab~aba bi", which means "to cause", has an equivalent TD word "تْسَبِّبْ فِي/tsab~ib fiy" with just different vowels and new preposition.

In some cases, the SA words are linked to TD expressions which have the same meaning, since there are no TD simple equivalent words, as illustrates the following table:

Arabic	Tunisian dialect		Translation
أَزَّمَ, صَعَّبَ	طَلَّعْ الما لِلصَّعْدَة	Tal~aEo AlmA lilS~aEodap	To aggravate

Table 10. TD expressions equivalent to SA words

We deduce from this study and the given examples that the Tunisian dialect is marked by a lexical variety which escapes from the standard rules of the Standard Arabic.

5 Conclusion and future works

We have described an approach for building a Tunisian dialect lexical resource which takes advantages of online TD resources and reuses Wordnets of other languages.

The proposed TunDiaWN can be considered as parallel TD-SA resource since it preserves the AWN content. Thanks to the novel added TD attributes, the TunDiaWN design provides, also, great opportunities to deal with the lack of a standard written form and other specificities of the Tunisian dialect.

The construction process begins with the MultiTD corpus construction from many sources. After preprocessing the collected texts, the TD extracted words are gathered according to their common TD roots.

Arabic		أفْقَرَ	أضْعَفَ	اِنْتَعَشَ	اِنْتَفَخَ
Tunisian dialect	Arabic Letters	فَقْرْ	ضَعِّفْ	تْنَعْوِشْ	تِنْفَخْ
	Transliteration	faq~ir	DaE~if	tonaEowi$	tinofax
Root		فقر	ضعف	نعش	نفخ
Translation		To beggar	To impoverish	To refresh	To swell

Table 8. Examples of TD words having SA roots and applying specific TD patterns

Our aim at this level is to support the TD experts in the database enrichment task, by giving suggestions of the possible TD words organizations. Now, the proposed TD resource is under construction and evaluation. We plan to improve the coverage of TunDiaWN and looking for other TD specificities not yet covered. We plan also to incorporate the French language into the TunDiaWN content, taking advantages of the available lexical French resource WOLF (Sagot and Fišer, 2008).

Reference

Benoît Sagot and Darja Fišer. 2008. Construction d'un wordnet libre du français à partir de ressources multilingues. In proceeding of TALN conference, Avignon, France.

Christiane Fellbaum. 1998. WordNet: An Electronic Lexical Database. Cambridge, MA: MIT Press.

Dan Tufis, Dan Cristea and Sofia Stamou. 2004. BalkaNet: Aims, Methods, Results and Perspectives. *A General Overview. Romanian Journal on Information Science and Technology*, Dan Tufiş (ed.), Special Issue on BalkaNet, Romanian Academy, 7 (1–2), 7–41.

David Parapar, Álvaro Barreiro and David E. Losada. 2005. Query expansion using wordnet with a logical model of information retrieval. IADIS AC: 487-494.

E. W. Forgy. 1965. Cluster analysis of multivariate data: efficiency versus interpretability of classifications. *Biometrics - A Journal of the International Biometric Society*, 21: 768–769.

Ganesh Ramakrishnan, Kedar Bellare, Chirag Shah and Deepa Paranjpe. 2003. Generic Text Summarization Using Wordnet for Novelty and Hard. TREC: 303-304.

Giannis Varelas, Epimenidis Voutsakis, Euripides G. M. Petrakis, Evangelos E. Milios, Paraskevi Raftopoulou. 2005. Semantic similarity methods in wordNet and their application to information retrieval on the web. In proceedings of, the 7th annual ACM international workshop on Web information and data management WIDM'07, Bremen, Germany: 10-16.

Grzegorz Kondrak. 2005. N-gram similarity and distance". Proceedings of the Twelfth International Conference on String Processing and Information Retrieval, SPIRE 2005, Buenos Aires, Argentina: 115-126.

Horacio Rodríguez, David Farwell, Javi Farreres, Manuel Bertran, M. Antonia Martí, William Black , Sabri Elkateb, James Kirk, Piek Vossen, Christiane Fellbaum. 2008. Arabic WordNet: current state and future extensions. In Proceedings of The Fourth Global WordNet Conference, Szeged, Hungary.

J. MacQueen. 1967. Some Methods for classification and Analysis of Multivariate Observations. In Proceedings of 5th Berkeley Symposium on Mathematical Statistics and Probability 1. University of California Press: 281–297.

Ines Zribi, Mariem Ellouze Khemekhem and Lamia Hadrich Belguith. 2013. Morphological Analysis of Tunisian dialect. In proceeding of the International Joint Conference on Natural Language Processing, Nagoya, Japan: 992–996.

Marwa Graja, Maher Jaoua and Lamia Hadrich Belguith. 2010. Lexical Study of A Spoken Dialogue Corpus in Tunisian dialect. In proceeding of the International Arab Conference on Information Technology ACIT'2010, Benghazi-Libya.

Mona Diab and Nizar Habash. 2007. Arabic Dialect Processing Tutorial. In Proceedings of the Human Language Technology Conference of the NAACL, Companion Volume: Tutorial Abstracts: 5-6.

Paolo Rosso, Edgardo Ferretti, Daniel Jiménez and Vicente Vidal. 2004. Text Categorization and Information Retrieval using WordNet senses. In Proceeding of the 2nd Global WordNet International conference, Brno, Czech Republic: 299-304.

Piek Vossen. 1998. Introduction to EuroWorNet. *Computers and the Humanities,* 32(2-3), 73-89.

Rihab Bouchlaghem, Aymen Elkhlifi and Rim Faiz. 2010. Automatic extraction and classification approach of opinions in texts. In Proceeding of the 10th International Conference on Intelligent Systems Design and Applications, ISDA 2010, Cairo, Egypt. IEEE 2010: 918-922.

Rahma Boujelbane, Mariem Ellouze Khemekhem and Lamia Hadrich Belguith. 2013. Mapping Rules for Building a Tunisian dialect Lexicon and Generating Corpora. In Proceedings of the International Joint Conference on Natural Language Processing. Nagoya, Japan: 419–428.

Sabri Elkateb , William Black , Horacio Rodríguez , Musa Alkhalifa , Piek Vossen , Adam Pease and Christiane Fellbaum. 2006. Building a WordNet for Arabic. In Proceedings of The fifth international conference on Language Resources and Evaluation; Genoa-Italy: 29-34.

Shehroz S. Khan and Amir Ahmad. 2013. Cluster center initialization algorithm for K-modes clustering. *International journal of Expert Systems with Applications*, 40(18): 7444-7456.

Soo-Min Kim and Eduard Hovy.(2004). Determining the sentiment of opinions. In Proceedings of the

20th international conference on Computational Linguistics COLING '04: 1267–1373.

Violetta Cavalli-Sforza, Hind Saddiki, Karim Bouzoubaa, Lahsen Abouenour, Mohamed Maamouri and Emily Goshey. 2013. Bootstrapping a WordNet for an Arabic dialect from other WordNets and dictionary resources. In Proceedings of the 10th IEEE International Conference on Computer Systems and Applications, Fes/Ifrane, Morocco.

William Black, Sabri Elkateb, Horacio Rodriguez, Musa Alkhalifa, Piek Vossen, Adam Pease, Christiane Fellbaum. 2006. Introducing the Arabic WordNet project. In Proceedings of the Third International WordNet Conference, Fellbaum and Vossen (eds).

Zengyou He, Xaiofei Xu and Shengchun Deng. 2011. Attribute value weighting in k-modes clustering. *International journal of Expert Systems with Applications*, 38(12): 15365-15369.

.Zhexue Huang. 1997. A fast clustering algorithm to cluster very large categorical data sets in data mining. In Proceeding of SIGMOD Workshop on Research Issues on Data Mining and Knowledge Discovery: 1-8

A Pipeline Approach to Supervised Error Correction for the QALB-2014 Shared Task

Nadi Tomeh[†] **Nizar Habash**[‡] **Ramy Eskander**[*] **Joseph Le Roux**[†]

{nadi.tomeh,leroux}@lipn.univ-paris13.fr[†]
nizar.habash@nyu.edu[‡], ramy@ccls.columbia.edu[*]

[†]Université Paris 13, Sorbonne Paris Cité, LIPN, Villetaneuse, France

[‡]Computer Science Department, New York University Abu Dhabi

[*]Center for Computational Learning Systems, Columbia University

Abstract

This paper describes our submission to the ANLP-2014 shared task on automatic Arabic error correction. We present a pipeline approach integrating an error detection model, a combination of character- and word-level translation models, a reranking model and a punctuation insertion model. We achieve an F_1 score of 62.8% on the development set of the QALB corpus, and 58.6% on the official test set.

1 Introduction

Devising algorithms for automatic error correction generated considerable interest in the community since the early 1960s (Kukich, 1992) for at least two reasons. First, typical NLP tools lack in robustness against errors in their input. This sensitivity jeopardizes their usefulness especially for unedited text, which is prevalent on the web. Second, automated spell and grammar checkers facilitate text editing and can be of great help to non-native speakers of a language. Several resources and shared tasks appeared recently, including the HOO task (Dale and Kilgarriff, 2010) and the CoNLL task on grammatical error correction (Ng et al., 2013b). In this paper we describe our participation to the first shared task on automatic error correction for Arabic (Mohit et al., 2014).

While non-word errors are relatively easy to handle, the task is more challenging for grammatical and semantic errors. Detecting and correcting such errors require context-sensitive approaches in order to capture the dependencies between the words of a text at various lexical and semantic levels. All the more so for Arabic which brings dependence down to the morphological level (Habash, 2010).

A particularity interesting approach to error correction relies on statistical machine translation (SMT) (Brockett et al., 2006), due to its context-sensitivity and data-driven aspect. Therefore, the pipeline system which we describe in Section 2 has as its core a phrase-based SMT component (PBSMT) (Section 2.3). Nevertheless, several factors may hinder the success of this approach, such as data sparsity, discrepancies between translation and error correction tasks, and the difficulty of incorporating context-sensitive features into the SMT decoder.

We address all these issues in our system which achieves a better correction quality than a simple word-level PBSMT baseline on the QALB corpus (Zaghouani et al., 2014) as we show in our experiments in Section 3.

2 Pipeline Approach to Error Correction

The PBSMT system accounts for context by learning, from a parallel corpus of annotated errors, mappings from erroneous multi-word segments of text to their corrections, and using a language model to help select the suitable corrections in context when multiple alternatives are present. Furthermore, since the SMT approach is data-driven, it is possible to address multiple types of errors at once, as long as examples of them appear in the training corpus. These errors may include non-word errors, wrong lexical choices and grammatical errors, and can also handle normalization issues (Yvon, 2010).

One major issue is data sparsity, since large amount of labeled training data is necessary to provide reliable statistics of all error types. We ad-

Proceedings of the EMNLP 2014 Workshop on Arabic Natural Langauge Processing (ANLP), pages 114–120,
October 25, 2014, Doha, Qatar.

dress this issue by backing-off the word-level PB-SMT model with a character-level correction component, for which richer statistics can be obtained.

Another issue may stem from the inherent difference in nature between error correction and translation. Unlike translation, the input and output vocabularies in the correction task overlap significantly, and the majority of input words are typically correct and are copied unmodified to the output. The SMT system should handle correct words by selecting their identities from all possible options, which may fail resulting in over-correction. To help the SMT decoder decide, we augment our pipeline with a problem zone detection component, which supplies prior information on which input words need to be corrected.

The final issue concerns the difficulty of incorporating features that require context across phrase boundaries into the SMT decoder. A straightforward alternative is to use such features to rerank the hypotheses in the SMT n-best hypotheses lists.

Since punctuation is particularity noisy in Arabic data, we add a specialized punctuation insertion component to our pipeline, depicted in Figure 1.

2.1 Error Detection

We formalize the error detection problem as a sequence labeling problem (Habash and Roth, 2011). Errors are classified into substitution, insertion and deletion errors. Substitutions involve an incorrect word form that should be replaced by another correct form. Insertions are words that are incorrectly added into the text and should be deleted. Deletions are simply missing words that should be added.

We group all error classes into a simple binary problem tag: a word from the input text is tagged as "PROB" if it is the result of an insertion or a substitution of a word. Deleted words, which cannot be tagged themselves, cause their adjacent words to be marked as PROB instead. In this way, the subsequent components in the pipeline can be alerted to the possibility of a missing word via its surroundings. Any words not marked as PROB are given an "OK" tag.

Gold tags, necessary for training, can be generated by comparing the text to its correction using some sequence alignment technique, for which we use SCLITE (Fiscus, 1998).

For this task, we use Yamcha (Kudo and Matsumoto, 2003) to train an SVM classifier using morphological and lexical features. We employ a quadratic polynomial kernel. The static feature window context size is set to +/- 2 words; the previous two (dynamic) predicted tags are also used as features.

The feature set includes the surface forms and their normalization after "Alef", "Ya" and digit normalization, the POS tags and the lemmas of the words. These morphological features are obtained using MADA 3.0 (Habash et al., 2009).[1] We also use a set of word, POS and lemma 3-gram language models scores as features. These LMs are built using SRILM (Stolcke, 2002).

The error detection component is integrated into the pipeline by concatenating the predicted tags with the words of the input text. The SMT model uses this additional information to learn distinct mappings conditional on the predicted correctness of words.

2.2 Character-level Back-off Correction

Each word that is labeled as error (PROB) in the output of the error detection component is mapped to multiple possible corrections using a weighted finite-state transducer similar to the transducers used in speech recognition (Mohri et al., 2002). The WFST, for which we used OpenFST (Allauzen et al., 2007), operates on the character level, and the character mapping is many-to-many (similar to the phrase-based SMT framework).

The score of each proposed correction is a combination of the scores of character mappings used to build it. The list is filtered using WFST scores and an additional character-level LM score. The result is a list of error-tagged words and their correction suggestions, which constitutes a small on-the-fly phrase table used to back-off primary PB-SMT table.

During training, the mapping dictionary is learned from the training after aligning it at the character level using SCLITE. Mapping weights are computed as their normalized frequencies in the aligned training corpus.

2.3 Word-level PBSMT Correction

We formalize the correction process as a phrase-based statistical machine translation problem (Koehn et al., 2003), at the word-level, and solve

[1]We did not use MADAMIRA (the newest version of MADA) since it was not available when this component was built.

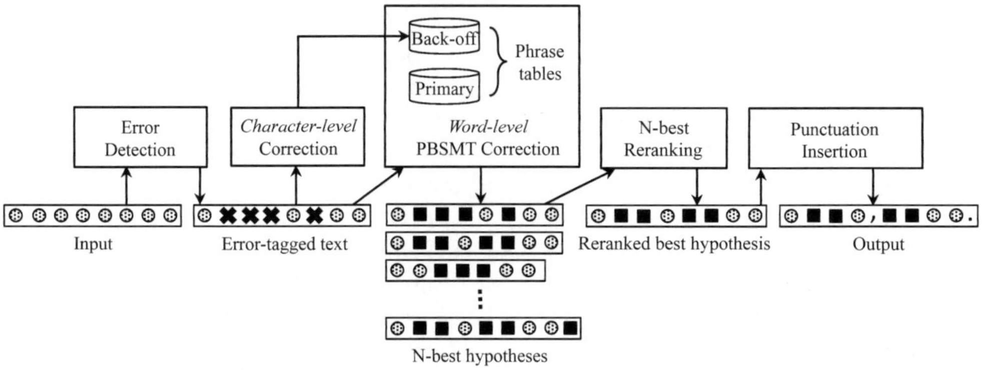

Figure 1: Input text is run through the error detection component which labels the problematic words. The labeled text is then fed to the character-level correction components which constructs a back-off phrase table. The PBSMT component then uses two phrase tables to generate n-best correction hypotheses. The reranking component selects the best hypothesis, and pass it to the punctuation insertion component in order to produce the final output.

it using Moses, a well-known PBSMT tool (Koehn et al., 2007). The decoder constructs a correction hypothesis by first segmenting the input text into phrases, and mapping each phrase into its best correction using a combination of scores including a context-sensitive LM score.

Unlike translation, error correction is mainly monotonic, therefore we set disallow reordering by setting the distortion limit in Moses to 0.[2]

When no mapping can be found for a given phrase in the primary phrase table, the decoder looks it up in the back-off model. The decoder searches the space of all possible correction hypotheses, resulting from alternative segmentations and mappings, and returns the list of n-best scoring hypotheses.

2.4 N-best List Reranking

In this step, we combine LM information with linguistically and semantically motivated features using learning to rank methods (Tomeh et al., 2013). Discriminative reranking (Liu, 2009) allows each hypothesis to be represented as an arbitrary set of features without the need to explicitly model their interactions. Therefore, the system benefits from global and potentially complex features which are not available to the baseline decoder.

Each hypothesis in an n-best list is represented by a d-dimensional feature vector. Word error rate (WER) is computed for each hypotheses by comparing it to the reference correction. The resulting scored n-best list is used for supervised training of a reranking model. We employ a pairwise approach to ranking which takes pairs of hypotheses as instances in learning, and formalizes the ranking problem as pairwise classification.

For this task we use RankSVM (Joachims, 2002) which is a method based on Support Vector Machines (SVMs). We use only linear kernels to keep complexity low. We use a rich set of features including LM scores on surface forms, POS tags and lemmas. We also use a feature based on a global model of the semantic coherence of the hypotheses (Tomeh et al., 2013). The new top ranked hypothesis is the output of this step which is then fed to the next component.

2.5 Punctuation Insertion

We developed a model that predicts the occurrence of periods and commas in a given Arabic text. The core model is a decision tree classifier trained on the QALB parallel training data using WEKA (Hall et al., 2009). For each space between two words, the classifier decides whether or not to insert a punctuation mark, using a window size of three words surrounding the underlying space.

The model uses the following features:

- A class punctuation feature, that is whether to insert a period, a comma or none at the current space location;
- The part-of-speech of the previous word;
- The existence of a conjunctive or connective proclitic in the following word; that is a "wa"

[2]Only 0.14% of edits in the QALB corpus are actually reordering.

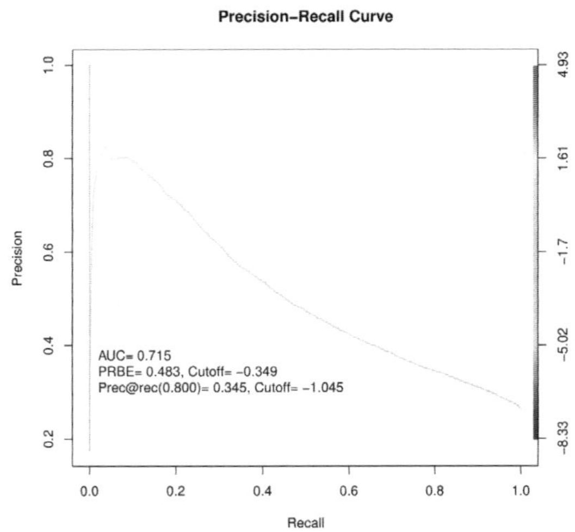

Figure 2: Evaluation of the error detection component. AUC: Area Under the Curve, PRBE: precision-recall break-even point. Classifier thresholds are displayed on the right vertical axis.

or "fa" proclitic that is either a conjunction, a sub-conjunction or a connective particle.

We obtain POS and proclitic information using MADAMIRA (Pasha et al., 2014). The output of this component is the final output of the system.

3 Experiments

All the models we use in our pipeline are trained in a supervised way using the training part of the QALB corpus (Zaghouani et al., 2014), while we reserve the development part of the corpus for testing.

3.1 Error detection

We evaluate the error detection binary classifier in terms of standard classification measures as shown in Figure 2. Each point on the curve is computed by selecting a threshold on the classifier score.

The threshold we use correspond to recall equal to 80%, at which the precision is very low which leaves much room for improvement in the performance of the error detection component.

3.2 Character-level correction

We evaluate the character-level correction model by measuring the percentage of erroneous phrases that have been mapped to their in-context reference corrections. We found this percentage to be 41% on QALB dev data. We limit the size of such phrases to one in order to focus on out-of-vocabulary words.

3.3 Punctuation insertion

To evaluate the punctuation insertion independently from the pipeline, we first remove the periods and commas from input text. Considering only the locations where periods and commas exist, our model gives a recall of 49% and a precision of 53%, giving an F_1-score of 51%.

When we apply our punctuation model in the correction pipeline, we find that it is always better to keep the already existing periods and commas in the input text instead of overwriting them by the model prediction.

While developing the model, we ran experiments where we train the complete list of features produced by MADAMIRA; that is part-of-speech, gender, number, person, aspect, voice, case, mood, state, proclitics and enclitics. This was done for two preceding words and two following words. However, the results were significantly outperformed by our final set-up.

3.4 The pipeline

The performance of the pipeline is evaluated in terms of precision, recall and F_1 as computed by the M^2 Scorer (Dahlmeier and Ng, 2012b). The results presented in Table 1 show that a simple PBSMT baseline achieves relatively good performance compared to more sophisticated models. The character-level back-off model helps by improving recall at the expense of decreased precision. The error detection component hurts the performance which could be explained by its intrinsic bad performance. Since more investigation is needed to clarify on this point, we drop this component from our submission. Both reranking and punctuation insertion improve the performance.

Our system submission to the shared task (back-off+PBSMT+Rank+PI) resulted in an F_1 score of 58.6% on the official test set, with a precision of 76.9% and a recall of 47.3%.

4 Related Work

Both rule-based and data-driven approaches to error correction can be found in the literature (Sidorov et al., 2013; Berend et al., 2013; Yi et al., 2013) as well as hybridization of them (Putra and Szabo, 2013). Unlike our approach, most of

System	PR	RC	F_1
PBSMT	75.5	49.5	59.8
backoff+PBSMT	74.1	51.8	60.9
ED+backoff+PBSMT	61.3	45.4	52.2
backoff+PBSMT+Rank	**75.7**	52.1	61.7
backoff+PBSMT+Rank+PI	74.9	**54.2**	**62.8**

Table 1: Pipeline precision, recall and F_1 scores. ED: error detection, PI: punctuation insertion.

the proposed systems build distinct models to address individual types of errors (see the CoNLL-2013, 2014 proceedings (Ng et al., 2013a; Ng et al., 2014), and combine them afterwords using Integer Linear Programming for instance (Rozovskaya et al., 2013). This approach is relatively time-consuming when the number of error types increases.

Interest in models that target all errors at once has increased, using either multi-class classifiers (Farra et al., 2014; Jia et al., 2013), of-the-shelf SMT techniques (Brockett et al., 2006; Mizumoto et al., 2011; Yuan and Felice, 2013; Buys and van der Merwe, 2013; Buys and van der Merwe, 2013), or building specialized decoders (Dahlmeier and Ng, 2012a).

Our system addresses the weaknesses of the SMT approach using additional components in a pipeline architecture. Similar work on word-level and character-level model combination has been done in the context of translation between closely related languages (Nakov and Tiedemann, 2012). A character-level correction model has also been considered to reduce the out-of-vocabulary rate in translation systems (Habash, 2008).

5 Conclusion and Future Work

We described a pipeline approach based on phrase-based SMT with n-best list reranking. We showed that backing-off word-level model with a character-level model improves the performance by ameliorating the recall of the system.

The main focus of our future work will be on better integration of the error detection model, and on exploring alternative methods for combining the character and the word models.

Acknowledgments

This material is partially based on research funded by grant NPRP-4-1058-1-168 from the Qatar National Research Fund (a member of the Qatar Foundation). The statements made herein are solely the responsibility of the authors.

Nizar Habash performed most of his contribution to this paper while he was at the Center for Computational Learning Systems at Columbia University.

References

Cyril Allauzen, Michael Riley, Johan Schalkwyk, Wojciech Skut, and Mehryar Mohri. 2007. Openfst: A general and efficient weighted finite-state transducer library. In *CIAA*, pages 11–23.

Gabor Berend, Veronika Vincze, Sina Zarrieß, and Richárd Farkas. 2013. Lfg-based features for noun number and article grammatical errors. In *Proceedings of the Seventeenth Conference on Computational Natural Language Learning: Shared Task*, pages 62–67, Sofia, Bulgaria, August. Association for Computational Linguistics.

Chris Brockett, William B. Dolan, and Michael Gamon. 2006. Correcting esl errors using phrasal smt techniques. In *Proceedings of the 21st International Conference on Computational Linguistics and the 44th Annual Meeting of the Association for Computational Linguistics*, ACL-44, pages 249–256, Stroudsburg, PA, USA. Association for Computational Linguistics.

Jan Buys and Brink van der Merwe. 2013. A tree transducer model for grammatical error correction. In *Proceedings of the Seventeenth Conference on Computational Natural Language Learning: Shared Task*, pages 43–51, Sofia, Bulgaria, August. Association for Computational Linguistics.

Daniel Dahlmeier and Hwee Tou Ng. 2012a. A beam-search decoder for grammatical error correction. In *EMNLP-CoNLL*, pages 568–578.

Daniel Dahlmeier and Hwee Tou Ng. 2012b. Better evaluation for grammatical error correction. In *HLT-NAACL*, pages 568–572.

Robert Dale and Adam Kilgarriff. 2010. Helping our own: Text massaging for computational linguistics as a new shared task. In *INLG*.

Noura Farra, Nadi Tomeh, Alla Rozovskaya, and Nizar Habash. 2014. Generalized character-level spelling error correction. In *ACL (2)*, pages 161–167.

Jon Fiscus. 1998. Speech Recognition Scoring Toolkit (SCTK). National Institute of Standard Technology (NIST). `http://www.itl.nist.gov/iad/mig/tools/`.

Nizar Habash and Ryan M. Roth. 2011. Using deep morphology to improve automatic error detection in arabic handwriting recognition. In *Proceedings of the 49th Annual Meeting of the Association for Computational Linguistics: Human Language Technologies - Volume 1*, HLT '11, pages 875–884, Stroudsburg, PA, USA. Association for Computational Linguistics.

Nizar Habash, Owen Rambow, and Ryan Roth. 2009. MADA+TOKAN: A toolkit for Arabic tokenization, diacritization, morphological disambiguation, POS tagging, stemming and lemmatization. In Khalid Choukri and Bente Maegaard, editors, *Proceedings of the Second International Conference on Arabic Language Resources and Tools*. The MEDAR Consortium, April.

Nizar Habash. 2008. Four Techniques for Online Handling of Out-of-Vocabulary Words in Arabic-English Statistical Machine Translation. In *Proceedings of ACL-08: HLT, Short Papers*, pages 57–60, Columbus, Ohio.

Nizar Habash. 2010. *Introduction to Arabic Natural Language Processing*. Morgan & Claypool Publishers.

Mark Hall, Eibe Frank, Geoffrey Holmes, Bernhard Pfahringer, Peter Reutemann, and Ian H. Witten. 2009. The weka data mining software: An update. *SIGKDD Explor. Newsl.*, 11(1):10–18, November.

Zhongye Jia, Peilu Wang, and Hai Zhao. 2013. Grammatical error correction as multiclass classification with single model. In *Proceedings of the Seventeenth Conference on Computational Natural Language Learning: Shared Task*, pages 74–81, Sofia, Bulgaria, August. Association for Computational Linguistics.

Thorsten Joachims. 2002. Optimizing search engines using clickthrough data. In *Proceedings of the eighth ACM SIGKDD international conference on Knowledge discovery and data mining*, KDD '02, pages 133–142.

Philipp Koehn, Franz Josef Och, and Daniel Marcu. 2003. Statistical Phrase-based Translation. In *Proceedings of the Human Language Technology and North American Association for Computational Linguistics Conference (HLT/NAACL)*, pages 127–133, Edmonton, Canada.

Philipp Koehn, Hieu Hoang, Alexandra Birch, Chris Callison-Burch, Marcello Federico, Nicola Bertoldi, Brooke Cowan, Wade Shen, Christine Moran, Richard Zens, Chris Dyer, Ondřej Bojar, Alexandra Constantin, and Evan Herbst. 2007. Moses: Open source toolkit for statistical machine translation. In *Proceedings of the 45th Annual Meeting of the ACL on Interactive Poster and Demonstration Sessions*, ACL '07, pages 177–180, Stroudsburg, PA, USA. Association for Computational Linguistics.

Karen Kukich. 1992. Techniques for automatically correcting words in text. *ACM Comput. Surv.*, 24(4):377–439, December.

Tie-Yan Liu. 2009. *Learning to Rank for Information Retrieval*. Now Publishers Inc., Hanover, MA, USA.

Tomoya Mizumoto, Mamoru Komachi, Masaaki Nagata, and Yuji Matsumoto. 2011. Mining revision log of language learning sns for automated japanese error correction of second language learners. In *IJCNLP*, pages 147–155.

Behrang Mohit, Alla Rozovskaya, Nizar Habash, Wajdi Zaghouani, and Ossama Obeid. 2014. The First QALB Shared Task on Automatic Text Correction for Arabic. In *Proceedings of EMNLP Workshop on Arabic Natural Language Processing*, Doha, Qatar, October.

Mehryar Mohri, Fernando Pereira, and Michael Riley. 2002. Weighted finite-state transducers in speech recognition. *Computer Speech & Language*, 16(1):69–88.

Preslav Nakov and Jörg Tiedemann. 2012. Combining word-level and character-level models for machine translation between closely-related languages. In *ACL (2)*, pages 301–305.

Hwee Tou Ng, Joel Tetreault, Siew Mei Wu, Yuanbin Wu, and Christian Hadiwinoto, editors. 2013a. *Proceedings of the Seventeenth Conference on Computational Natural Language Learning: Shared Task*. Association for Computational Linguistics, Sofia, Bulgaria, August.

Hwee Tou Ng, Siew Mei Wu, Yuanbin Wu, Christian Hadiwinoto, and Joel Tetreault. 2013b. The conll-2013 shared task on grammatical error correction. In *Proceedings of the Seventeenth Conference on Computational Natural Language Learning: Shared Task*, pages 1–12, Sofia, Bulgaria, August. Association for Computational Linguistics.

Hwee Tou Ng, Siew Mei Wu, Ted Briscoe, Christian Hadiwinoto, Raymond Hendy Susanto, and Christopher Bryant, editors. 2014. *Proceedings of the Eighteenth Conference on Computational Natural Language Learning: Shared Task*. Association for Computational Linguistics, Baltimore, Maryland, June.

Arfath Pasha, Mohamed Al-Badrashiny, Mona T. Diab, Ahmed El Kholy, Ramy Eskander, Nizar Habash, Manoj Pooleery, Owen Rambow, and Ryan Roth. 2014. Madamira: A fast, comprehensive tool for morphological analysis and disambiguation of arabic. In *LREC*, pages 1094–1101.

Desmond Darma Putra and Lili Szabo. 2013. Uds at conll 2013 shared task. In *Proceedings of the Seventeenth Conference on Computational Natural Language Learning: Shared Task*, pages 88–95, Sofia, Bulgaria, August. Association for Computational Linguistics.

Alla Rozovskaya, Kai-Wei Chang, Mark Sammons, and Dan Roth. 2013. The university of illinois system in the conll-2013 shared task. In *Proceedings of the Seventeenth Conference on Computational Natural Language Learning: Shared Task*, pages 13–19, Sofia, Bulgaria, August. Association for Computational Linguistics.

Grigori Sidorov, Anubhav Gupta, Martin Tozer, Dolors Catala, Angels Catena, and Sandrine Fuentes. 2013. Rule-based system for automatic grammar correction using syntactic n-grams for english language learning (l2). In *Proceedings of the Seventeenth Conference on Computational Natural Language Learning: Shared Task*, pages 96–101, Sofia, Bulgaria, August. Association for Computational Linguistics.

Andreas Stolcke. 2002. SRILM - an Extensible Language Modeling Toolkit. In *Proceedings of the International Conference on Spoken Language Processing (ICSLP)*, volume 2, pages 901–904, Denver, CO.

Nadi Tomeh, Nizar Habash, Ryan Roth, Noura Farra, Pradeep Dasigi, and Mona Diab. 2013. Reranking with linguistic and semantic features for arabic optical character recognition. In *Proceedings of the 51st Annual Meeting of the Association for Computational Linguistics (Volume 2: Short Papers)*, pages 549–555, Sofia, Bulgaria, August. Association for Computational Linguistics.

Bong-Jun Yi, Ho-Chang Lee, and Hae-Chang Rim. 2013. Kunlp grammatical error correction system for conll-2013 shared task. In *Proceedings of the Seventeenth Conference on Computational Natural Language Learning: Shared Task*, pages 123–127, Sofia, Bulgaria, August. Association for Computational Linguistics.

Zheng Yuan and Mariano Felice. 2013. Constrained grammatical error correction using statistical machine translation. In *Proceedings of the Seventeenth Conference on Computational Natural Language Learning: Shared Task*, pages 52–61, Sofia, Bulgaria, August. Association for Computational Linguistics.

François Yvon. 2010. Rewriting the orthography of sms messages. *Natural Language Engineering*, 16:133–159, 3.

Wajdi Zaghouani, Behrang Mohit, Nizar Habash, Ossama Obeid, Nadi Tomeh, Alla Rozovskaya, Noura Farra, Sarah Alkuhlani, and Kemal Oflazer. 2014. Large scale arabic error annotation: Guidelines and framework. In *Proceedings of the Ninth International Conference on Language Resources and Evaluation (LREC'14)*, Reykjavik, Iceland, May. European Language Resources Association (ELRA).

Arabic Spelling Correction using Supervised Learning

Youssef Hassan
Dept Computer Engineering
Cairo University
Giza, Egypt
youssefhassan13@gmail.com

Mohamed Aly
Dept Computer Engineering
Cairo University
Giza, Egypt
mohamed@mohamedaly.info

Amir Atiya
Dept Computer Engineering
Cairo University
Giza, Egypt
amir@alumni.caltech.edu

Abstract

In this work, we address the problem of spelling correction in the Arabic language utilizing the new corpus provided by QALB (Qatar Arabic Language Bank) project which is an annotated corpus of sentences with errors and their corrections. The corpus contains edit, add before, split, merge, add after, move and other error types. We are concerned with the first four error types as they contribute more than 90% of the spelling errors in the corpus. The proposed system has many models to address each error type on its own and then integrating all the models to provide an efficient and robust system that achieves an overall recall of 0.59, precision of 0.58 and F1 score of 0.58 including all the error types on the development set. Our system participated in the QALB 2014 shared task "Automatic Arabic Error Correction" and achieved an F1 score of 0.6, earning the sixth place out of nine participants.

1 Introduction

The Arabic language is a highly inflected natural language that has an enormous number of possible words (Othman et al., 2003). And although it is the native language of over 300 million people, it suffers from the lack of useful resources as opposed to other languages, specially English and until now there are no systems that cover the wide range of possible spelling errors. Fortunately the QALB corpus (Zaghouani et al., 2014) will help enrich the resources for Arabic language generally and the spelling correction specifically by providing an annotated corpus with corrected sentences from user comments, native student essays, non-native data and machine translation data. In this work, we are trying to use this corpus to build an error correction system that can cover a range of spelling errors.

This paper is a system description paper that is submitted in the EMNLP 2014 conference shared task "Automatic Arabic Error Correction" (Mohit et al., 2014) in the Arabic NLP workshop. The challenges that faced us while working on this system was the shortage of contribution in the area of spelling correction in the Arabic language. But hopefully the papers and the work in this shared task specifically and in the workshop generally will enrich this area and flourish it.

Our system targets four types of spelling errors, edit errors, add before errors, merge errors and split errors. For each error type, A model is built to correct erroneous words detected by the error detection technique. Edit errors and add before errors are corrected using classifiers with contextual features, while the merge and split errors are corrected by inserting or omitting a space between words and choosing the best candidate based on the language model score of each candidate.

The rest of this paper is structured as follows. In section 2, we give a brief background on related work in spelling correction. In section 3, we introduce our system for spelling correction with the description of the efficient models used in the system. In section 4, we list some experimental results on the development set. In section 5, we give some concluding remarks.

2 Related Work

The work in the field of spelling correction in the Arabic language is not yet mature and no system achieved a great error correction efficiency. Even Microsoft Word, the most widely used Arabic spelling correction system, does not achieve good results. Our work was inspired by a number of papers. (Shaalan et al., 2012) addressed the problem of Arabic Word Generation for spell checking and they produced an open source and

Proceedings of the EMNLP 2014 Workshop on Arabic Natural Langauge Processing (ANLP), pages 121–126,
October 25, 2014, Doha, Qatar.

large coverage word list for Arabic containing 9 million fully inflected surface words and applied language models and Noisy Channel Model and knowledge-based rules for error correction. This word list is used in our work besides using language models and Noisy Channel Model.

(Shaalan et al., 2010) proposed another system for cases in which the candidate generation using edit algorithm only was not enough, in which candidates were generated based on transformation rules and errors are detected using BAMA (Buckwalter Arabic Morphological Analyzer)(Buckwalter, 2002).

(Khalifa et al., 2011) proposed a system for text segmentation. The system discriminates between waw wasl and waw fasl, and depending on this it can predict if the sentence to be segmented at this position or not, they claim that they achieved 97.95% accuracy. The features used in this work inspired us with the add before errors correction.

(Schaback, 2007) proposed a system for the English spelling correction, that is addressing the edit errors on various levels: on the phonetic level using *Soundex* algorithm, on the character level using edit algorithm with one operation away, on the word level using bigram language model, on the syntactic level using collocation model to determine how fit the candidate is in this position and on the semantic level using co-occurrence model to determine how likely a candidate occurs within the given context, using all the models output of candidate word as features and using SVM model to classify the candidates, they claim reaching recall ranging from 90% for first candidate and 97% for all five candidates presented and outperforming MS Word, Aspell, Hunspell, FST and Google.

3 Proposed System

We propose a system for detecting and correcting various spelling errors, including edit, split, merge, and add before errors. The system consists of two steps: error detection and error correction. Each word is tested for correctness. If the word is deemed incorrect, it is passed to the correction step, otherwise it remains unchanged. The correction step contains specific handling for each type of error, as detailed in subsection 3.3.

3.1 Resources

Dictionary: Arabic wordlist for spell checking[1] is a free dictionary containing 9 million Arabic words. The words are automatically generated from the AraComLex[2] open-source finite state transducer.

The dictionary is used in the generation of candidates and using a special version of MADAMIRA[3] (Pasha et al., 2014) created for the QALB shared task using a morphological database based on BAMA 1.2.1[4] (Buckwalter, 2002). Features are extracted for each word of the dictionary to help in the proposed system in order that each candidate has features just like the words in the corpus.

Stoplist: Using stop words list available on sourceforge.net[5]. This is used in the collocation algorithm described later.

Language Model: We use SRILM (Stolcke, 2002) to build a language model using the Ajdir Corpora[6] as a corpus with the vocabulary from the dictionary stated above. We train a language model containing unigrams, bigrams, and trigrams using modified Kneser-Ney smoothing (James, 2000).

QALB Corpus: QALB shared task offers a new corpus for spelling correction. The corpus contains a large dataset of manually corrected Arabic sentences. Using this corpus, we were able to implement a spelling correction system that targets the most frequently occurring error types which are **(a) edit errors** where a word is replaced by another word, **(b) add before errors** where a word was removed, **(c) merge errors** where a space was inserted mistakenly and finally **(d) split errors** where a space was removed mistakenly. The corpus provided also has three other error types but they occur much less frequently happen which are **(e) add after errors** which is like the add before but the token removed should be put after the word, **(f) move errors** where a word should be moved to other place within the sentence and **(g) other errors** where any other error that does

[1]http://sourceforge.net/projects/arabic-wordlist/

[2]http://aracomlex.sourceforge.net/

[3]MADAMIRA-release-20140702-1.0

[4]AraMorph 1.2.1 - http://sourceforge.net/projects/aramorph/

[5]http://sourceforge.net/projects/arabicstopwords/

[6]http://aracorpus.e3rab.com/argistestsrv.nmsu.edu/AraCorpus/

not lie in the six others is labeled by it.

3.2 Error Detection

The training set, development set and test set provided by QALB project come with the "columns file" and contains very helpful features generated by MADAMIRA. Using the Buckwalter morphological analysis (Buckwalter, 2002) feature, we determine if a word is correct or not. If the word has no analysis, we consider the word as *incorrect* and pass it through the correction process.

3.3 Edit Errors Correction

The edit errors has the highest portion of total errors in the corpus. It amounts to more than 55% of the total errors. To correct this type of errors, we train a classifier with features like the error model probability, collocation and co-occurrence as follows:

Undiacriticized word preprocessed: Utilizing the MADAMIRA features of each word, the undiacriticized word fixes some errors like hamzas, the pair of haa and taa marboutah and the pair of yaa and alif maqsoura.

We apply some preprocessing on the undiacriticized word to make it more useful and fix the issues associated with it. For example we remove the incorrect redundant characters from the word e.g (الرجاااال → الرجال, AlrjAAAAl → AlrjAl). We also replace the Roman punctuation marks by the Arabic ones e.g (? → ؟).

Language Model: For each candidate, A unigram, bigram and trigram values from the language model trained are retrieved. In addition to a feature that is the product of the unigram, bigram and trigram values.

Likelihood Model: The likelihood model is trained by iterating over the training sentences counting the occurrences of each edit with the characters being edited and the type of edit. The output of this is called a confusion matrix.

The candidate score is based on the Noisy Channel Model (Kernighan et al., 1990) which is the multiplication of probabilty of the proposed edit using the confusion matrix trained which is called the error model, and the language model score of that word. The language model used is unigram, bigram and trigram with equal weights. Add-1 smoothing is used for both models in the counts.

$$Score = p(x|w).p(w)$$

where x is the wrong word and w is the candidate correction.

For substitution edit candidates, we give higher score for substitution of a character that is close on the keyboard or the substitution pair belongs to the same group of letter groups (Shaalan et al., 2012) by multiplying the score by a constant greater than one.

(آ، إ، أ، ا)، (ي، ن، ث، ت، ب)، (خ، ح، ج)،
(ذ، د)، (ز، ر)، (ش، س)، (ض، ص)، (ظ، ط)،
(غ، ع)، (ق، ف)، (ة، ه)، (ؤ، و)، (ى، ي).

(|, < , >, A), (y, n, v, t, b), (x, H, j), (*, d), (z, r), ($, s), (D, S), (Z, T), (g, E), (q, f), (p h), (&, w), (Y, y)

For each candidate , the likelihood score is computed and added to the feature vector of the candidate.

Collocation: The collocation model targets the likelihood of the candidate inside the sentence. This is done using the lemma of the word and the POS tags of words in the sentence.

We use the algorithm in (Schaback, 2007) for training the collocation model. Specifically, by retrieving the 5,000 most occurring lemmas in the training corpus and put it in list L. For each lemma in L, three lists are created, each record in the list is a sequence of three POS tags around the target lemma. For training, we shift a window of three POS tags over the training sentence. If a lemma belongs to L, we add the surrounding POS tags to the equivalent list of the target lemma depending on the position of the target lemma within the three POS tags.

Given a misspelled word in a sentence, for each candidate correction, if it is in the L list, we count the number of occurrences of the surrounding POS tags in each list of the three depending on the position of of the candidate.

The three likelihoods are stored in the feature vector of the candidate in addition to the product of them.

Co-occurrence: Co-occurrence is used to measure how likely a word fits inside a context. Where L is the same list of most frequent lemmata from collocation.

We use the co-occurrence algorithm in (Schaback, 2007). Before training the model, we transform each word of our training sentence into its lemma form and remove stop-words. For example, consider the original text:

حيث لأفرق بين الاستعمار والحكومة الحالية بما أنها

Hyv l>frq byn AlAstEmAr wAlHkwmp AlHAlyp bmA >nhA

After removing stop-words and replacing the remaining words by their lemma form we end up with:

أفرق استعمار حكومة حالي

>frq AstEmAr Hkwmp HAly

which forms C.

From that C, we get all lemmata that appear in the radius of 10 words around the target lemma b where b belongs to L. We count the number of occurrences of each lemma in that context C.

By using the above model, three distances are calculated for target lemma b: d_1, the ratio of actually found context words in C and possibly findable context words. This describes how similar the trained context and the given context are for candidate b; d_2 considers how significant the found context lemmata are by summing the normalized frequencies of the context lemmata. As a third feature; $d_3(b)$ that simply measures how big the vector space model for lemma b is.

For each candidate, the model is applied and the three distances are calculated and added to the feature vector of that candidate.

The Classifier: After generating the candidate corrections within 1 and 2 edit operations (insert, delete, replace and transpose) distance measured by Levenshtein distance (Levenshtein, 1966), we run them through a Naive-Bayes classifier using python NLTK's implementation to find out which one is the most likely to be the correction for the incorrect word.

The classifier is trained using the training set provided by QALB project. For each edit correction in the training set, all candidates are generated for the incorrect word and a feature vector (as shown in table1) is calculated using the techniques aforementioned. If the candidate is the correct one, the label for the training feature vector is correct else it is incorrect.

Then using the trained classifier, the same is done on the development set or the test set where we replace the incorrect word with the word suggested by the classifier.

3.4 Add before Errors Correction

The add before errors are mostly punctuation errors. A classifier is trained on the QALB training

Table 1: The feature set used by the edit errors classifier.

Feature name
Likelihood model probability
unigram probability
previous bigram probability
next bigram probability
trigram probability
language model product
collocation left
collocation right
collocation mid
collocation product
cooccurrence distance 1
cooccurrence distance 2
cooccurrence distance 3
previous gender
previous number
next gender
next number

corpus. A classifier is implemented with contextual features C. C is a 4-gram around the token being investigated. Each word of these four has the two features: The token itself and Part-of-speech tag and for the next word only pregloss because if the word's pregloss is "and" it is more probable that a new sentence began. Those features are available thanks to MADAMIRA features provided with the corpus and the generated for dictionary words.

The classifier is trained on the QALB training set. We iterate over all the training sentences word by word and getting the aforementioned features (as shown in table 2) and label the training with the added before token if there was a matching add before correction for this word or the label will be an empty string.

For applying the model, the same is done on the QALB development sentences after removing all punctuations as they are probably not correct and the output of the classifier is either empty or suggested token to add before current word.

3.5 Merge Errors Correction

The merge errors occurs due to the insertion of a space between two words by mistake. The approach is simply trying to attach every word with its successor word and checking if it is a valid

Table 2: The feature set used by the add before errors classifier.

Feature name
before previous word
before previous word POS tag
previous word
previous word POS tag
next word
next word POS tag
next word pregloss
after next word
after next POS tag

Arabic word and rank it with the language model score.

3.6 Split Errors Correction

The split errors occurs due to the deletion of a space between two words. The approach is simply getting all the valid partitions of the word and try to correct both partitions and give them a rank using the language model score. The partition is at least two characters long.

4 Experimental Results

In order to know the contribution of each error type models to the overall system performance, we adopted an incremental approach of the models. We implemented the system using python[7] and NLTK[8] (Loper and Bird, 2002) toolkit. The models are trained on the QALB corpus training set and the results are obtained by applying the trained models on the development set. Our goal was to achieve high recall but without losing too much precision. The models were evaluated using M2 scorer (Dahlmeier and Ng, 2012).

First, we start with only the preprocessed undiacriticized word, then we added our edit error classifier. Adding the add before classifier was a great addition to the system as the system was able to increase the number of corrected errors significantly, notably the add before classifier proposed too many incorrect suggestions that decreased the precision. Then we added the merging correction technique. Finally we added the split error correction technique. The system corrects 9860 errors versus 16659 golden error corrections and proposed 17057 correction resulting in the final system recall of 0.5919, precision of 0.5781 and F1 score of 0.5849. Details are shown in Table 3.

Table 3: The incremental results after adding each error type model and applying them on the development set.

Model name	Recall	Precision	F1 score
Undiacriticized	0.32	0.833	0.4715
+ Edit	0.3515	0.7930	0.5723
+ Add before	0.5476	0.5658	0.5567
+ Merge	0.5855	0.5816	0.5836
+ Split	**0.5919**	**0.5781**	**0.5849**

We tried other combinations of the models by removing one or more of the components to get the best results possible. Noting that all the systems results are using the undiacriticized word. Details are shown in Table 4

Table 4: The results of some combinations of the models and applying them on the development set. The models are abbreviated as Edit E, Merge M, Split S, and Add before A.

Model name	Precision	Recall	F1 score
M Only	0.8441	0.3724	0.5167
S Only	0.7838	0.338	0.5167
A Only	0.6008	0.4887	0.539
E Only	0.8143	0.3472	0.4868
M & S	0.8121	0.3814	0.5191
E & S	0.62	0.3542	0.4508
M & E	0.6184	0.5403	0.5767
S & M & A	0.6114	0.5396	0.5733
M & E & A	0.6186	0.5404	0.5768
E & S & A	0.5955	0.507	0.5477
E & S & M	0.6477	0.3969	0.4922
E & S & M & A	**0.5919**	**0.5781**	**0.5849**

5 Conclusion and Future Work

We propose an all-in-one system for error detection and correction. The system addresses four types of spelling errors (edit, add before, merge and split errors). The system achieved promising results by successfully getting corrections for about 60% of the spelling errors in the development set. Also, There is still a big room for improvements in all types of error correction models.

We are planning to improve the current system by incorporating more intelligent techniques and models for split and merge. Also, the add before classifier needs much work to improve the coverage as the errors are mostly missing punctuation marks. For the edit classifier, real-word errors need to be addressed.

[7]https://www.python.org/

[8]http://www.nltk.org/

References

Tim Buckwalter. 2002. Buckwalter arabic morphological analyzer version 1.0. November.

Daniel Dahlmeier and Hwee Tou Ng. 2012. Better evaluation for grammatical error correction. In *Proceedings of the 2012 Conference of the North American Chapter of the Association for Computational Linguistics: Human Language Technologies*, NAACL HLT '12, pages 568–572, Stroudsburg, PA, USA. Association for Computational Linguistics.

Frankie James. 2000. Modified kneser-ney smoothing of n-gram models. RIACS.

Mark D. Kernighan, Kenneth W. Church, and William A. Gale. 1990. A spelling correction program based on a noisy channel model. In *Proceedings of the 13th Conference on Computational Linguistics - Volume 2*, COLING '90, pages 205–210, Stroudsburg, PA, USA. Association for Computational Linguistics.

Iraky Khalifa, Zakareya Al Feki, and Abdelfatah Farawila. 2011. Arabic discourse segmentation based on rhetorical methods.

VI Levenshtein. 1966. Binary Codes Capable of Correcting Deletions, Insertions and Reversals. volume 10, page 707.

Edward Loper and Steven Bird. 2002. NLTK: The Natural Language Toolkit.

Behrang Mohit, Alla Rozovskaya, Nizar Habash, Wajdi Zaghouani, and Ossama Obeid. 2014. The First QALB Shared Task on Automatic Text Correction for Arabic. In *Proceedings of EMNLP Workshop on Arabic Natural Language Processing*, Doha, Qatar, October.

Eman Othman, Khaled Shaalan, and Ahmed Rafea. 2003. A chart parser for analyzing modern standard arabic sentence. In *To appear in In proceedings of the MT Summit IX Workshop on Machine Translation for Semitic Languages: Issues and Approaches*, Louisiana, U.S.A.

Pasha, Arfath, Mohamed Al-Badrashiny, Mona Diab, Ahmed El Kholy, Ramy Eskander, Nizar Habash, Manoj Pooleery, Owen Rambow, and Ryan M. Roth. 2014. Madamira: A fast, comprehensive tool for morphological analysis and disambiguation of arabic. In *In Proceedings of the Language Resources and Evaluation Conference (LREC)*, Reykjavik, Iceland.

Johannes Schaback. 2007. Multi-level feature extraction for spelling correction. Hyderabad, India.

K. Shaalan, R. Aref, and A Fahmy. 2010. An approach for analyzing and correcting spelling errors for non-native arabic learners. In *Informatics and Systems (INFOS), 2010 The 7th International Conference on*, pages 1–7, March.

Khaled Shaalan, Mohammed Attia, Pavel Pecina, Younes Samih, and Josef van Genabith. 2012. Arabic word generation and modelling for spell checking. In Nicoletta Calzolari (Conference Chair), Khalid Choukri, Thierry Declerck, Mehmet Uur Doan, Bente Maegaard, Joseph Mariani, Asuncion Moreno, Jan Odijk, and Stelios Piperidis, editors, *Proceedings of the Eight International Conference on Language Resources and Evaluation (LREC'12)*, Istanbul, Turkey, may. European Language Resources Association (ELRA).

A. Stolcke. 2002. Srilm – an extensible language modeling toolkit. In *Proc. Intl. Conf. on Spoken Language Processing*, Denver,U.S.A.

Wajdi Zaghouani, Behrang Mohit, Nizar Habash, Ossama Obeid, Nadi Tomeh, Alla Rozovskaya, Noura Farra, Sarah Alkuhlani, and Kemal Oflazer. 2014. Large scale arabic error annotation: Guidelines and framework. In *Proceedings of the Ninth International Conference on Language Resources and Evaluation (LREC'14)*, Reykjavik, Iceland, May. European Language Resources Association (ELRA).

Autocorrection Of Arabic Common Errors For Large Text Corpus

QALB-2014 Shared Task

Taha Zerrouki
Bouira University, Bouira, Algeria
The National Computer Science Engineering School (ESI), Algiers, Algeria
t_zerrouki@esi.dz

Khaled Alhawaity
Tabuk University, KSA
al-howity@hotmail.com

Amar Balla
The National Computer Science Engineering School (ESI), Algiers, Algeria
a_balla@esi,dz

Abstract

Automatic correction of misspelled words means offering a single proposal to correct a mistake, for example, switching two letters, omitting letter or a key press. In Arabic, there are some typical common errors based on letter errors, such as confusing in the form of Hamza همزة, confusion between Daad ضاد and Za ظاء, and the omission dots with Yeh ياء and Teh تاء.

So we propose in this paper a system description of a mechanism for automatic correction of common errors in Arabic based on rules, by using two methods, a list of words and regular expressions.

Keywords: *AutoCorrect, spell checking, Arabic language processing.*

1 Introduction

Spell check is the most important functions of correct writing, whether manual or assisted by programs, it detects errors and suggests corrections.

Conventional spelling checkers detect typing errors simply by comparing each token of a text against a dictionary of words that are known to be correctly spelled.

Any token that matches an element of the dictionary, possibly after some minimal morphological analysis, is deemed to be correctly spelled; any token that matches no element is flagged as a possible error, with near-matches displayed as suggested corrections (Hirst, 2005).

2 Auto-correction

An auto-correction mechanism watches out for certain predefined "errors" as the user types, replacing them with a "correction" and giving no indication or warning of the change.

Such mechanisms are intended for undoubted typing errors for which only one correction is plausible, such as correcting accomodate* to accommodate (Hirst, 2005).

In Arabic, we found some common errors types, like the confusion in Hamza forms, e.g. the word Isti'maal (إستعمال*) must be written by a simple Alef, not Alef with Hamza below. This error can be classed as a kind of errors and not a simple error in a word (Shaalan, 2003, Habash, 2011).

Spellchecking and autocorrection are widely applicable for tasks such as:

- word- processing
- Post-processing Optical Character Recognition.
- Correction of large content site like Wikipedia.
- Correction of corpora.
- Search queries
- Mobile auto-completion and autocorrection programs.

3 Related works

Current works on autocorrection in Arabic are limited; there are some works on improving spell checking to select one plausible correction especially for correcting large texts like corpus. In English, Deorowicz (2005) had worked on correcting spelling errors by modeling their causes, he propose to classify mis-

Proceedings of the EMNLP 2014 Workshop on Arabic Natural Langauge Processing (ANLP), pages 127–131,
October 25, 2014, Doha, Qatar. ©2014 Association for Computational Linguistics

takes causes in order to improve replacement suggestion.

In Arabic, Microsoft office provides an autocorrect word list of common errors, which is limited and not studied.

Google search engine had improved its search algorithm for Arabic query by using some rules on letters which can be mistaken, for better words split based on letters properties, for example if we type [رائعةالجمال]*, the engine can give results for "Rae'at alJamaal" [رائعةالجمال]*and [رائعة الجمال]. , some other example: "Altarbia wa alta'lim", "Google", "Jaridat alahraam", [، *[قووقل] ،*[جريدةالاهرام التربيةوالتعليم]]*.

Google Arabia says in its blog, that "this improvement which looked very simple, enhance search in Arabic language by 10% which is in real an impressive change" (Hammad, 2010).

4 Our approach

We have launched our first project about autocorrection for a special objective to enhance Wikipedia article spell checking. Wikipedia is a large text database written by thousands of persons with different language skill levels and with multiple origins, which make a lot of mistakes. The idea is to provide an automatic script which can detect common errors by using regular expressions and a word replacement list[1].

This objective can be extended to answer other needs for users in office, chat, tweets, etc.

The idea is to use a non-ambiguous regular expressions or word list, to prevent common errors, while writing or as an automated script for large texts data.

As we say above, our method is based on:

- Regular expressions which can be used to identify errors and give one replacement.

- Replacement list which contains the misspelled word, and the exact correction for this case, this way is used for cases which can't be modeled as regular expression.

4.1 Regular Expressions

We use regular expression pattern to detect.errors in words by using word weight (Wazn) and affixes. For example we can detect that words with the weight INFI'AL انفعال must be written by Hamza Wasl, and we consider the form إنفعال* as wrong. Then, we represent all forms of this weight with all possible affixes.

Suffixes	Weight	prefixes
[illegible]	[illegible]	[illegible]

Table 1 Infi'aal wheight with its affixation

rules for انفعال
ur'\b(إن|ال|)(ك|ب|)(و|ف|)(\w\w)ا(\w)(ين|ات|ة|تين)(ي|)\b'
ur'\b(إن|لل|)(و|ف|)(\w\w)ا(\w)(ين|ات|تين|ة)(ي|)\b'
ur'\b(إن|ال|ب|ك|)(و|ف|)(\w\w)ا(\w)(ي|)(هما|كما|هم|كم|هن|كن|نا|ه|ك|ها|تهما|تكما|تهم|تكم|تهن|تكن|تنا|ته|تها|تك|اته اتك|اتها|اته|اتنا|اتكن|اتهن|اتكم|اتهم|اتكما|ما|)\b'
ur'\b(إن|ال|)(و|ف|)(\w\w)ا(\w)(ين|ان|تين|تان|ون)(ي|)\b'
ur'\b(إن|)(و|ف|)(\w\w)ا(\w)(ا|أ|ً)(ي|)\b'

Table 2 Rules for the Infi'al weight in all forms

By regular expressions we have modeled the following cases (cf.):

- words with weights (infi'al and ifti'al انفعال و افتعال)
- Words with Alef Maksura followed by Hamza, for example سئ will be corrected ad سيء.
- words with Teh Marbuta misplaced, like مدرسةالعلم to be corrected to مدرسة العلم.

Regular expression	replacement
# removing kashida (Tatweel)	
ur'([\u0621-\u063F\u0641-\u064A])\u0640+([\u0621-\u063F\u0641-\u064A])'	ur'\1\2'
# rules for انفعال	
ur'\b(إن|ال|)(ك|ب|)(و|ف|)(\w\w)ا(\w)(ين|ات|ة|تين)(ي|)\b'	ur'\1\2\3\ان4\ا5\6\7'
ur'\b(إن|لل|)(و|ف|)(\w\w)ا(\w)(ين|ات|تين|ة)(ي|)\b'	ur'\1\2\ان3\ا4\5\6'
ur'\b(إن|ال|ب|ك|)(و|ف|)(\w\w)ا(\w)(ي|)(هما|كما|هم|كم|هن|كن|نا|ه|ك|ها|تهما|تكما|تهم|تكم|تهن|تكن|تنا|ته|تها|تك|اتهما|اتكما|اتهم|اتكم|اتهن|اتكن|اتنا|اته|اتها|اتك|ما|)\b'	ur'\1\2\ان3\ا4\5\6'
ur'\b(إن|ال|)(و|ف|)(\w\w)ا(\w)(ين|ان|تين|تان|ون)(ي|)\b'	ur'\1\2\ان3\ا4\5\6'
ur'\b(إن|)(و|ف|)(\w\w)ا(\w)(ا|أ|ً)(ي|)\b'	ur'\1\ان2\ا3\4\5'

Table 3 Rules expressed by regular expressions.

4.2 Wordlist

Most common mistakes cannot be represented as regular expressions, such as errors in

[1] The script is named AkhtaBot, which is applied to arabic wikipedia, the Akhtabot is available on http://ar.wikipedia.org/wiki/مستخدم:AkhtaBot

the confusion between the Dhad and Za, and omitted dots on Teh and Yeh, such as in the المكتبه * and فى*, So we resort to build a list of common misspelled words.

To build an autocorrect word list, we suppose to use statistical extraction from a corpus, but we think that's not possible in Arabic language, because the common mistakes can have certain pattern and style, for example, people who can't differentiate between Dhad and Zah, make mistakes in all words containing these letters. Mistakes on Hamzat are not limited to some words, but can be typical and occur according to letters not especially for some words.

For this reason, we propose to build a word list based on Attia (2012) spell-checking word list, by generating errors for common letters errors, then filter resulted word list to obtain an autocorrect word list without ambiguity.

How to build generated word list:

1- take a correct word list

2- select candidate words:

- words start by Hamza Qat' or Wasl.
- words end by Yeh or Teh marbuta.
- Words contain Dhad or Zah.

3- Make errors on words by replacing candidate letters by errors.

4- Spell check the wordlist, and eliminate correct words, because some modified words can be correct, for example, if we take the word ضل Dhalla ، then modify it to ظل Zalla , the modified word exists in the dictionary, then we exclude it from autocorrect wordlist, and we keep only misspelled modified words.

words	modified	Spellcheck	Add to word list
بمكتبة	بمكتبه	True	
المكتبة	المكتبه	False	المكتبه
بالمكتبة	بالمكتبه	False	بالمكتبه
وبالمكتبة	وبالمكتبه	False	وبالمكتبه
ومكتبة	ومكتبه	True	

Table 4 Example of word errors generating

For example, if we have the word إسلام Islam, it can be written as اسلام Islam by mistake because that have the same pronociation. We can generate errors on words by appling some rule:

- Alef with Hamza above همزة قطع <=> Alef همزة وصل
- Alef with Hamza below همزة تحت الألف <=> Alef همزة وصل
- Dhah ض <=> Zah ظ
- The Marbuta ة <=> Heh ـه
- Yeh ي <=> Alef Maksura ى

We suppose that we have the following word list, this list is chosen to illustrate some cases.

إسلام
ظلام
ظل
مكتبة
المكتبة
إعلام

For every word, we map an mistaken word, then we get a list like this:

Word	candidate word
إسلام	اسلام
ظلام	ضلام
ظل	ضل
مكتبة	مكتبه
المكتبة	المكتبه
إعلام	اعلام

We note that some candidate words are right, then we remove it, and the remaining words consititute the autocorrect wordlist

Word	candidate word
إسلام	اسلام
ظلام	ضلام
المكتبة	المكتبه
إعلام	اعلام

The following list (cf. Table**5**) shows the number of words in each type of errors,

Error type	**Words count**
words started by Hamza Qat'	101853
words ended by Yeh	700198
words ended by Teh marbuta	152210
words contained Dhad	396506
words contained Zah	94395
Total	1445162

Table 5 Errors categories in wordlist

The large number of words is due to the multiple forms per word, which avoids the morphological analysis, in such programs.

Customized Wordlist

Large number of replacement cases in generated autocorrect list encourages us to make an improvement to generate customized list for specific cases in order to reduce list length. We apply the following algorithm to generate customized list from large text data set:

1. Extract misspelled words from dataset by using Hunspell spellchecker.
2. Generate suggestions given by Hunspell

3. Study suggestions to choose the best one in hypothesis that words have common errors on letters according to modified letters.
4. Exclude ambiguous cases.

The automatically generated word list is used to autocorrect the dataset instead of default word list

5 Tools and resources

In our program we have used the following resources:

- Arabic word list for spell checking containing 9 million Arabic words, from Attia works (2012).
- a simple Python script to generate errors.
- Hunspell spellchecker program with Ayaspell dictionary (Hadjir 2009, Zerrouki, 2013). and Attia spellchecking wordlist (2012).
- our autocorrect program named Ghalatawi[2] (cf. a screenshot on Figure 1) ،
- A script to select best suggestion from Hunspell correction suggestions to generate customized autocorrect list.

Example

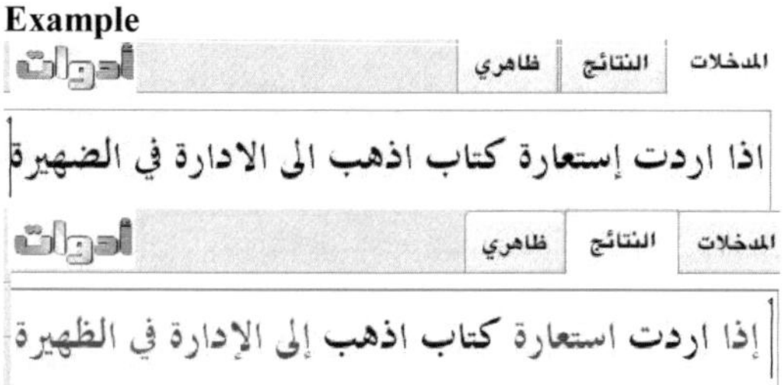

Figure 1 Ghalatawi program, autocorrection example

6 Evaluation

In order to evaluate the performance of automatic correction program, we used the data set provided in the shared task test (Behrang, 2014). After that autocorrect the texts by Galatawi program based on regular expressions and a wordlist.

For this evaluation we have used two autocorrect word lists:

- a generic word list generated from Attia wordlist, this wordlist is used for general purposes. This word list is noted in evaluation as "STANDARD".

- a customized wordlist based on dataset, by generating a special word list according to data set, in order to improve auto correction and avoid unnecessary replacement. this wordlist is noted in evaluation as "CUSTOMIZED".

The customized autocorrect word list is built in the same way as STANDARD, by replacing the source dictionary by misspelled words from QALB corpus (Zaghouani, 2014).

How customized list is built from dataset?

1- Hunspell detects 3463 unrepeated misspelled word in the dataset, like

للامريكيين*، الاف *
اإثيوبي
, ااسف
االشعب
االقاتل
,االمتظاهرين
,االمدعو
,االمدنين، االمرسوم

2- Hunspell generates suggestions for misspelled words, like

```
@(#) International Ispell Version 3.2.06 (but really Hunspell 1.3.2)
& للامريكيين 1 4: للأمريكيين

& الاف 15 1: الأف، الآف، ألاف، ألاق، الأأف، ألآف، إلاف، إلاق، آلاف، آلأف، آلآف، لافا، للاف، تلاف، غلاف
```

3- the script can select all words with one suggestion, and words with near suggestion as a common error. The script has select only 1727 non ambiguous case (not repeated).

The customized autocorrected list is used in test as CUSTOMIZED.

We got the following results (cf. Table 6) by using the M2 scorer (Dahlmeier et al 2012):

	Training		Test	
	STAND.	CUST.	STAND.	CUST.
Precision	0.6785	0.7383	0.698	0.7515
Recall	0.1109	0.2280	0.1233	0.2315
F_1.0	0.1906	0.3484	0.2096	0.35

Table 6 Training dataset evaluation

We note that the customized wordlist give us precision and recall better than the use of standard wordlist.

7 Conclusion

AutoCorrect for words is to propose a one correction for common errors in writing.

---

2 The Ghalatawi autocorrect program is available as an open source program at http://ghalatawi.sourceforge.net

In Arabic there are the following common mistakes: failure to differentiate between Hamza Wasl and Qat', confusion between the Dhah and Zah, and the omission of dots on Teh and under Yeh.

We have tried in this paper to find a way to adjust these errors automatically without human review, using a list of words and regular expressions to detect and correct errors.

This technique has been tried on the QALB corpus and gave mentioned results.

References

Hadjir،I، "Towards an open source arabic spell checker", magister in Natural language processing, scientific and technique research center to arabic language development, 2009.

Zerrouki T, "Improving the spell checking dictionary by users feedback" A meeting of experts check the spelling and grammar and composition automation, Higher Institute of Applied Science and Technology of Damascus, the Arab Organization for Education, Science and Culture, Damascus, April 18 to 20, 2011.

Deorowicz S،, Marcin G. Ciura, Correcting Spelling Errors By Modeling Their Causes. Int. J. Appl. Math. Comput. Sci., 2005, Vol. 15, No. 2, 275–285

Hammad M، and Mohamed Alhawari, recent improvement of arabic language search, Google Arabia Blog, Google company, 2010 http://google-arabia.blogspot.com/.

K Shaalan, A Allah, Towards automatic spell checking for Arabic... - Conference on Language Engineering, 2003 - claes.sci.eg

Graeme Hirst And Alexander Budanitsky, Correcting real-word spelling errors by restoring lexical cohesion, Natural Language Engineering 11 (1): 87–111, 2005 Cambridge University Press

Nizar Habash, Ryan M. Roth, Using Deep Morphology to Improve Automatic Error Detection in Arabic Handwriting Recognition, ACL, page 875-884. The Association for Computer Linguistics, (2011)

Behrang Mohit, Alla Rozovskaya, Wajdi Zaghouani, Ossama Obeid, and Nizar Habash , 2014. The First shared Task on Automatic Text Correction for Arabic.

Wajdi Zaghouani, Behrang Mohit, Nizar Habash, Ossama Obeid, Nadi Tomeh, Alla Rozovskaya, Noura Farra, Sarah Alkuhlani, and Kemal Oflazer. 2014. Large Scale Arabic Error Annotation: Guidelines and Framework. In Proceedings of the Ninth International Conference on Language Resources and Evaluation (LREC'14), Reykjavik, Iceland.

Golding and Roth. "A Winnow based approach to Context-Sensitive Spelling Correction". 1999.

Dahlmeier, Daniel and Ng, Hwee Tou. 2012. Better evaluation for grammatical error correction. In Proceedings of NAACL.

Habash, Nizar Y. "Introduction to Arabic natural language processing." Synthesis Lectures on Human Language Technologies 3.1 (2010): 1-187

Automatic Correction of Arabic Text: a Cascaded Approach

Hamdy Mubarak, Kareem Darwish
Qatar Computing Research Institute
Qatar Foundation
{hmubarak,kdarwish}@qf.org.qa

Abstract

This paper describes the error correction model that we used for the Automatic Correction of Arabic Text shared task. We employed two correction models, namely a character-level model and a case-specific model, and two punctuation recovery models, namely a simple statistical model and a CRF model. Our results on the development set suggest that using a cascaded correction model yields the best results.

1 Introduction

In This paper, we describe our system for automatic Arabic error correction shared task (QALB-2014 Shared Task on Automatic Correction of Arabic) as part of the Arabic NLP workshop (Mohit et al., 2014). Our system is composed of two main steps. The first involves correcting word level errors, and the second pertains to performing punctuation recovery. For word level correction, we used two approaches, namely: 1) a statistical character level transformation model that is aided by a language model (LM) to handle letter insertions, deletions, and substitutions and word merges; and 2) a case-specific system that is aided by a LM to handle specific error types such as dialectal word substitutions and word splits. For punctuation recovery, we used two approaches, namely a simple statistical word-based system, and a conditional random fields (CRF) sequence labeler (Lafferty et al., 2001) that attempts to recover punctuation based on POS and word sequences. We performed all experiments on the QALB dataset (Zaghouani et al., 2014).

2 Word Error Correction

In this section we describe two approaches for word correction. The first approach involves using a character level model, and the second handles specific correction cases.

2.1 Character-level Correction Model

For the character level model, we treated correction as a Transliteration Mining (TM) task. In TM, a sequence in a source alphabet is used to find the most similar sequence in a lexicon that is written in a target alphabet. TM has been fairly well studied with multiple evaluation campaigns such as the Named Entities Workshop (NEWS) (Zhang et al., 2011; Zhang et al., 2012). In our work, we adopted a TM system to find corrections appearing in a large Arabic corpus. The system involved learning character (or character-sequence) level mappings between erroneous words and their correct counterparts. Given the character mappings between the erroneous and correct words, we used a generative model that attempts to generate all possible mappings of a source word while restricting the output to words in the target language (El-Kahki et al., 2011; Noeman and Madkour, 2010). Specifically, we used the baseline system of El-Kahky et al. (2011). To train character-level mappings, we extracted all the parallel word-pairs in the original (uncorrected) and corrected versions in the training set. If a word in the original version of the training set was actually correct, the word would be mapped to itself. We then aligned the parallel word pairs at character level using GIZA++ (Och and Ney, 2003), and symmetrized the alignments using grow-diag-

Proceedings of the EMNLP 2014 Workshop on Arabic Natural Langauge Processing (ANLP), pages 132–136,
October 25, 2014, Doha, Qatar.

final-and heuristic (Koehn et al., 2007). In all, we aligned a little over one million word pairs. As in the baseline of El-Kahki et al. (2011), given a possibly misspelled word w_{org}, we produced all its possible segmentations along with their associated mappings that we learned during alignment. Valid target sequences were retained and sorted by the product of the constituent mapping probabilities. The top n (we picked n = 10) candidates, $w_{trg_{1..n}}$ with the highest probability were generated. Using Bayes rule, we computed:

$$\underset{w_{trg_{i\in 1..n}}}{argmax}\, p(w_{trg_i}|w_{org}) = p(w_{org}|w_{trg_i})p(w_{trg_i}) \quad (1)$$

where $p(w_{org}|w_{trg_i})$ is the posterior probability of mapping, which is computed as the product of the mappings required to generate w_{org} from w_{trg_i}, and $p(w_{trg_i})$ is the prior probability of the word. Then we used a trigram LM to pick the most likely candidate in context. We used a linear combination of the the character-level transformation probability and the LM probability using the following formula: $score = \lambda log(Prob_{LM}) + (1-\lambda)log(Prob_{char})$
We built the lexicon from a set of 234,638 Aljazeera articles[1] that span 10 years and all of Arabic Wikipedia. We also built a trigram language model on the same corpus. The combined corpus contains 576 million tokens including 1.6 million unique ones. Spelling mistakes in Aljazeera articles (Mubarak et al., 2010) and Wikipedia were infrequent.

We varied the value of λ between 0 and 1 with increments of 0.1 and found that the values 0.6 and 0.7 yielded the best results. This indicates that LM probability is more important than character-mapping probability.

2.2 Case-specific Correction

In this method we attempted to address specific types of errors that are potentially difficult for the character-based model to handle. Some of these errors include dialectal words and words that were erroneously split. Before applying any correction, we consulted a bigram LM that was trained the aforementioned set of Aljazeera articles. The following cases are handled (in order):

- Switching from English punctuations to Arabic ones, namely changing: "?" → "؟" and "," → "،".

- Handling common dialectal words and common word-level mistakes. An example dialectal word is اللي (Ally)[2] (meaning "this" or "that") which could be mapped to الذي (Al*y) , التي (Alty) or الذين (Al*yn). An example of a common mistake is انشاء الله (An$A' Allh) (meaning "God willing") which is corrected to إن شاء الله (>n $A' Allh). The sentence is scored with and without the word replacement, and the replacement is done if it yields higher LM probability.

- Handling errors pertaining to the different forms of *alef*, *alef maqsoura* and *ya*, and *ta marbouta* and *ha* (Nizar Habash, 2010). We reimplemented the baseline system in (Moussa et al., 2012) where words are normalized and the different possible denormalized forms are scored in context using the LM. We also added the following cases, namely attempting to replace: ؤ (&) with ؤو (&w) or ئو (}w); and ئ (}) with يء (y') or vice versa (ex: مرؤس (mr&s) → مرؤوس (mr&ws)).

- Handling merges and splits. Often words are concatenated erroneously. Thus, we attempted to split all words that were at least 5 letters long after letters that don't change their shapes when they are connected to the letters following them, namely different alef forms, د (d), ذ (*), ر (r), ز (z), و (w), ة (p), and ى (Y) (ex: يارينا (yArbnA) → يا ربنا (yA rbnA)). If the bigram was observed in the LM and the LM score was higher (in context) than when they were concatenated, then the word was split. Conversely, some words were split in the middle. We attempted to merge every two words in sequence. If the LM score was higher (in context) after the merge, then the two words would be merged (ex:

[1] http://www.aljazeera.net

[2] Buckwalter transiteration

انتصار ات (AntSAr At) → انتصارات (AntSArAt)).

• Removing repeated letters. Often people repeat letters, particularly long vowels, for emphasis as in أخييييراااا (>xyyyyrAAA) (meaning "at last"). We corrected for elongation in a manner similar to that of Darwish et al. (Darwish et al., 2012). When a long vowel are repeated, we replaced it with a either the vowel (ex. أخيرا (>xyrA) or the vowel with one repetition (ex. أخييرا (>xyyrA) and scored using the LM. If a repeated *alef* appeared in the beginning of the word, we attempted to replace it with alef lam (ex. اا حضارة (AAHDArp) → الحضارة (AlHDArp) (meaning "civilization")). A trailing alef-hamza-alef sequence was replaced by alef-hamza (ex. سماء ا (smA'A) → سماء (smA') (meaning "sky")).

• Correcting out-of-vocabulary words. For words that were not observed in the LM, we attempted the following corrections: 1) replacing phonetically or visually confusable letters, namely ض (D) and ظ (Z), د (d) and ذ (*), and ذ (*) and ز; (z) (ex: ظابط (ZAbT) → ضابط (DAbT)) 2) removing the letters ب (b) and د (d) that are added to verbs in present tense in some dialects (ex: بيكتب (byktb) → يكتب (yktb)); 3) replacing the letters ح (H) and ه (h), which are added in some dialects to indicate future tense, with س (s) (ex: حيشرب (Hy$rb) → سيشرب (sy$rb)); and 4) replacing a leading ها (hAl) with either هذا ال (h*A Al) or هذه ال (h*h Al) (ex. هالكتاب (hAlktAb) → هذا الكتاب (h*A AlktAb)) and the leading عال (EAl) with على ال (ElY Al) (ex. عالأرض (EAl>rD) → على الأرض(ElY Al>rD)). After replacement, the LM was always consulted.

2.3 Correction Results

Table 1 reports on the results of performing both correction methods on the development set. Also, since

Method	F-measure
Character-level	0.574
Case-specific	0.587
Character-level → Case-specific	0.615
Case-specific → Character-level	0.603

Table 1: The correction results using the character-level model, case-specific correction, or their cascades.

the case-specific corrections handle cases that were not handled by the character-level model, we attempted to cascade both methods together. It seems that when applying the character-level model first followed by the case-specific correction yielded the best results.

3 Punctuation Recovery

In this section, we describe two methods for punctuation recovery. The first is a simple word-based model and the other is a CRF based model.

3.1 Simple Statistical Model

In this approach, we identified words that were preceded or followed by punctuations in the training set. If a word was preceded or followed by a particular punctuation mark more than 40% of the time, then we automatically placed the punctuation before or after the word in the dev set. Also, if a sentence did not have a period at the end of it, we added a period.

3.2 CRF Model

In this approach we trained a CRF sequence labeling to attempt to recover punctuation. CRF combines state and transition level features making it a possibly better choice than an HMM or a simple classifier. We used the CRF++ implementation[3] of the sequence labeler. We trained the labeler on the training part of the QALB dataset. We used the following features:

Word features: the current word, the previous and next words, and the two previous and two next words.

Part-of-speech (POS) tags: the POS of the current

[3] http://crfpp.googlecode.com/svn/trunk/doc/index.html

Method	Precision	Recall	F-measure
Stat model	0.306	0.153	0.204
CRF model	0.373	0.141	0.204

Table 2: The punctuation recovery results using the simple statistical model and the CRF model.

Method	F-measure
Stat model (before correction)	0.593
Stat model (after correction)	0.614
CRF model (before correction)	0.607
CRF model (after correction)	0.615

Table 3: Cascaded correction (Character-level → Case-specific) combined with punctuation recovery.

word and the POS of the two previous and two following words.

3.3 Punctuation Recovery Results

Table 2 reports on the results of using the two different methods for punctuation recovery. Note that no other correction is applied.

4 Combining Correction with Punctuation Recovery

Given that cascading both correction models yielded the best results, we attempted to combine the cascaded correction model with the two punctuation recovery methods. We tried to put punctuation recovery before and after correction. Table 3 summarizes the results. As the results suggest, combining correction with punctuation recovery had a negative effect on overall F-measure. This requires further investigation.

5 Official Shared Task Experiments and Results

For the official submissions to the shared task, we submitted 3 runs as follows:

1. QCRI-1: character-level correction, then case-based correction.
2. QCRI-2: case-based correction, then statistical punctuation recovery
3. QCRI-3: exactly like 2, but preceded also by statistical punctuation recovery

Run	Precision	Recall	F-measure
QCRI-1	0.717	0.5686	0.6343
QCRI-2	0.6286	0.6032	0.6157
QCRI-3	0.6066	0.5928	0.5996

Table 4: Official Results.

Table 4 reports on the officially submitted results against the test set. It seems that our attempts to add punctuation recovery worsened results.

6 Conclusion

In this paper, we presented automatic approaches for correcting Arabic text and punctuation recovery. Our results on the development set shows that using a cascaded approach that involves a character-level model and another model that handles specific errors yields the best results. Incorporating punctuation recovery did not improve correction.

References

Kareem Darwish, Walid Magdy, and Ahmed Mourad. 2012. Language processing for arabic microblog retrieval. Proceedings of the 21st ACM international conference on Information and knowledge management. ACM, 2012.

Ali El-Kahky, Kareem Darwish, Ahmed Saad Aldein, Mohamed Abd El-Wahab, Ahmed Hefny, and Waleed Ammar. 2001. Improved transliteration mining using graph reinforcement. In Proceedings of the Conference on Empirical Methods in Natural Language Processing, pp. 1384-1393, 2011.

Nizar Habash. 2010. Introduction to Arabic natural language processing. Synthesis Lectures on Human Language Technologies 3.1 (2010): 1-187

Philipp Koehn, Hieu Hoang, Alexandra Birch, Chris Callison-Burch, Marcello Federico, Nicola Bertoldi, Brooke Cowan, Wade Shen, Christine Moran, Richard Zens, Chris Dyer, Ondrej Bojar, Alexandra Constantin, Evan Herbst, Moses: Open Source Toolkit for Statistical Machine Translation, Annual Meeting of the Association for Computational Linguistics (ACL), demonstration session, Prague, Czech Republic, June 2007.

J. Lafferty, A. McCallum, and F. Pereira. 2001. Conditional random fields: Probabilistic models for segmenting and labeling sequence data, In Proc. of ICML, pp.282-289, 2001.

Behrang Mohit, Alla Rozovskaya, Nizar Habash, Wajdi Zaghouani, and Ossama Obeid, 2014. The First QALB

Shared Task on Automatic Text Correction for Arabic. In Proceedings of EMNLP workshop on Arabic Natural Language Processing. Doha, Qatar.

Mohammed Moussa, Mohamed Waleed Fakhr, and Kareem Darwish. 2012. Statistical denormalization for Arabic Text. In Empirical Methods in Natural Language Processing, pp. 228. 2012.

Hamdy Mubarak, Ahmed Metwali, Mostafa Ramadan. 2010. Spelling Mistakes in Arabic Newspapers. Arabic Language and Scientific Researches conference, Faculty of Arts, Ain Shams University, Cairo, Egypt

Sara Noeman and Amgad Madkour. 2010. Language Independent Transliteration Mining System Using Finite State Automata Framework. ACL NEWS workshop 2010.

Franz J. Och and Hermann Ney. 2003. A Systematic Comparison of Various Statistical Alignment Models. Computational Linguistics, Vol. 1(29), 2003.

Wajdi Zaghouani, Behrang Mohit, Nizar Habash, Ossama Obeid, Nadi Tomeh, Alla Rozovskaya, Noura Farra, Sarah Alkuhlani, and Kemal Oflazer. 2014. Large Scale Arabic Error Annotation: Guidelines and Framework. In Proceedings of the Ninth International Conference on Language Resources and Evaluation (LREC14), Reykjavik, Iceland.

Min Zhang, A Kumaran, Haizhou Li. 2011. Whitepaper of NEWS 2012 Shared Task on Machine Transliteration. IJCNLP-2011 NEWS workshop.

Min Zhang, Haizhou Li, Ming Liu, A Kumaran. 2012. Whitepaper of NEWS 2012 Shared Task on Machine Transliteration. ACL-2012 NEWS workshop.

CMUQ@QALB-2014: An SMT-based System for Automatic Arabic Error Correction

Serena Jeblee[1] , Houda Bouamor[2], Wajdi Zaghouani[2] and Kemal Oflazer[2]
[1]**Carnegie Mellon University**
sjeblee@cs.cmu.edu
[2]**Carnegie Mellon University in Qatar**
{hbouamor,wajdiz}@qatar.cmu.edu, ko@cs.cmu.edu

Abstract

In this paper, we describe the CMUQ system we submitted to The ANLP-QALB 2014 Shared Task on Automatic Text Correction for Arabic. Our system combines rule-based linguistic techniques with statistical language modeling techniques and machine translation-based methods. Our system outperforms the baseline and reaches an F-score of 65.42% on the test set of QALB corpus. This ranks us 3rd in the competition.

1 Introduction

The business of text creation and editing represents a large market where NLP technologies might be applied naturally (Dale, 1997). Today's users of word processors get surprisingly little help in checking spelling, and a small number of them use more sophisticated tools such as grammar checkers, to provide help in ensuring that a text remains grammatically accurate after modification. For instance, in the Arabic version of Microsoft Word, the spelling checker for Arabic, does not give reasonable and natural proposals for many real-word errors and even for simple probable errors (Haddad and Yaseen, 2007).

With the increased usage of computers in the processing of natural languages comes the need for correcting errors introduced at different stages. Natural language errors are not only made by human operators at the input stage but also by NLP systems that produce natural language output. Machine translation (MT), or optical character recognition (OCR), often produce incorrect output riddled with odd lexical choices, grammar errors, or incorrectly recognized characters. Correcting human/machine-produced errors, or post-editing, can be manual or automated. For morphologically and syntactically complex languages, such as Modern Standard Arabic (MSA), correcting texts automatically requires complex human and machine processing which makes generation of correct candidates a challenging task.

For instance, the Automatic Arabic Text Correction Shared Task is an interesting testbed to develop and evaluate spelling correction systems for Arabic trained either on naturally occurring errors in texts written by humans (e.g., non-native speakers), or machines (e.g., MT output). In such tasks, participants are asked to implement a system that takes as input Modern Standard Arabic texts with various spelling errors and automatically correct them. In this paper, we describe the CMUQ system we developed to participate in the The First Shared Task on Automatic Text Correction for Arabic (Mohit et al., 2014). Our system combines rule-based linguistic techniques with statistical language modeling techniques and machine translation-based methods. Our system outperforms the baseline, achieves a better correction quality and reaches an F-score of 62.96% on the development set of QALB corpus (Zaghouani et al., 2014) and 65.42% on the test set.

The remainder of this paper is organized as follows. First, we review the main previous efforts for automatic spelling correction, in Section 2. In Section 3, we describe our system, which consists of several modules. We continue with our experiments on the shared task 2014 dev set (Section 4). Then, we give an analysis of our system output in Section 5. Finally, we conclude and hint towards future improvement of the system, in Section 6.

2 Related Work

Automatic error detection and correction include automatic spelling checking, grammar checking and post-editing. Numerous approaches (both supervised and unsupervised) have been explored to improve the fluency of the text and reduce the percentage of out-of-vocabulary words using NLP tools, resources, and heuristics, e.g., morphological analyzers, language models, and edit-distance measure (Kukich, 1992; Oflazer, 1996; Zribi and Ben Ahmed, 2003; Shaalan et al., 2003; Haddad and Yaseen, 2007; Hassan et al., 2008; Habash, 2008; Shaalan et al., 2010). There has been a lot of work on error correction for English (e.g., (Golding and Roth, 1999)). Other approaches learn models of correction by training on paired examples of errors and their corrections, which is the main goal of this work.

For Arabic, this issue was studied in various directions and in different research work. In 2003, Shaalan et al. (2003) presented work on the specification and classification of spelling errors in Arabic. Later on, Haddad and Yaseen (2007) presented a hybrid approach using morphological features and rules to fine

Proceedings of the EMNLP 2014 Workshop on Arabic Natural Langauge Processing (ANLP), pages 137–142,
October 25, 2014, Doha, Qatar. ©2014 Association for Computational Linguistics

tune the word recognition and non-word correction method. In order to build an Arabic spelling checker, Attia et al. (2012) developed semi-automatically, a dictionary of 9 million fully inflected Arabic words using a morphological transducer and a large corpus. They then created an error model by analyzing error types and by creating an edit distance ranker. Finally, they analyzed the level of noise in different sources of data and selected the optimal subset to train their system. Alkanhal et al. (2012) presented a stochastic approach for spelling correction of Arabic text. They used a context-based system to automatically correct misspelled words. First of all, a list is generated with possible alternatives for each misspelled word using the Damerau-Levenshtein edit distance, then the right alternative for each misspelled word is selected stochastically using a lattice search, and an n-gram method. Shaalan et al. (2012) trained a Noisy Channel Model on word-based unigrams to detect and correct spelling errors. Dahlmeier and Ng (2012a) built specialized decoders for English grammatical error correction. More recently, (Pasha et al., 2014) created MADAMIRA, a system for morphological analysis and disambiguation of Arabic, this system can be used to improve the accuracy of spelling checking system especially with Hamza spelling correction.

In contrast to the approaches described above, we use a machine translation (MT) based method to train an error correction system. To the best of our knowledge, this is the first error correction system for Arabic using an MT approach.

3 Our System

Our system is a pipeline that consists of several different modules. The baseline system uses a spelling checking module, and the final system uses a phrase-based statistical machine translation system. To preproces the text, we use the provided output of MADAMIRA (Pasha et al., 2014) and a rule-based correction. We then do a rule-based post-processing to fix the punctuation.

3.1 Baseline Systems

For the baseline system, we try a common spelling checking approach. We first pre-process the data using the features from MADAMIRA (see Feature 14 Replacement), then we use a noisy channel model for spelling checking.

Feature 14 Replacement

The first step in the pipeline is to extract MADAMIRA's 14th feature from the *.column file* and replace each word in the input text with this form. MADAMIRA uses morphological disambiguation and SVM analysis to select the most likely fully diacritized Arabic word for the input word. The 14th feature represents the undiacritized form of the most likely word. This step corrects many Hamza placement or omission errors, which makes a good base for other correction modules.

Spelling Correction

The spelling checker is based on a noisy channel model - we use a word list and language model to determine the most probable correct Arabic word that could have generated the incorrect form that we have in the text. For detecting spelling errors we use the AraComLex word list for spelling checking (Attia et al., 2012), which contains about 9 million Arabic words.[1] We look up the word from the input sentence in this list, and attempt to correct those that are not found in the list. We also train a mapping of incorrect words and possible corrections from the edits in the training data. If the word is in this map, the list of possible corrections from the training data becomes the candidate list. If the word is not in the trained map, the candidate list is created by generating a list of words with common insertions, substitutions, and deletions, according to the list in (Attia et al., 2012). Each candidate is generated by performing these edits and has a weight according to the edit distance weights in the list. We then prune the candidate list by keeping only the lowest weight words, and removing candidates that are not found in the word list. The resulting sentence is scored with a 3-gram language model built with KenLM (Heafield et al., 2013) on the correct side of the training data. The top one sentence is then kept and considerd as the "corrected" one.

This module handles spelling errors of individual words; it does not handle split/merge errors or word reordering. The spelling checker sometimes attempts to correct words that were already correct, because the list does not contain named entities or transliterations, and it does not contain all possible correct Arabic words. Because the spelling checker module decreased the overall performance, it is not included in our final system.

3.2 Final System

Feature 14 Replacement

The first step in our final system is Feature 14 Replacement, as described above.

Rule-based Clitic Correction

With the resulting data, we apply a set of rules to reattach clitics that may have been split apart from the base word. After examining the train dataset, we realized that 95% of word merging cases involve "و" attachment. When found by themselves, the clitics are attached to either the previous word or next word, based on whether they generally appear as prefixes or suffixes. The clitics handled by this module are specified in Table 2.

We also remove extra characters by replacing a sequence of 3 or more of the same character with a single

[1] http://sourceforge.net/projects/arabic-wordlist/

	Dev					
	Exact Match			No Punct		
	Precision	Recall	F1	Precision	Recall	F1
Feature 14	0.7746	0.3210	0.4539	0.8100	0.5190	0.6326
Feature 14 + Spelling checker (baseline)	0.4241	0.3458	0.3810	0.4057	0.4765	0.4382
Feature 14 + Clitic Rules	0.7884	0.3642	0.4983	0.8149	0.5894	0.6841
Feature 14 + Phrase-based MT	0.7296	0.5043	0.5964	0.7797	0.6397	0.7028
Feature 14 + Clitic Rules + Phrase-based MT	0.7571	0.5389	**0.6296**	0.8220	0.6850	**0.7473**
	Test					
Feature 14 + Clitic Rules + Phrase-based MT	0.7797	0.5635	**0.6542**	0.7438	0.6855	**0.7135**

Table 1: System results on the dev set (upper part) and on the test set (lower part).

Attach clitic to...	Clitics
Beginning of next word	{س, ف, ب, ال, و}
End of previous word	{ا, كم, ي, ني, نا, ها, ك}

Table 2: Clitics handled by the rule-based module.

instance of that character (e.g. !!!!!!! would be replaced with !).

Statistical Phrase-based Model

We use the Moses toolkit (Koehn et al., 2007) to create a statistical phrase-based machine translation model built on the best pre-processed data, as described above. We treat this last step as a translation problem, where the source language is pre-processed incorrect Arabic text, and the reference is correct Arabic. Feature 14 extraction, rule-based correction, and character de-duplication are applied to both the train and dev sets. All but the last 1,000 sentences of the train data are used at the training set for the phrase-based model, the last 1,000 sentences of the train data are used as a tuning set, and the dev set is used for testing and evaluation. We use fast_align, the aligner included with the cdec decoder (Dyer et al., 2010) as the word aligner with grow-diag as the symmetrization heuristic (Och and Ney, 2003), and build a 5-gram language model from the correct Arabic training data with KenLM (Heafield et al., 2013). The system is evaluated with BLEU (Papineni et al., 2002) and then scored for precision, recall, and F1 measure against the dev set reference.

We tested several different reordering window sizes since this is not a standard translation task, so we may want shorter distance reordering. Although 7 is the default size, we tested 7, 5, 4, 3, and 0, and found that a window of size 4 produces the best result according to BLEU score and F1 measure.

4 Experiments and Results

We train and evaluate our system with the training and development datasets provided for the shared task and the m2Scorer (Dahlmeier and Ng, 2012b). These datasets are extracted from the QALB corpus of human-edited Arabic text produced by native speakers, non-native speakers and machines (Zaghouani et al., 2014).

We conducted a small scale statistical study on the 950K tokens training set used to build our system. We realized that 306K tokens are affected by a correction action which could be a word edit, insertion, deletion, split or merge. 169K tokens were edited to correct the spelling errors and 99K tokens were inserted (mostly punctuation marks). Furthermore, there is a total of 6,7K non necessary tokens deleted and 10.6K attached tokens split and 18.2 tokens merged. Finally, there are only 427 tokens moved in the sentence and 1563 multiple correction action.

We experiment with different configurations and reach the sweet spot of performance when combining the different modules.

4.1 Results

To evaluate the performance of our system on the development data, we compare its output to the reference (gold annotation). We then compute the usual measures of precision, recall and f-measure. Results for various system configurations on the dev and test sets are given in Table 1. Using the baseline system consisting in replacing words by their non diacritized form (Feature 14), we could correct 51.9% of the errors occurring in the dev set, when punctuation is not considered. This result drops when we consider the punctuation errors which seem to be more complex to correct: Only 32.1% of the errors are corrected in the dev set. It is important to notice that adding the clitic rules to the Feature 14 baseline yields an improvement of + 5.15 in F-measure. We reach the best F-measure value when using the phrase-based MT system after pre-processing the data and applying the Feature 14 and clitic rules. Using this combination we were able to correct 68.5% of the errors (excluding punctuation) on the development set with a precision of 82.2% and 74.38% on the test set. When we consider the punctuation, 53.89% of the errors of different types were corrected on the dev set and 56.35% on the test set with a precision of 75.71% and 77.97%, respectively.

5 Error Analysis and Discussion

When building error correction systems, minimizing the number of cases where correct words are marked as incorrect is often regarded as more important than covering a high number of errors. Therefore, a higher precision is often preferred over higher recall. In order to understand what was affecting the performance, we took a closer look at our system output and translation tables to present some samples of errors that our system makes on development set.

5.1 Out-of-vocabulary Words

This category includes words that are not seen by our system during the training which is a common problem in machine translation systems. In our system, most of out-of-vocabulary words were directly transferred unchanged from source to target. For example the word افلمسؤولية was not corrected to المسؤولية.

5.2 Unnecessary Edits

In some cases, our system made some superfluous edits such as adding the definite article in cases where it is not required such as :

Source	أطياف المدينة
Hypothesis	**الأطياف** المدينة
Reference	(unchanged) أطياف المدينة

Table 3: An example of an unnecessary addition of the definite article.

5.3 Number Normalization

We observed that in some cases, the system did not normalize the numbers such as in the following case which requires some knowledge of the real context to understand that these numbers require normalization.

Source	450000 ميغاوات
Hypothesis	450**000** ميغاوات
Reference	450 ميغاوات

Table 4: An example of number normalization.

5.4 Hamza Spelling

Even though our system corrected most of the Hamza spelling errors, we noticed that in certain cases they were not corrected, especially when the words without the Hamza were valid entries in the dictionary. These cases are not always easy to handle since only context and semantic rules can handle them.

5.5 Grammatical Errors

In our error analysis we encountered many cases of uncorrected grammatical errors. The most frequent type is the case endings correction such as correcting the verbs in jussive mode when there is a prohibition particle (negative imperative) like the (لا) in the following examples :

Source	واد الوطنية
Hypothesis	**واد** الوطنية
Reference	وأد الوطنية

Table 5: A sentence where the Hamza was not added above the Alif in the first word because both versions are valid dictionary entries.

Source	لا يضربوا على أياديهم
Hypothesis	لا **يضربوا** على أياديهم
Reference	لا يضربون على أياديهم

Table 6: An example of a grammatical error.

5.6 Unnecessary Word Deletion

According to the QALB annotation guidelines, extra words causing semantic ambiguity in the sentence should be deleted. The decision to delete a given word is usually based on the meaning and the understanding of the human annotator, unfortunately this kind of errors is very hard to process and our system was not able to delete most of the unnecessary words.

Source	هل سنشهد وضعا أيديهما مشينا آخر
Hypothesis	هل سنشهد وضعا **أيديهما** مشينا آخر
Reference	هل سنشهد وضعا مشينا آخر

Table 7: An example of word deletion.

5.7 Adding Extra Words

Our analysis revealed cases of extra words introduced to some sentences, despite the fact that the words added are coherent with the context and could even improve the overall readability of the sentence, they are uncredited correction since they are not included in the gold standard. For example :

Source	ضرب سمعة الجيش السوري
Hypothesis	ضرب سمعة الجيش السوري **الحر**
Reference	ضرب سمعة الجيش السوري

Table 8: An example of the addition of extra words.

5.8 Merge and Split Errors

In this category, we show some sample errors of necessary word splits and merge not done by our system. The word خصوصابعد should have been split as خصوصا بعد and the word لا بد should have been merged to appear as one word as in لابد.

5.9 Dialectal Correction Errors

Dialectal words are usually converted to their Modern Standard Arabic (MSA) equivalent in the QALB corpus, since dialectal words are rare, our system is unable to detect and translate the dialectal words to the MSA as in the expression مب زين that is translated in the gold standard to غير زين.

6 Conclusion

We presented our CMUQ system for automatic Arabic text correction. Our system combines rule-based linguistic techniques with statistical language modeling techniques and a phrase-based machine translation method. We experiment with different configurations. Our experiments have shown that the system we submitted outperforms the baseline and we reach an F-score of 74.73% on the development set from the QALB corpus when punctuation is excluded, and 65.42% on the test set when we consider the punctuation errors . This placed us in the 3rd rank. We believe that our system could be improved in numerous ways. In the future, we plan to finalize a current module that we are developing to deal with merge and split errors in a more specific way. We also want to focus in a deeper way on the word movement as well as punctuation problems, which can produce a more accurate system. We will focus as well on learning further error correction models from Arabic Wikipedia revision history, as it contains natural rewritings including spelling corrections and other local text transformations.

Acknowledgements

This publication was made possible by grants NPRP-09-1140-1-177 and NPRP-4-1058- 1-168 from the Qatar National Research Fund (a member of the Qatar Foundation). The statements made herein are solely the responsibility of the authors.

References

Mohamed I. Alkanhal, Mohamed Al-Badrashiny, Mansour M. Alghamdi, and Abdulaziz O. Al-Qabbany. 2012. Automatic Stochastic Arabic Spelling Correction With Emphasis on Space Insertions and Deletions. *IEEE Transactions on Audio, Speech & Language Processing*, 20(7):2111–2122.

Mohammed Attia, Pavel Pecina, Younes Samih, Khaled Shaalan, and Josef van Genabith. 2012. Improved Spelling Error Detection and Correction for Arabic. In *Proceedings of COLING 2012: Posters*, pages 103–112, Mumbai, India.

Daniel Dahlmeier and Hwee Tou Ng. 2012a. A Beam-Search Decoder for Grammatical Error Correction. In *Proceedings of the 2012 Joint Conference on Empirical Methods in Natural Language Processing and Computational Natural Language Learning*, pages 568–578, Jeju Island, Korea.

Daniel Dahlmeier and Hwee Tou Ng. 2012b. Better Evaluation for Grammatical Error Correction. In *NAACL HLT '12 Proceedings of the 2012 Conference of the North American Chapter of the Association for Computational Linguistics: Human Language Technologies*, pages 568–572.

Robert Dale. 1997. Computer Assistance in Text Creation and Editing. In *Survey of the state of the art in Human Language Technology*, chapter 7, pages 235–237. Cambridge University Press.

Chris Dyer, Jonathan Weese, Hendra Setiawan, Adam Lopez, Ferhan Ture, Vladimir Eidelman, Juri Ganitkevitch, Phil Blunsom, and Philip Resnik. 2010. cdec: A Decoder, Alignment, and Learning Framework for Finite-state and Context-free Translation Models. In *Proceedings of the ACL 2010 System Demonstrations*, pages 7–12, Uppsala, Sweden.

A. R. Golding and D. Roth. 1999. A Winnow Based Approach to Context-Sensitive Spelling Correction. *Machine Learning*, 34(1-3):107–130.

Nizar Habash. 2008. Four Techniques for Online Handling of Out-of-Vocabulary Words in Arabic-English Statistical Machine Translation. In *Proceedings of ACL-08: HLT, Short Papers*, pages 57–60, Columbus, Ohio.

Bassam Haddad and Mustafa Yaseen. 2007. Detection and Correction of Non-words in Arabic: a Hybrid Approach. *International Journal of Computer Processing of Oriental Languages*, 20(04):237–257.

Ahmed Hassan, Sara Noeman, and Hany Hassan. 2008. Language Independent Text Correction using Finite State Automata. In *Proceedings of the Third International Joint Conference on Natural Language Processing (IJCNLP 2008)*, pages 913–918, Hyderabad, India.

Kenneth Heafield, Ivan Pouzyrevsky, Jonathan H. Clark, and Philipp Koehn. 2013. Scalable Modfied Kneser-Ney Language Model Estimation. In *In Proceedings of the Association for Computational Linguistics*, Sofia, Bulgaria.

Philipp Koehn, Hieu Hoang, Alexandra Birch, Christopher Callison-Burch, Marcello Federico, Nicola Bertoldi, Brooke Cowan, Wade Shen, Christine Moran, Richard Zens, Christopher Dyer, Ondrej Bojar, Alexandra Constantin, and Evan Herbst. 2007. Moses: Open Source Toolkit for Statistical Machine Translation. In *Proceedings of the 45th Annual Meeting of the Association for Computational Linguistics Companion Volume Proceedings of the Demo and Poster Sessions*, pages 177–180, Prague, Czech Republic.

Karen Kukich. 1992. Techniques for Automatically Correcting Words in Text. *ACM Computing Surveys (CSUR)*, 24(4):377–439.

Behrang Mohit, Alla Rozovskaya, Nizar Habash, Wajdi Zaghouani, and Ossama Obeid. 2014. The First QALB Shared Task on Automatic Text Correction for Arabic. In *Proceedings of EMNLP Workshop on Arabic Natural Language Processing*, Doha, Qatar, October.

Franz Josef Och and Hermann Ney. 2003. A Systematic Comparison of Various Statistical Alignment Models. In *Computational Linguistics*, page 1951.

Kemal Oflazer. 1996. Error-Tolerant Finite-State Recognition with Applications to Morphological Analysis and Spelling Correction. *Computational Linguistics*, 22(1):73–89.

Kishore Papineni, Salim Roukos, Todd Ward, and Wei-Jing Zhu. 2002. BLEU: A Method for Automatic Evaluation of Machine Translation. In *Proceedings of the Association for Computational Linguistics*, Philadelphia, Pennsylvania.

Arfath Pasha, Mohamed Al-Badrashiny, Mona Diab, Ahmed El Kholy, Ramy Eskander, Nizar Habash, Manoj Pooleery, Owen Rambow, and Ryan Roth. 2014. MADAMIRA: A Fast, Comprehensive Tool for Morphological Analysis and Disambiguation of Arabic. In *Proceedings of the Ninth International Conference on Language Resources and Evaluation (LREC'14)*, pages 1094–1101, Reykjavik, Iceland.

Khaled Shaalan, Amin Allam, and Abdallah Gomah. 2003. Towards Automatic Spell Checking for Arabic. In *Proceedings of the 4th Conference on Language Engineering, Egyptian Society of Language Engineering (ELSE)*, Cairo, Egypt.

Khaled Shaalan, Rana Aref, and Aly Fahmy. 2010. An Approach for Analyzing and Correcting Spelling Errors for Non-native Arabic Learners. In *Proceedings of The 7th International Conference on Informatics and Systems, INFOS2010, the special track on Natural Language Processing and Knowledge Mining*, pages 28–30, Cairo, Egypt.

Khaled Shaalan, Mohammed Attia, Pavel Pecina, Younes Samih, and Josef van Genabith. 2012. Arabic Word Generation and Modelling for Spell Checking. In *Proceedings of the Eighth International Conference on Language Resources and Evaluation (LREC-2012)*, pages 719–725, Istanbul, Turkey.

Wajdi Zaghouani, Behrang Mohit, Nizar Habash, Ossama Obeid, Nadi Tomeh, Alla Rozovskaya, Noura Farra, Sarah Alkuhlani, and Kemal Oflazer. 2014. Large Scale Arabic Error Annotation: Guidelines and Framework. In *Proceedings of the Ninth International Conference on Language Resources and Evaluation (LREC'14)*, Reykjavik, Iceland.

Chiraz Zribi and Mohammed Ben Ahmed. 2003. Efficient Automatic Correction of Misspelled Arabic Words Based on Contextual Information. In *Proceedings of the Knowledge-Based Intelligent Information and Engineering Systems Conference*, pages 770–777, Oxford, UK.

Fast and Robust Arabic Error Correction System

Michael N. Nawar
Computer Engineering Department
Cairo University
Giza, Egypt
michael.nawar@eng.cu.edu.eg

Moheb M. Ragheb
Computer Engineering Department
Cairo University
Giza, Egypt
moheb.ragheb@eng.cu.edu.eg

Abstract

In this paper we describe the implementation of an Arabic error correction system developed for the EMNLP2014 shared task on automatic error correction for Arabic text. We proposed a novel algorithm, where we find some correction rules and calculate their probability based on the training data, they we rank the correction rules, then we apply them on the text to maximize the overall F-score for the provided data. The system achieves and F-score of 0.6573 on the test data.

1 Introduction

Traditional techniques in text correction is the generation of a large set of candidates for an incorrect word using different approaches like enumerating all possible candidates in edit distance of one. Then, all the candidates are ranked such that the best candidates are ranked on the top of the list. Finally, the best candidate is chosen to replace incorrect word.

The traditional techniques are slow, since the generation of a large set of candidates is time consuming task. Also, it doesn't take into consideration the overall score of the system. While, in this paper we apply a novel technique in automatic error correction, where we take into consideration the correction rules, not the variants. In the propose technique, we order corrections to be applied on text to maximize the F-score.

This shared task was on automatic Arabic text correction. For this task, the Qatar Arabic Language Bank (QALB) corpus (Mohit et. al, 2014) was provided. The QALB corpus contains a preprocessed input text with some features extracted and the corrected output. The main issue in the shared task, that the tools used for the extraction of the provided features wasn't provided. So, we had a choice, to create an algorithm that can deal with missing features, or to generate our own set of features. Finally, we have chosen to generate our own set of features.

The proposed framework could be described as a probabilistic rule-based framework. During the training of this framework, we extracted some rules and assign a probability to each rule as shown later in section 3. The extracted rules are then sorted based on their probabilities. And during the test, we apply the rules from the highest probability to the lowest probability one by one, on the entire test data till a stopping criteria is satisfied. During the algorithm we have some kind of heuristic to estimate the F-score after each rule is apply. The stopping criteria for the algorithm is that the estimated F-score start to decrease.

This paper is organized as follow, in section 2, an overview of the related work in the field of error correction is discussed. In section 3, the proposed system and its main components are explained. The evaluation process is presented in section 4. Finally, concluding remarks and future work are presented in section 5.

2 Related Work

Most of the work done in the field automatic error correction for text, is made for English language (Kukich, 1992; Golding and Roth, 1999; Carlson and Fette, 2007; Banko and Brill, 2001). Arabic spelling correction has also received considerable interest, Ben Othmane Zribi and Ben Ahmed, (2003) have proposed a new aiming to reduce the number of proposals given by automatic Arabic spelling correction tools, which have reduced the proposals by about 75%. Haddad and Yaseen (2007) took into consideration the complex nature of the Arabic language and the effect of the root-pattern relationship to lo-

Proceedings of the EMNLP 2014 Workshop on Arabic Natural Langauge Processing (ANLP), pages 143–147,
October 25, 2014, Doha, Qatar. ©2014 Association for Computational Linguistics

cate, reduce and rank the most probable correction candidates in Arabic derivative words to improve the process of error detection and correction. Hassan et al. (2008) used a finite state automata to propose candidates corrections, then assign a score to each candidate and choose the best correction in the context. Shaalan et al. (2010) developed an error correction system to Arabic learners. Alkanhal et al. (2012) have developed an error correction system and they emphasized on space insertion and deletion. Zaghouani et al. (2014) provided a large scale dataset for the task of automatic error correction for Arabic text.

3 The Proposed System

The main system idea is explained by the algorithm, in figure 1. The algorithm has two inputs: the set of sentences that need to be modified T[1..n], and the set of correction rules C[1..m] that could be applied to text. The algorithm has one single output: the set of modified sentences T'[1..n]. The algorithm could be divided into two main component: the initialization and the main loop.

```
Input: T[1..n], C[1..m]
Output: T'[1..n]
1: T' = T
2: Gold Edits = #Words in Test * # Gold Edits in
Train / # Words in Train
3: Correct Edits = 0
4: Performed Edits = 0
5: Precision = 0
6: Recall = 0
7: Old F-score = 0
8: F-score = 0
9: Do
10:     T' = T
11:     Old F-score = F-score
12:     Get next correction "c" with the highest
        probability "p" from C
13:     Apply the correction "c" on T
14:     N = number of changes between T and
        T'
15:     Performed Edits = Performed Edits + N
16:     Correct Edits = Correct Edits + p * N
17:     Precision = Correct Edits / Performed
        Edits
18:     Recall = Correct Edits / Gold Edits
19:     F-score = 2*Precision*Recall / (Precision+Recall)
20: while F-score > Old F-score do
21: return T'
```

Figure 1: Proposed Algorithm

First, the initialization part of the algorithm starts from line 1 to line 8. In the first line, the sentences are copied from T[1..n] to T'[1..n]. In line number 2, the number of errors in the test set T[1..n] is expected using the rate of errors in the train set (#error / #words). In lines 3 to 8, the variables used in the algorithm are initialized to zero.

The main loop of the algorithm starts from line 9 to line 20. In line 9, the loop begins, and the sentences are copied from T[1..n] to T'[1..n] and the F-score is copied to old F-score, in linarae 10 and 11. Then the first not applied correction with the highest probability to be correct is correct is chosen in line 12. In line 13, the correction is applied on the text T[1..n]. Then we calculate the number of changes between T[1..n] and T'[1..n], in line 14. And based on the expected number of changes, we update the expected number of performed edits in line 14. Also, we update the expected number of the correct edits based on the number of change and the probability of a change to be correct in line 15. In lines 17 to 19, we calculate the expected precision, recall and F-score based on the expected gold edits, performed edits, and correct edits calculated at lines 2, 14, and 15. If the F-score is higher than the old F-score, which means that applying the correction c on the text T[1..n] will increase the expected F-score, then go to line 9 and start a new iteration in the loop. And if the F-score is lower than the old F-score, which means that applying the correction c on the text T[1..n] will decrease the expected F-score, then exit the loop and return the modified text T'[1..n].

After we have discussed the main idea of algorithm, in the following subsections we will discuss some of the extracted corrections rules and the calculation of the probability of each rule. These rules and their probabilities are compiled by analyzing the training data.

3.1 Morphological Analyzer Corrections Rules

We used a morphological analyzer, BAMA-v2.0 (Buckwalter Arabic morphological analyzer version 2.0) (Buckwalter, 2010), in the extraction of a correction rule. This rule will be used to solve the errors caused by the exchange between some characters like: ("ا", "A"), ("أ", ">"), ("إ", "<") and ("ه", "h"), ("ة", "p") and ("ي", "y"), ("ى", "Y").

RULE: We analyze a word with the morphological analyzer, if all the solutions of the word have the same form that is different from the word, then change the word by the solutions form.

For example, the word ("احمد", "AHmd"), when the word is analyzed by the morphological analyzer, there are 20 different solutions, 14 are proper noun ("أحمد", ">Hmd", "Ahmed") and the remaining 6 of them are verb ("أحمد", ">Hmd", "I praise"). Since all the solution of the word ("احمد", "AHmd") have the form ("أحمد", ">Hmd"), then we will change ("احمد", "AHmd") to ("أحمد", ">Hmd"). Another example, the word ("امام", "AmAm"), when the word is analyzed by the morphological analyzer, there are 24 different solutions, 12 of them have the form ("أمام", ">mAm"), and the other 12 have the form ("إمام", "<mAm"), so we leave it unchanged.

To calculate the correctness probability of the rule, we apply the following rule to all the training set, then we calculate the number of correct edits, and the number of performed edits, finally we calculate the probability as the ratio between the correct and the performed edits.

3.2 Colloquial to Arabic Corrections Rules

To convert the colloquial Arabic words to Arabic words, we have compiled some rules as shown below:

RULE: Replace a word or a phrase by a specific word or phrase from a list extracted from the training set provided in Qalb shared task (Mohit et. al, 2014).

From example replace the word ("احنا", "AHnA", "we") by the word ("نحن", "nHn", "we").

RULE: Replace a word or phrase with a specific word or phrase based on its context.

RULE: Replace a word or phrase with a specific pattern to another word or phrase.

From example replace the word ("بيلعب", "bylEb", "is playing") by the word ("يلعب", "ylEb", "is playing").

The correctness probability of each rule is the ratio between the correct and the performed edits when this rule is applied on the train data.

3.3 The Single Character Spelling Errors Correction

The single character spelling errors are divided into four main subcategories: replace character by another character, insert character, delete character, and transpose two adjacent characters. For these four errors, we have conducted four types of rules.

RULE 1: We analyze a word with the morphological analyzer, if it is outside the corpus, and it not defined in the correct words in qalb corpus (the words that don't change) try to change one character by a specific character, if the new word is recognized by the morphological analyzer or it is inside the corpus, then change the word and keep the new solution.

For example, if we have a word ("بعظ", "bEZ") and a rule that change the character ('ظ', 'Z') to ('ض', 'D'). And the word ("بعض", "bED") is recognized by the morphological analyzer, then we change the word ("بعظ", "bEZ") to ("بعض", "bED"). Another example, if we have the word ("بعظ", "bEZ") and a rule that change the character ('ع', 'E') to ('غ', 'g'). And the word ("بغظ", "bgZ") is not recognized by the morphological analyzer and it is outside the Qalb corpus, then we don't change the word.

RULE 2: We analyze a word with the morphological analyzer, if it is outside the corpus, and it not defined in the correct words in qalb corpus (the words that don't change) try to insert one specific character between a pair of specific characters, if the new word is recognized by the morphological analyzer or it is inside the corpus, then change the word and keep the new solution.

RULE 3: We analyze a word with the morphological analyzer, if it is outside the corpus, and it not defined in the correct words in qalb corpus (the words that don't change) try to delete one specific character from a triplet of specific characters, if the new word is recognized by the morphological analyzer or it is inside the corpus, then change the word and keep the new solution.

RULE 4: We analyze a word with the morphological analyzer, if it is outside the corpus, and it not defined in the correct words in Qalb corpus (the words that don't change) try to replace a pair of characters to the transpose of the pair of characters, if the new word is recognized by the morphological analyzer or it is inside the corpus, then change the word and keep the new solution.

The correctness probability of each rule is the ratio between the correct and the performed edits when this rule is applied on the train data, and it differs from one character to another (i.e. the two examples in rule 1, will have different correctness probabilities based on the training data).

3.4 The Space Insertion Errors Correction

The space insertion error correction is the process of splitting an incorrect word to multiple correct word.

RULE: If there is a character concatenated after taa marbouta ('ة', 'p'), insert a space between them.

RULE: If the word starts with negation particle, split negation particle from it.

RULE: If the word starts with vocative particle, split vocative particle from it.

RULE: If the word starts with vocative particle, split vocative particle from it.

RULE: We analyze a word with the morphological analyzer, if it is outside the corpus, and it not defined in the correct words in Qalb corpus (the words that don't change) try to find the long substring from the word, that keep another substring, where both of them are recognized by the morphological analyzer.

The correctness probability of each rule is the ratio between the correct and the performed edits when this rule is applied on the train data.

3.5 The Space Deletion Errors Correction

The space deletion errors correction is the process of merging multiple tokens into one correct word.

RULE: Merge conjunction particles, with their succeeding token.

RULE: If two out of corpus tokens could be merged to an inside the corpus word, then merge them.

The correctness probability of each rule is the ratio between the correct and the performed edits when this rule is applied on the train data.

3.6 Punctuation Errors Corrections

The punctuation errors are hard to correct because they depends on the meaning of the sentence, and require almost full understanding of the sentence. However, we have conducted some rules for the punctuation, for example:

RULE: If the sentence doesn't end with a punctuation point from (".", "!", "؟"), then add a point at the end of the sentence.

RULE: Insert a punctuation mark before a certain word.

For example, insert a semicolon before the word ("لأنه", "l>nH", "because he").

The correctness probability of each rule is the ratio between the correct and the performed edits when this rule is applied on the train data.

3.7 Syntactic Errors Corrections

The syntactic errors is one of the most difficult error to correct. For this task we apply a simple kind of a grammatical analyzer to assign simple grammatical tag to some words. One simple grammatical system, is the one to determine genitive noun. Nouns are genitive mainly if they occur after a preposition, or if they are possessives (definite noun after indefinite noun) or if they are adjectives of genitive nouns, or if they are conjunction with genitive noun.

RULE: Plural and Dual genitive nouns that end with ("ون", "wn") or ("ان", "An") should end with ("ين", "yn").

The correctness probability of each rule is the ratio between the correct and the performed edits when this rule is applied on the train data.

3.8 Additional Corrections Rules

Finally, we generated some rules that present the data on a correct format as the training data and we will assign their correctness probability manually to be equal to 1.

RULE: Remove kashida (tatweel) from text.

RULE: Replace "*" if between parenthesis by the Arabic character ('ذ', '*').

RULE: If a character is repeated consecutively more than twice inside a word, remove the extra characters except if the word consists of only one char like ("ههههه", "hhhhh").

RULE: Write a comma between two numbers.

4 Evaluation of the System

For the evaluation of the system, we used the M2 scorer by Dahlmeier and Ng (2012). When we evaluated the system with the development dataset, we have reached an F-score of 0.6817; and when the system is evaluated the test dataset, we have reached and F-score of 0.6573.

The proposed algorithm is very fast compared to traditional error correction algorithm. In traditional error correction algorithm, you generate all possible variants of an incorrect word, then you rank the solutions and choose the best solution. But, in the proposed algorithm, you rank the rules during the training time, and you apply one rule at the time until you find an appropriate solution of an incorrect word.

For example, let's consider single character replace spelling error, if the incorrect word length is five characters, so you need to make ((28-1)*5) iterations to generate all possible variants of a word, while in the proposed algorithm you generate one variant at the time, and you might stop after that.

5 Conclusion

In this paper we have presented a novel and fast algorithm for the automatic text correction for Arabic. The proposed algorithm has a good F-score, and the system has the potential to be further improved. As a future work, the punctuation error correction might need to be further improved. And the expected number of gold edits, could be improved or calculated on the sentence level. And finally, the rules used in the framework could be extended by further analysis of the training data.

References

Mohamed I. Alkanhal, Mohammed A. Al-Badrashiny, Mansour M. Alghamdi, and Abdulaziz O. AlQabbany. 2012. Automatic Stochastic Arabic Spelling Correction with Emphasis on Space Insertions and Deletions. *IEEE Transactions on Audio, Speech & Language Processing*, 20:2111–2122.

Michele Banko and Eric Brill, 2001. Scaling to very very large corpora for natural language disambiguation. In *Proceedings of 39th Annual Meeting of the Association for Computational Linguistics*. Toulouse, France.

Chiraz Ben Othmane Zribi and Mohammed Ben Ahmed. 2003. Efficient Automatic Correction of Misspelled Arabic Words Based on Contextual Information. In *Proceedings of the Knowledge-Based Intelligent Information and Engineering Systems Conference*, Oxford, UK.

Tim Buckwalter. 2010. Buckwalter Arabic Morphological Analyzer Version 2.0. Linguistic Data Consortium, University of Pennsylvania, 2002. LDC Catalog No.: LDC2004L02. ISBN 1-58563-324-0.

Andrew Carlson and Ian Fette. 2007. Memory-based context-sensitive spelling correction at web scale. In *Proceedings of the IEEE International Conference on Machine Learning and Applications (ICMLA)*.

Daniel Dahlmeier and Hwee Tou Ng. 2012. Better evaluation for grammatical error correction. In *Proceeding of the 2012 Conference of the North American Chapter of the Association for Computational Linguistics: Human Language Technologies.*

Andrew R. Golding and Dan Roth. 1999. A Winnow based approach to context-sensitive spelling correction. *Machine Learning*, 34(1-3):107–130.

Bassam Haddad and Mustafa Yaseen. 2007. Detection and Correction of Non-Words in Arabic: A Hybrid Approach. *International Journal of Computer Processing Of Languages (IJCPOL).*

Ahmed Hassan, Sara Noeman, and Hany Hassan. 2008. Language Independent Text Correction using Finite State Automata. In *Proceedings of the International Joint Conference on Natural Language Processing (IJCNLP 2008).*

Karen Kukich. 1992. Techniques for Automatically Correcting Words in Text. *ACM Computing Surveys*, 24(4).

Behrang Mohit, Alla Rozovskaya, Nizar Habash, Wajdi Zaghouani, and Ossama Obeid, 2014. The First shared Task on Automatic Text Correction for Arabic. In *Proceedings of EMNLP workshop on Arabic Natural Language Processing*. Doha, Qatar.

Khaled Shaalan, Rana Aref, and Aly Fahmy. 2010. An approach for analyzing and correcting spelling errors for non-native Arabic learners. In *Proceedings of Informatics and Systems (INFOS).*

Wajdi Zaghouani, Behrang Mohit, Nizar Habash, Ossama Obeid, Nadi Tomeh, Alla Rozovskaya, Noura Farra, Sarah Alkuhlani, and Kemal Oflazer. 2014. Large Scale Arabic Error Annotation: Guidelines and Framework. In *Proceedings of the Ninth International Conference on Language Resources and Evaluation (LREC'14)*, Reykjavik, Iceland.

GWU-HASP: Hybrid Arabic Spelling and Punctuation Corrector[1]

Mohammed Attia, Mohamed Al-Badrashiny, Mona Diab
Department of Computer Science
The George Washington University
{Mohattia;badrashiny;mtdiab}@gwu.edu

Abstract

In this paper, we describe our Hybrid Arabic Spelling and Punctuation Corrector (HASP). HASP was one of the systems participating in the QALB-2014 Shared Task on Arabic Error Correction. The system uses a CRF (Conditional Random Fields) classifier for correcting punctuation errors, an open-source dictionary (or word list) for detecting errors and generating and filtering candidates, an n-gram language model for selecting the best candidates, and a set of deterministic rules for text normalization (such as removing diacritics and kashida and converting Hindi numbers into Arabic numerals). We also experiment with word alignment for spelling correction at the character level and report some preliminary results.

1 Introduction

In this paper we describe our system for Arabic spelling error detection and correction, Hybrid Arabic Spelling and Punctuation Corrector (HASP). We participate with HASP in the QALB-2014 Shared Task on Arabic Error Correction (Mohit et al., 2014) as part of the Arabic Natural Language Processing Workshop (ANLP) taking place at EMNLP 2014.

The shared task data deals with "errors" in the general sense which comprise: a) punctuation errors; b) non-word errors; c) real-word spelling errors; d) grammatical errors; and, e) orthographical errors such as elongation (kashida) and speech effects such as character multiplication for emphasis. HASP in its current stage only handles types (a), (b), and (e) errors. We assume that the various error types are too distinct to be treated with the same computational technique. Therefore, we treat each problem separately, and for each problem we select the approach that seems most efficient, and ultimately all components are integrated in a single framework.

1.1 Previous Work

Detecting spelling errors in typing is one of the earliest NLP applications, and it has been researched extensively over the years, particularly for English (Damerau, 1964; Church and Gale, 1991; Kukich, 1992; Brill and Moore, 2000; Van Delden et al., 2004; Golding, 1995; Golding and Roth, 1996; Fossati and Di Eugenio, 2007; Islam in Inkpen, 2009; Han and Baldwin, 2011; Wu et al., 2013).

The problem of Arabic spelling error correction has been investigated in a number of papers (Haddad and Yaseen, 2007; Alfaifi and Atwell, 2012; Hassan et al., 2008; Shaalan et al., 2012; Attia et al., 2012; Alkanhal et al., 2012).

In our research, we address the spelling error detection and correction problem with a focus on non-word errors. Our work is different from previous work on Arabic in that we cover punctuation errors as well. Furthermore, we fine-tune a Language Model (LM) disambiguator by adding probability scores for candidates using forward-backward tracking, which yielded better results than the default Viterbi. We also develop a new and more efficient splitting algorithm for merged words.

1.2 Arabic Morphology, Orthography and Punctuation

Arabic has a rich and complex morphology as it applies both concatenative and non-concatenative morphotactics (Ratcliffe, 1998; Beesley, 1998; Habash, 2010), yielding a wealth of morphemes that express various morpho-

[1] This work was supported by the Defense Advanced Research Projects Agency (DARPA) Contract No. HR0011-12-C-0014, BOLT program with subcontract from Raytheon BBN.

Proceedings of the EMNLP 2014 Workshop on Arabic Natural Langauge Processing (ANLP), pages 148–154,
October 25, 2014, Doha, Qatar.

syntactic features, such as tense, person, number, gender, voice and mood.

Arabic has a large array of orthographic variations, leading to what is called ‘typographic errors’ or ‘orthographic variations’ (Buckwalter, 2004a), and sometimes referred to as substandard spellings, or spelling soft errors. These errors are basically related to the possible overlap between orthographically similar letters in three categories: a) the various shapes of *hamzahs* (ا A[2], أ >, إ <, آ |, ئ }, ء ', ؤ &); b) *taa marboutah* and *haa* ة p, ه h); and c) *yaa* and *alif maqsoura* (ي y, ى Y).

Ancient Arabic manuscripts were written in *scriptura continua*, meaning running words without punctuation marks. Punctuation marks were introduced to Arabic mainly through borrowing from European languages via translation (Alqinai, 2013). Although punctuation marks in Arabic are gaining popularity and writers are becoming more aware of their importance, yet many writers still do not follow punctuation conventions as strictly and consistently as English writers. For example, we investigated contemporaneous same sized tokenized (simple tokenization with separation of punctuation) English and Modern Standard Arabic Gigaword edited newswire corpora, we found that 10% of the tokens in the English Gigaword corresponded to punctuation marks, compared to only 3% of the tokens in the Arabic counterpart.

	Train.	%	Dev.	%
Word Count	925,643	--	48,471	--
Total Errors	306,757	33.14	16,659	34.37
Word errors	187,040	60.97	9,878	59.30
Punc. errors	618,886	39.03	6,781	40.70
Split	10,869	3.48	612	3.67
Add_before	99,258	32.36	5,704	34.24
Delete	6,778	2.21	338	2.03
Edit	169,769	55.34	8,914	53.51
Merge	18,267	5.95	994	5.97
Add_after	20	0.01	2	0.01
Move	427	0.14	13	0.08

Table 1. Distribution Statistics on Error Types

1.3 Data Analysis

In our work, we use the QALB corpus (Zaghouani et al. 2014), and the training and development set provided in the QALB shared task (Mohit et. al 2014). The shared task addresses a large array of errors, and not just typical spelling errors. For instance, as Table 1 illustrates punctuation errors make up to 40% of all the errors in the shared task.

For further investigation, we annotated 1,100 words from the development set for error types, and found that 85% of the word errors (excluding punctuation marks) are typical spelling errors (or non-word errors), while 15% are real-word errors, or lexical ambiguities (that is, they are valid words outside of their context), and they range between dialectal words, grammatical errors, semantic errors, speech effects and elongation, examples shown in Table 2.

<table>
<tr><td>Error Type</td><td>Example</td><td>Correction</td></tr>
<tr><td>dialectal words</td><td>بهاي bhAy
‘by this’ [Syrian]</td><td>بهذه bh*h
‘by this’ [MSA]</td></tr>
<tr><td>grammatical errors</td><td>كبير kbyr
‘big.masc’</td><td>كبيرة kbyrp
‘big.fem’</td></tr>
<tr><td>semantic errors</td><td>آتيه |tyh
‘come to him’</td><td>آتية |typ
‘coming’</td></tr>
<tr><td>speech effects</td><td>الرجاااال
AlrjAAAAl ‘men’</td><td>الرجال
AlrjAl ‘men’</td></tr>
<tr><td>elongation</td><td>دمـــاء dm__A'
‘blood’</td><td>دماء dmA'
‘blood’</td></tr>
</table>

Table 2. Examples of real word errors

2 Our Methodology

Due to the complexity and variability of errors in the shared task, we treat each problem individually and use different approaches that prove to be most appropriate for each problem. We specifically address three subtypes of errors: orthographical errors; punctuation errors; and non-word errors.

2.1 Orthographical Errors

There are many instances in the shared task's data that can be treated using simple and straightforward conversion via regular expression replace rules. We estimate that these instances cover 10% of the non-punctuation errors in the development set. In HASP we use deterministic heuristic rules to normalize the text, including the following:

1. Hindi numbers (٠١٢٣٤٥٦٧٨٩) are converted into Arabic numerals [0-9] (occurs 495 in the training data times);
2. Speech effects are removed. For example, الرجاااال AlrjAAAAl ‘men’ is converted to الرجال AlrjAl. As a general rule letters repeated three times or more are reduced to one letter (715 times);
3. Elongation or kashida is removed. For example, دمـــاء dm__A' ‘blood’ is converted to

[2] In this paper, we use the Buckwalter Transliteration Scheme as described in www.qamus.com.

دماء dmA' (906 times);

4. Special character U+06CC, the Farsi yeh: ی is converted to U+0649, the visually similar Arabic *alif maqsoura* ى Y (293 times).

2.2 Punctuation Errors

Punctuation errors constitute 40% of the errors in the QALB Arabic data. It is worth noting that by comparison, punctuation errors only constituted 4% of the English data in CoNLL 2013 Shared Task on English Grammatical Error Correction (Ng et al., 2013) and were not evaluated or handled by any participant. In HASP, we focus on 6 punctuation marks: comma, colon, semi-colon, exclamation mark, question mark and period.

The 'column' file in the QALB shared task data comes preprocessed with the MADAMIRA morphological analyzer version 04092014-1.0-beta (Pasha et al., 2014). The features that we utilize in our punctuation classification experiments are all extracted from the 'column' file, and they are as follows:

(1) The original word, that is the word as it appears in the text without any further processing, (e.g., للتشاور llt$Awr 'for consulting');
(2) The tokenized word using the Penn Arabic Treebank (PATB) tokenization (e.g., ل+ التشاور l+Alt$Awr);
(3) Kulick POS tag (e.g., IN+DT+NN).
(4) Buckwalter POS tag (e.g., PREP+DET+ NOUN+CASE_DEF_GN) as produced by MADAMIRA;
(5) Classes to be predicted: colon_after, comma_after, exclmark_after, period_after, qmark_after, semicolon_after and NA (when no punctuation marks are used);

Window Size	Recall	Precision	F-measure
4	36.24	54.09	43.40
5	**37.95**	59.61	**46.37**
6	36.65	**59.99**	45.50
7	34.50	59.53	43.68

Table 3. Yamcha results on the development set

For classification, we experiment with Support Vector Machines (SVM) as implemented in Yamcha (Kudo and Matsumoto, 2003) and Conditional Random Field (CRF++) classifiers (Lafferty et al. 2001). In our investigation, we vary the context window size from 4 to 8 and we use all 5 features listed for every word in the window. As Tables 3 and 4 show, we found that window size 5 gives the best f-score by both Yamcha and CRF. When we strip clitics from tokenized tag, reducing it to stems only, the performance of the system improved. Overall CRF yields significantly higher results using the same experimental setup. We assume that the performance advantage of CRF is a result of the way words in the context and their features are interconnected in a neat grid in the template file.

#	Window Size	Recall	Precision	f-measure
1	4	44.03	74.33	55.31
2	5	**44.50**	**75.49**	**55.99**
3	6	44.22	74.93	55.62
4	7	43.81	75.09	55.34
5	8	43.49	75.41	55.17
6	8*	43.31	75.37	55.00

Table 4. CRF results on the development set
* with full tokens; other experiments use stems only, i.e., clitics are removed.

2.3. Non Word Errors

This type of errors comprises different subtypes: merges where two or more words are merged together; splits where a space is inserted within a single word; or misspelled words (which underwent substitution, deletion, insertion or transposition) that should be corrected. We handle these problems as follows.

2.3.1. Word Merges

Merged words are when the space(s) between two or more words is deleted, such as هذاالنظام h*AAlnZAm 'this system', which should be هذا النظام h*A AlnZAm. They constitute 3.67% and 3.48% of the error types in the shared task's development and training data, respectively. Attia et al. (2012) used an algorithm for dealing with merged words in Arabic, that is, $l - 3$, where l is the length of a word. For a 7-letter word, their algorithm generates 4 candidates as it allows only a single space to be inserted in a string. Their algorithm, however, is too restricted. By contrast Alkanhal et al. (2012) developed an algorithm with more generative power, that is 2^{l-1}. Their algorithm, however, is in practice too general and leads to a huge fan out. For a 7-letter word, it generates 64 solutions. We develop a splitting algorithm by taking into account that the minimum length of words in Arabic is two. Our modified algorithm is 2^{l-4}, which creates an effective balance between comprehensiveness and compactness. For the 7-letter word, it generates 8 candidates. However, from Table 5 on merged words and their gold splits, one would question the feasibility of producing more than two splits for any given string. Our splitting algorithm is evaluated in 2.3.3.1.c and compared to Attia et al.'s (2012) algorithm.

	Development	Training
Total Count	631	11,054
1 split	611	10,575
2 splits	15	404
3 splits	3	57
4 splits	1	13
5 splits	1	5

Table 5. Merged words and their splits

2.3.2. Word Splits

Beside the problem of merged words, there is also the problem of split words, where one or more spaces are inserted within a word, such as صم ام Sm Am 'valve' (correction is صمام SmAm). This error constitutes 6% of the shared task's both training and development set. We found that the vast majority of instances of this type of error involve the clitic conjunction *waw* "and", which should be represented as a word prefix. Among the 18,267 splits in the training data 15,548 of them involved the *waw*, corresponding to 85.12%. Similarly among the 994 splits in the development data, 760 of them involved the *waw* (76.46%).

Therefore, we opted to handle this problem in our work in a partial and shallow manner using deterministic rules addressing specifically the following two phenomena:

1. Separated conjunction morpheme *waw* و w 'and' is attached to the succeeding word (occurs 15,915 times in the training data);
2. Literal strings attached to numbers are separated with space(s). For example, "دماء2000شهيدا" "dmA'2000$hydF" 'blood of 2000 martyrs' is converted to "دماء 2000 شهيدا" "dmA' 2000 $hydF" (824 times).

2.3.3. Misspelled Word Errors

This is more akin to the typical spelling correction problem where a word has the wrong letters, rendering it a non-word. We address this problem using two approaches: Dictionary-LM Correction, and Alignment Based Correction.

2.3.3.1. Dictionary-LM Correction

Spelling error detection and correction mainly consists of three phases: a) error detection; b) candidate generation; and c) error correction, or best candidate selection.

a. Error Detection

For non-word spelling error detection and candidate generation we use AraComLex Extended, an open-source reference dictionary (or word list) of full-form words. The dictionary is developed by Attia et al. (2012) through an amalgamation of various resources, such as a wordlist from the Arabic Gigaword corpus, wordlist generated from the Buckwalter morphological analyzer, and AraComLex (Attia et al., 2011), a finite-state morphological transducer. AraComLex Extended consists of 9.2M words and, as far as we know, is the largest wordlist for Arabic reported in the literature to date.

We enhance the AraComLex Extended dictionary by utilizing the annotated data in the shared task's training data. We add 776 new valid words to the dictionary and remove 4,810 misspelt words, leading to significant improvement in the dictionary's ability to make decisions on words. Table 6 shows the dictionary's performance on the training and development set in the shared task as applied only to non-words and excluding grammatical, semantic and punctuation errors.

data set	R	P	F
Training	98.84	96.34	97.57
Development	98.72	96.04	97.36

Table 6. Results of dictionary error detection

b. Candidate Generation

For candidate generation we use Foma (Hulden, 2009), a finite state compiler that is capable of producing candidates from a wordlist (compiled as an FST network) within a certain edit distance from an error word. Foma allows the ranking of candidates according to customizable transformation rules.

#	Error Type	Count	Ratio %
1.	أ > typed as ا A	59,507	31.82
2.	Insert	28.945	15.48
3.	إ < typed as ا A	25.392	13.58
4.	Delete	18.246	9.76
5.	ة p typed as ه h	14.639	7.83
6.	Split	11.419	6.11
7.	ي y typed as ى Y	6.419	3.43

Table 7. Error types in the training set

We develop a re-ranker based on our observation of the error types in the shared task's training data (as shown in Table 7) and examining the character transformations between the misspelt words and their gold corrections. Our statistics shows that soft errors (or variants as explained in Section 1.2) account for more than 62% of all errors in the training data.

c. Error Correction

For error correction, namely selecting the best solution among the list of candidates, we use an n-gram language model (LM), as implemented in the SRILM package (Stolcke et al., 2011). We use the 'disambig' tool for selecting candidates from a map file where erroneous words are provided with a list of possible corrections. We also use the 'ngram' utility in post-processing for deciding on whether a split-word solution has a better probability than a single word solution. Our bigram language model is trained on the Gigaword Corpus 4th edition (Parker et al., 2009).

For the LM disambiguation we use the '–fb' option (forward-backward tracking), and we provide candidates with probability scores. We generate these probability scores by converting the edit distance scores produced by the Foma FST re-ranker explained above. Both of the forward-backward tracking and the probability scores in in tandem yield better results than the default values. We evaluate the performance of our system against the gold standard using the *Max-Match* (M^2) method for evaluating grammatical error correction by Dahlmeier and Ng (2012).

The best f-score achieved in our system is obtained when we combine the CRF punctuation classifier (merged with the original punctuations found in data), knowledge-based normalization (norm), dictionary-LM disambiguation and split-1, as shown in Table 8. The option split-1 refers to using the splitting algorithm $l-3$ as explained in Section 2.3.1, while split-2 refers to using the splitting algorithm 2^{l-4}.

#	Experiment	R	P	F
1	LM+split-1	33.32	**73.71**	45.89
2	+CRF_punc+split-1	49.74	65.38	56.50
3	+ norm+split-1	38.81	69.08	49.70
4	+CRF_punc+norm +split-1	**54.79**	67.65	60.55
5	+CRF_punc+norm +orig_punc+split-1	53.18	73.15	**61.59**
6	+CRF_punc+norm +orig_punc+split-2	53.13	73.01	61.50

Table 8. LM correction with 3 candidates

In the QALB Shared Task evaluation, we submit two systems: System 1 is configuration 5 in Table 8, and System 2 corresponds to configuration 6, and the results on the test set are shown in Table 9. As Table 9 shows, the best scores are obtained by System 1, which is ranked 5th among the 9 systems participating in the shared task.

#	Experiment	R	P	F
1	System 1	52.98	**75.47**	**62.25**
2	System 2	**52.99**	75.34	62.22

Table 9. Final official results on the test set provided by the Shared Task

2.3.3.2. Alignment-Based Correction

We formatted the data for alignment using a window of 4 words: one word to each side (forming the contextual boundary) and two words in the middle. The two words in the middle are split into characters so that character transformations can be observed and learned by the aligner. The alignment tool we use is Giza++ (Och and Ney, 2003). Results are reported in Table 10.

#	Experiment	R	P	F
1	for all error types	36.05	45.13	37.99
2	excluding punc	32.37	54.65	40.66
3	2 + CRF_punc+norm	46.11	62.02	52.90

Table 10. Results of character-based alignment

Although these preliminary results from Alignment are significantly below results yielded from the Dictionary-LM approach, we believe that there are several potential improvements that need to be explored:

- Using LM on the output of the alignment;
- Determining the type of errors that the alignment is most successful at handling: punctuation, grammar, non-words, etc;
- Parsing training data errors with the Dictionary-LM disambiguation and retraining, so instead of training data consisting of errors and gold corrections, it will consist of corrected errors and gold corrections.

3 Conclusion

We have described our system HASP for the automatic correction of spelling and punctuation mistakes in Arabic. To our knowledge, this is the first system to handle punctuation errors. We utilize and improve on an open-source full-form dictionary, introduce better algorithm for handing merged word errors, tune the LM parameters, and combine the various components together, leading to cumulative improved results.

References

Alfaifi, A., and Atwell, E. (2012) Arabic Learner Corpora (ALC): a taxonomy of coding errors. In Proceedings of the 8th International Computing Conference in Arabic (ICCA 2012), Cairo, Egypt.

Alkanhal, Mohamed I., Mohamed A. Al-Badrashiny, Mansour M. Alghamdi, and Abdulaziz O. Al-Qabbany. (2012) Automatic Stochastic Arabic Spelling Correction With Emphasis on Space Insertions and Deletions. IEEE Transactions on Audio, Speech, and Language Processing, Vol. 20, No. 7, September 2012.

Alqinai, Jamal. (2013) Mediating punctuation in English Arabic translation. Linguistica Atlantica. Vol. 32.

Attia, M., Pecina, P., Tounsi, L., Toral, A., and van Genabith, J. (2011) An Open-Source Finite State Morphological Transducer for Modern Standard Arabic. International Workshop on Finite State Methods and Natural Language Processing (FSMNLP). Blois, France.

Attia, Mohammed, Pavel Pecina, Younes Samih, Khaled Shaalan, Josef van Genabith. 2012. Improved Spelling Error Detection and Correction for Arabic. COLING 2012, Bumbai, India.

Beesley, Kenneth R. (1998). Arabic Morphology Using Only Finite-State Operations. In The Workshop on Computational Approaches to Semitic languages, Montreal, Quebec, pp. 50–57.

Ben Othmane Zribi, C. and Ben Ahmed, M. (2003) Efficient Automatic Correction of Misspelled Arabic Words Based on Contextual Information, Lecture Notes in Computer Science, Springer, Vol. 2773, pp.770–777.

Brill, Eric and Moore, Robert C. (2000) An improved error model for noisy channel spelling correction. Proceedings of the 38th Annual Meeting of the Association for Computational Linguistics, Hong Kong, pp. 286–293.

Brown, P. F., Della Pietra, V. J., de Souza, P. V., Lai, J. C. and Mercer, R. L. (1992) Class-Based n-gram Models of Natural Language. *Computational Linguistics*, 18(4), 467–479.

Buckwalter, T. (2004b) Buckwalter Arabic Morphological Analyzer (BAMA) Version 2.0. Linguistic Data Consortium (LDC) catalogue number: LDC2004L02, ISBN1-58563-324-0.

Buckwalter, Tim. (2004a) Issues in Arabic orthography and morphology analysis. Proceedings of the Workshop on Computational Approaches to Arabic Script-based Languages. Pages 31-34. Association for Computational Linguistics Stroudsburg, PA, USA.

Church, Kenneth W. and William A. Gale. (1991) Probability scoring for spelling correction. *Statistics and Computing*, 1, pp. 93–103.

Dahlmeier, Daniel and Ng, Hwee Tou. 2012. Better evaluation for grammatical error correction. In Proceedings of NAACL.

Damerau, Fred J. (1964) A Technique for Computer Detection and Correction of Spelling Errors. Communications of the ACM, Volum 7, issue 3, pp. 171–176.

Gao, Jianfeng, Xiaolong Li, Daniel Micol, Chris Quirk, and Xu Sun. (2010) A large scale ranker-based system for search query spelling correction. Proceedings of the 23rd International Conference on Computational Linguistics (COLING 2010), pages 358–366, Beijing, China

Golding, Andrew R. A Bayesian Hybrid Method for Context-sensitive Spelling Correction. In Proceedings of the Third Workshop on Very Large Corpora. MIT, Cambridge, Massachusetts, USA. 1995, pp.39–53.

Golding, Andrew R., and Dan Roth. (1996) Applying Winnow to Context-Sensitive Spelling Correction. In Proceedings of the Thirteenth International Conference on Machine Learning, Stroudsburg, PA, USA, pp. 182–190

Habash, Nizar Y. (2010) *Introduction to Arabic Natural Language Processing*. Synthesis Lectures on Human Language Technologies 3.1: 1-187.

Haddad, B., and Yaseen, M. (2007) Detection and Correction of Non-Words in Arabic: A Hybrid Approach. International Journal of Computer Processing of Oriental Languages. Vol. 20, No. 4.

Han, Bo and Timothy Baldwin. (2011) Lexical Normalisation of Short Text Messages: Makn Sens a #twitter. Proceedings of the 49th Annual Meeting of the Association for Computational Linguistics, pages 368–378, Portland, Oregon, June 19-24, 2011

Hassan, A, Noeman, S., and Hassan, H. (2008) Language Independent Text Correction using Finite State Automata. IJCNLP. Hyderabad, India.

Hulden, M. (2009) Foma: a Finite-state compiler and library. EACL '09 Proceedings of the 12th Conference of the European Chapter of the Association for Computational Linguistics. Association for Computational Linguistics Stroudsburg, PA, USA

Islam, Aminul, Diana Inkpen. (2009) Real-Word Spelling Correction using Google Web 1T n-gram with Backoff. International Conference on Natural Language Processing and Knowledge Engineering, Dalian, China, pp. 1–8.

Kiraz, G. A. (2001) *Computational Nonlinear Morphology: With Emphasis on Semitic Languages*. Cambridge University Press.

Kudo, Taku, Yuji Matsumoto. (2003) Fast Methods for Kernel-Based Text Analysis. 41st Annual Meeting of the Association for Computational Linguistics (ACL-2003), Sapporo, Japan.

Kukich, Karen. (1992) Techniques for automatically correcting words in text. Computing Surveys, 24(4), pp. 377–439.

Lafferty, John, Andrew McCallum, and Fernando Pereira. (2001) Conditional random fields: Probabilistic models for segmenting and labeling sequence data, In Proceedings of the International Conference on Machine Learning (ICML 2001), , MA, USA, pp. 282-289.

Levenshtein, V. I. (1966) Binary codes capable of correcting deletions, insertions, and reversals. In: Soviet Physics Doklady, pp. 707-710.

Magdy, W., and Darwish, K. (2006) Arabic OCR error correction using character segment correction, language modeling, and shallow morphology. EMNLP '06 Proceedings of the 2006 Conference on Empirical Methods in Natural Language Processing.

Mohit, Behrang, Alla Rozovskaya, Nizar Habash, Wajdi Zaghouani, and Ossama Obeid, 2014. The First QALB Shared Task on Automatic Text Correction for Arabic. In Proceedings of EMNLP workshop on Arabic Natural Language Processing. Doha, Qatar.

Ng, Hwee Tou, Siew Mei Wu, Yuanbin Wu, Christian Hadiwinoto, and Joel Tetreault. (2013) The CoNLL-2013 Shared Task on Grammatical Error Correction. Proceedings of the Seventeenth Conference on Computational Natural Language Learning: Shared Task, pages 1–12, Sofia, Bulgaria, August 8-9 2013.

Norvig, P. (2009) Natural language corpus data. In Beautiful Data, edited by Toby Segaran and Jeff Hammerbacher, pp. 219- "-242. Sebastopol, Calif.: O'Reilly.

Och, Franz Josef, Hermann Ney. (2003) A Systematic Comparison of Various Statistical Alignment Models. In Computational Linguistics, volume 29, number 1, pp. 19-51 March 2003.

Parker, R., Graff, D., Chen, K., Kong, J., and Maeda, K. (2009) Arabic Gigaword Fifth Edition. LDC Catalog No.: LDC2009T30, ISBN: 1-58563-532-4.

Parker, R., Graff, D., Chen, K., Kong, J., and Maeda, K. (2011) Arabic Gigaword Fifth Edition. LDC Catalog No.: LDC2011T11, ISBN: 1-58563-595-2.

Pasha, Arfath, Mohamed Al-Badrashiny, Ahmed El Kholy, Ramy Eskander, Mona Diab, Nizar Habash, Manoj Pooleery, Owen Rambow, Ryan Roth. (2014) Madamira: A fast, comprehensive tool for morphological analysis and disambiguation of Arabic. In Proceedings of the 9th International Conference on Language Resources and Evaluation, Reykjavik, Iceland.

Ratcliffe, Robert R. (1998) *The Broken Plural Problem in Arabic and Comparative Semitic: Allomorphy and Analogy in Non-concatenative Morphology*. Amsterdam studies in the theory and history of linguistic science. Series IV, Current issues in linguistic theory ; v. 168. Amsterdam ; Philadelphia: J. Benjamins.

Roth, R. Rambow, O., Habash, N., Diab, M., and Rudin, C. (2008) Arabic Morphological Tagging, Diacritization, and Lemmatization Using Lexeme Models and Feature Ranking. Proceedings of ACL-08: HLT, Short Papers, pp. 117–120.

Shaalan, K., Samih, Y., Attia, M., Pecina, P., and van Genabith, J. (2012) Arabic Word Generation and Modelling for Spell Checking. Language Resources and Evaluation (LREC). Istanbul, Turkey. pp. 719–725.

Stolcke, A., Zheng, J., Wang, W., and Abrash, V. (2011) SRILM at sixteen: Update and outlook. in Proc. IEEE Automatic Speech Recognition and Understanding Workshop. Waikoloa, Hawaii.

van Delden, Sebastian, David B. Bracewell, and Fernando Gomez. (2004) Supervised and Unsupervised Automatic Spelling Correction Algorithms. In proceeding of Information Reuse and Integration (IRI). Proceedings of the 2004 IEEE International Conference on Web Services, pp. 530–535.

Wu, Jian-cheng, Hsun-wen Chiu, and Jason S. Chang. (2013) Integrating Dictionary and Web N-grams for Chinese Spell Checking. Computational Linguistics and Chinese Language Processing. Vol. 18, No. 4, December 2013, pp. 17–30.

Zaghouani, Wajdi, Behrang Mohit, Nizar Habash, Ossama Obeid, Nadi Tomeh, Alla Rozovskaya, Noura Farra, Sarah Alkuhlani, and Kemal Oflazer. 2014. Large Scale Arabic Error Annotation: Guidelines and Framework. In Proceedings of the Ninth International Conference on Language Resources and Evaluation (LREC'14), Reykjavik, Iceland.

TECHLIMED system description for the Shared Task on Automatic Arabic Error Correction

Djamel MOSTEFA
Techlimed
42 rue de l'Université
Lyon, France

Omar ASBAYOU
Techlimed
42 rue de l'Université
Lyon, France

Ramzi ABBES
Techlimed
42 rue de l'Université
Lyon, France

{firstname.lastname}@techlimed.com

Abstract

This article is a system description paper and reports on the participation of Techlimed in the "QALB-2014 shared task" on evaluation of automatic arabic error correction systems organized in conjunction with the EMNLP 2014 Workshop on Arabic Natural Language Processing. Correcting automatically texts in Arabic is a challenging task due to the complexity and rich morphology of the Arabic language and the lack of appropriate resources, (e.g. publicly available corpora and tools). To develop our systems, we considered several approaches from rule based systems to statistical methods. Our results on the development set show that the statistical system outperforms the lexicon driven approach with a precision of 71%, a recall of 50% and a F-measure of 59%.

1 Introduction

Automatic error correction is an important task in Natural Language Processing (NLP). It can be used in a wide range of applications such as word processing tools (e.g. Microsoft Office, Openoffice, ...), machine translation, information retrieval, optical character recognition ... Automatic error correction tools on Arabic are underperforming in comparison with other languages like English or French. This can be explained by the lack of appropriate resources (e.g. publicly available corpora and tools) and the complexity of the Arabic language. Arabic is a challenging language for any NLP tool for many reasons. Arabic has a rich and complex morphology compared to other latin languages. Short vowels are missing in the texts but are mandatory from a grammatical point of view. Moreover they are needed to disambiguate between several possibilities of words. Arabic is a rich language.There are many synonyms and Arabic is a highly agglutinative, inflectional and derivational language and uses clitics (proclitics and enclitics). Arabic has many varieties. Modern Standard Arabic includes the way Arabic is written in the news or in formal speech. Classical Arabic refers to religious and classical texts. Dialectal Arabic has no standard rules for orthography and is based on the pronunciation. Therefore a same word can be written using many different surface forms depending on the dialectal origin of the writer. Another very popular way of writing Arabic on the Internet and the social media like Facebook or Tweeter is to use "Arabizi", a latinized form of writing Arabic using latin letters and digits (Aboelezz, 2009).

For our participation in this evaluation task, we tried to implement two different approaches. The first approach is a lexicon driven spell checker. For this, we have plan to adapt and test state-of-the-art spell checkers. The second approach is a pure statistical approach by considering the correction problem as a statical machine translation task.

The paper is organized as follows: section 2 gives an overview of the automatic error correction evaluation task and resources provided by the organizers; section 3 describes the systems we have developed for the evaluations; and finally in section 4 we discuss the results and draw some conclusion.

2 Task description and language resources

The aim of the QALB Shared Task on Automatic Arabic Error Correction (Mohit, 2014) is to evaluate automatic text correction systems for the Arabic language. The objective of the task is to correct automatically texts in Arabic provided by the organizers. The QALB corpus is used for the evaluation task. A training set and a development set with gold standard is provided for system train-

Proceedings of the EMNLP 2014 Workshop on Arabic Natural Langauge Processing (ANLP), pages 155–159,
October 25, 2014, Doha, Qatar.

ing and development. The training and development sets are made of sentences with errors coming from newspapers articles and the gold standard is made of manual annotations of the sentences. The annotations were made by human annotators who used a correction guidelines described in (Zaghouani, 2014). The corrections are made of substitutions, insertions, deletions, splits, merges, moves of words and punctuation marks.

The training set is made of 19,411 sentences and 1M tokens. The development set includes 1,017 sentences for around 53k tokens.

The evaluation is performed by comparing the gold standard with the hypothesis using the Levenshtein edit distance (Levenshtein, 1966) and the implementation of the M2 scorer (Dahlmeier, 2012). Then for each sentence the Precision, Recall and F-measure are calculated.

Finally a test set of 968 sentences for 52k tokens with no gold standard has to be corrected automatically for the evaluation.

3 System description

For our participation in this evaluation campaign, we studied two main approaches. The first one is a lexical driven approach using dictionaries to correct the errors. Different lexicons were evaluated using Hunspell as spellchecking and correction tool.
The second approach is a statistical machine translation point of view by considering the automatic error correction problem as a translation task. For this we used the statistical machine translation system Moses (Koehn, 2007), to train a model on the training data provided by the organizers.

3.1 Baseline system

Since this the time first we are trying to develop a spellchecker and correction tool for Arabic, we wanted to have some figures about the performance of spellcheckers on Arabic.

We used the development set to test the performance of various spellchecker and correction tools. We corrected the development set automatically using the spellchecker module of the following softwares:

- Microsoft Word 2013
- OpenOffice 2014
- Hunspell

For Microsoft Word and OpenOffice we used the default configuration for correcting Arabic text and disabled the grammar correction.

Hunspell is an open source spellchecker widely used in the open source community. It is the spellchecker of many well-known applications such as OpenOffice, LibreOffice, Firefox, Thunderbird, Chrome, etc. It is the next generation of lexical based spellcheckers in line with Myspell, Ispell and Aspell. It is highly configurable, supports Unicode and rich morphology languages like Arabic or Hungarian. Hunspell uses mainly two files for spellchecking and correction. The first one is a dictionary file *.dic which contains basically a wordlist and for each word, a list of applicable rules that can be applied to the word. The second one is an affix file *.aff which contains a list of possible affixes and the rules of application. More information on these files can be found in the Hunspell manual[1].

Hunspell is an interactive spellchecker. It takes as an input a text to be corrected and for each word that is not found using the loaded dictionary and affix files, it gives a list of suggestions to correct the word. For the correction which must be fully automatic, we forced Hunspell to always correct the word with the first suggestion without any human intervention.

The dictionaries/affixes used for the evaluation is coming from the Ayaspell project(Ayaspell, 2008). The dictionary contains 52 725 entries and the affix file contains 11859 rules.

The results are given in Table 1

Dictionary	Precision	Recall	F-measure
Word	45.7	16.6	24.3
Hunspell	51.8	18.8	27.6
OpenOffice	56.1	20.7	30.2

Table 1: Results on the development set for Word, Hunspell/Ayaspell and OpenOffice(in percentage)

The best results are the ones obtained by OpenOffice with a precision of 56.1%, a recall of 20.7% and a F-measure of 30.2%.

We would like to mention that these spellcheckers do not correct the punctuations which may explain the relative low recall scores.

[1] http://sourceforge.net/projects/hunspell/files/Hunspell/Documentation/

3.2 Statistical machine translation system

Our second approach is to consider the automatic correction problem as a translation problem by considering the sentences to be corrected as a source language and the correct sentences as a target language. Since the organizers provided us with a 1 million tokens corpora with and without spelling errors, we tried to build a statistical machine translation system using the parallel data. We used the Moses (Koehn, 2007), a Statistical Machine Translation (SMT) system to train a phrase based translation model with the training data. The training data provided is made of erroneous sentences and for each sentence a list of corrections to be applied. To build the parallel error/correct text corpus we applied the corrections to the sentences. We came up with a parallel corpus of 19421 sentences and 102k tokens for the error version and 112k tokens for the corrected version. Moses requires a parallel corpus to train a translation model, a development set to tune the translation model and also a monolingual language model in the target language. Since we had to evaluate the performance on the development data provided by the organizers, we had to use part of the training data as a development data for Moses. So we split the 20k sentences included in the training data in a new training set of 18k and a new development data of 2k sentences. We trained standard phrase based models using the surface word form with no morphological analysis or segmentation. For the word alignment in the training process, we used GIZA++ (Och, 2003). The 2k sentences were used to tune the SMT models.

Corpus	# Sentences	Usage
train18k	18000	train
dev-train2k	1411	dev
dev	1017	test

Table 2: Bitexts used for the SMT system

For the language models we used corpora of newspapers publicly available or collected by Techlimed. The sources are coming from the Open Source Arabic Corpora (Saad, 2010) (20M words), the Adjir corpus (Adjir, 2005) (147M words) and other corpora we collected from various online newspapers for a total of 300M words. The language model was created with the IRSTLM toolkit (Federico, 2008).

We evaluated the translation models on the development set using different sizes of monolingual corpus. The 3 systems were trained on the same parallel corpus but with different size for fir monolingual data for System100, System200 and System300 with respectively 100M words, 200M words and 300M words. The results are given in table 3.

System	Precision	Recall	F-measure
System100	70.7	48.8	57.8
System200	70.7	49.6	58.3
System300	70.8	50.1	58.7

Table 3: Results on the development set (in percentage) for the 3 SMT systems

We can see from table 3 that the size of the language model has no impact on the precision but increases slightly the recall of 1.3% in absolute (2.6% in relative).

The BLEU scores (Papineni, 2002) measured on Sytem100, System200, System300 are respectively 65.45, 65.82 and 65.98.

We also tried to combine Hunspell/Ayaspell with the SMT system by correcting the output of the SMT system with Hunspell/Ayaspell but didn't get any improvement.

4 Discussion

The results obtained by the SMT system is much more better than the ones obtained with Hunspell/Ayaspell with a F-measure of 58.7% for the best SMT system and 27,6 for Hunspell/Ayaspell. We have to mention that the training corpus provided by the organizers of 1 million words with the manual annotations enabled us to train a statistical system that learn automatically the correction made by the annotators while Hunspell/Ayaspell was not adapted to the correction guidelines. In particular the punctuations are not corrected by Hunspell/Ayaspell and this explains the difference of recall between the SMT system (50.1%) and Hunspell/Ayaspell (20.7%). If we have a look at the gold standard of the development set, 38.6% of the manual annotations concern punctuation marks with 6266 punctuation marks annotations for an overall total of 16,231 annotations. While there are clear rules for strong punctuation marks like period, question or exclamation marks, there are no clear grammatical rules for the weak punctuation marks, especially for commas which concern 4,117 annotations of the gold standard of the development set (25.4%). Another point that we would like to mention is that a spell checker and correction tool is usually used in an interactive mode by proposing n-best candidates for the correction of a word. When looking at Hunspell/Ayspell correction candidates for an error, we saw the correction was not in position 1 but in the list of candidates. So it would be interesting to compare the correction on the n-best candidates and not only on the first candidate for Hunspell and the SMT system.

5 Conclusion

This paper has reported on the participation of Techlimed in the QALB Shared Task on Automatic Arabic Error Correction. This is the first time we tried to develop a spellchecker for Arabic and have investigated two approaches. The first one is a lexicon driven approach using Hunspell as a spellchecker and correction tool and the second one is a SMT systems using Moses for training a statistical machine translation model on the 1 million tokens corpus provided by the organizers. The best results were obtained with the SMT system which, especially, was able to deal with the punctuation marks corrections. We also tested an hybrid system by combining Hunspell and the SMT system but didn't get better results than the SMT system alone. Our perspective is to improve the results by using hybrid systems based on the DiiNAR lexical database (Abbes, 2004) and also a large arabic named entity dictionary, both owned and developped by Techlimed We will also try to used factored translation models with the Techlimed Part-Of-Speech taggers. And more training data will also improve the quality of the corrections.

Acknowledgments

We would like to thank the QALB Shared Task organizers for setting up this evaluation campaign on automatic error correction tool for Arabic and for providing us with the language resources and tools that we used for the development of our systems.

References

Ramzi Abbès, Joseph Dichy, and Mohamed Hassoun. 2004. The architecture of a standard arabic lexical database: some figures, ratios and categories from the Diinar. 1 source program. In *Proceedings of the Workshop on Computational Approaches to Arabic Script-based Languages*, pages 15–22. Association for Computational Linguistics, 2004.

Mariam Aboelezz. 2009. Latinised arabic and connections to bilingual ability. In *Papers from the Lancaster University Postgraduate Conference in Linguistics and Language Teaching*, 2009.

Ahmed Abdelali. 2005. http://aracorpus.e3rab.com/

Ayaspell Arabic dictionary project, 2008. http://ayaspell.sourceforge.net

Daniel Dahlmeier and Hwee Tou Ng. 2012. Better evaluation for grammatical error correction. In *Proceedings of the 2012 Conference of the North American Chapter of the Association for Computational Linguistics: Human Language Technologies*, pages 568–572. Association for Computational Linguistics, 2012.

Marcello Federico, Nicola Bertoldi, and Mauro Cettolo. 2008. Irstlm: an open source toolkit for handling large scale language models. In *Interspeech*, pages 1618–1621, 2008.

Hunspell, 2007. http://hunspell.sourceforge.net/

Philipp Koehn, Hieu Hoang, Alexandra Birch, Chris Callison-Burch, Marcello Federico, Nicola Bertoldi, Brooke Cowan, Wade Shen, Christine Moran, Richard Zens, et al. 2007. Moses: Open source toolkit for statistical machine translation. In *Proceedings of the 45th Annual Meeting of the ACL on Interactive Poster and Demonstration Sessions*, pages 177–180. Association for Computational Linguistics, 2007.

Vladimir Levenshtein. 1966. Binary codes capable of correcting deletions, insertions and reversals. In *Soviet physics doklady*, volume 10, page 707, 1966.

Behrang Mohit, Alla Rozovskaya, Nizar Habash, Wajdi Zaghouani, and Ossama Obeid. 2014. The First QALB Shared Task on Automatic Text Correction for Arabic. In *Proceedings of EMNLP Workshop on Arabic Natural Language Processing*, Doha, Qatar, October 2014.

Franz Josef Och and Hermann Ney. 2003. A systematic comparison of various statistical alignment models. *Computational Linguistics*, 29(1):19–51, 2003.

Kishore Papineni, Salim Roukos, Todd Ward, and Wei-Jing Zhu. 2002. Bleu: a method for automatic evaluation of machine translation. In *Proceedings of the 40th annual meeting on association for computational linguistics*, pages 311–318. Association for Computational Linguistics, 2002.

Motaz K Saad and Wesam Ashour. 2010 Osac: Open source arabic corpora. In *6th ArchEng Int. Symposiums, EEECS*, volume 10, 2010.

Wajdi Zaghouani, Behrang Mohit, Nizar Habash, Ossama Obeid, Nadi Tomeh, Alla Rozovskaya, Noura Farra, Sarah Alkuhlani, and Kemal Oflazer. 2014. Large scale arabic error annotation: Guidelines and framework. In *Proceedings of the Ninth International Conference on Language Resources and Evaluation (LREC'14)*, Reykjavik, Iceland, May 2014. European Language Resources Association (ELRA).

The Columbia System in the QALB-2014 Shared Task on Arabic Error Correction

Alla Rozovskaya Nizar Habash[†] Ramy Eskander Noura Farra Wael Salloum

Center for Computational Learning Systems, Columbia University
[†]New York University Abu Dhabi

{alla,ramy,noura,wael}@ccls.columbia.edu
[†]nizar.habash@nyu.edu

Abstract

The QALB-2014 shared task focuses on correcting errors in texts written in Modern Standard Arabic. In this paper, we describe the Columbia University entry in the shared task. Our system consists of several components that rely on machine-learning techniques and linguistic knowledge. We submitted three versions of the system: these share several core elements but each version also includes additional components. We describe our underlying approach and the special aspects of the different versions of our submission. Our system ranked first out of nine participating teams.

1 Introduction

The topic of text correction has seen a lot of interest in the past several years, with a focus on correcting grammatical errors made by learners of English as a Second Language (ESL). The two most recent CoNLL shared tasks were devoted to grammatical error correction for non-native writers (Ng et al., 2013; Ng et al., 2014).

The QALB-2014 shared task (Mohit et al., 2014) is the first competition that addresses the problem of text correction in Modern Standard Arabic (MSA) texts. The competition makes use of the recently developed QALB corpus (Zaghouani et al., 2014). The shared task covers all types of mistakes that occur in the data.

Our system consists of statistical models, linguistic resources, and rule-based modules that address different types of errors.

We briefly discuss the task in Section 2. Section 3 gives an overview of the Columbia system and describes the system components. In Section 4, we evaluate the complete system on the development data and show the results obtained on test. Section 5 concludes.

2 Task Description

The QALB-2014 shared task addresses the problem of correcting errors in texts written in Modern Standard Arabic (MSA). The task organizers released training, development, and test data. All of the data comes from online commentaries written to Aljazeera articles.[1] The training data contains 1.2 million words; the development and the test data contain about 50,000 words each. The data was annotated and corrected by native Arabic speakers. For more detail on the QALB corpus, we refer the reader to Zaghouani et al. (2014). The results in the subsequent sections are reported on the development set.

It should be noted that in the annotation process, the annotators did not assign error categories but only specified an appropriate correction. In spite of this, it is possible, to isolate certain error types automatically, by using the corrections in coordination with the input words. The first type concerns punctuation errors. Errors involving punctuation account for about 39% of all errors in the data. In addition to punctuation mistakes, another very common source of errors refers to suboptimal spelling for two groups of letters – *Alif* (and its *Hamzated versions*) and *Ya* (and its *undotted* or *Alif Maqsura versions*). For more detail on this and other Arabic phenomena, we refer the reader to Habash (2010; Buckwalter (2007; El Kholy and Habash (2012). Mistakes associated with *Alif* and

[1] http://www.aljazeera.net/

Proceedings of the EMNLP 2014 Workshop on Arabic Natural Langauge Processing (ANLP), pages 160–164, October 25, 2014, Doha, Qatar.

Component	System		
	CLMB-1	CLMB-2	CLMB-3
MADAMIRA	✓	✓	
MLE	✓	✓	
Naïve Bayes	✓		
GSEC			✓
MLE-unigram			✓
Punctuation	✓	✓	✓
Dialectal		✓	
Patterns	✓	✓	✓

Table 1: **The three versions of the Columbia system and their components.**

Ya spelling constitute almost 30% of all errors.

3 System Overview

The Columbia University system consists of several components designed to address different types of errors. We submitted three versions of the system. We refer to these as CLMB-1, CLMB-2, and CLMB-3. Table 1 lists all of the components and indicates which components are included in each version. The components are applied in the order shown in the table. Below we describe each component in more detail.

3.1 MADAMIRA Corrector

MADAMIRA (Pasha et al., 2014) is a tool designed for morphological analysis and disambiguation of Modern Standard Arabic. MADAMIRA performs morphological analysis in context. This is a knowledge-rich resource that requires a morphological analyzer and a large corpus where every word is marked with its morphological features. The task organizers provided the shared task data pre-processed with MADAMIRA, including all of the features generated by the tool for every word. In addition to the morphological analysis and contextual morphological disambiguation, MADAMIRA also performs *Alif* and *Ya* spelling correction for the phenomena associated with these letters discussed in Section 2. The corrected form was included among the features and can be used for correcting the input. We use the corrections proposed by MADAMIRA and apply them to the data. As we show in Section 4, while the form proposed by MADAMIRA may not necessarily be correct, MADAMIRA performs at a very high precision. MADAMIRA corrector is used in the CLMB-1 and CLMB-2 systems.

3.2 Maximum Likelihood Model

The Maximum Likelihood Estimator (MLE) is a supervised component that is trained on the training data of the shared task. Given the annotated training data, a map is defined that specifies for every word n-gram in the source text the most likely n-gram corresponding to it in the target text. The MLE model considers source n-grams of lengths between 1 to 3; the MLE-unigram model that is part of the CLMB-3 version only considers n-grams of length 1.

The MLE approach performs well on errors that have been observed in the training data and can be unambiguously corrected without using the surrounding context, i.e. do not have many alternative corrections. Consequently, MLE fails on words that have many possible corrections, as well as words not seen in training.

3.3 Naïve Bayes for Unseen Words

The Naïve Bayes component addresses errors for words that were not seen in training. The system uses the approach proposed in Rozovskaya and Roth (2011) that proved to be successful for correcting errors made by English as a Second Language learners. The model operates at the word level and targets word replacement errors that involve single tokens. Candidate corrections are generated using a character confusion table that is based on the training data. The model is a Naïve Bayes classifier trained on the Arabic Gigaword corpus (Parker et al., 2011) with word n-gram features in the 4-word window around the word to be corrected. The Naïve Bayes component is used in the CLMB-1 system.

3.4 The GSEC Model

The CLMB-3 system implements a Generalized Character-Level Error Correction model (GSEC) proposed in Farra et al. (2014). GSEC is a supervised model that operates at the character level. Because of this, the source and the target side of the training data need to be aligned at the character level. We use the alignment tool Sclite (Fiscus, 1998). The alignment maps each source character to itself, a different character, a pair of characters, or an empty string. For the shared task, punctuation corrections are ignored since punctuation errors are handled by the punctuation corrector described in the following section. It should also be noted that the model was not trained to insert missing characters. The model is a multi-class SVM classifier (Kudo, 2005) that makes use of character-level features using a window of four characters that may occur within the word boundaries as well as in the surrounding context. Due to a long training time, GSEC was trained on a quarter of the training data. The system is post-processed with a unigram word-level maximum-likelihood model described in Section 3.2. For more detail on the GSEC approach, we refer the reader to Farra et al. (2014).

3.5 Punctuation Corrector

The shared task data contains a large number of punctuation mistakes. Punctuation errors, such as missing periods and commas, account for about 30% of all errors in the data. Most of these errors involve incorrectly omitting a punctuation symbol. Our punctuation corrector is a statistical model that inserts periods and commas. The system is a decision tree model trained on the shared task training data using WEKA (Hall et al., 2009). For punctuation insertion, every space that is not followed or preceded by a punctuation mark is considered.

To generate features, we use a window of size three around the target space. The features are defined as follows:

- The part-of-speech of the previous word
- The existence of a conjunctive or connective proclitic in the following word; that is a "w" or "f" proclitic that is either a conjunction, a sub-conjunction or a connective particle

The part-of-speech and proclitic information is obtained by running MADAMIRA on the text.

We also ran experiments where the model is trained with a complete list of features produced by MADAMIRA; that is part-of-speech, gender, number, person, aspect, voice, case, mood, state, proclitics and enclitics. This was done for two preceding words and two following words. However, this model did not perform as well as the one described above, which we used in the final system.

Note that the punctuation model predicts presence or absence of a punctuation mark in a specific location and is applied to the source data from which all punctuation marks have been removed. However, when we apply our punctuation model in the correction pipeline, we find that it is always better to keep the already existing periods and commas in the input text instead of overwriting them with the model prediction. In other words, we only attempt to add missing punctuation.

3.6 Dialectal Usage Corrector

Even though the shared task data is written in MSA, MSA is not a native language for Arabic speakers. Typically, an Arabic speaker has a native proficiency in one of the many Arabic dialects and learns to write and read MSA in a formal setting. For this reason, even in MSA texts produced by native Arabic speakers, one typically finds words and linguistic features specific to the writer's native dialect that are not found in the standard language.

To address such errors, we use Elissa (Salloum and Habash, 2012), which is Dialectal to Standard Arabic Machine Translation System. Elissa uses a rule-based approach that relies on the existence of a dialectal morphological analyzer (Salloum and Habash, 2011), a list of hand-written transfer rules, and dialectal-to-standard Arabic lexicons. Elissa uses different dialect identification techniques to select dialectal words and phrases (dialectal multi-word expressions) that need to be handled. Then equivalent MSA paraphrases of the selected words/phrases are generated and an MSA lattice for each input sentence is constructed. The paraphrases within the lattice are then ranked using language models and the n-best sentences are extracted from lattice. We use 5-gram language models trained using SRILM (Stolcke, 2002) on about 200 million untokenized, *Alif/Ya* normalized words extracted from Arabic GigaWord. This component is employed in the CLMB-2 system.

3.7 Pattern-Based Corrector

We created a set of rules that account for very common phenomena involving incorrectly split or merged tokens. The MADAMIRA corrector described above does not handle splits and merges; however, some of the cases are handled in the MLE method. Note that the MLE method is restrictive since it does not correct words not seen in training, while the pattern-based corrector is more general. The rules were created through analysis of samples of the QALB Shared Task training data. Some of the rules use regular expressions, while others make use of the rule-based Standard Arabic Morphological Analyzer (SAMA) (Maamouri et al., 2010), the same out-of-context analyzer used inside of MADAMIRA.

Rules for splitting words

- All digits are separated from words.
- A space is added after all word medial *Ta-Marbuta* characters.
- A space is added after the very common "ElY" 'at/about/on' preposition if it is attached to the following word.
- If a word has a morphological analysis that includes "lmA" (as negation particle, relative pronoun or pseudo verb), "hA" (a demonstrative pronoun), or "Ebd" and ">bw" in proper nouns, a space is inserted after those parts of the analysis.
- If a word has no morphological analysis, but starts with a set of commonly mis-attached words, and the rest of the word has an analysis, the word is split after the mis-attached word sequence.

Rules for merging words

- All lone occurrences of the conjunction *w* 'and' are attached to the following word.
- All sequences of the punctuation marks (., ?, !) that occur between two and six times are merged: e.g ! ! ! $\rightarrow$!!!.

4 Experimental Results

In Section 3, we described the individual system components that address different types of errors. In this section, we show how the system improves when each component is added into the system. System output is scored with the M2 scorer (Dahlmeier and Ng, 2012), the official scorer of the shared task.

Table 2 reports performance results of each version of the Columbia system on the development data. Table 3 shows the performance results for the best-performing system, CLMB-1, as each system component is added.

System	P	R	F1
CLMB-1	**72.22**	**62.79**	**67.18**
CLMB-2	69.49	61.72	65.38
CLMB-3	69.71	59.42	64.15

Table 2: **Performance of the Columbia systems on the development data.**

System	P	R	F1
MADAMIRA	83.33	32.94	47.21
+ MLE	86.52	42.52	57.02
+ NB	85.80	43.27	57.53
+ Punc.	73.66	59.51	65.83
+ Patterns	72.22	62.79	67.18

Table 3: **Performance of the CLMB-1 system on the development data and the contribution of its components.**

System	P	R	F1
CLMB-1	**73.34**	**63.23**	**67.91**
CLMB-2	70.86	62.21	66.25
CLMB-3	71.45	60.00	65.22

Table 4: **Performance of the Columbia systems on the test data.**

Finally, Table 4 reports results obtained on the test data. These results are comparable to the performance observed on the development data. In particular, CLMB-1 achieves the highest score.

5 Conclusion

We have described the Columbia University system that participated in the first shared task on grammatical error correction for Arabic and ranked first out of nine participating teams. We have presented three versions of the system; all of these incorporate several components that target different types of mistakes, which we presented and evaluated in this paper.

Acknowledgments

This material is based on research funded by grant NPRP-4-1058-1-168 from the Qatar National Research Fund (a member of the Qatar Foundation). The statements made herein are solely the responsibility of the authors. Nizar Habash performed most of his contribution to this paper while he was at the Center for Computational Learning Systems at Columbia University.

References

T. Buckwalter. 2007. Issues in Arabic Morphological Analysis. In A. van den Bosch and A. Soudi, editors, *Arabic Computational Morphology: Knowledge-based and Empirical Methods*. Springer.

D. Dahlmeier and H. T. Ng. 2012. Better evaluation for grammatical error correction. In *Proceedings of NAACL*.

A. El Kholy and N. Habash. 2012. Orthographic and morphological processing for English–Arabic statistical machine translation. *Machine Translation*, 26(1-2).

N. Farra, N. Tomeh, A. Rozovskaya, and N. Habash. 2014. Generalized character-level spelling error correction. In *Proceedings of ACL*.

J. Fiscus. 1998. Sclite scoring package version 1.5. US National Institute of Standard Technology (NIST), URL http://www. itl. nist. gov/iaui/894.01/tools.

N. Y. Habash. 2010. *Introduction to Arabic natural language processing*. Synthesis Lectures on Human Language Technologies 3.1.

M. Hall, F. Eibe, G. Holmes, B. Pfahringer, P. Reutemann, and I. H. Witten. 2009. The WEKA data mining software: an update. *SIGKDD Explorations*, 11(1):10–18.

T. Kudo. 2005. YamCha: Yet another multipurpose chunk annotator. http://chasen.org/ taku/software/.

M. Maamouri, D. Graff, B. Bouziri, S. Krouna, A. Bies, and S. Kulick. 2010. *LDC Standard Arabic Morphological Analyzer (SAMA) Version 3.1*. Linguistic Data Consortium.

B. Mohit, A. Rozovskaya, N. Habash, W. Zaghouani, and O. Obeid. 2014. The first QALB shared task on automatic text correction for Arabic. In *Proceedings of EMNLP Workshop on Arabic Natural Language Processing*.

H. T. Ng, S. M. Wu, Y. Wu, Ch. Hadiwinoto, and J. Tetreault. 2013. The CoNLL-2013 shared task on grammatical error correction. In *Proceedings of CoNLL: Shared Task*.

H. T. Ng, S. M. Wu, T. Briscoe, C. Hadiwinoto, R. H. Susanto, and C. Bryant. 2014. The CoNLL-2014 shared task on grammatical error correction. In *Proceedings of CoNLL: Shared Task*.

R. Parker, D. Graff, K. Chen, J. Kong, and K. Maeda. 2011. *Arabic Gigaword Fifth Edition*. Linguistic Data Consortium.

A. Pasha, M. Al-Badrashiny, A. E. Kholy, R. Eskander, M. Diab, N. Habash, M. Pooleery, O. Rambow, and R. Roth. 2014. MADAMIRA: A fast, comprehensive tool for morphological analysis and disambiguation of arabic. In *Proceedings of LREC*.

A. Rozovskaya and D. Roth. 2011. Algorithm selection and model adaptation for ESL correction tasks. In *Proceedings of ACL*.

W. Salloum and N. Habash. 2011. Dialectal to standard arabic paraphrasing to improve arabic-english statistical machine translation. In *Proceedings of the First Workshop on Algorithms and Resources for Modelling of Dialects and Language Varieties*.

W. Salloum and N. Habash. 2012. Elissa: A dialectal to standard arabic machine translation system. In *Proceedings of COLING (Demos)*.

A. Stolcke. 2002. Srilm-an extensible language modeling toolkit. In *Proceedings of International Conference on Spoken Language Processing*.

W. Zaghouani, B. Mohit, N. Habash, O. Obeid, N. Tomeh, A. Rozovskaya, N. Farra, S. Alkuhlani, and K. Oflazer. 2014. Large scale arabic error annotation: Guidelines and framework. In *Proceedings of the Ninth International Conference on Language Resources and Evaluation (LREC'14)*.

A Large Scale Arabic Sentiment Lexicon for Arabic Opinion Mining

Gilbert Badaro, Ramy Baly, Hazem Hajj
Electrical and Computer Engineering Department
American University of Beirut, Lebanon
{ggb05,rgb15,hh63}@aub.edu.lb

Nizar Habash
Computer Science Department
New York University Abu Dhabi, UAE
nizar.habash@nyu.edu

Wassim El-Hajj
Computer Science Department
American University of Beirut, Lebanon
we07@aub.edu.lb

Abstract

Most opinion mining methods in English rely successfully on sentiment lexicons, such as English SentiWordnet (ESWN). While there have been efforts towards building Arabic sentiment lexicons, they suffer from many deficiencies: limited size, unclear usability plan given Arabic's rich morphology, or non-availability publicly. In this paper, we address all of these issues and produce the first publicly available large scale Standard Arabic sentiment lexicon (ArSenL) using a combination of existing resources: ESWN, Arabic WordNet, and the Standard Arabic Morphological Analyzer (SAMA). We compare and combine two methods of constructing this lexicon with an eye on insights for Arabic dialects and other low resource languages. We also present an extrinsic evaluation in terms of subjectivity and sentiment analysis.

1 Introduction

Opinion mining refers to the extraction of subjectivity and polarity from text (Pang and Lee, 2005). With the growing availability and popularity of opinion rich resources such as online review sites and personal blogs, opinion mining is capturing the interest of many researchers due to its significant role in helping people make their decisions (Taboada et al., 2011). Some opinion mining methods in English rely on the English lexicon SentiWordnet (ESWN) (Esuli and Sebastiani, 2006; Baccianella et al., 2010) for extracting word-level sentiment polarity. Some researchers used the stored positive or negative connotation of the words to combine them and derive the polarity of the text (Esuli and Sebastiani, 2005).

Recently, special interest has been given to mining opinion from Arabic texts, and as a result, there has also been interest in developing an Arabic Lexicon for word-level sentiment evaluation. The availability of a large scale Arabic based SWN is still limited (Alhazmi et al., 2013; Abdul-Mageed and Diab, 2012; Elarnaoty et al., 2012). In fact, there is no publicly available large scale Arabic sentiment lexicon similar to ESWN. Additionally there are limitations with existing Arabic lexicons including deficiency in covering the correct number and type of lemmas.

In this paper, we propose to address these challenges, and create a large-scale sentiment lexicon benefiting from available Arabic lexica. We compare two methods with an eye towards creating such resources for other Arabic dialects and low resource languages. One lexicon is created by matching Arabic WordNet (AWN) (Black et al., 2006) to ESWN. This path relies on the existence of a wordnet, a rather expensive resource; while the second lexicon is developed by matching lemmas in the SAMA (Graff et al., 2009) lexicon to ESWN directly. This path relies on the existence of a mere dictionary, still expensive but more likely available than a wordnet. Finally, the combination of the two lexicons is used to create the proposed large-scale Arabic Sentiment Lexicon (ArSenL). Each lemma entry in the lexicon has three scores associated with the level of matching for each of the three sentiment labels: positive, negative, and objective.

The paper is organized as follows. A literature review presented in section 2 is conducted on work that involved developing multilingual lexi-

Proceedings of the EMNLP 2014 Workshop on Arabic Natural Langauge Processing (ANLP), pages 165–173,
October 25, 2014, Doha, Qatar. ©2014 Association for Computational Linguistics

cal resources. In section 3, the steps followed to create ArSenL are detailed. Extrinsic evaluation of ArSenL is discussed in section 4. In section 5, we conclude our work and outline possible extensions.

2 Literature Review

There have been numerous efforts for creating sentiment lexica in English and Arabic. Esuli and Sebastiani (2006) introduced English SentiWordNet (ESWN), a resource that associates synsets in the English WordNet (EWN) with scores for objectivity, positivity, and negativity. ESWN has been widely used for opinion mining in English (Denecke, 2008; Ohana and Tierney, 2009). Staiano and Guerini (2014) introduced DepecheMood, a 37K entry lexicon assigning emotion scores to words. This lexicon was created automatically by harvesting social media data and affective annotated data.

In the context of developing sentiment lexica and resources for Arabic, Abdul-Mageed et al. (2011) evaluated the use of an adjective polarity lexicon on a manually annotated portion of the Penn Arabic Treebank. They describe the process of creating the adjective polarity lexicon (named SIFAAT) in Abdul-Mageed and Diab (2012) using a combination of manual and automatic annotations. The manual annotation consisted of extracting 3,982 Arabic adjectives from the Penn Arabic Tree (part 1) and manually labeling them into three tags: positive, negative or neutral. The automated annotation relied on the automatic translation of the ESWN synsets and glosses using Google translate. More recently, Abdul-Mageed and Diab (2014) extended their lexicons creating SANA, a subjectivity and sentiment lexicon for Arabic. SANA combines different pre-existing lexica and involves extensive manual annotation, automatic machine translation and statistical formulation based on pointwise mutual information. The process also involved gloss matching across several resources such as THARWA (Diab et al., 2014) and SAMA (Graff et al., 2009). SANA included 224,564 entries which cover Modern Standard Arabic (MSA) as well as Egyptian and Levantine dialects. These entries are not distinct and possess many duplicates. Through these different publications, the authors heavily rely on two types of techniques: manual annotations, which can be rather expensive (yet accurate) and automatic translation which is cheap (but very noisy since the Arabic output is not diacritized and no POS information was used). Their SANA lexicon has a mix of lemmas and inflected forms, many of which are not diacritized. This is not a problem in itself, but it limits the usability of the resource. That said, we use their annotated PATB corpus and SIFAAT lexicon for evaluating our lexicon. We focus on these two resources because they were manually created and are of good quality.

Alhazmi et al. (2013) linked the Arabic WordNet to ESWN through the provided synset offset information. Their approach had limited coverage (~10K lemmas only) and did not define a process for using the lexicon in practical application given Arabic's complex morphology. Furthermore it is not yet publicly available and was not evaluated in the context of an application.

In addition to English and Arabic sentiment lexica development, recent efforts were put to develop a multilingual sentiment lexicon. Chen and Skienna (2014) proposed an automatic approach for creating sentiment lexicons for 136 major languages that include Arabic by integrating several resources to create a graph across words in different languages. The resources used were Wiktionary, Machine translation (Google), Transliteration and WordNet. They created links across 100,000 words by retrieving five binary fields using the above four resources. Then using a seed list obtained from Liu's English lexicon (2010) the sentiment labels are propagated based on the links in the developed graph. The resulting Arabic sentiment lexicon which is of small size was compared to SIFAAT (Abdul-Mageed and Diab, 2012).

We are inspired by these efforts for Arabic sentiment lexicon creation. We extend them by comparing different methods for creating such a resource with implications for other languages. Our lexicon is not only large-scale with high coverage and high accuracy, but it is also publicly available. Finally, our lemma-based lexicon is linked to a morphological analyzer for ease of use in conjunction with Arabic lemmatizer such as MADA (Habash and Rambow, 2005).

3 Approaches to Lexicon Creation

We define our target Arabic Sentiment Lexicon (or ArSenL) as a resource, pairing Arabic lemmas used in the morphological analyzer SAMA with sentiment scores such as those used in ESWN (positive, negative and neutral scores). We briefly describe next the different resources we use, followed by two methods for creating ArSenL: using an existing Arabic WordNet or using English glosses in a dictionary.

3.1 Resources

We rely on four existing resources to create ArSenL: English WordNet (EWN), Arabic WordNet (AWN), English SentiWordNet (ESWN) and SAMA. A high level summary of characteristics is shown in Table 1.

Lexicon	Language	Sentiment	#Synsets	#Lemmas
EWN	English	No	~90K	~120K
AWN	Arabic	No	~10K	~7K
ESWN	English	**Yes**	~90K	~120K
SAMA	Arabic-English	No	N/A	~40K
ArSenL	**Arabic**	**Yes**	157,969	**28,760**

Table 1. The different resources used to build ArSenL.

The English WordNet (EWN) (Miller et al., 1990) is perhaps one of the most used resources for English NLP. Several offset-linked versions of EWN have been released (2.0, 2.1, 3.0 and 3.1). The offset is a unique identifier for a synset in EWN. EWN includes a dictionary augmented with lexical relations (synonymy, antonymy, etc.) and part-of-speech (POS) tags.

Arabic WordNet (AWN 2.0) (Black et al., 2006) was part of a Global WordNet project whose aim was to develop WordNets similar to EWN but for different languages. AWN entries are connected by offsets to EWN 2.0. AWN does not include Arabic examples or glosses as EWN, but include POS tags.

English SentiWordNet (ESWN 3.0) (Esuli and Sebastiani, 2006) is a large-scale English Sentiment lexicon that provides for each synset in EWN 3.0 three sentiment scores whose sum is equal to 1: Pos, Neg, and Obj. ESWN has the same offset mappings of EWN across its different versions.

Standard Arabic Morphological Analyzer (SAMA 3.1) (Graff et al., 2009) is a commonly used morphological analyzer for Arabic. Each lemma has a POS tag and English gloss. The analyzer produces for a given word all of its possible readings out of context.

3.2 Arabic WordNet-based Approach

In this approach, we rely on the existence of a richly annotated resource, namely a wordnet, which is aligned to the ESWN. For Arabic, this approach requires two steps: mapping AWN to ESWN and mapping SAMA to AWN. The mapping between AWN to EWSN provides us with the sentiment scores and the mapping between AWN and SAMA provides us with the correct lemma forms for the words in AWN. We refer to the resulting lexicon as **ArSenL-AWN**.

Mapping AWN to ESWN. The entries in the various Wordnet resources we use are nicely linked through offsets to allow backward compatibility and linkage (see Figure 1). Figure 1 shows the connection with a walking example for the word **شعر $aEor**[1] 'hair'. We use the available offset maps to link synsets in AWN 2.0 to those in ESWN 3.0 and thus are able to assign sentiment scores to the AWN 2.0 entries. We make use of sense map files provided by WordNet that connect its three different versions 2.0, 2.1 and 3.0. Since some of the offsets were used to refer to different entries in WordNet, POS tags were also checked to validate the mapping. The process of aligning AWN to ESWN yielded very reliable links.

We manually checked each of the 9,692 terms in AWN and their ESWN English complements. Out of the 9,692, there were only 9 AWN words that did not match with anything in ESWN; and 48 entries in AWN that had no lemmas to start with although they were linked to ESWN. These terms were dropped for the next processing performed. Thus, this technique only allowed us to line 9,635 synsets corresponding to 6,967 Arabic lemmas. Through this process, we noticed that there were no sense map files for adjectives in WordNet which limited the mappings performed in this approach to nouns and verbs only.

Mapping SAMA to AWN. The alignment of Arabic lemmas in SAMA and AWN is complicated due to several issues:

a. SAMA and AWN do not always agree on lemma orthography, e.g., long vowel A is represented as A in SAMA and aA in AWN, and the two resources do not always agree on Hamzated Alif forms (Habash, 2010). The issue of Hamzated Alif is solved by replacing it in both resources by the letter A. The definition of lemmas varies between the two, e.g., SAMA does not use the definite article in nouns, and uses the stem of the 3rd person masculine singular verb (as opposed to full form): katab not kataba 'to write'.

b. AWN has multi-word lemmas, which SAMA lacks.

---

[1] Arabic transliteration is provided in the Buckwalter Scheme (Buckwalter, 2004).

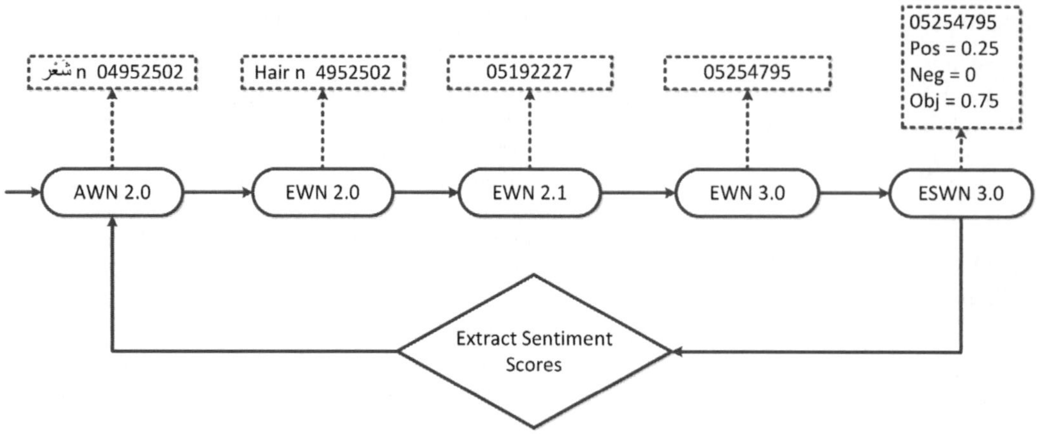

Figure 1. Steps to map AWN 2.0 to ESWN 3.0 with a walking example for the word شعر $aEor 'hair'.

To address these issues, we first exclude the multi-word lemmas in AWN, which account for 1,695 lemmas out of 6,967 (24%). Of the rest, exact matching against SAMA yields pairings for 1,736 lemmas. After applying a set of orthographic and lemma-form normalization rules as indicated in Table 2, exact matching yields additional 1927 lemma matches. Finally, we back off to using the SAMA morphological analyzer on AWN terms and selecting the lemma with the lowest edit distance. This step adds 1,094 lemma matches. Overall, 7,326 synsets entries corresponding to 5,002 lemmas in AWN are linked to 4,507 lemmas in SAMA. The linked lemmas account for 95% of all single word lemmas in AWN, but only correspond to 12% of SAMA lemmas. Moreover, we manually validated the mapping between SAMA and AWN lemmas, specifically the ones that were mapped using SAMA back off with minimum edit distance computation. 10% were not correct matches. We corrected them and created a gold reference for the lexicon, which we use in the evaluation section. In Table 3, we report some entries that were mapped wrongly between AWN and SAMA and which were removed from the lexicon.

In AWN	After Modification	Example
aA	A	(struggle) kifaAH → kifAH
If (pos = = v and lemma ends with a)	Remove "a"	(circulate) $aAEa →$aAE
If lemma ends with K	Replace K by iy	(past) mADK → mADiy

Table 2. Summary of modifications performed to AWN lemmas in order to match them to SAMA.

Examples of entries in ArSenL-AWN are shown in Table 4. Each row represents a field in ArSenL-AWN. AWN-Offset represents the offset of the Arabic word in AWN 2.0. SWN-Offset is the mapped SWN 3.0 entry's offset. The AWN lemma is the lemma form that is found in AWN 2.0 and SAMA lemma field is its corresponding lemma in SAMA form after performing the cleanup. Positive and negative score fields are the ones retrieved from SWN 3.0. The confidence is a percentage that represents our confidence in the entry.

AWN Offset	114276721	112853471	200548789
SWN Offset	15133621	13619764	00564300
POS tag	N	n	v
AWN Lemma	>amad_n1AR	AlgaAluwn_n1AR	Haloma>a_v1AR
SAMA Lemma	>amobiyr_1	gAliy_1	Halum-u_1
Positive Score	0	0	0
Negative Score	0	0	0
Confidence	100	100	100
English Gloss	Duration	gallon	hydrolize

Table 3. Examples of entries that were mapped incorrectly from AWN to SAMA

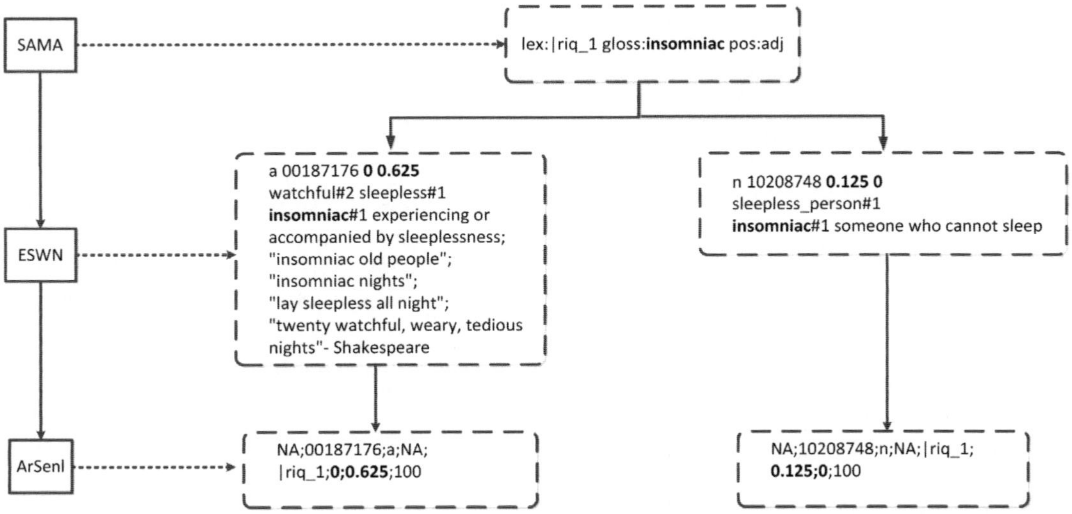

Figure 2. Steps to map SAMA to ESWN 3.0 with a walking example for the word أرق.

Since AWN was connected to SWN through a direct mapping all the entries of ArSenL-AWN were assigned 100% confidence. In table 5, row 3 summarizes the numbers obtained through the automated process and row 7, the results obtained after manual correction.

AWN Offset	100392523	201014980
SWN Offset	00410247	01048569
POS tag	n	v
AWN Lemma	EaAdap_n1AR	SaAHa_v2AR
SAMA Lemma	EAdap_1	SAH-i_1
Positive Score	0.25	0
Negative Score	0.125	0
Confidence	100	100
English Gloss	habit, custom, practice	scream, call

Table 4. Examples of entries in ArSenL-AWN.

3.3 English Gloss-based Approach

In this approach, we make use of the English glosses associated with the SAMA lemma entries. For each entry, we find the synset in ESWN with the highest overlap in SAMA English glosses. A walking example of the described method is shown in Figure 2. The recall of the SAMA gloss is used as a confidence measure of the mapping. We refer to the resulting lexicon as **ArSenL-Eng**.

Each lemma in SAMA is appended with a gloss list that varies in size from 1 up to 6 words. Let *n* denote the number of words available in the gloss list. We first attempt to match all the words in the list to the glosses of each entry in ESWN. If one or more matches are found, the scores are retrieved and a new entry in SAMA is processed as described. In case there were no matches, we try to find an overlap between a combination of *n-1* words of the SAMA gloss list and the glosses of ESWN. If one or more matches are found, the scores are retrieved and each match is recorded in ArSenL-Eng. Again, if no matches were obtained, the same process is repeated for the combination of *n-2* words of the SAMA gloss list.

Lexicon	#Lemmas	#Related Synsets
Automatic Process		
ArSenL-AWN	4,507	7,326
ArSenL-Eng	28,540	150,700
ArSenL-Union	28,812	158,026
Manual Correction		
ArSenL-AWN	4,492	7,269
ArSenL-Union	28,780	157,969

Table 5. Sizes of the created sentiment lexica.

This procedure is followed until we span all the words in the gloss list. As the number of words used in the combination to check for overlap between the two resources decreases, the confidence percentage decreases. In ArSenL-Eng, the confidence measure is equal to the ratio of the number of words overlapping between SAMA and ESWN over the total number of words available in the gloss list of the corresponding SAMA entry. Besides checking the overlap of glosses, POS tags are also used to make sure that verbs are not mapped to nouns and vice versa. This technique results in mapping 150,700 ESWN synsets corresponding to 28,540 distinct lemmas in SAMA (76%). The validation of ArSenL-Eng was performed (a) automatically by using **ArSenL-AWN** and (b) manually by randomly validating 400 distinct lemmas. For the automated part, we check for each common lemma between the two lexicons if the sentiment scores match. A total of 3,833 lemmas (out of 4,507) from ArSenL-AWN were matched in ArSenL-Eng.

Thus, we can inspect that the precision of the remaining scores is of 85%. For the manual validation, we check if the meaning of the SAMA lemma corresponds to the one in ESWN. 70% of the 400 randomly selected lemmas were accurately mapped to ESWN. The main issue of the remaining 30% is the unavailability of enough glosses per SAMA lemma, which makes the connection weaker. This approach did not involve manual correction and the lemma numbers are reported in row 4 of Table 5 along with their corresponding number of related synsets.

3.4 Combining the Two Approaches

We combine the two lexica created above by taking their union. We refer to the resulting lexicon as ArSenL. The details of the sizes of the three lexica are shown in Table 5.

The union of the two lexicons consisted of combining the two resources and adding a field in the lexicon to distinguish the original source of the entry. For instance, an entry from the first approach, i.e. ArSenL-AWN, will have an AWN offset while an entry in ArSenL-Eng will have the same field set to N.A (Not Available). Furthermore, due to manual correction performed to ArSenL-AWN, the gold version of the union lexicon includes 28,780 lemmas with the corresponding number of 157,969 synsets.

A public interface to browsing ArSenL is available at http://oma-project.com. The interface allows the user to search for an Arabic word. The output would show the different scores for the Arabic word along with the corresponding sentiment scores, English glosses and examples that help in disambiguating different sentiment scores for the same Arabic lemma. Work is also being done to allow searching for English words and finding the corresponding Arabic words. Snapshot of the homepage is shown in Figure 3.

4 Evaluation

We conduct an extrinsic evaluation to compare the different versions of ArSenL on the task of subjectivity and sentiment analysis (SSA). We also compare the performance of the SIFAAT lexicon (Abdul-Mageed et al., 2011) discussed in Section 2.

Experimental Settings We perform our experiments on the same corpus used by Abdul-Mageed et al. (2011). The corpus consists of 400 documents form the Penn Arabic Treebank (part 1 version 3) that are gold segmented and lemmatized. The sentences are tagged as objective, subjective-positive, subjective-negative and subjective-neutral.

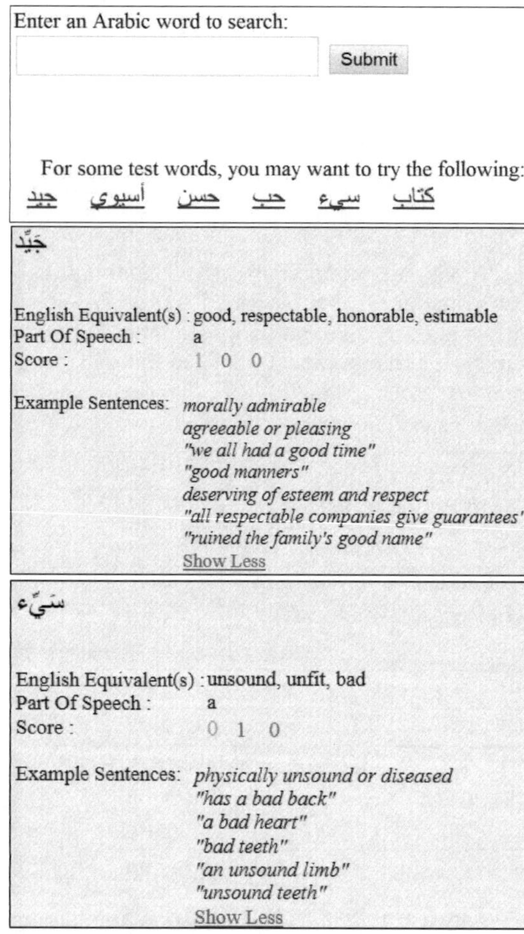

Figure 3. Homepage of the lexicon interface and snapshots of examples searched through the interface. Positive, negative and objective scores are represented in green, red and gray respectively.

We use nonlinear SVM implementation in MATLAB, with the radial basis function (RBF) kernel, to evaluate the different lexicons in the context of SSA. The classification model is developed in two steps. In the first step, the kernel parameters (kernel's width γ and regularization parameter C) are selected, and in the second step the classification model is developed and evaluated based on the selected parameters. To decide on the choice of RBF kernel parameters, we use the first 80% of the dataset to tune the kernel parameters to the values that produce the best F1-score using 5-fold cross-validation. The resulting parameters are then used to develop and evaluate the SVM model using 5-fold cross-validation on the whole dataset.

Two experiments were conducted to evaluate the impact of the different lexicons on opinion mining. The first experiment considers subjectivity classification where sentences are classified as either subjective or objective. In this experiment, the SVM kernel parameters were tuned to maximize the F1-score for predicting subjective sentences. The second experiment considers sentiment classification, where only subjective sentences are classified as either positive or negative. Subjective-neutral sentences are ignored. In this experiment, the classifier's parameters are tuned to maximize the average F1-score of positive and negative labels. We report the performance measures of the individual classes, as well as their average.

For baseline comparison, the majority class is chosen in each of the experiments, where all sentences are assigned to the majority class. For subjective versus objective baseline classification, all sentences were classified as subjective since the majority (55.1%) of the sentences were subjective. To further emphasize the importance of detecting subjectivity, we chose the F1-score for subjective as baseline. For positive versus negative baseline classification, all sentences were classified as negative since the majority (58.4%) of the dataset was annotated as negative. The resulting baseline performance measures are captured in Table 6, and serve as basis for comparison with our developed models. For the subjective versus objective the baseline F1-score is 71.1%, and for positive versus negative, the baseline F1-score is averaged as 36.9%.

Features We train the SVM classifier using sentence vectors consisting of three numerical features that reflect the sentiments expressed in each sentence, namely positivity, negativity and objectivity. The value of each feature is calculated by matching the lemmas in each sentence to each of the lexicons separately: ArSenL-AWN, ArSenL-Eng, ArSenL-Union and SIFAAT. The corresponding scores are then accumulated and normalized by the length of the sentence. We remove all stop words in the process. For words that occur in the lexicon multiple times, the average sentiment score is used. It is worth noting that the choice of aggregation for the different scores and the choice of nonlinear SVM was concluded after a set of experiments, but not reported in the paper. In this regards, we conducted a suite of experiments to evaluate the impact of using: (a) linear versus Gaussian nonlinear SVM kernels, (b) normalization based on sentence length, (c) normalization using z-score versus not, and (d) using the confidence score from the lexicons. Our best results across the different configurations reflected the best results with the non-linear Gaussian RBF kernels, with sentence length-based normalization and without confidence weighting.

		Base-line	ArSenL			Sifaat
			AWN	Eng	Union	
Coverage %		NA	56.6	88.8	**89.9**	32.1
Subjective	F1	71.1	71.2	72.1	**72.3**	66
	Pre	55.1	58.1	58.5	58.3	**61.5**
	Rec	100	92	93.9	**95.1**	71.4
Positive	F1	0	52.9	59.7	**61.6**	55.4
	Pre	0	44.7	55	**55.2**	51.8
	Rec	0	64.8	65.6	**70.1**	60.2
Negative	F1	73.7	55	65.1	**67.3**	63
	Pre	58.4	67	70.7	**75.6**	67.6
	Rec	100	46.9	60.6	**61**	59.4
Average F1 (Pos/Neg)		36.9	53.9	62.4	**64.5**	59.2

Table 6. Results of extrinsic evaluation. Numbers that are highlighted reflect the best performances obtained by the lexicons, without considering the baseline

Results Three evaluations were conducted to compare the performances of the developed sentiment lexicons. The results of the experiments are shown in Table 6. First, we evaluate the coverage of the different lexicons. We define coverage as the percentage of lemmas (excluding stop words) covered by each lexicon. ArSenL-AWN and SIFAAT have lower coverage than the ArSenL-Eng lexicon. The union lexicon has the highest coverage. This is normally due to the larger number of lemmas included in the English and union lexicons, as shown in Table 5.

In subjectivity classification, ArSenL lexicons perform better than the majority baseline and outperform SIFAAT in terms of F1-score. Overall, the developed ArSenL-Union gives the best performance among all lexicons. The only exception of better performance for SIFAAT for subjectivity is in terms of precision, which is associated with a much lower recall resulting in an F1-score that is lower than that of ArSenL's.

Similarly, sentiment classification experiment reveals that ArSenL lexicons produce results that are consistently better than SIFAAT and the majority baseline. The ArSenL-Union lexicon outperforms all lexicons in all measures without exceptions.

In summary, it can be observed that the English-based lexicon produces results that are superior to the AWN-based lexicon. Combining both resources, through the union, allows further improvement in SSA performance. It is also worth noting that the English and union lexicons consistently outperform SIFAAT despite the fact that the latter was manually derived from the same corpus we are using for evaluation. We close by showing examples of ArSenL in Table 7.

The lemmas are in their Buckwalter (2004) format for easier integration in any NLP task. The word NA stands for Not Applicable. In the case where AWN Offset is NA and AWN lemma is NA, this means that the entry is retrieved from ArSenL-Eng. Otherwise, the entries are from ArSenL-AWN. The additions to the lemmas such as "_v1AR" , "_n1AR", "_1" or "_2" can be dropped when data processing is performed. They were kept for easier retrieval in the original sources (AWN and SAMA). We added the "English Gloss" field for easier understanding of the Arabic word in the table. Moreover, it can be seen that only positive and negative scores are reported in the lexicon since the objective score can be easily derived by subtracting the sum of positive and negative scores from 1.

5 Conclusion and Future Work

We create a large sentiment lexicon for Arabic sentiments using different approaches linking to ESWN. We compared the two methods. Our results show that using English-based linking produces, on average, superior performance in comparison to using the WordNet-based approach. A union of the two resources is better than either and outperforms a high-quality manually-derived adjective sentiment lexicon for Arabic.

In the future, we plan to make use of this lexicon to develop more powerful SSA systems. We also plan to extend the effort to Arabic dialects and other languages.

6 Acknowledgments

This work was made possible by NPRP 6-716-1-138 grant from the Qatar National Research Fund (a member of Qatar Foundation). The statements made herein are solely the responsibility of the authors. Nizar Habash performed most of his contribution to this paper while he was at the Center for Computational Learning Systems at Columbia University.

AWN Offset	SWN Offset	POS tag	AWN Lemma	SAMA Lemma	Positive Score	Negative Score	Confidence	English Gloss
NA	04151581	n	NA	Aap_1	0	0	100	screen
NA	01335458	a	NA	$ATir_1	0.75	0	33	smart;bright
NA	05820620	n	NA	$Ahidap_1	0	0	50	proof
NA	00792921	v	NA	$Al-u_1	0	0	50	lift
NA	01285136	a	NA	$Amix_1	0.75	0	33	superior
NA	04730580	n	NA	danA'ap_1	0.222	0.778	33	inferiority
NA	01797347	v	NA	Hazin-a_1	0	0.5	50	sorrow
NA	00811421	a	NA	sAxin_1	0.75	0.125	50	hot
NA	07527352	n	NA	faraH_1	0.5	0.25	33	joy
NA	00064787	a	NA	Hasan_1	0.625	0	100	good
200300610	00310386	v	<izodahara_v1AR	{izodahar_1	0.125	0	100	flourish
200844607	00873682	v	>a$oEara_v1AR	>a$oEar_1	0	0	100	notify
201766276	01819147	v	>aHobaTa_v1AR	>aHobaT_1	0.125	0.5	100	discourage
114279405	15136453	n	nahaAr_n1AR	nahAr_2	0	0	100	day
100059106	00064504	n	najaAH_n1AR	najAH_2	0.625	0	100	success
113808178	14646610	n	naykl_n1AR	niykol_1	0	0	100	nickle
104540432	04748836	n	tabaAyun_n1AR	tabAyun_1	0.25	0.625	100	difference
200705236	00729378	v	tasaA'ala_v1AR	tasA'al_1	0.375	0	100	wonder
NA	01983162	a	NA	$ariyf_2	1	0	67	respectable
NA	05144663	n	NA	$ariyr_1	0	0.75	33	evil

Table 7. Samples of ArSenL showing entries originating from ArSenL-Eng and ArSenL-AWN.

References

Abdul-Mageed, M., Diab, M. and Korayem, M. (2011). Subjectivity and sentiment analysis of modern standard Arabic. *In Proceedings of the 49th Annual Meeting of the Association for Computational Linguistics: Human Language Technologies: short papers*-Volume 2. Association for Computational Linguistics.

Abdul-Mageed, M., & Diab, M. (2012). Toward building a large-scale Arabic sentiment lexicon. In *Proceedings of the 6th International Global WordNet Conference* (pp. 18-22).

Abdul-Mageed, M., & Diab, M. (2014) SANA: A Large Scale Multi-Genre, Multi-Dialect Lexicon for Arabic Subjectivity and Sentiment Analysis. *In Proceedings of the Language Resources and Evaluation Conference (LREC)*, Reykjavik, Iceland

Alhazmi, S., Black, W., & McNaught, J. (2013). Arabic SentiWordNet in Relation to SentiWordNet 3.0. *2180-1266*, *4*(1), 1-11.

Baccianella, S., Esuli, A., & Sebastiani, F. (2010, May). SentiWordNet 3.0: An Enhanced Lexical Resource for Sentiment Analysis and Opinion Mining. In *LREC* (Vol. 10, pp. 2200-2204).

Black, W., Elkateb, S., & Vossen, P. (2006). Introducing the Arabic wordnet project. In *In Proceedings of the third International WordNet Conference (GWC-06).*

Buckwalter, T. 2004. Buckwalter Arabic morphological analyzer version 2.0. LDC catalog number LDC2004L02, ISBN 1-58563-324-0

Chen, Y., & Skienna, S. (2014). Building Sentiment Lexicons for All Major Languages. *In Proceedings of the 52nd Annual Meeting of the Association for Computational Linguistics (Short Papers)* (pp. 383-389). 2014 Association for Computational Linguistics.

Denecke, K. (2008, April). Using sentiwordnet for multilingual sentiment analysis. *In Data Engineering Workshop, 2008. ICDEW 2008. IEEE 24th International Conference* on (pp. 507-512). IEEE.

Diab, M., Al-Badrashiny, M., Aminian, M., Attia, M., Dasigi, P., Elfardy, H., Eskander, R., Habash, N., Hawwari, A., & Salloum, W. (2014). Tharwa: A Large Scale Dialectal Arabic - Standard Arabic - English Lexicon. *In Proceedings of the Language Resources and Evaluation Conference (LREC)*, Reykjavik, Iceland.

Elarnaoty, M., AbdelRahman, S., & Fahmy, A. (2012). A Machine Learning Approach for Opinion Holder Extraction in Arabic Language. *International Journal of Artificial Intelligence & Applications*, *3*(2).

Esuli, A., & Sebastiani, F. (2005). Determining the semantic orientation of terms through gloss classification. In *Proceedings of the 14th ACM international conference on Information and knowledge management* (pp. 617-624). ACM.

Esuli, A., & Sebastiani, F. (2006). Sentiwordnet: A publicly available lexical resource for opinion mining. In *Proceedings of LREC* (Vol. 6, pp. 417-422).

Graff, D., Maamouri, M., Bouziri, B., Krouna, S., Kulick, S., & Buckwalter, T. (2009). Standard Arabic Morphological Analyzer (SAMA) Version 3.1, 2009. Linguistic Data Consortium LDC2009E73.

Habash, N., & Rambow, O., (2005). Arabic tokenization, part-of-speech tagging and morphological disambiguation in one fell swoop. Proceedings of the 43rd Annual Meeting on Association for Computational Linguistics. Association for Computational Linguistics.

Habash, N. (2010). Introduction to Arabic natural language processing. *Synthesis Lectures on Human Language Technologies*, *3*(1), 1-187.

Liu, B. (2010). Sentiment Analysis and Subjectivity. *Handbook of Natural Language Proccessing*, 2:568.

Maamouri, M., Bies, A., Buckwalter, T., & Mekki, W. (2004, September). The penn arabic treebank: Building a large-scale annotated arabic corpus. In *NEMLAR Conference on Arabic Language Resources and Tools* (pp. 102-109).

Miller, G. A., Beckwith, R., Fellbaum, C., Gross, D., & Miller, K. J. (1990). Introduction to wordnet: An on-line lexical database. *International journal of lexicography*, *3*(4), 235-244.

Ohana, B., & Tierney, B. (2009, October). Sentiment classification of reviews using SentiWordNet. *In 9th. IT & T Conference* (p. 13).

Pang, B., & Lee, L. (2004, July). A sentimental education: Sentiment analysis using subjectivity summarization based on minimum cuts. In *Proceedings of the 42nd annual meeting on Association for Computational Linguistics* (p. 271). Association for Computational Linguistics.

Pang, B., & Lee, L. (2005, June). Seeing stars: Exploiting class relationships for sentiment categorization with respect to rating scales. In *Proceedings of the 43rd Annual Meeting on Association for Computational Linguistics* (pp. 115-124). Association for Computational Linguistics.

Staiano, J., & Guerini, M. (2014). DepecheMood: a Lexicon for Emotion Analysis from Crowd-Annotated News. *arXiv preprint arXiv:1405.1605*.

Taboada, M., Brooke, J., Tofiloski, M., Voll, K., & Stede, M. (2011). Lexicon-based methods for sentiment analysis. *Computational linguistics*, *37*(2), 267-307.

Evaluating Distant Supervision for Subjectivity and Sentiment Analysis on Arabic Twitter Feeds

Eshrag Refaee and Verena Rieser
Interaction Lab, School of Mathematical and Computer Sciences,
Heriot-Watt University,
EH14 4AS Edinburgh, United Kingdom.
eaar1@hw.ac.uk, v.t.rieser@hw.ac.uk

Abstract

Supervised machine learning methods for automatic subjectivity and sentiment analysis (SSA) are problematic when applied to social media, such as Twitter, since they do not generalise well to unseen topics. A possible remedy of this problem is to apply distant supervision (DS) approaches, which learn from large amounts of automatically annotated data. This research empirically evaluates the performance of DS approaches for SSA on Arabic Twitter feeds. Results for emoticon- and lexicon-based DS show a significant performance gain over a fully supervised baseline, especially for detecting subjectivity, where we achieve 95.19% accuracy, which is a 48.47% absolute improvement over previous fully supervised results.

1 Introduction

Subjectivity and sentiment analysis (SSA) aims to determine the attitude of an author with respect to some topic, e.g. objective or subjective, or the overall contextual polarity of an utterance, e.g. positive or negative. Previous work on automatic SSA has used manually annotated gold standard data sets to analyse which feature sets and models perform best for this task, e.g. (Wilson et al., 2009; Wiebe et al., 1999). Most of this work is in English, but there have been first attempts to apply similar techniques to Arabic, e.g. (Abdul-Mageed et al., 2011; Mourad and Darwish, 2013). While these models work well when tested using cross-validation on limited static data sets, our previous results reveal that these models do not generalise to new data sets, e.g. collected at a later point in time, due to their limited coverage (Refaee and Rieser, 2014). While there is a growing interest within the NLP community in building Arabic corpora by harvesting the web, e.g. (Al-Sabbagh and Girju, 2012; Abdul-Mageed and Diab, 2012; Zaidan and Callison-Burch, 2013), these resources have not been publicly released yet and only small amounts of these data-sets are (manually) annotated. We therefore turn to an approach known as *distant supervision* (DS), as first proposed by (Read, 2005), which uses readily available features, such as emoticons, as noisy labels in order to efficiently annotate large amounts of data for learning domain-independent models. This approach has been shown to be successful for English SSA, e.g. (Go et al., 2009), and SSA for under-resourced languages, such as Chinese (Yuan and Purver, 2012).

The contributions of this paper are as follows: we first collect two large corpora using emoticons and lexicon-based features as noisy labels, which we plan to release as part of this submission. Second, this work is the first to apply and empirically evaluate DS approaches on Arabic Twitter feeds. We find that DS significantly outperforms fully supervised SSA on our held-out test set. However, compared to a majority baseline, predicting negative sentiment proves to be difficult using DS approaches. Third, we conduct an error analysis to critically evaluate the results and give recommendations for future directions.

2 Arabic Twitter SSA Corpora

We start by collecting three corpora at different times over one year to account for the cyclic effects of topic change in social media (Eisenstein, 2013). Table 1 shows the distributions of labels in our data-sets:

1. A gold standard data-set which we use for training and evaluation (spring 2013);
2. A data-set for DS using emoticon-based queries (autumn 2013);
3. Another data-set for DS using a lexicon-based approach (winter 2014).

Proceedings of the EMNLP 2014 Workshop on Arabic Natural Langauge Processing (ANLP), pages 174–179,
October 25, 2014, Doha, Qatar.

Data set	Neutral	Polar	Positive	Negative	Total
Gold standard training	1,157	937	470	467	3,031
Emoticon-based training	55,076	62,466	32,842	33,629	184,013
Lexicon-based training	55,076	55,538	18,442	5,013	134,069
Manually labelled test	422	579	278	301	1,580

Table 1: Sentiment label distribution of the gold standard manually annotated and distant supervision data sets.

Gold Standard Data-set: We harvest two gold standard data sets at different time steps, which we label manually. We first harvest a data set of 3,031 multi-dialectal Arabic tweets randomly retrieved over the period from February to March 2013. We use this set as a training set for our fully supervised approach. We also manually label 1,580 tweets collected in autumn 2013, which we use as an independent held-out test set. Two native speakers were recruited to manually annotate the collected data for subjectivity and sentiment, where we define sentiment as a positive or negative emotion, opinion or attitude, following (Wilson et al., 2009). Our gold standard annotations reached a weighted $\kappa = 0.76$, which indicates reliable annotations (Carletta, 1996). We also automatically annotate the corpus with a rich set of linguistically motivated features using freely available processing tools for Arabic, such as MADA (Nizar Habash and Roth, 2009), see Table 2. For more details on gold standard corpus annotation please see (Refaee and Rieser, 2014). [1]

Type	Feature-sets
Morphological	diacritic, aspect, gender, mood, person, part_of_speech (POS), state, voice, has_morphological_analysis.
Syntactic	n-grams of words and POS, lemmas, including bag_of_words (BOW), bag_of_lemmas.
Semantic	has_positive_lexicon, has_negative_lexicon, has_neutral_lexicon, has_negator, has_positive_emoticon, has_negative_emoticon.

Table 2: Annotated Feature-sets

Emoticon-Based Queries: In order to investigate DS approaches to SSA, we also collect a much larger data set of Arabic tweets, where we use emoticons as noisy labels, following e.g. (Read, 2005; Go et al., 2009; Pak and Paroubek, 2010; Yuan and Purver, 2012; Suttles and Ide, 2013). We query Twitter API for tweets with variations of positive and negative emoticons to obtain pairs of micro-blog texts (statuses) and using

Emoticon	Sentiment label
:) , :-) , :)), (: , (-: , ((:	positive
:(, :-(, :((, :((,): ,)):)-:	negative

Table 3: Emoticons used to automatically label the training data-set.

emoticons as author-provided emotion labels. In following (Purver and Battersby, 2012; Zhang et al., 2011; Suttles and Ide, 2013), we also utilise some sentiment-bearing hash tags to query emotional tweets, e.g. فرح *happiness* and حزن *sadness*. Note that emoticons and hash-tags are merely used to collect and build the training set and were replaced by the standard (positive/ negative) labels. In order to collect neutral instances, we query a set of official news accounts, following an approach by (Pak and Paroubek, 2010). Examples of the accounts queried are: BBC-Arabic, Al-Jazeera Arabic, SkyNews Arabia, Reuters Arabic, France24-Arabic, and DW Arabic. We then automatically extract the same set of linguistically motivated features as for the gold standard corpus.

Lexicon-Based Annotation: We also investigate an alternative approach to DS, which combines rule-driven lexicon-based SSA, e.g. (Taboada et al., 2011), with machine learning approaches, following (Zhang et al., 2011). We build a new training dataset by combining three lexica. We first exploit two existing subjectivity lexica: a manually annotated Arabic subjectivity lexicon (Abdul-Mageed and Diab, 2012) and a publicly available English subjectivity lexicon, MPQA (Wilson et al., 2009), which we automatically translate using Google Translate, following a

[1]This GS data-set has been shared via a special LREC repository available at http://www.resourcebook.eu/shareyourlr/index.php

similar technique to (Mourad and Darwish, 2013). The translated lexicon is manually corrected by removing translations with neutral or no clear sentiment indicator.[2] This results in 2,627 translated instances after correction. We then construct a third dialectal lexicon of 484 words that we extracted from an independent Twitter development set and manually annotated for sentiment. All lexicons were merged into a combined lexicon of 4,422 annotated sentiment words (duplicates removed). In order to obtain automatic labels for positive and negative instances, we follow a simplified version of the rule-based aggregation approach of Taboada et al. (2011). First, all lexicons and tweets are lemmatised. For each tweet, matched sentiment words are marked with either (+1) or (-1) to incorporate the semantic orientation of individual constituents. This achieves a coverage level of 76.62% (which is computed as a percentage of tweets with at least one lexicon word) using the combined lexicon. The identified sentiment words are replaced by place-holders to avoid bias. To account for negation, we reverse the polarity (switch negation) following (Taboada et al., 2011). The sentiment orientation of the entire tweet is then computed by summing up the sentiment scores of all sentiment words in a given tweet into a single score that automatically determines the label as being: positive or negative. Instances where the score equals zero are excluded from the training set as they represent mixed-sentiment instances with an even number of sentiment words. We validate this lexicon-based labelling approach against a separate development set by comparing the automatically computed labels against manually annotated ones, reaching an accuracy of 69.06%.

3 Classification Experiments Using Distant Supervision

We experiment with a number of machine learning methods and we report the results of the best performing scheme, namely Support Vector Machines (SVMs), where we use the implementation provided by WEKA (Witten and Frank, 2005). We report the results on two metrics: F-score and accuracy. We use paired t-tests to establish significant differences ($p < .05$). We experiment with different feature sets and report on the best results (*Bag-of-Words (BOW) + morphological + semantic*). We compare our results against a majority baseline and against a fully supervised approach. It is important to mention the most prominent previous work on SSA of Arabic tweets like (Abdul-Mageed et al., 2012) who trained SVM classifiers on a nearly 3K manually labelled data-set to curry out two-stage binary classification attaining accuracy up to 65.87% for the sentiment classification task. In a later work, (Mourad and Darwish, 2013) employ SVM and Naive Bayes classifiers trained on a set of 2,300 manually labelled Arabic tweets. With 10-fold cross-validation settings, the author reported an accuracy score of 72.5% for the sentiment classification task (positive vs. negative).

We evaluate the approaches on a separate held-out test-set that is collected at a later point in time, as described in Section 2.

3.1 Emoticon-Based Distant Supervision

We first evaluate the potential of exploiting training data that is automatically labelled using emoticons. The results are summarised in Table 4.

Polar vs. neutral: The results show a significant improvement over the majority baseline, as well as over the classifier trained on the gold standard data set: We achieve 95.19% accuracy on the held-out set, which is a 48.47% absolute improvement over our previous fully supervised results. We attribute this improvement to two factors. First, the emoticon-based data set is about 60 times bigger than the gold standard data set (see Table 1) and thus the emoticon-based model better generalises to unseen events. Note that this performance is comparable with (Suttles and Ide, 2013) who achieved up to 98% accuracy using emoticon-based DS on English tweets using 5.9 million tweets. Second, neutral instances were sampled from news accounts, which are mainly written in modern standard Arabic (MSA), whereas we assume that tweets including emoticons (which we use for acquiring polar instances) are mainly written in dialectal Arabic (DA). In future work, we plan to investigate this hypothesis further by automatically detecting MSA/DA for a given tweet, e.g. (Zaidan and Callison-Burch, 2013). Abdul-Mageed et al. (2012) show that having such a feature can result in no significant impact on the overall performance of both subjectivity and sentiment analysis tasks.

Positive vs. negative: For sentiment classification, the performance of the emoticon-based approach degrades notably to 51%, which is still

[2] For instance, *the day of judgement* is assigned with a negative label while its Arabic translation is neutral considering the context-independent polarity.

Data-set	majority baseline		fully supervised		emoticon DS		lexicon-presence		lexicon-aggr.	
	F	Acc.	F	Acc.	F	Acc.	F	Acc.	F	Acc.
polar vs. neutral	0.69	53.0	0.43	46.62	**0.95**	**95.19**	**0.95**	**95.09**	0.91	91.09
positive vs. negative	**0.67**	50.89	0.41	49.65	0.51	51.25	0.53	**57.06**	0.52	52.98

Table 4: 2-level and single-level SSA classification using distant supervision (DS).

significantly better that the fully supervised baseline, but nevertheless worse than a simple majority baseline. These results are much lower than previous results on emoticon-based sentiment analysis on English tweets by (Go et al., 2009; Bifet and Frank, 2010) which both achieved around 83% accuracy. The confusion matrix shows that mostly negative instances are misclassified as positive, with a very low recall on negative instances, see Table 5. Next, we investigate possible reasons in a detailed error analysis.

Data set	Precision	Recall
emoticon DS		
positive	0.479	0.81
negative	0.556	0.212
lexicon-presence DS		
positive	0.521	0.866
negative	0.733	0.317
lexicon-aggregation DS		
positive	0.496	0.650
negative	0.583	0.426

Table 5: Recall and precision for Sentiment Analysis

3.1.1 Error Analysis for Emoticon-Based DS

In particular, we investigate the use of sarcasm and the direction emoticons face in right-to-left alphabets.

Use of sarcasm and irony: Using an emoticon as a label is naturally noisy, since we cannot know for sure the intended meaning the author wishes to express. This is especially problematic when emoticons are used in a sarcastic way, i.e. their intended meaning is the opposite of the expressed emotion. An example from our data set is:

(1) جميل يا اهلي :(*great job Ahli :(— referring to a famous football team.*

Research in psychology shows that up to 31% of the time, emoticons are used sarcastically (Wolf, 2000). In order to investigate this hypothesis we manually labelled a random sample of 303 misclassified instances for neutral, positive, negative, as well as sarcastic, mixed and unclear sentiments, see Table 6. Interestingly, the sarcastic instances represent only 4.29%, while tweets with mixed (positive and negative) sentiments represent 5.94% of the manually annotated sub-set. In 34.32% of the instances, the manual labels have matched the automatic emoticon-based labels. Surprisingly, automatic emoticon-based label contrasts the manual labels in 36.63% of the instances. Instances labelled as neutral represent 4.95%. The rest of the instances were assigned 'unclear sentiment orientation'.

Emoticon Label	Predicted label	Manual label	# instances
Positive	Negative	Mixed	8
Negative	Positive	Mixed	10
Positive	Negative	Negative	59
Negative	Positive	Negative	42
Positive	Negative	Neutral	29
Negative	Positive	Neutral	7
Positive	Negative	Positive	62
Negative	Positive	Positive	52
Positive	Negative	Sarcastic	8
Negative	Positive	Sarcastic	5
Positive	Negative	Unclear sentiment indicator	19
Negative	Positive	Unclear sentiment indicator	2

Table 6: Results of labelling sarcasm, mixed emotions and unclear sentiment for misclassified instances.

Facing of emoticons: We therefore investigate another possible error source following (Mourad and Darwish, 2013), who claim that the right-to-left alphabetic writing of Arabic might result in emoticons being mistakenly interchanged while typing. On some Arabic keyboards, typing ")" will produce the opposite " (" parentheses. The following example (2) illustrates a case of a misclassified instance, where we assume that the facing of emoticons might have been interchanged or mistyped.

(2) خلاص مافي امل :) *no hope anymore :)*

3.2 Lexicon-Based Distant Supervision

To avoid the issue of ambiguity in the direction of facing, we experiment with a lexicon-based approach to DS: instead of using emoticons, we now utilise the adjectives in our sentiment lexicon as noisy labels. We experiment with two different settings for the lexicon-based DS approach. First, we experiment with a lexicon-presence approach that automatically labels a tweet as a positive instance if it only includes positive lexicon(s) and the same for the negative class. Data instances having mixed positive and negative lexicons or no sentiment lexicons are excluded from the training set. The second approach is based on assigning a numerical value to sentiment words and aggregating the value into a single score, see Section 2. The results are summarised in Table 4.

Polar vs. neutral: We can observe that the models trained with the lexicon-presence approach significantly outperform the majority baseline, the fully supervised learning, as well as the lexicon-aggregation approach. The lexicon-presence and the emoticon-based DS approaches reach almost identical performance on our test set.

Positive vs. negative: Again, we observe that it is difficult to discriminate negative instances for both lexicon-based approaches. The lexicon-presence approach significantly outperforms the majority baseline, the fully supervised learning, and the lexicon-aggregation approach. But this time it also significantly outperforms the emoticon-based approach, which allows us to conclude that lexicon-based labelling introduces less noise for sentiment analysis. However, our results are significantly worse than the lexicon-based approach of Taboada et al. (2011), with up to 80% accuracy, and the learning-based approach of Zhanh et al. (2011), with up to 85% accuracy on English tweets. The lexicon-presence approach achieves the highest precision for negative tweets, see table 5, but still has a low recall. The lexicon-aggregation approach has the highest recall for negative tweets, but its precision is almost identical to the emoticon-based approach.

3.2.1 Error Analysis for Lexicon-Based DS

We conduct an error analysis in order to further investigate the difference in performance between the lexicon-presence and the lexicon-aggregation approach. We hypothesise that the lexicon-aggregation might perform better on instances with mixed emotions, i.e. tweets with positive and negative indicators, but a clear overall sentiment. We therefore manually add 36 instances to the test set which contain mixed emotions (but a unique sentiment label). However, the results on the new test set confirm the superiority of the lexicon-presence approach. In general, both lexicon-based approaches perform worse for sentiment classification. Taboada et al. (2011) highlight the issue of "positive bias" associated with lexicon-based approaches of sentiment analysis, as people tend to prefer using positive expressions and understate negative ones.

4 Conclusion and Future Work

We address the task of subjectivity and sentiment analysis (SSA) for Arabic Twitter feeds. We empirically investigate the performance of distant supervision (DS) approaches on a manually labelled independent test set, in comparison to a fully supervised baseline, trained on a manually labelled gold standard data set. Our experiments reveal:

(1) DS approaches to SSA for Arabic Twitter feeds show significantly higher performance in accuracy and F-score than a fully supervised approach. Despite providing noisy labels, they allow larger amounts of data to be rapidly annotated, and thus, can account for the topic shifts observed in social media.

(2) DS approaches which use a subjectivity lexicon for labelling outperform approaches using emoticon-based labels for sentiment analysis, but achieve a very similar performance for subjectivity detection. We hypothesise that this can be attributed to unclear facings of the emoticons.

(3) We also find that both our DS approaches achieve good results of up to 95% accuracy for subjectivity analysis, which is comparable to previous work on English tweets. However, we detect a decrease in performance for sentiment analysis, where negative instances repeatedly get misclassified as positive. We assume that this can be attributed to the more indirect ways adopted by people to express their emotions verbally via social media (Taboada et al., 2011). Other possible reasons for this, which we will explore in future work, include culturally specific differences (Hong et al., 2011), as well as pragmatic/ context-dependent aspects of opinion (Sayeed, 2013).

References

Muhammad Abdul-Mageed and Mona Diab. 2012. AWATIF: A multi-genre corpus for modern standard Arabic subjectivity and sentiment analysis. In *Proceedings of the Eight International Conference on Language Resources and Evaluation (LREC'12)*, Istanbul, Turkey. European Language Resources Association (ELRA).

Muhammad Abdul-Mageed, Mona T. Diab, and Mohammed Korayem. 2011. Subjectivity and sentiment analysis of modern standard Arabic. In *Proceedings of the 49th Annual Meeting of the Association for Computational Linguistics: Human Language Technologies: short papers - Volume 2*, HLT '11, pages 587–591, Stroudsburg, PA, USA. Association for Computational Linguistics.

Muhammad Abdul-Mageed, Sandra Kuebler, and Mona Diab. 2012. SAMAR: A system for subjectivity and sentiment analysis of Arabic social media. In *Proceedings of the 3rd Workshop in Computational Approaches to Subjectivity and Sentiment Analysis*, pages 19–28. Association for Computational Linguistics.

Rania Al-Sabbagh and Roxana Girju. 2012. YADAC: Yet another dialectal Arabic corpus. In *Proceedings of the Eight International Conference on Language Resources and Evaluation (LREC'12)*, Istanbul, Turkey. European Language Resources Association (ELRA).

Albert Bifet and Eibe Frank. 2010. Sentiment knowledge discovery in twitter streaming data. In *Discovery Science*, pages 1–15. Springer.

J. Carletta. 1996. Assessing agreement on classification tasks: the kappa statistic. *Computational Linguistics*, 22(2):249–254.

Jacob Eisenstein. 2013. What to do about bad language on the internet. In *Proceedings of NAACL-HLT*, pages 359–369.

Alec Go, Richa Bhayani, and Lei Huang. 2009. Twitter sentiment classification using distant supervision. *CS224N Project Report, Stanford*, pages 1–12.

Lichan Hong, Gregorio Convertino, and Ed H Chi. 2011. Language matters in twitter: A large scale study. In *ICWSM*.

Ahmed Mourad and Kareem Darwish. 2013. Subjectivity and sentiment analysis of modern standard Arabic and Arabic microblogs. *WASSA 2013*, page 55.

Owen Rambow Nizar Habash and Ryan Roth. 2009. MADA+TOKAN: A toolkit for Arabic tokenization, diacritization, morphological disambiguation, pos tagging, stemming and lemmatization. In Khalid Choukri and Bente Maegaard, editors, *Proceedings of the Second International Conference on Arabic Language Resources and Tools*, Cairo, Egypt, April. The MEDAR Consortium.

A. Pak and P. Paroubek. 2010. Twitter as a corpus for sentiment analysis and opinion mining. In *Proceedings of LREC*.

Matthew Purver and Stuart Battersby. 2012. Experimenting with distant supervision for emotion classification. In *Proceedings of the 13th Conference of the European Chapter of the Association for Computational Linguistics (EACL)*, pages 482–491, Avignon, France, April. Association for Computational Linguistics.

Jonathon Read. 2005. Using emoticons to reduce dependency in machine learning techniques for sentiment classification. In *Proceedings of the ACL Student Research Workshop*, pages 43–48. Association for Computational Linguistics.

Eshrag Refaee and Verena Rieser. 2014. An Arabic twitter corpus for subjectivity and sentiment analysis. In *Proceedings of the Ninth International Conference on Language Resources and Evaluation (LREC'14)*, Reykjavik, Iceland, may. European Language Resources Association (ELRA).

Asad Sayeed. 2013. An opinion about opinions about opinions: subjectivity and the aggregate reader. In *Proceedings of NAACL-HLT*, pages 691–696.

Jared Suttles and Nancy Ide. 2013. Distant supervision for emotion classification with discrete binary values. In *Computational Linguistics and Intelligent Text Processing*, pages 121–136. Springer.

Maite Taboada, Julian Brooke, Milan Tofiloski, Kimberly Voll, and Manfred Stede. 2011. Lexicon-based methods for sentiment analysis. *Computational linguistics*, 37(2):267–307.

Janyce M. Wiebe, Rebecca F. Bruce, and Thomas P. O'Hara. 1999. Development and use of a gold-standard data set for subjectivity classifications. In *Proceedings of the 37th annual meeting of the Association for Computational Linguistics on Computational Linguistics*, ACL '99, pages 246–253, Stroudsburg, PA, USA. Association for Computational Linguistics.

Theresa Wilson, Janyce Wiebe, and Paul Hoffmann. 2009. Recognizing contextual polarity: An exploration of features for phrase-level sentiment analysis. *Computational Linguistics*, 35(3):399–433.

Ian H Witten and Eibe Frank. 2005. *Data Mining: Practical machine learning tools and techniques*. Morgan Kaufmann.

Alecia Wolf. 2000. Emotional expression online: Gender differences in emoticon use. *CyberPsychology & Behavior*, 3(5):827–833.

Zheng Yuan and Matthew Purver. 2012. Predicting emotion labels for chinese microblog texts. In *Proceedings of the 1st International Workshop on Sentiment Discovery from Affective Data (SDAD)*, pages 40–47, Bristol, UK, September.

Omar F. Zaidan and Chris Callison-Burch. 2013. Arabic dialect identification. *Computational Linguistics*.

Ley Zhang, Riddhiman Ghosh, Mohamed Dekhil, Meichun Hsu, and Bing Liu. 2011. Combining lexiconbased and learning-based methods for twitter sentiment analysis. *HP Laboratories, Technical Report HPL-2011*, 89.

Arabic Native Language Identification

Shervin Malmasi
Centre for Language Technology
Macquarie University
Sydney, NSW, Australia
shervin.malmasi@mq.edu.au

Mark Dras
Centre for Language Technology
Macquarie University
Sydney, NSW, Australia
mark.dras@mq.edu.au

Abstract

In this paper we present the first application of Native Language Identification (NLI) to Arabic learner data. NLI, the task of predicting a writer's first language from their writing in other languages has been mostly investigated with English data, but is now expanding to other languages. We use L2 texts from the newly released Arabic Learner Corpus and with a combination of three syntactic features (CFG production rules, Arabic function words and Part-of-Speech n-grams), we demonstrate that they are useful for this task. Our system achieves an accuracy of 41% against a baseline of 23%, providing the first evidence for classifier-based detection of language transfer effects in L2 Arabic. Such methods can be useful for studying language transfer, developing teaching materials tailored to students' native language and forensic linguistics. Future directions are discussed.

1 Introduction

Researchers in Second Language Acquisition (SLA) investigate the multiplex of factors that influence our ability to acquire new languages and chief among these factors is the role of the learner's mother tongue. Recently this fundamental factor has been studied in Native Language Identification (NLI), which aims to infer the native language (L1) of an author based on texts written in a second language (L2). Machine Learning methods are usually used to identify language use patterns common to speakers of the same L1.

The motivations for NLI are manifold. The use of such techniques can help SLA researchers identify important L1-specific learning and teaching issues. In turn, the identification of such issues can enable researchers to develop pedagogical material that takes into consideration a learner's L1 and addresses them. It can also be applied in a forensic context, for example, to glean information about the discriminant L1 cues in an anonymous text.

While almost all NLI research to date has focused on English L2 data, there is a growing need to apply the techniques to other language in order to assess the cross-language applicability. This need is partially driven by the increasing number of learners of various other languages.

One such case is the teaching of Arabic as a Foreign Language, which has experienced unparalleled growth in the past two decades. For a long time the teaching of Arabic was not considered a priority, but this view has now changed. Arabic is now perceived as a critical and strategically useful language (Ryding, 2013), with enrolments rising rapidly and already at an all time high (Wahba et al., 2013). This trend is also reflected in the NLP community, evidenced by the continuously increasing research focus on Arabic tools and resources (Habash, 2010).

A key objective of this study is to investigate the efficacy of syntactic features for Arabic, a language which is significantly different to English.

Arabic orthography is very different to English with right-to-left text that uses connective letters. Moreover, this is further complicated due to the presence of word elongation, common ligatures, zero-width diacritics and allographic variants. The morphology of Arabic is also quite rich with many morphemes that can appear as prefixes, suffixes or even circumfixes. These mark grammatical information including case, number, gender, and definiteness amongst others. This leads to a sophisticated morphotactic system.

Given the aforementioned differences with English, the main objective of this study is to determine if NLI techniques can be effective for detecting L1 transfer effects in L2 Arabic.

Proceedings of the EMNLP 2014 Workshop on Arabic Natural Langauge Processing (ANLP), pages 180–186,
October 25, 2014, Doha, Qatar.

2 Background

NLI has drawn the attention of many researchers in recent years. With the influx of new researchers, the most substantive work in this field has come in the last few years, leading to the organization of the inaugural NLI Shared Task in 2013 which was attended by 29 teams from the NLP and SLA areas. A detailed exposition of the shared task results and a review of prior NLI work can be found in Tetreault et al. (2013).

While there exists a large body of literature produced in the last decade, almost all of this work has focused exclusively on L2 English. The most recent work in this field successfully presented the first application of NLI to a large non-English dataset (Malmasi and Dras, 2014a), evidencing the usefulness of syntactic features in distinguishing L2 Chinese texts.

3 Data

Although the majority of currently available learner corpora are based on English L2 (Granger, 2012), data from learners of other languages such as Chinese have also attracted attention in the past several years.

No Arabic learner corpora were available for a long time. This paucity of data has been noted by researchers (Abuhakema et al., 2008; Zaghouani et al., 2014) and is thought to be due to issues such as difficulties with non-Latin script and a lack of linguistic and NLP software to work with the data.

More recently, the first version of the Arabic Learner Corpus[1] (ALC) was released by Alfaifi and Atwell (2013). The corpus includes texts by Arabic learners studying in Saudi Arabia, mostly timed essays written in class. In total, 66 different L1 backgrounds are represented. While texts by native Arabic speakers studying to improve their writing are also included, we do not utilize these.

We use the more recent second version of the ALC (Alfaifi et al., 2014) as the data for our experiments. While there are 66 different L1s in the corpus, the majority of these have less than 10 texts and cannot reliably be used for NLI. Instead we use a subset of the corpus consisting of the top seven native languages by number of texts. The languages and document counts in each class are shown in Table 1.

Both plain text and XML versions of the learner texts are provided with the corpus. Here we use text versions and strip the metadata information from the files, leaving only the author's writings.

Native Language	Texts
Chinese	76
Urdu	64
Malay	46
French	44
Fulani	36
English	35
Yoruba	28
Total	329

Table 1: The L1 classes included in this experiment and the number of texts within each class.

4 Experimental Methodology

In this study we employ a supervised multi-class classification approach. The learner texts are organized into classes according on the author's L1 and these documents are used for training and testing in our experiments. A diagram conceptualizing our NLI system is shown in Figure 1.

4.1 Word Segmentation

The tokenization and word segmentation of Arabic is an important preprocessing step for addressing the orthographic issues discussed in §1. For this task we utilize the Stanford Word Segmenter[2].

4.2 Parsing and Part-of-Speech Tagging

To extract the syntactic information required for our models, the Arabic texts are POS tagged and parsed using the Stanford Arabic Parser[3].

4.3 Classifier

We use a linear Support Vector Machine to perform multi-class classification in our experiments. In particular, we use the LIBLINEAR[4] package (Fan et al., 2008) which has been shown to be efficient for text classification problems such as this.

4.4 Evaluation Methodology

In the same manner as many previous NLI studies and also the NLI 2013 shared task, we report our results as classification accuracy under k-fold cross-validation, with $k = 10$. In recent years this

[1]http://www.arabiclearnercorpus.com/

[2]http://nlp.stanford.edu/software/segmenter.shtml

[3]http://nlp.stanford.edu/projects/arabic.shtml

[4]http://www.csie.ntu.edu.tw/%7Ecjlin/liblinear/

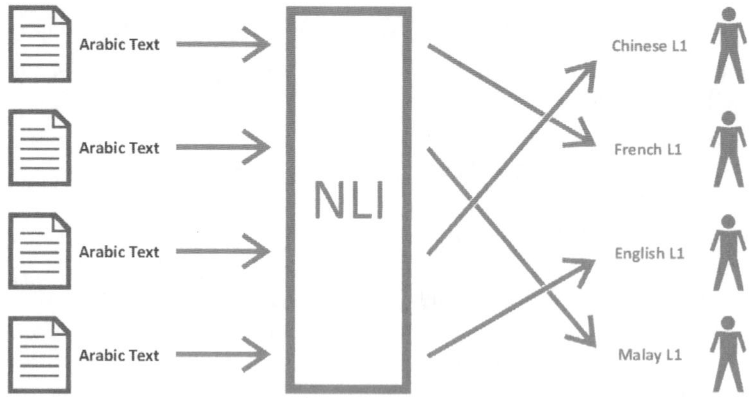

Figure 1: Illustration of our NLI system that identifies the L1 of Arabic learners from their writing.

has become a *de facto* standard for reporting NLI results.

5 Experiments

We experiment using three syntactic feature types described in this section. As the ALC is not balanced for topic, we do not consider the use of lexical features such as word n-grams in this study. Topic bias can occur as a result of the subject matters or topics of the texts to be classified not not evenly distributed across the classes. For example, if in our training data all the texts written by English L1 speakers are on topic A, while all the French L1 authors write about topic B, then we have implicitly trained our classifier on the topics as well. In this case the classifier learns to distinguish our target variable through another confounding variable.

5.1 Context-free Grammar Production Rules

Context-free phrase structure rules (without lexicalizations) are extracted from parse trees of the sentences in each learner text. One such constituent parse tree and extracted rules are shown in Figure 2. These production rules are used as classification features[5]. Linguistically, they capture the global syntactic structures used by writers.

5.2 Arabic Function Words

The distributions of grammatical function words such as determiners and auxiliary verbs have proven to be useful in NLI. This is considered to be a useful syntactic feature as these words indicate the relations between content words and are topic independent. The frequency distributions of a set of 150 function words were extracted from the learner texts and used as features in this model.

السبب ق اختيار الطب هو أنني أحب أن أدخِل السرور ﻓﻲ قلوب الناس
وأساعدهم ﻓﻲ أزمنة خطيرة.

```
DTNN IN NN DTNN PRP VBD VBP IN VBN DTNN
IN NN DTNN CC NN PRP$ IN NN JJ PUNC
```

Figure 3: An example of a sentence written by a learner and its Part-of-Speech tag sequence. Unigrams, bigrams and trigrams are then extracted from this tag sequence.

5.3 Part-of-Speech n-grams

In this model POS n-grams of size 1–3 were extracted. These n-grams capture small and very local syntactic patterns of language production and were used as classification features.

6 Results

The results from all experiments are shown in Table 2. The majority baseline is calculated by using the largest class, in this case Chinese[6], as the default classification. The frequency distributions of the production rules yield 31.7% accuracy, demonstrating their ability to identify structures that are characteristic of L1 groups. Similarly, the distribution of function words is helpful, with 29.2% accuracy.

While all the models provide results well above the baseline, POS tag n-grams are the most useful features, with bigrams providing the highest accuracy for a single feature type with 37.6%. This

[5] All models use relative frequency feature representations

[6] $76/329 = 23.1\%$

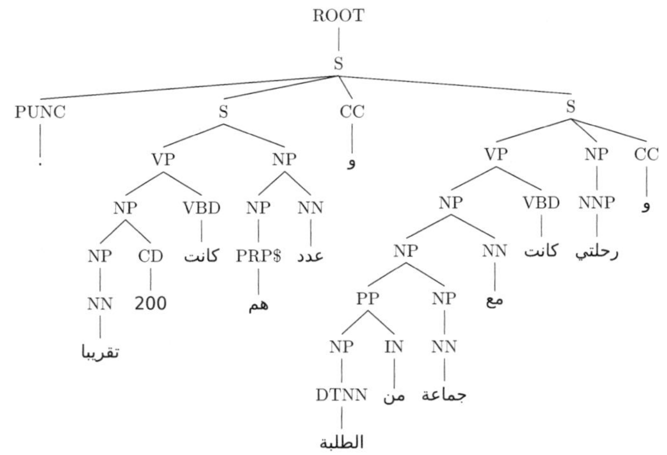


```
S → S CC S PUNC      VP → VBD NP
NP → DTNN            PP → IN NP
```

Figure 2: A constituent parse tree for a sentence from the corpus along with some of the context-free grammar production rules extracted from it.

Feature	Accuracy (%)
Majority Baseline	23.1
CFG Production Rules	31.7
Function Words	29.2
Part-of-Speech unigrams	36.0
Part-of-Speech bigrams	37.6
Part-of-Speech trigrams	36.5
All features combined	41.0

Table 2: Arabic Native Language Identification accuracy for the three experiments in this study.

seems to suggest that the greatest difference between groups lies in their word category ordering.

Combining all of the models into a single feature space provides the highest accuracy of 41%. This demonstrates that the information captured by the various models is complementary and that the feature types are not redundant.

7 Discussion

The most prominent finding here is that NLI techniques can be successfully applied to Arabic, a morphologically complex language differing significantly from English, which has been the focus of almost all previous research.

This is one of the very first applications of NLI to a language other than English and an important step in the growing field of NLI, particularly with the current drive to investigate other languages. This research, though preliminary, presents an approach to Arabic NLI and can serve as a step towards further research in this area.

NLI technology has practical applications in various fields. One potential application of NLI is in the field of forensic linguistics (Gibbons, 2003; Coulthard and Johnson, 2007), a juncture where the legal system and linguistic stylistics intersect (Gibbons and Prakasam, 2004; McMenamin, 2002). In this context NLI can be used as a tool for Authorship Profiling (Grant, 2007) in order to provide evidence about the linguistic background of an author.

There are a number of situations where a text, such as an anonymous letter, is the central piece of evidence in an investigation. The ability to extract additional information from an anonymous text can enable the authorities and intelligence agencies to learn more about threats and those responsible for them. Clues about the native language of a writer can help investigators in determining the source of anonymous text and the importance of this analysis is often bolstered by the fact that in such scenarios, the only data available to users and investigators is the text itself. One recently studied example is the analysis of extremist related activity on the web (Abbasi and Chen, 2005).

Accordingly, we can see that from a forensic point of view, NLI can be a useful tool for intelligence and law enforcement agencies. In fact, recent NLI research such as that related to the work presented by (Perkins, 2014) has already attracted interest and funding from intelligence agencies (Perkins, 2014, p. 17).

In addition to applications in forensic linguistics, Arabic NLI can aid the development of research tools for SLA researchers investigating language transfer and cross-linguistic effects. Similar data-driven methods have been recently applied to generate potential language transfer hypotheses from the writings of English learners (Malmasi and Dras, 2014c). With the use of an error annotated corpus, which was not the case in this study, the annotations could be used in conjunction with similar linguistic features to study the syntactic contexts in which different error types occur (Malmasi and Dras, 2014b).

Results from such approaches could be used to create teaching material that is customized for the learner's L1. This approach has been previously shown to yield learning improvements (Laufer and Girsai, 2008). The need for such SLA tools is particularly salient for a complex language such as Arabic which has several learning stages (Mansouri, 2005), such as phrasal and interphrasal agreement morphology, which are hierarchical and generally acquired in a specific order (Nielsen, 1997).

The key shortcoming of this study, albeit beyond our control, is the limited amount of data available for the experiments. To the best of our knowledge, this is the smallest dataset used for this task in terms of document count and length. In this regard, we are surprised by relatively high classification accuracy of our system, given the restricted amount of training data available.

While it is hard to make comparisons with most other experiments due to differing number of classes, one comparable study is that of Wong and Dras (2009) which used some similar features on 7-class English dataset. Despite their use of a much larger dataset[7], our individual models are only around 10% lower in accuracy.

We believe that this is a good result, given our limited data. In their study of NLI corpora, Brooke and Hirst (2011) showed that increasing the amount of training data makes a very significant difference in NLI accuracy for both syntactic and lexical features. This was verified by Tetreault et al. (2012) who showed that there is a very steep rise in accuracy as the corpus size is increased towards 11,000 texts[8]. Based on this, we are confident that given similarly sized training data, an Arabic NLI system can achieve similar accuracies. On a broader level, this highlights the need for more large-scale L2 Arabic corpora.

Future work includes the application of our methods to large-scale Arabic learner data as it becomes available. With the ongoing development of the Arabic Learner Corpus and other projects like the Qatar Arabic Language Bank (Mohit, 2013), this may happen in the very near future.

The application of more linguistically sophisticated features also merits further investigation, but this is limited by the availability of Arabic NLP tools and resources. From a machine learning perspective, classifier ensembles have been recently used for this task and shown to improve classification accuracy (Malmasi et al., 2013; Tetreault et al., 2012). Their application here could also increase system accuracy.

We also leave the task of interpreting the linguistic features that differentiate and characterize L1s to future work. This seems to be the next logical phase in NLI research and some methods to automate the detection of language transfer features have been recently proposed (Swanson and Charniak, 2014; Malmasi and Dras, 2014c). This research, however, is still at an early stage and could benefit from the addition of more sophisticated machine learning techniques.

More broadly, additional NLI experiments with different languages are needed. Comparative studies using equivalent syntactic features but with distinct L1-L2 pairs can help us better understand Cross-Linguistic Influence and its manifestations. Such a framework could also help us better understand the differences between different L1-L2 language pairs.

8 Conclusion

In this work we identified the appropriate data and tools to perform Arabic NLI and demonstrated that syntactic features can be successfully applied, despite a scarcity of available L2 Arabic data. Such techniques can be used to generate cross-linguistic hypotheses and build research tools for Arabic SLA. As the first machine learning based investigation of language transfer effects in L2 Arabic, this work contributes important additional evidence to the growing body of NLI work.

[7]Wong and Dras (2009) had 110 texts per class, with average text lengths of more than 600 words.

[8]Equivalent to 1000 texts per L1 class.

References

Ahmed Abbasi and Hsinchun Chen. 2005. Applying authorship analysis to extremist-group Web forum messages. *IEEE Intelligent Systems*, 20(5):67–75.

Ghazi Abuhakema, Reem Faraj, Anna Feldman, and Eileen Fitzpatrick. 2008. Annotating an Arabic Learner Corpus for Error. In *LREC*.

Abdullah Alfaifi and Eric Atwell. 2013. Arabic Learner Corpus v1: A New Resource for Arabic Language Research.

Abdullah Alfaifi, Eric Atwell, and I Hedaya. 2014. Arabic learner corpus (ALC) v2: a new written and spoken corpus of Arabic learners. In *Proceedings of the Learner Corpus Studies in Asia and the World (LCSAW)*, Kobe, Japan.

Julian Brooke and Graeme Hirst. 2011. Native language detection with 'cheap' learner corpora. In *Conference of Learner Corpus Research (LCR2011)*, Louvain-la-Neuve, Belgium. Presses universitaires de Louvain.

Malcolm Coulthard and Alison Johnson. 2007. *An introduction to Forensic Linguistics: Language in evidence*. Routledge.

Rong-En Fan, Kai-Wei Chang, Cho-Jui Hsieh, Xiang-Rui Wang, and Chih-Jen Lin. 2008. LIBLINEAR: A library for large linear classification. *Journal of Machine Learning Research*, 9:1871–1874.

John Gibbons and Venn Prakasam. 2004. *Language in the Law*. Orient Blackswan.

John Gibbons. 2003. Forensic Linguistics: An Introduction To Language In The Justice System.

Sylviane Granger. 2012. Learner corpora. *The Encyclopedia of Applied Linguistics*.

Tim Grant. 2007. Quantifying evidence in forensic authorship analysis. *International Journal of Speech Language and the Law*, 14(1):1–25.

Nizar Y Habash. 2010. Introduction to Arabic natural language processing. *Synthesis Lectures on Human Language Technologies*, 3(1):1–187.

Batia Laufer and Nany Girsai. 2008. Form-focused instruction in second language vocabulary learning: A case for contrastive analysis and translation. *Applied Linguistics*, 29(4):694–716.

Shervin Malmasi and Mark Dras. 2014a. Chinese Native Language Identification. *Proceedings of the 14th Conference of the European Chapter of the Association for Computational Linguistics*.

Shervin Malmasi and Mark Dras. 2014b. From Visualisation to Hypothesis Construction for Second Language Acquisition. In *Graph-Based Methods for Natural Language Processing*, Doha, Qatar, October. Association for Computational Linguistics.

Shervin Malmasi and Mark Dras. 2014c. Language Transfer Hypotheses with Linear SVM Weights. *Proceedings of the 2014 Conference on Empirical Methods in Natural Language Processing (EMNLP)*.

Shervin Malmasi, Sze-Meng Jojo Wong, and Mark Dras. 2013. Nli shared task 2013: Mq submission. In *Proceedings of the Eighth Workshop on Innovative Use of NLP for Building Educational Applications*, pages 124–133, Atlanta, Georgia, June. Association for Computational Linguistics.

Fethi Mansouri. 2005. Agreement morphology in Arabic as a second language. *Cross-linguistic aspects of Processability Theory*, pages 117–253.

Gerald R McMenamin. 2002. *Forensic linguistics: Advances in Forensic Stylistics*. CRC press.

Behrang Mohit. 2013. QALB: Qatar Arabic language bank. In *Qatar Foundation Annual Research Conference*, number 2013.

Helle Lykke Nielsen. 1997. On acquisition order of agreement procedures in Arabic learner language. *Al-Arabiyya*, 30:49–93.

Ria Perkins. 2014. *Linguistic identifiers of L1 Persian speakers writing in English: NLID for authorship analysis*. Ph.D. thesis, Aston University.

Karin C. Ryding. 2013. Teaching Arabic in the United States. In Kassem M Wahba, Zeinab A Taha, and Liz England, editors, *Handbook for Arabic language teaching professionals in the 21st century*. Routledge.

Ben Swanson and Eugene Charniak. 2014. Data Driven Language Transfer Hypotheses. *EACL 2014*, page 169.

Joel Tetreault, Daniel Blanchard, Aoife Cahill, Beata Beigman-Klebanov, and Martin Chodorow. 2012. Native Tongues, Lost and Found: Resources and Empirical Evaluations in Native Language Identification. In *Proc. Internat. Conf. on Computat. Linguistics (COLING)*.

Joel Tetreault, Daniel Blanchard, and Aoife Cahill. 2013. A report on the first native language identification shared task. In *Proceedings of the Eighth Workshop on Innovative Use of NLP for Building Educational Applications*, pages 48–57, Atlanta, Georgia, June. Association for Computational Linguistics.

Kassem M Wahba, Zeinab A Taha, and Liz England. 2013. *Handbook for Arabic language teaching professionals in the 21st century*. Routledge.

Sze-Meng Jojo Wong and Mark Dras. 2009. Contrastive analysis and native language identification. In *Proc. Australasian Language Technology Workshop (ALTA)*, pages 53–61.

Wajdi Zaghouani, Behrang Mohit, Nizar Habash, Ossama Obeid, Nadi Tomeh, Alla Rozovskaya, Noura Farra, Sarah Alkuhlani, and Kemal Oflazer. 2014. Large Scale Arabic Error Annotation: Guidelines and Framework. In Nicoletta Calzolari (Conference Chair), Khalid Choukri, Thierry Declerck, Hrafn Loftsson, Bente Maegaard, Joseph Mariani, Asuncion Moreno, Jan Odijk, and Stelios Piperidis, editors, *Proceedings of the Ninth International Conference on Language Resources and Evaluation (LREC'14)*, Reykjavik, Iceland, may. European Language Resources Association (ELRA).

AIDArabic
A Named-Entity Disambiguation Framework for Arabic Text

Mohamed Amir Yosef, Marc Spaniol, Gerhard Weikum
Max-Planck-Institut für Informatik, Saarbrücken, Germany
{mamir|mspaniol|weikum}@mpi-inf.mpg.de

Abstract

There has been recently a great progress in the field of automatically generated knowledge bases and corresponding disambiguation systems that are capable of mapping text mentions onto canonical entities. Efforts like the before mentioned have enabled researchers and analysts from various disciplines to semantically "understand" contents. However, most of the approaches have been specifically designed for the English language and - in particular - support for Arabic is still in its infancy. Since the amount of Arabic Web contents (e.g. in social media) has been increasing dramatically over the last years, we see a great potential for endeavors that support an entity-level analytics of these data. To this end, we have developed a framework called AIDArabic that extends the existing AIDA system by additional components that allow the disambiguation of Arabic texts based on an automatically generated knowledge base distilled from Wikipedia. Even further, we overcome the still existing sparsity of the Arabic Wikipedia by exploiting the interwiki links between Arabic and English contents in Wikipedia, thus, enriching the entity catalog as well as disambiguation context.

1 Introduction

1.1 Motivation

Internet data including news articles and web pages, contain mentions of named-entities such as people, places, organizations, etc. While in many cases the intended meanings of the mentions is obvious (and unique), in many others, the mentions are ambiguous and have many different possible meanings. Therefore, Named-Entity Disambiguation (NED) is essential for many application in the domain of Information Retrieval (such as information extraction). It also enables producing more useful and accurate analytics. The problem has been exhaustively studied in the literature. The essence of all NED techniques is using background information extracted from various sources (e.g. Wikipedia), and use such information to know the correct/intended meaning of the mention.

The Arabic content is enormously growing on the Internet, nevertheless, background ground information is clearly lacking behind other languages such as English. Consider Wikipedia for example, while the English Wikipedia contains more than 4.5 million articles, the Arabic version contains less than 0.3 million ones [1]. As a result, and up to our knowledge, there is no serious work that has been done in the area of performing NED for Arabic input text.

1.2 Problem statement

NED is the problem of mapping ambiguous names of entities (mentions) to canonical entities registered in an entity catalog (knowledgebase) such as Freebase (www.freebase.com), DBpedia (Auer et al., 2007), or Yago (Hoffart et al., 2013). For example, given the text "I like to visit Sheikh Zayed. Despite being close to Cairo, it is known to be a quiet district", or in Arabic,"أحب زيارة الشيخ زايد. فهي تّتميز بالهدوء بالرغم من قربها من القاهرة". When processing this text automatically, we need to be able to tell that Sheikh Zayed denotes the the city in Egypt[2], not the mosque in Abu Dhabi[3] or the President of the United Arab

[1] as of July 2014
[2] http://en.wikipedia.org/wiki/Sheikh_Zayed_City
http://ar.wikipedia.org/wiki/مدينة_الشيخ_زايد
[3] http://en.wikipedia.org/wiki/Sheikh_Zayed_Mosque
http://ar.wikipedia.org/wiki/جامع_الشيخ_زايد

Proceedings of the EMNLP 2014 Workshop on Arabic Natural Langauge Processing (ANLP), pages 187–195,
October 25, 2014, Doha, Qatar.

Emirates[4]. In order to automatically establish such mappings, the machine needs to be aware of the characteristic description of each entity, and try to find the most suitable one given the input context. In our example, knowing that the input text mentioned the city of Cairo favors the Egyptian city over the mosque in Abu Dhabi, for example. In principle, state-of-the-art NED frameworks require main four ingredients to solve this problem:

- **Entity Repository**: A predefined universal catalog of all entities known to the NED framework. In other words, each mention in the input text must be mapped to an entity in the repository, or to null indicating the correct entity is not included in the repository.
- **Name-Entity Dictionary**: It is a many-to-many relation between possible mentions and the entities in the repository. It connects an entity with different possible mentions that might be used to refer to this entity, as well as connecting a mention with all potential candidate entity it might denote.
- **Entity-Descriptions**: It keeps per entity a bag of characteristic keywords or keyphrases that distinguishes an entity from another. In addition, they come with scoring scheme that signify the specificity of such keyword to that entity.
- **Entity-Entity Relatedness Model**: For coherent text, the entities that are used for mapping all the mentions in the input text, should be semantically related. For that reason, an entity-entity relatedness model is required to asses the coherence.

For the English language, all of the ingredients mentioned above are richly available. For instance, the English Wikipedia is a comprehensive up-to-date resource. Many NED systems use Wikipedia as their entity repository. Furthermore, many knowledge bases are extracted from Wikipedia as well. When trying to apply the existing NED approaches on the Arabic text, we face the following challenges:

- **Entity Repository**: There is no such comprehensive entity catalog. Arabic Wikipedia is an order of magnitude smaller than the English one. In addition, many entities in the Arabic Wikipedia are specific to the Arabic culture with no corresponding English counterpart. As a consequence, even many prominent entities are missing from the Arabic Wikipedia.
- **Name-Entity Dictionary**: Most of the name-entity dictionary entries originate from manual input (e.g. anchor links). Like outlined before, Arabic Wikipedia has fewer resources to extract name-entity mappings, caused by the lack of entities and lack of manual input.
- **Entity-Descriptions**: As already mentioned, there is a scarcity of anchor links in the Arabic Wikipedia. Further, the categorization system of entities is insufficient, Both are essential sources of building the entities descriptions. Hence, it is more challenging to produce comprehensive description of each entity.
- **Entity-Entity Relatedness Model**: Relatedness estimation among entities is usually computed using the overlap in the entities description and/or link structure of Wikipedia. Due to the previously mentioned scarcity of contents in the Arabic Wikipedia, it is also difficult to accurately estimate the entity-entity relatedness.

As a consequence, the main challenge in performing NED on Arabic text is the lack of a comprehensive entity catalog together with rich descriptions of each entity. We considered our open source AIDA system[5] (Hoffart et al., 2011)- mentioned as state-of-the-art NED System by (Ferrucci, 2012) - as a starting point and modified its data acquisition pipeline in order to generate a schema suitable for performing NED on Arabic text.

1.3 Contribution

We developed an approach to exploit and fuse cross-lingual evidences to enrich the background information we have about entities in Arabic to build a comprehensive entity catalog together with their context that is not restricted to the Arabic Wikipedia. Our contributions can be summarized in the following points:

- **Entity Repository**: We switched to YAGO3(Mahdisoltani et al., 2014), the

[4]http://en.wikipedia.org/wiki/Zayed_bin_Sultan_Al_Nahyan
http://ar.wikipedia.org/wiki/زايد_بن_سلطان_آل_نهيان

[5]https://www.github.com/yago-naga/aida

multilingual version of YAGO2s. YAGO3 comes with a more comprehensive catalog that covers entities from different languages (extracted from different Wikipedia dumps). While we selected YAGO3 to be our background knowledge base, any multi-lingual knowledge base such as Freebase could be used as well.

- **Name-Entity Dictionary**: We compiled a dictionary from YAGO3 and Freebase to provide the potential candidate entities for each mention string. While the mention is in Arabic, the entity can belong to either the English or the Arabic Wikipedia.

- **Entity-Descriptions**: We harnessed different ingredients in YAGO3, and Wikipedia to produce a rich entity context schema. For the sake of precision, we did not employ any automated translation.

- **Entity-Entity Relatedness Model**: We fused the link structure of both the English and Arabic Wikipedia's to compute a comprehensive relatedness measure between the entities.

2 Related Work

NED is one of the classical NLP problems that is essential for many Information Retrieval tasks. Hence, it has been extensively addressed in NLP research. Most of NED approaches use Wikipedia as their knowledge repository. (Bunescu and Pasca, 2006) defined a similarity measure that compared the context of a mention to the Wikipedia categories of the entity candidate. (Cucerzan, 2007; Milne and Witten, 2008; Nguyen and Cao, 2008) extended this framework by using richer features for similarity comparison. (Milne and Witten, 2008) introduced the notion of semantic relatedness and estimated it using the the co-occurrence counts in Wikipedia. They used the Wikipedia link structure as an indication of occurrence. Below, we give a brief overview on the most recent NED systems:

The **AIDA** system is an open source system that employs contextual features extracted from Wikipedia (Hoffart et al., 2011; Yosef et al., 2011). It casts the NED problem into a graph problem with two types of nodes (mention nodes, and entity nodes). The weights on the edges between the mentions and the entities are the contextual similarity between mention's context and entity's context. The weights on the edges between the entities are the semantic relatedness among those entities. In a subsequent process, the graph is iteratively reduced to achieve a dense sub-graph where each mention is connected to exactly one entity.

The **CSAW** system uses local scores computed from 12 features extracted from the context surrounding the mention, and the candidate entities (Kulkarni et al., 2009). In addition, it computes global scores that captures relatedness among annotations. The NED is then formulated as a quadratic programming optimization problem, which negatively affects the performance. The software, however, is not available.

DBpedia Spotlight uses Wikipedia anchors, titles and redirects to search for mentions in the input text (Mendes et al., 2011). It casts the context of the mention and the entity into a vector-space model. Cosine similarity is then applied to identify the candidate with the highest similarity. Nevertheless, their model did not incorporate any semantic relatedness among entities. The software is currently available as a service.

TagMe 2 exploits the Wikipedia link structure to estimate the relatedness among entities (Ferragina and Scaiella, 2010). It uses the measure defined by (Milne and Witten, 2008) and incorporates a voting scheme to pick the right mapping. According to the authors, the system is geared for short input text with limited context. Therefore, the approach favors coherence among entities over contextual similarity. TagMe 2 is available a service.

Illinois Wikifier formulates NED as an optimization problem with an objective function designed for higher global coherence among all mentions (Ratinov et al., 2011). In contrast to AIDA and TagMe 2, it does not incorporate the link structure of Wikipedia to estimate the relatedness among entities. Instead, it uses normalized Google similarity distance (NGD) and pointwise mutual information. The software is as well available as a service.

Wikipedia Miner is a machine-learning based approach (Milne and Witten, 2008). It exploits three features in order to train the classifier. The features it employs are prior probability that a mention refers to a specific entity, properties extracted from the mention context, and finally the entity-entity relatedness. The software of Wikipedia

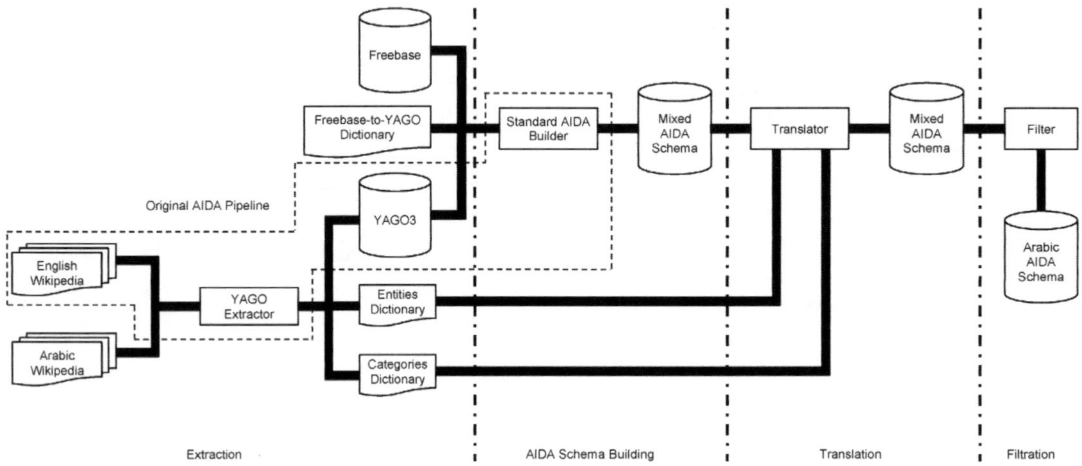

Figure 1: AIDArabic Architecture

Miner is available on their Website.

The approaches mentioned before have been developed for English language NED. As such, none of them is ready to handle Arabic input without major modification.

As of now, no previous research exploits cross-lingual resources to enable NED for Arabic text. Nevertheless, cross-lingual resources have been used to improve Arabic NER (Darwish, 2013). They used Arabic and English Wikipedia together with DBpedia in order to build a large Arabic-English dictionary for names. This augments the Arabic names with a capitalization feature, which is missing in the Arabic language.

3 Architecture

In order to build AIDArabic, we have extended the pipeline used for building an English AIDA schema from the YAGO knowledge base. The new architecture is shown in Figure 1 and indicates those components, that have been added for AIDArabic. These are pre- and post-processing stages to the original AIDA schema extractor. The new pipeline can be divided into the following stages:

Extraction

We have configured a dedicated YAGO3 extractor to provide the data necessary for AIDArabic. To this end, we feed the English and Arabic Wikipedia's into YAGO3 extractor to provide three major outputs:

- **Entity Repository**: A comprehensive set of entities that exist in both, the English and Arabic Wikipedia's. In addition, the corresponding anchortexts, categories as well as links from and/to each entity.
- **Entity Dictionary**: This is an automatically compiled mappings that captures the inter-wiki links among the English and the Arabic Wikipedia's.
- **Categories Dictionary**: This is also an automatically harvested list of mappings between the English and Arabic Wikipedia categories.

More details about data generated by each and every extractor will be given in Section 4.

AIDA Schema Building

In this stage we invoke the original AIDA schema builder without any language information. However, we additionally add the Freebase knowledge base to AIDA and map Freebase entities to YAGO3 entities. Freebase is used here solely to harness its coverage of multi-lingual names of different entities. It is worth noting that Freebase is used merely to enrich YAGO3, but the set of entities are gathered from YAGO. In other words, if there is an entity in Freebase without a YAGO counter part, it gets discarded.

Translation

Although it is generally viable to use machine translation or "off the shelf" English-Arabic dictionaries to translate the context of entities. However, we confine ourselves to the dictionaries extracted from Wikipedia that maps entities as well as categories from English to Arabic. This is done in order to achieve a high precision derived from the manual labor inherent in interwiki links and assigned categories.

Filtration

This is a final cleaning stage. Despite translating the context of entities using the Wikipedia-based dictionaries as comprehensive as possible, a considerable amount of context information remains in English (e.g. those English categories that do not have an Arabic counterpart). To this end, any remaining leftovers in English are being discarded.

4 Implementation

This section explains the implementation of the pipeline described in Section 3. We first highlight the differences between YAGO2 and YAGO3, which justify the switch of the underlying knowledge base. Then, we present the techniques we have developed in order to build the dictionary between mentions and candidate entities. After that, we explain the context enrichment for Arabic entities by exploiting cross-lingual evidences. Finally, we briefly explain the entity-entity relatedness measure applied for disambiguation. In the following table (cf. Table 1 for details) we summarize the terminology used in the following section.

4.1 Entity Repository

YAGO3 has been specifically designed as a multilingual knowledge base. Hence, standard YAGO3 extractors take as an input a set of Wikipedia dumps from different languages, and produce a unified repository of named entities across all languages. This is done by considering inter-wiki links. If an entity in language $l \in L - \{en\}$ has an English counter part, the English one is kept instead of that in language l, otherwise, the original entity is kept. For example, in our repository, the entity used to represent Egypt is "Egypt" coming from the English Wikipedia instead of "ar/مصر" coming from the Arabic Wikpedia. However, the entity that refers to the western part of Cairo is identified as "ar/غرب القاهرة" because it has no counter-part in the English Wikipedia. Formally, the set of entities in YAGO3 are defined as follows:

$$E = E_{en} \cup E_{ar}$$

After the extraction is done, YAGO3 generates an entity dictionary for each and every language. This dictionary translates any language specific entity into the one that is used in YAGO3 (whether the original one, or the English counter part). Based on the the previous example, the following entries are created in the dictionary:

ar/مصر	→	Egypt
ar/غرب القاهرة	→	ar/غرب القاهرة

Such a dictionary is essential for all further processing we do over YAGO3 to enrich the Arabic knowledge base using the English one. It is worth noting here, that this dictionary is completely automatically harvested from the inter-wiki links in Wikipedia, and hence no automated machine translation and/or transliteration are invoked (e.g. for Person Names, Organization Names, etc.). While this may harm the coverage of our linkage, it guarantees the precision of our mapping at the same time. This is thanks to the high quality of inter-wiki between named-entities in Wikipedia.

4.2 Name-Entity Dictionary

The dictionary in the context of NED refers to the relation that connects strings to canonical entities. In other words, given a mention string, the dictionary provides a list of potential canonical entities this string may refer to. In our original implementation of AIDA, this dictionary was compiled from four sources extracted from Wikipedia (titles, disambiguation pages, redirects, and anchor texts). We used the same sources after adapting them to the Arabic domain, and added to them entries coming from Freebase. In the following, we briefly summarize the main ingredients used to populate our dictionary:

- **Titles**: The most natural possible name of a canonical entity is the title of its corresponding page in Wikipedia. This is different from the entity ID itself. For example, in our example for the entity "Egypt" that gets its id from the English Wikipeida, we consider the title "مصر" coming from the Arabic Wikipedia.
- **Disambiguation Pages**: These pages are called in the Arabic Wikipedia "صفحات التوضيح". They are dedicated pages to list the different possible meanings of a specific name. We harness all the links in a disambiguation page and add them as

l	A language in Wikipedia
L	Set of all languages in Wikipedia
e_{en}	An entity originated from the English WIkipedia
e_{ar}	An entity originated from the Arabic WIkipedia
e	An entity in the final collection of YAGO3
E	Set of the corresponding entities
$Cat_{en}(e)$	Set of Categories of an entity e in the English Wikipedia
$Cat_{ar}(e)$	Set of Categories of an entity e in the Arabic Wikipedia
$Inlink_{en}(e)$	Set of Incoming Links to an entity e in the English Wikipedia
$Inlink_{ar}(e)$	Set of Incoming Links to an entity e in the Arabic Wikipedia
$\underset{en\rightarrow ar}{\text{Trans}}(S)$	Translation of each element in S from English to Arabic using the appropriate dictionaries

Table 1: Terminology

potential entities for that name. To this end, we extract our content solely from the Arabic Wikipedia. For instance, the phrase "مدينة زايد" has a disambiguation page that lists all the cities that all called Zayed including the ones in Egypt, Bahrain and United Arab Emirates.

- **Redirects**: "تحويلات" denotes redirects in Arabic Wikipedia. Those are pages where you search for a name and it redirects you to the most prominent meaning of this name. This we extract from the Arabic Wikipedia as well. For example, if you search in the Arabic Wikipedia for the string "زايد", you will be automatically redirected to page of the president of the United Arabic Emirates.

- **Anchor Text**: When people create links in Wikipedia, sometimes they use different names from the title of the entity page as an anchor text. This indicates that this new name is also a possible name for that entity. Therefore, we collect all anchors in the Arabic Wikipedia and associate them with the appropriate entities. For example, in the Arabic Wikipedia page of Sheikh Zayed, there is a anchor link to the city of Al Ain "ar/العين", while the anchor text reads "المنطقة الشرقية" (in English: "The Eastern Area"). Therefore, when there is a mention called "The Eastern Area", one of the potential candidate meanings is the city of Al-Ain in United Arab Emirates.

- **Freebase**: Freebase is a comprehensive resource which comes with multi-lingual labels of different entities. In addition, there is a one-to-one mapping between (most of) Freebase entities and YAGO3 entities, because Freebase is extracted from Wikipedia as well. Therefore, we carry over the Arabic names of the entities from Freebase to our AIDA schema after mapping the entities to their corresponding ones in YAGO3.

4.3 Entity-Descriptions

The context of an entity is the cornerstone in the data required to perform NED task with high quality. Having a comprehensive and "clean" context for each entity facilitates the task of the NED algorithm by providing good clues for the correct mapping. We follow the same approach that we used in the original AIDA framework by representing an entity context as a set of characteristic keyphrases that captures the specifics of such entity. The keyphrases are further decomposed into keywords with specificity scores assigned to each of them in order to estimate the global and entity-specific prominence of this keyword. The original implementation of AIDA extracted keyphrases from 4 different sources (anchor text, inlink titles, categories, as well as citation titles and external links). Below we summarize how we adopted the extraction to accommodate the disambiguation of Arabic text.

- **Anchor Text**: Anchors in a Wikipedia page are usually good indicators of the most important aspects of that page. In the original implementation of AIDA, all anchors in a page are associated with the corresponding entity of this page, and added to the set of its keyphrases.The same holds for AIDArabic. However, we extract the anchors from the Arabic Wikipedia to get Arabic context.

- **Inlink Titles**: In the same fashion that links to other entities are good clues for the aspects of the entity, links coming from other entities are as well. In AIDA, the set of the titles of the pages that has links to an entity were considered among the keyphrases of such an entity. We pursued the same approach here, and fused incoming links to an entity from both English and Arabic Wikipedia. Once set of the incoming links was fully built, we applied - when applicable - interwiki links to get the translation of titles of the entities coming from the English Wikipedia into the Arabic language. Formally:

$$Inlink(e) = Inlink_{ar}(e) \cup \underset{en \rightarrow ar}{\text{Trans}}(Inlink_{en}(e))$$

- **Categories**: Each Wikipedia page belongs to one or more categories, which are mentioned at the bottom part of the page. We configured YAGO3 to provide the union of the categories from both, the English and Arabic Wikipedia. We exploit the interwiki links among categories to translate the English categories to Arabic. This comes with two benefits, we use the category mappings which result in fairly accurate translation in contrast to machine translation. In addition, we enrich the category system of the Arabic Wikipedia by categories from the English for entities that have corresponding English counterpart.

$$Cat(e) = Cat_{ar}(e) \cup \underset{en \rightarrow ar}{\text{Trans}}(Cat_{en}(e))$$

- **Citation Titles and External Links**: Those were two sources of entities context in the original Wikipedia. Due to the small coverage in the Arabic Wikipedia, we ignored them in AIDArabic.

Table 2 summarizes which context resource has been translated and/or enriched from the English Wikipedia.

4.4 Entity-Entity Relatedness Model

For coherent text, there should be connection between all entities mentioned in the text. In other words, a piece of text cannot cover too many aspects at the same time. Therefore, recent NED techniques exploit entity-entity relatedness to further improve the quality of mapping mentions to entities. The original implementation of AIDA used for that purpose a measure introduced by (Milne and Witten, 2008) that estimates the relatedness or coherence between two entities using the overlap in the incoming links to them in the English Wikipedia.

Despite the cultural difference, it is fairly conceivable to assume that if two entities are related in the English Wikipedia, they should also be related in the Arabic one. In addition, we enrich the link structure used in AIDA with the link structure of the Arabic Wikipedia. Hence, we estimate the relatedness between entities using overlap in incoming links in both the English and Arabic Wikipedia's together.

5 Experimentation

5.1 Setup and Results

Up to our knowledge, there is no standard Arabic data set available for a systematic evaluation of NED. In order to assess the quality of our system, we manually prepared a small benchmark collection. To this end, we gathered 10 news articles from www.aljazeera.net from the domains of sports and politics including regional as well as international news. We manually annotated the mentions in the text, and disambiguated the text by using AIDArabic. In our setup, we used the LOCAL configuration setting of AIDA together with the original weights. The data set contains a total of **103 mentions**. AIDArabic managed to annotate **34 of them correctly**, and assigned **68 to NULL**, while **one mention was mapped wrongly**.

5.2 Discussion

AIDArabic performance in terms of precision is impressive (%97.1). Performance in that regard is positively influenced by testing on a "clean" input of news articles. Nevertheless, AIDArabic loses on recall. Mentions that are mapped to NULL, either

Context Source	Arabic Wikipedia	English Wikipedia
Anchor Text	+	-
Categories	+	+
Title of Incoming Links	+	+

Table 2: Entities Context Sources

have no correct entity in the entity repository, or the entity exists but lacks the corresponding name-entity dictionary entry.

This observation confirms our initial hypothesis that lack of data is one of the main challenges for applying NED on Arabic text. Another aspect that harms recall is the nature of Arabic language. Letters get attached to the beginning and/or the end of words (e.g. connected prepositions and pronouns). In such a case, when querying the dictionary, AIDArabic is not able to retrieve the correct candidates for a mention like "بفرنسا", because of the "ب" in the beginning. Similar difficulties arise when matching the entities description. Here, many keywords do not be to match the input text because they appear in a modified version augmented with some extra letters.

6 Conclusion & Outlook

In this paper, we have introduced the AIDArabic framework, which allows named entity disambiguation of Arabic texts based on an automatically generated knowledge based derived from Wikipedia. Our proof-of-concept implementation shows that entity disambiguation for Arabic texts becomes viable, although the underlying data sources (in particular Wikipedia) still is relatively sparse. Since our approach "integrates" knowledge encapsulated in interwiki links from the English Wikipedia, we are able to boost the amount of context information available compared to a solely monolingual approach.

As a next step, intend to build up a proper dataset that we will use for a systematic evaluation of AIDArabic. In addition, we plan to apply machine translation/transliteration techniques for keyphrases and/or dictionary lookup for keywords in order to provide even more context information for each and every entity. In addition, we may employ approximate matching approaches for keyphrases to account for the existence of additional letter connected to words. As a byproduct we will be able to apply AIDArabic on less formal text (e.g. social media) which contains a considerable amount of misspellings for example. Apart from assessing and improving AIDArabic, a natural next step is to extend the framework by extractors for other languages, such as French or German. By doing so, we are going to create a framework, which will be in its final version fully language agnostic.

Acknowledgments

We would like to thank Fabian M. Suchanek and Joanna Biega for their help with adopting YAGO3 extraction code to fulfill AIDArabic requirements.

References

[Auer et al.2007] Sören Auer, Christian Bizer, Georgi Kobilarov, Jens Lehmann, and Zachary Ives. 2007. DBpedia: A nucleus for a web of open data. In *Proceedings of the 6th Intl Semantic Web Conference*, pages 11–15, Busan, Korea.

[Bunescu and Pasca2006] Razvan Bunescu and Marius Pasca. 2006. Using encyclopedic knowledge for named entity disambiguation. In *Proceedings of the 11th Conference of the European Chapter of the Association for Computational Linguistics (EACL 2006)*, pages 9–16, Trento, Italy.

[Cucerzan2007] S. Cucerzan. 2007. Large-scale named entity disambiguation based on Wikipedia data. In *Proceedings of EMNLP-CoNLL 2007*, pages 708–716, Prague, Czech Republic.

[Darwish2013] Kareem Darwish. 2013. Named entity recognition using cross-lingual resources: Arabic as an example. In *Proceedings of the 51st Annual Meeting of the Association for Computational Linguistics (ACL 2013)* , pages 1558–1567, Sofia, Bulgaria.

[Ferragina and Scaiella2010] Paolo Ferragina and Ugo Scaiella. 2010. Tagme: On-the-fly annotation of short text fragments (by Wikipedia entities). In *Proceedings of the 19th ACM International Conference on Information and Knowledge Management (CIKM 2010)*, pages 1625–1628, New York, NY, USA.

[Ferrucci2012] D. A. Ferrucci. 2012. Introduction to "This is Watson". *IBM Journal of Research and Development (Volume 56, Issue 3)*, pages 235–249.

[Hoffart et al.2011] Johannes Hoffart, Mohamed Amir Yosef, Ilaria Bordino, Hagen Fürstenau, Manfred Pinkal, Marc Spaniol, Bilyana Taneva, Stefan Thater, and Gerhard Weikum. 2011. Robust disambiguation of named entities in text. In *Proceedings of the Conference on Empirical Methods in Natural Language Processing (EMNLP 2011)*, pages 782–792, Edinburgh, Scotland.

[Hoffart et al.2013] Johannes Hoffart, Fabian M. Suchanek, Klaus Berberich, and Gerhard Weikum. 2013. YAGO2: A spatially and temporally enhanced knowledge base from Wikipedia. *Artificial Intelligence (Volume 194)*, pages 28–61.

[Kulkarni et al.2009] Sayali Kulkarni, Amit Singh, Ganesh Ramakrishnan, and Soumen Chakrabarti. 2009. Collective annotation of Wikipedia entities in web text. In *Proceedings of the 15th ACM International Conference on Knowledge Discovery and Data Mining (SIGKDD 2009)*, pages 457–466, New York, NY, USA.

[Mahdisoltani et al.2014] Farzane Mahdisoltani, Joanna Biega, and Fabian M. Suchanek. 2014. A knowledge base from multilingual Wikipedias – yago3. Technical report, Telecom ParisTech. http://suchanek.name/work/publications/yago3tr.pdf.

[Mendes et al.2011] Pablo N. Mendes, Max Jakob, Andrés García-Silva, and Christian Bizer. 2011. DBbpedia Spotlight: Shedding light on the web of documents. In *Proceedings of the 7th International Conference on Semantic Systems (I-Semantics 2011)*, pages 1–8, New York, NY, USA.

[Milne and Witten2008] David N. Milne and Ian H. Witten. 2008. Learning to link with Wikipedia. In *Proceedings of the 17th ACM International Conference on Information and Knowledge Management (CIKM 2008)*, pages 509–518, New York, NY, USA.

[Nguyen and Cao2008] Hien T. Nguyen and Tru H. Cao. 2008. Named entity disambiguation on an ontology enriched by Wikipedia. In *Proceedings of IEEE International Conference on Research, Innovation and Vision for the Future (RIVF 2008)*, pages 247–254, Ho Chi Minh City, Vietnam.

[Ratinov et al.2011] Lev Ratinov, Dan Roth, Doug Downey, and Mike Anderson. 2011. Local and global algorithms for disambiguation to wikipedia. In *Proceedings of the 49th Annual Meeting of the Association for Computational Linguistics: Human Language Technologies (HLT 2011)*, pages 1375–1384, Stroudsburg, PA, USA.

[Yosef et al.2011] Mohamed Amir Yosef, Johannes Hoffart, Ilaria Bordino, Marc Spaniol, and Gerhard Weikum. 2011. AIDA: An online tool for accurate disambiguation of named entities in text and tables. In *Proceedings of the 37th International Conference on Very Large Data Bases (VLDB 2011)*, pages 1450–1453, Seattle, WA, USA.

Domain and Dialect Adaptation for Machine Translation into Egyptian Arabic

Serena Jeblee[1], Weston Feely[1], Houda Bouamor[2]
Alon Lavie[1], Nizar Habash[3] and Kemal Oflazer[2]

[1]**Carnegie Mellon University**
{sjeblee, wfeely, alavie}@cs.cmu.edu
[2]**Carnegie Mellon University in Qatar**
hbouamor@qatar.cmu.edu, ko@cs.cmu.edu
[3]**New York University Abu Dhabi**
nizar.habash@nyu.edu

Abstract

In this paper, we present a statistical machine translation system for English to Dialectal Arabic (DA), using Modern Standard Arabic (MSA) as a pivot. We create a core system to translate from English to MSA using a large bilingual parallel corpus. Then, we design two separate pathways for translation from MSA into DA: a two-step domain and dialect adaptation system and a one-step simultaneous domain and dialect adaptation system. Both variants of the adaptation systems are trained on a 100k sentence tri-parallel corpus of English, MSA, and Egyptian Arabic generated by a rule-based transformation. We test our systems on a held-out Egyptian Arabic test set from the 100k sentence corpus and we achieve our best performance using the two-step domain and dialect adaptation system with a BLEU score of 42.9.

1 Introduction

While MSA is the shared official language of culture, media and education in the Arab world, it is not the native language of any speakers of Arabic. Most native speakers are unable to produce sustained spontaneous discourse in MSA - they usually resort to repeated code-switching between their dialect and MSA (Abu-Melhim, 1991). Arabic speakers are quite aware of the contextual factors and the differences between their dialects and MSA, although they may not always be able to pinpoint exact linguistic differences. In the context of natural language processing (NLP), some Arabic dialects have started receiving increasing attention, particularly in the context of machine translation (Zbib et al., 2012; Salloum and Habash, 2013; Salloum et al., 2014; Al-Mannai et al., 2014) and in terms of data collection (Cotterell and Callison-Burch, 2014; Bouamor et al., 2014; Salama et al., 2014) and basic enabling technologies (Habash et al., 2012; Pasha et al., 2014). However, the focus is on a small number of iconic dialects, (e.g., Egyptian). The Egyptian media industry has traditionally played a dominant role in the Arab world, making the Egyptian dialect the most widely understood and used dialect. DA is now emerging as the language of informal communication online. DA differs phonologically, lexically, morphologically, and syntactically from MSA. And while MSA has an established standard orthography, the dialects do not: people write words reflecting their phonology and sometimes use roman script. Thus, MSA tools cannot effectively model DA; for instance, over one-third of Levantine verbs cannot be analyzed using an MSA morphological analyzer (Habash and Rambow, 2006). These differences make the direct use of MSA NLP tools and applications for handling dialects impractical.

In this work, we design an MT system for English to Egyptian Arabic translation by using MSA as an intermediary step. This includes different challenges from those faced when translating into English. Because MSA is the formal written variety of Arabic, there is an abundance of written data, including parallel corpora from sources like the United Nations and newspapers, as well as various treebanks. Using these resources, many researchers have created fairly reliable MSA translation systems. However, these systems are not designed to deal with the other Arabic variants.

Egyptian Arabic is much closer to MSA than it is to English, so one can get a system bet-

Proceedings of the EMNLP 2014 Workshop on Arabic Natural Langauge Processing (ANLP), pages 196–206,
October 25, 2014, Doha, Qatar.

ter performance by translating first into MSA and then translating from MSA to Egyptian Arabic, which are far more similar. Our approach consists of a core MT system trained on a large amount of out-of-domain English-MSA parallel data, followed by an adaptation system. We design and implement two adaptation systems: a two-step system first adapts to in-domain MSA and then separately adapts from MSA to Egyptian Arabic, and a one-step system that adapts directly from out-of-domain MSA to in-domain Egyptian Arabic.

Our research contributions are summarized as follows:

(a) We build a machine translation system to translate into, rather than out of, dialectal Arabic (from English), using MSA as a pivot point.
(b) We apply a domain adaptation technique to improve the MSA results on our in-domain dataset.
(c) We automatically generate the Egyptian side of a 100k tri-parallel corpus covering MSA, English and Egyptian.
(d) We use this domain adaptation technique to adapt MSA into dialectal Arabic.

The remainder of this paper is structured as follows. We first review the main previous efforts for dealing with DA in NLP, in Section 2. In Section 3,we give a general description about using phrase-based MT as an adaptation system. Section 4 presents the dataset used in the different experiments. Our approach for translating English text into Egyptian Arabic is explained in Section 5. Section 6 presents our experimental setup and the results obtained. Then, we give an analysis of our system output in Section 7. Finally, we conclude and describe our future work in Section 8.

2 Related work

Machine translation (MT) for dialectal Arabic (DA) is quite challenging given the limited resources to build rule-based models or train statistical models for MT. While there has been a considerable amount of work in the context of standard Arabic NLP (Habash, 2010), DA is impoverished in terms of available tools and resources compared to MSA, e.g., there are few parallel DA-English corpora (Zbib et al., 2012; Bouamor et al., 2014). The majority of DA resources are for speech recognition, although more and more resources for machine translation and enabling technologies such as morphological analyzers are becoming available for specific dialects (Habash et al., 2012; Habash et al., 2013).

For Arabic and its dialects, several researchers have explored the idea of exploiting existing MSA rich resources to build tools for DA NLP. Different research work successfully translated DA to MSA as a bridge to translate to English (Sawaf, 2010; Salloum and Habash, 2013), or to enhance the performance of Arabic-based information retrieval systems (Shatnawi et al., 2012). Among the efforts on translation from DA to MSA, Abo Bakr et al. (2008) introduced a hybrid approach to transfer a sentence from Egyptian Arabic to MSA. Sajjad et al. (2013) used a dictionary of Egyptian/MSA words to transform Egyptian to MSA and showed improvement in the quality of machine translation. A similar but rule-based work was done by Mohamed et al. (2012). Boujelbane et al. (2013) and Hamdi et al. (2014) built a bilingual dictionary using explicit knowledge about the relation between Tunisian Arabic and MSA. These works are limited to a dictionary or rules that are not available for all dialects. Zbib et al. (2012) used crowdsourcing to translate sentences from Egyptian and Levantine into English, and thus built two bilingual corpora. The dialectal sentences were selected from a large corpus of Arabic web text. Then, they explored several methods for dialect/English MT. Their best Egyptian/English system was trained on dialect/English parallel data. They argued that differences in genre between MSA and DA make bridging through MSA of limited value. For this reason, while pivoting through MSA, it is important to consider the domain and add an additional step: domain adaptation.

The majority of previous efforts in DA MT has been focusing on translating from dialectal Arabic into other languages (mainly MSA or English). In contrast, in this work we focus on building a system to translate from English and MSA into DA. Furthermore, to the best of our knowledge, this is the first work in which we adapt the domain in addition to the dialect (Egyptian specifically).

3 Using Phrase-Based MT as an Adaptation System

For commercial use, MT output is usually post-edited by a human translator in order to fix the errors generated by the MT system. This is often faster and cheaper than having a human translate the document from scratch. However, we can apply statistical phrase-based MT to create an automatic machine post-editor (what we refer to in this paper as an adaptation system) to improve the output of an MT system, and make it more closely resemble the references. Simard et al. (2007) used a phrase-based MT system as an automatic post-editor for the output of a commercial rule-based MT system, showing that it produced better results than both the rule-based system alone and a single pass phrase-based MT system. This technique is also useful for adapting to a specific domain or dataset. Isabelle et al. (2007) used a statistical MT system to automatically post-edit the output of a generic rule-based MT system, to avoid manually customizing a system dictionary and to reduce the amount of manual post-editing required.

For our adaptation systems, we build a core phrase-based MT system with a large amount of out-of-domain data, which allows us to have better coverage of the target language. For an adaptation system, we then build a second phrase-based MT system by translating the in-domain train, tune, and test sets through the core translation system, then using that data to build the second system. This system uses only in-domain data: parallel MT output from the core and the references. In this system, instead of learning to translate one language into another, the model learns to translate erroneous MT output into more fluent output of the same language, which more closely resembles the references.

In this work, we apply this technique for domain and dialect adaptation, treating Egyptian Arabic as the target language, and the MT-generated MSA as the erroneous MT output. We use this approach to adapt to the domain of the MSA data, and also to adapt to the Egyptian dialect. What we refer to as the "one-step" system is a core system plus one adaptation system, whereas the "two-step" system consists of the core plus two subsequent adaptation systems. We describe the systems in more detail in Section 5.

4 Data

For the core English to MSA system, we use the 5 million parallel sentences of English and MSA from NIST 2012 as the training set. The tuning set consists of 1,356 sentences from the NIST 2008 Open Machine Translation Evaluation (MT08) data (NIST Multimodal Information Group, 2010a), and the test set consists of 1,313 sentences from NIST MT09 (NIST Multimodal Information Group, 2010b).

We use a 5-gram MSA language model built using the SRILM toolkit (Stolcke, 2002) on 260 million words of MSA from the Arabic Gigaword (Parker et al., 2011). All our MSA parallel data and monolingual MSA language modeling data were tokenized with MADA v3.1 (Habash and Rambow, 2005) using the ATB (Arabic Treebank) tokenization scheme.

For the adaptation systems, we build a 100k tri-parallel corpus Egyptian-MSA-English corpus. The MSA and English parts are extracted from the NIST corpus distributed by the Linguistic Data Consortium. The Egyptian sentences are obtained automatically by extending Mohamed et al. (2012) method for generating Egyptian Arabic from morphologically disambiguated MSA sentences. This rule-based method relies on 103 transformation rules covering essentially nouns, verbs and pronouns as well as certain lexical items. For each MSA sentence, this method provides more than one possible candidate, in its original version, the Egyptian sentence kept was chosen randomly. We extend the selection algorithm by scoring the different sentences using a language model. For this, we use SRILM with modified Kneser-Ney smoothing to build a 5-gram language model. The model is trained on a corpus including articles extracted from the Egyptian version of Wikipedia[1] and the Egyptian side of the AOC corpus (Zaidan and Callison-Burch, 2011). We chose to include Egyptian Wikipedia for the formal level of sentences in it different from the regular DA written in blogs or microblogging websites (e.g., Twitter) and closer to the ones generated by our system.

We split this data into train, tune, and test sets of 98,027, 960, and 961 sentences respectively, after removing duplicates across sets. The MSA corpus was tokenized using MADA and the Egyptian Arabic data was tokenized with MADA-ARZ v0.4 (Habash et al., 2013), both using the ATB tokenization scheme, with alif/ya normalization.

5 System Design

Figure 1 shows a diagram of our three English to Egyptian Arabic MT systems: (1) the baseline MT system, (2) the one-step adaptation MT system, and (3) the two-step adaptation MT system. We describe each system below.

[1] `http://arz.wikipedia.org/`

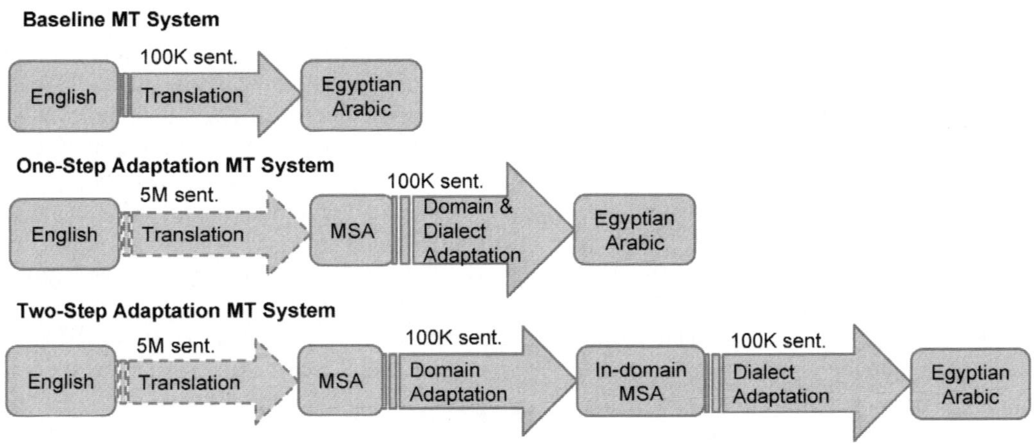

Figure 1: An overview of the different system architectures.

Baseline System

Our baseline system is a single phrase-based English to Egyptian Arabic MT system, built using Moses (Koehn et al., 2007) on the 100k corpus described in Section 4. This system does not include any MSA data, nor does it have an adaptation system; it is a typical, one-pass MT system that translates English directly into Egyptian Arabic. We will show that using adaptation systems improves the results significantly.

Core System

We base our systems on a core system built using Moses with the NIST data, a large amount of parallel English-MSA data from different sources than our in-domain data (the 100k dataset). Our core system is also built using Moses. We use this core system to translate the English side of our 100k train, tune, and test sets into MSA, the output of which we refer to as MSA'. This MSA' data is what we use as the source side for the adaptation systems.

One-Step Adaptation System

To adapt to the domain and dialect of the 100k corpus, we first build a single adaptation system that translates the MSA' output of the core directly into Egyptian Arabic using the 100k corpus. The training data consists of parallel MSA' (the output of the core) and the Egyptian Arabic from the 100k dataset. With this system, we can take an English test set, translate it through the core to get MSA' output, which we can translate through the adaptation system to get Egyptian Arabic.

Two-Step Adaptation System

We also build a two-step adaptation system that consists of two adaptation steps: one to adapt the MSA output of the core system to the domain of the MSA in the 100k corpus, and a second system to translate the MSA output of the domain adaptation system into Egyptian Arabic. We use the first adaptation system to translate the MSA' train, tune, and test sets (the output of the core, which is out-of-domain MSA), into in-domain MSA. This system is trained on the MSA' output parallel with the MSA references from the 100k dataset. We refer to the output of this system as MSA", because it has been translated from English into out-of-domain MSA (MSA'), and then from out-of-domain MSA to in-domain MSA.

The first adaptation system is used to translate the MSA' train, tune, and test sets into MSA". Then we use these MSA" sets with their parallel Egyptian Arabic from the 100k dataset to build the second adaptation system from in-domain MSA to Egyptian Arabic. We do not use the dialect transformation from (Mohamed et al., 2012) because it is designed to work with gold-standard annotation of the MSA text, which we do not have.

System Variants

Since MSA and Egyptian are more similar to each other than they are to English, we tried several different reordering window sizes to find the optimal reordering distance for adapting MSA to Egyptian Arabic, including the typical reordering window of length 7, a smaller window of length 4, and no reordering at all. We found a reordering window size of 7 to work best for all our systems, except for the one-step adaptation system, where no reordering produced the best result.

We also tested two different heuristics for symmetrizing the word alignments: grow-diag and grow-diag-final-and (Och and Ney, 2003). We found that using grow-diag as our symmetrization heuristic produced slightly better scores on the 100k datasets. For the baseline and adaptation systems we built 5-gram language models with KenLM (Heafield et al., 2013) using the target side of the training set, and for the core system we used the large MSA language model described in section 4. We use KenLM because it has been shown (Heafield, 2011) to be faster and use less memory than SRILM (Stolcke, 2002) and IRSTLM (Federico et al., 2008).

6 Evaluation and Results

For evaluation we use multeval (Clark et al., 2011) to calculate BLEU (Papineni et al., 2002), METEOR (Denkowski and Lavie, 2011), TER (Snover et al., 2006), and length of the test set for each system. We evaluate the core and adaptation systems on the MSA and Egyptian sides of the test set drawn from the 100k corpus, which we refer to as the 100k sets. The data used for evaluation is a genuine Egyptian Arabic generated from MSA, just like the data the systems were trained on. It is not practical to evaluate on naturally-generated Egyptian Arabic in this case because the domain of our datasets is very formal, since most of the text comes from news sources, and dialectal Arabic is generally used in informal situations.[2]

Below we report BLEU scores from our evaluation using tokenized and detokenized system output. We separate our results into the baseline system results, the results of the core, the results of the adaptation systems, and a comparison section. We specify scores of intermediate system output, such as MSA, as BLEU (A), and the scores of final system output as BLEU (B). For error analysis, we use METEOR X-ray (Denkowski and Lavie, 2011) to visualize the alignments of our system results with the references and each other.

For all MT systems we used grow-diag as our symmetrization heuristic. For each system, we report only the BLEU score of the best reordering window variant, which is specified in the caption below each table. The difference in scores between the different reordering window sizes (7, 4, and 0) we tried for the adaptation systems was not large (between 0 and 0.7 BLEU). In the following tables we present the best results for each adaptation system, which is a reordering window size of 7 for all systems, except for the phrase-based one-step domain and dialect adaptation system, which performs better with no reordering (0.2 BLEU better than a window of 7, 0.6 BLEU better than a window of 4), but these small differences in BLEU scores are within noise. The greatest difference in scores from the reordering windows was in the two-step systems domain adaptation step (MSA to MSA) on top of the phrase-based core, where a reordering window of 7 was 0.7 BLEU better than a window of 0.

6.1 Baseline System Results

	BLEU (B)	
	Tokenized	**Detokenized**
100k EGY Tune	22.6	22.3
100k EGY Test	21.5	21.1

Table 1: Baseline results (English → EGY) with a reordering window size of 7.

The baseline system demonstrates the results of building a basic MT system directly from English to Egyptian Arabic. The goal of the core and adaptation systems is to achieve better scores than this initial approach.

6.2 Core System Results

In Table 2, we report BLEU scores for our core system on its own tuning set, NIST MT08, and NIST MT09 as a held-out MSA test set. We also report scores on the tune and test sets used to build our adaptation systems, both MSA and Egyptian Arabic. This is not the final system output, but rather these scores are for intermediate output only, which becomes the input for our adapatation systems.

We notice that unsurprisingly the core system performs much better on the 100k MSA test set than on the 100k Egyptian Arabic test set, which is to be expected because the core system is not trained on any Egyptian Arabic data. This shows the impact that the dialectal differences make on MT output. The results on the Egyptian test set here are the result of evaluating MSA output against Egyptian Arabic references.

[2]It is important to note that the Egyptian Arabic data we use is more MSA-like than typical Egyptian because it was generated directly from MSA.

	BLEU (A)	
	Tokenized	**Detokenized**
NIST MT08 (Tune)	23.6	22.8
NIST MT09 (Test)	29.3	28.5
100k MSA Tune	39.8	39.3
100k MSA Test	39.4	39.0
100k EGY Tune	28.1	28.1
100k EGY Test	27.7	27.7

Table 2: Core system (English → MSA) results using a reordering window size of 7.

6.3 Adaptation System Results

The adaptation systems take as input the MSA output of the core and attempt to improve the scores on the Egyptian test set by adapting to the domain of the 100k dataset, as well as to Egyptian Arabic, in either one or two steps.

	BLEU (B)	
	Tokenized	**Detokenized**
100k EGY Tune	40.8	40.5
100k EGY Test	40.3	40.1

Table 3: One-Step Adaptation system (MSA' → Egyptian Arabic) results using a reordering window size of 0.

Table 3 shows the results of the single adaptation system, which adapts directly from the MSA output of the core to Egyptian Arabic. These BLEU scores are already much better than the core systems performance on the same test sets, improving from 28.1 BLEU to 40.5 BLEU on the Egyptian Arabic tuning set (a difference of 12.4 BLEU) and improving from 22.7 BLEU to 40.1 BLEU on the Egyptian Arabic test set (a difference of 17.4 BLEU).

Tables 4 and 5 below illustrate the results of the first and second steps of the two-step adaptation system: Table 4 contains the results of the first domain adaptation step from out-of-domain MSA to in-domain MSA and Table 5 contains the results of the second dialect adaptation step from in-domain MSA to Egyptian Arabic.

An example of our system output for an English sentence is given in Table 6. Its METEOR X-ray alignment is illustrated in Figure 2.

6.4 System Comparisons on 100k Test Sets

In Table 7, we compare the results from the core and the results from the first step of the two-step adaptation system on the MSA test set and we see that adapting to the domain improves BLEU scores on MSA.

Since our goal is to improve the output for

	BLEU (A)	
	Tokenized	**Detokenized**
100k MSA Tune	45.2	44.6
100k MSA Test	44.8	44.2
100k EGY Tune	32.2	32.2
100k EGY Test	32.0	32.0

Table 4: Domain Adaptation system (MSA' → MSA") for Two-Step Adaptation System Results using a reordering window size of 7.

	BLEU (B)	
	Tokenized	**Detokenized**
100k EGY Tune	43.3	43.2
100k EGY Test	43.1	42.9

Table 5: Dialect Adaptation system (MSA" → Egyptian) for Two-Step Adaptation System Results using a reordering window size of 7.

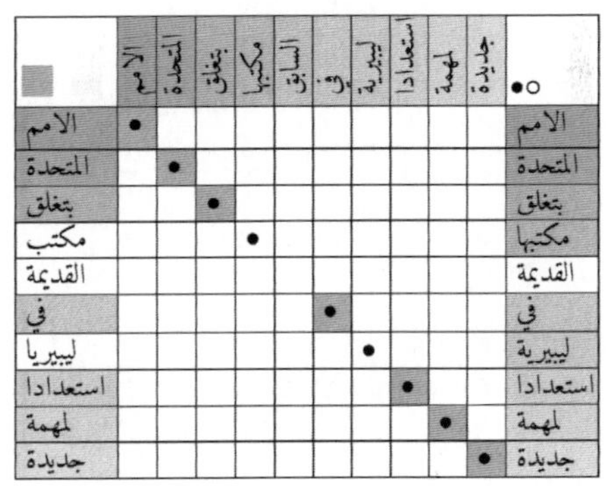

Figure 2: METEOR X-ray alignment of the sentence in table 6. The left side is the output of the one-step system, the right side is the output of the two-step system, and the top is the reference. The shaded cells represent matches between the reference and the one-step system, and the dots represent matches between the reference and the two-step system.

[1]One-Step System: Core + Domain and Dialect Adaptation (MSA' → EGY)

[2]Two Step Adaptation System (Step 1): Core + Domain Adaptation (MSA' → MSA")

[3]Two Step Adaptation System (Step 2): Core + Domain Adaptation (MSA' → MSA") + Dialect Adaptation (MSA" → EGY)

English	UN closes old office in Liberia in preparation for new mission
Egyptian Reference	الامم المتحدة بتغلق مكتبها السابق في ليبيرية استعدادا لمهمة جديدة *AAlAmm AAlmtHdp btglq mktbhA AAlsAbq fy lybyryp AAstEdAdA lmhmp jdydp*
1-Step System	الامم المتحدة بتغلق مكتب القديمة في ليبيريا استعدادا لمهمة جديدة *AAlAmm AAlmtHdp btglq mktb AAlqdymp fy lybyryA AAstEdAdA lmhmp jdydp*
2-Step System (step2)	الامم المتحدة بتغلق مكتبها القديمة في ليبيرية استعدادا لمهمة جديدة *AAlAmm AAlmtHdp btglq mktbhA AAlqdymp fy lybyryp AAstEdAdA lmhmp jdydp*

Table 6: An example of system output from the Egyptian test set.

	BLEU (A)	
	Tokenized	**Detokenized**
Core (English → MSA')	39.4	39.0
Core + Domain Adaptation (MSA' → MSA")	44.8	44.2

Table 7: Comparison of results on 100k MSA test set.

	BLEU (A/B)	
	Tokenized	**Detokenized**
Baseline (English → EGY)	21.5 (B)	21.1
Core (English → MSA')	27.7 (A)	27.7
One-Step Adaptation System [1]	40.3 (B)	40.1
Two-Step Adaptation System (Step 1)[2]	32.0 (A)	32.0
Two-Step Adaptation System (Step 2)[3]	43.1 (B)	42.9

Table 8: Comparison of results on 100k EGY test data.

	BLEU (B)	**METEOR**	**TER**	**Length**
Baseline System	21.1	38.5	66.1	102.7
One-Step System	40.1	53.4	51.3	100.0
Two-Step System: Step 2 (Dialect)	42.9	55.2	50.4	100.1

Table 9: Detokenized BLEU, METEOR, TER, and length scores for the best system results.

Egyptian Arabic, we examine the improvement of scores through different steps of the system in Table 8. These scores are all based on the same Egyptian Arabic references, even though some of the systems are designed to produce MSA output. It is important to note that although the first step of the two-step adaptation system (domain adaptation) is still producing MSA output, it performs better on the Egyptian test set than the out-of-domain MSA core. The domain adaptation system built on top of the core performs better than the core alone on the 100k corpus MSA test set (+5.2 BLEU), as well as the 100k corpus Egyptian Arabic test set (+4.3 BLEU). The best score we achieve on the 100k corpus MSA test set is 44.2 BLEU, from the core plus the domain adaptation system.

Table 9 shows the other detokenized scores from multeval (Clark et al., 2011) from the final output on the EGY test set from each system, and Table 10 shows BLEU-1 through BLEU-4 scores on the same detokenized results, which shows an improvement at different n-gram levels in unigram coverage from the baseline system to the adaptation systems.

Overall, the two-step adaptation system built on top of the core performs 15.2 BLEU better than the core alone on the 100k corpus Egyptian Arabic test set and the one-step adaptation system performs 12.4 BLEU better than the core on the same test set. The best score on the 100k EGY test set is from the two-step adaptation system with 42.9 BLEU, which outperforms the one-step adaptation system by 2.8 BLEU points. We consider possible causes of these results in section 7.

	BLEU-1	BLEU-2	BLEU-3	BLEU-4
Baseline System	53.4	26.6	15.3	9.1
One-Step System	64.3	43.5	33.5	27.1
Two-Step System: Step 2 (Dialect)	65.2	46.0	36.8	30.7

Table 10: Detokenized BLEU (B) scores on the 100k EGY test set at different n-gram levels.

English	US , Indonesia commit to closer trade , investment ties
Egyptian Reference	الولايات المتحدة واندونيسيا بيلتزموا بعلاقات تجارية واستثمارية اوثق *AAlwlAyAt AAlmtHdp wAndwnysyA byltzmwA bElAqAt tjAryp wAstvmAryp AAwvq*
Baseline output	+نا ، فان اندونيسيا بتّعهد بتوثيق العلاقات التجارية والاستثمارية *+nA , fAn AAndwnysyA bt Ehd btwvyq AAlElAqAt AAltjAryp wAlAstvmAryp*

Table 11: An example of a Baseline system output sentence with no word matches.

English	Pakistan sends envoys to Arab countries
Egyptian Reference	باكستان بترسل مبعوثين الي الدول العربية *bAkstAn btrsl mbEwvyn AAly AAldwl AAlErbyp*
One-Step System	باكستان بيرسل عنثيس الي الدول العربية *bAkstAn byrsl Envys AAly AAldwl AAlErbyp*
Two-Step System (Step 2)	باكستان بترسل عنثيس الي الدول العربية *bAkstAn btrsl Envys AAly AAldwl AAlErbyp*

Table 12: An example of system output from the Egyptian test set.

7 Error Analysis

In some of the output sentences, there are no exact matches and the sentence gets a score of 0, such as in the example from the Baseline system output in Table 11. But there are actually four words in the output that are present in the reference, but they have different clitics attached to them. The third word in the reference, واندونيسيا/*wAndwnysyA* "and Indonesia", is present in the output as just اندونيسيا/*AndwnysyA* "Indonesia". The same is true of the fifth, sixth, and seventh words in the reference: بعلاقات/*bElAqAt* "with relationships" is العلاقات/*AlElAqAt* "the relationships" in the output, تجارية/*tjAryp* "commercial" is التجارية/*AltjAryp* "commercial(definite)", and واستثمارية/*wAstvmAryp* "and investment" is والاستثمارية/*wAlAstvmAryp* "and the investment". In tokenized output the base words would be matched because the clitics would be separate. This is one of the drawbacks of evaluating on detokenized data.

Table 12 and Figure 3 show the output for a sentence from the Egyptian test set from the two different adaptation systems. In Figure 3, the results from the one-step and two-step adaptation systems are almost the same, except that the two-step adaptation system (which scored 2.8 BLEU higher than the one-step system overall) has one more word correct (the second word). This word is actually the same verb, but the two-step adaptation system has produced the correct conjugation of the verb (3rd person feminine), while the one-step system produced the wrong conjugation (3rd person masculine). In adapting to the domain first, the system seems to produce better subject-verb agreement.

In Table 6 and Figure 2 in Section 6.3, the transliteration of "Liberia" in the output of the two-step system matches the reference. The one-step system produces a different transliteration which is also valid, but is not the same one the reference uses. It also produces the correct object clitic (مكتبها/*mktbhA* "its office" vs. مكتب/*mktb* "office"). The output of the two-step system more consistently matches the reference in transliteration, subject-verb agreement, and clitic attachment.

In general the output of the two-step adaptation system appears to be in the correct order more often than the output of the one-step adaptation sys-

English	man stabs nine at moscow synagogue
Egyptian Reference	شاب بيطعنن ٩ في كنيس يهودي في موسكوا *$Ab byTEnn 9 fy knys yhwdy fy mwskwA*
One-Step System	راجل طعن تسعه في كنيس يهودي في موسكوا *rAjl TEn tsEh fy knys yhwdy fy mwskwA*

Table 13: Comparison of reference and system output.

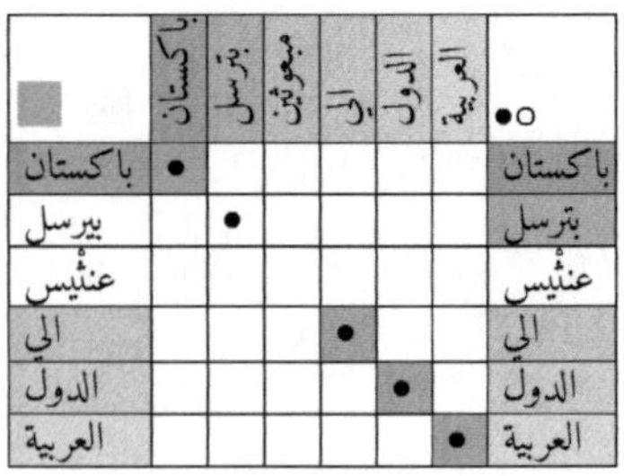

Figure 3: A comparison of the output of the one-step domain and dialect adaptation system (left column) and the two-step domain and dialect adaptation system (right column), both built on top of the phrase-based core. The top is the reference sentence.

tem, perhaps because we used a reordering window of 7 for the two-step system, whereas we used a window of 0 for the one step system. Additionally, the two-step system allows two passes of reordering, one in each step. Each step of the system produces a decrease in the fragmentation of the output: the output of the core on the Egyptian test set gets a fragmentation penalty of 0.204, the one-step system gets a fragmentation penalty of 0.159, and the two step system gets 0.189 for the first step (domain) and 0.139 for the second step (dialect). Since the output of the two-step system is less fragmented, there are longer sequences of words that are in the correct order.

Additionally, the one-step system misses more words, especially at the beginning of a sentence. There are many ways to introduce a sentence in Arabic, some of which correspond to the same English phrase. While the model will generate the most probable one, there may be several acceptable choices, and the reference may have a different one. For instance, in Table 13, the word "man" is translated as شاب/*$Ab* in the reference, and راجل/*rAjl* in the output of the one-step adaptation system. This word is penalized for not matching the reference, even though both are reasonable translations of "man". This problem could be helped by synonym matching in the evaluation metrics, which is not currently available for Arabic.

8 Conclusion and Future Work

We have shown that we can leverage a large amount of out-of-domain MSA data and a domain adaptation system to achieve better performance on an in-domain test set. We apply the same technique to translating Arabic dialects, by adapting from MSA to the Egyptian Arabic dialect as we would adapt between domains of the same language. Our results also show that when adapting to the domain, first by translating to MSA as an intermediary step and then adapting to the dialect, we can improve performance even more. Our results also show the importance of consistent and appropriate tokenization of the data. The tri-parallel corpus of English, MSA, and Egyptian gave us a unique opportunity to create this kind of system, as parallel data for Arabic dialects is hard to come by. However, this data is artificial Egyptian, not natural generated dialectal Arabic. In the future we hope to test our domain and dialect adaptation MT systems on more authentic Egyptian Arabic data sets and to be able to apply this technique to other Arabic dialects.

Acknowledgements

This publication was made possible by grant NPRP-09-1140-1-177 from the Qatar National Research Fund (a member of the Qatar Foundation) and by computing resources provided by the NSF-sponsored XSEDE program under grant TG-CCR110017. The statements made herein are solely the responsibility of the authors. We thank the reviewers for their comments. Nizar Habash performed most of his contribution to this paper while he was at the Center for Computational Learning Systems at Columbia University.

References

Hitham Abo Bakr, Khaled Shaalan, and Ibrahim Ziedan. 2008. A Hybrid Approach for Converting Written Egyptian Colloquial Dialect into Diacritized Arabic. In *Proceedings of the 6th International Conference on Informatics and Systems (INFOS2008)*. Cairo University.

Abdel-Rahman Abu-Melhim. 1991. Code-switching and Linguistic Accommodation in Arabic. In *Perspectives on Arabic Linguistics III: Papers from the Third Annual Symposium on Arabic Linguistics*, volume 80, pages 231–250. John Benjamins Publishing.

Kamla Al-Mannai, Hassan Sajjad, Alaa Khader, Fahad Al Obaidli, Preslav Nakov, and Stephan Vogel. 2014. Unsupervised Word Segmentation Improves Dialectal Arabic to English Machine Translation. In *Proceedings of EMNLP Workshop on Arabic Natural Language Processing*, Doha, Qatar.

Houda Bouamor, Nizar Habash, and Kemal Oflazer. 2014. A Multidialectal Parallel Corpus of Arabic. In *Proceedings of the Ninth International Conference on Language Resources and Evaluation (LREC'14)*, pages 1240–1245, Reykjavik, Iceland.

Rahma Boujelbane, Mariem Ellouze Khemekhem, and Lamia Hadrich Belguith. 2013. Mapping Rules for Building a Tunisian Dialect Lexicon and Generating Corpora. In *Proceedings of the Sixth International Joint Conference on Natural Language Processing*, pages 419–428, Nagoya, Japan.

Jonathan Clark, Chris Dyer, Alon Lavie, and Noah Smith. 2011. Better Hypothesis Testing for Statistical Machine Translation: Controlling for Optimizer Instability. In *Proceedings of the Association for Computational Linguistics (ACL)*, Portland, Oregon.

Ryan Cotterell and Chris Callison-Burch. 2014. A Multi-Dialect, Multi-Genre Corpus of Informal Written Arabic. In *Proceedings of the Ninth International Conference on Language Resources and Evaluation (LREC'14)*, pages 241–245, Reykjavik, Iceland.

Michael Denkowski and Alon Lavie. 2011. Meteor 1.3: Automatic metric for reliable optimization and evaluation of machine translation systems. In *Proceedings of the EMNLP 2011 Workshop on Statistical Machine Translation*, pages 1–4, Edinburgh, Scotland.

Marcello Federico, Nicola Bertoldi, and Mauro Cettolo. 2008. IRSTLM: an open source toolkit for handling large scale language models. In *INTERSPEECH*, pages 1618–1621.

Nizar Habash and Owen Rambow. 2005. Arabic Tokenization, Part-of-speech Tagging and Morphological Disambiguation in One Fell Swoop. In *Proceedings of the Association for Computational Linguistics*, Ann Arbor, Michigan.

Nizar Habash and Owen Rambow. 2006. MAGEAD: A Morphological Analyzer and Generator for the Arabic Dialects. In *Proceedings of the 21st International Conference on Computational Linguistics and 44th Annual Meeting of the Association for Computational Linguistics*, pages 681–688, Sydney, Australia.

Nizar Habash, Ramy Eskander, and Abdelati Hawwari. 2012. A Morphological Analyzer for Egyptian Arabic. In *Proceedings of the Twelfth Meeting of the Special Interest Group on Computational Morphology and Phonology*, pages 1–9, Montréal, Canada.

Nizar Habash, Ryan Roth, Owen Rambow, Ramy Eskander, and Nadi Tomeh. 2013. Morphological Analysis and Disambiguation for Dialectal Arabic. In *Proceedings of the 2013 Conference of the North American Chapter of the Association for Computational Linguistics: Human Language Technologies*, pages 426–432, Atlanta, Georgia.

Nizar Habash. 2010. *Introduction to Arabic Natural Language Processing*, volume 3. Morgan & Claypool Publishers.

Ahmed Hamdi, Nuria Gala, and Alexis Nasr. 2014. Automatically Building a Tunisian Lexicon for Deverbal Nouns. In *Proceedings of the First Workshop on Applying NLP Tools to Similar Languages, Varieties and Dialects*, pages 95–102, Dublin, Ireland.

Kenneth Heafield, Ivan Pouzyrevsky, Jonathan H. Clark, and Philipp Koehn. 2013. Scalable Modfied Kneser-Ney Language Model Estimation. In *In Proceedings of the Association for Computational Linguistics*, Sofia, Bulgaria.

Kenneth Heafield. 2011. KenLM: Faster and Smaller Language Model Queries. In *Proceedings of the EMNLP 2011 Sixth Workshop on Statistical Machine Translation*, pages 187–197, Edinburgh, Scotland, United Kingdom, July.

Pierre Isabelle, Cyril Goutte, and Michel Simard. 2007. Domain Adaptation of MT Systems through Automatic Post-Editing. In *Proceedings of MT Summit XI*, pages 255–261, Copenhagen, Denmark.

Philipp Koehn, Hieu Hoang, Alexandra Birch, Christopher Callison-Burch, Marcello Federico, Nicola Bertoldi, Brooke Cowan, Wade Shen, Christine Moran, Richard Zens, Christopher Dyer, Ondrej Bojar, Alexandra Constantin, and Evan Herbst. 2007. Moses: Open Source Toolkit for Statistical Machine Translation. In *Proceedings of the 45th Annual Meeting of the Association for Computational Linguistics Companion Volume Proceedings of the Demo and Poster Sessions*, pages 177–180, Prague, Czech Republic.

Emad Mohamed, Behrang Mohit, and Kemal Oflazer. 2012. Transforming Standard Arabic to Colloquial Arabic. In *Proceedings of the 50th Annual Meeting of the Association for Computational Linguistics (Volume 2: Short Papers)*, pages 176–180, Jeju Island, Korea.

NIST Multimodal Information Group. 2010a. NIST 2008 Open Machine Translation (OpenMT) Evaluation LDC2010T21. Web Download.

NIST Multimodal Information Group. 2010b. NIST 2009 Open Machine Translation (OpenMT) Evaluation LDC2010T23. Web Download.

Franz Josef Och and Hermann Ney. 2003. A Systematic Comparison of Various Statistical Alignment Models. In *Computational Linguistics*, pages 19–51.

Kishore Papineni, Salim Roukos, Todd Ward, and Wei-Jing Zhu. 2002. BLEU: a Method for Automatic Evaluation of Machine Translation. In *Proceedings of the Association for Computational Linguistics*, Philadelphia, Pennsylvania.

Robert Parker, David Graff, Ke Chen, Junbo Kong, and Kazuaki Maeda. 2011. Arabic Gigaword Fifth Edition LDC2011T11. Web Download.

Arfath Pasha, Mohamed Al-Badrashiny, Mona Diab, Ahmed El Kholy, Ramy Eskander, Nizar Habash, Manoj Pooleery, Owen Rambow, and Ryan Roth. 2014. MADAMIRA: A Fast, Comprehensive Tool for Morphological Analysis and Disambiguation of Arabic. In *Proceedings of the Ninth International Conference on Language Resources and Evaluation (LREC'14)*, pages 1094–1101, Reykjavik, Iceland.

Hassan Sajjad, Kareem Darwish, and Yonatan Belinkov. 2013. Translating Dialectal Arabic to English. In *Proceedings of the 51st Annual Meeting of the Association for Computational Linguistics (Volume 2: Short Papers)*, pages 1–6, Sofia, Bulgaria.

Ahmed Salama, Houda Bouamor, Behrang Mohit, and Kemal Oflazer. 2014. YouDACC: the Youtube Dialectal Arabic Comment Corpus. In *Proceedings of the Ninth International Conference on Language Resources and Evaluation (LREC'14)*, pages 1246–1251, Reykjavik, Iceland.

Wael Salloum and Nizar Habash. 2013. Dialectal Arabic to English Machine Translation: Pivoting through Modern Standard Arabic. In *Proceedings of the 2013 Conference of the North American Chapter of the Association for Computational Linguistics: Human Language Technologies*, pages 348–358, Atlanta, Georgia.

Wael Salloum, Heba Elfardy, Linda Alamir-Salloum, Nizar Habash, and Mona Diab. 2014. Sentence Level Dialect Identification for Machine Translation System Selection. In *Proceedings of the 52nd Annual Meeting of the Association for Computational Linguistics (Volume 2: Short Papers)*, pages 772–778, Baltimore, Maryland.

Hassan Sawaf. 2010. Arabic Dialect Handling in Hybrid Machine Translation. In *Proceedings of the Ninth Conference of the Association for Machine Translation in the Americas (AMTA 10)*, Denver, Colorado.

Mohammed Q Shatnawi, Muneer Bani Yassein, and Reem Mahafza. 2012. A Framework for Retrieving Arabic Documents Based on Queries Written in Arabic Slang Language. *Journal of Information Science*, 38(4):350–365.

Michel Simard, Cyril Goutte, and Pierre Isabelle. 2007. Statistical Phrase-Based Post-Editing. In *Proceedings of NAACL-HLT-2007 Human Language Technology: the Conference of the North American Chapter of the Association for Computational Linguistics*, pages 508–515, Rochester, NY.

Matthew Snover, Bonnie Dorr, Richard Schwartz, Linnea Micciulla, and John Makhoul. 2006. A Study of Translation Edit Rate with Targeted Human Annotation. In *Proceedings of Association for Machine Translation in the Americas*, Cambridge, Massachusetts.

Andreas Stolcke. 2002. SRILM - An Extensible Language Modeling Toolkit. In *Proceedings of the International Conference on Spoken Language Processing, vol. 2*, pages 901–904, Denver, CO, USA.

Omar F. Zaidan and Chris Callison-Burch. 2011. The Arabic Online Commentary Dataset: an Annotated Dataset of Informal Arabic with High Dialectal Content. In *Proceedings of the 49th Annual Meeting of the Association for Computational Linguistics: Human Language Technologies*, pages 37–41, Portland, Oregon, USA.

Rabih Zbib, Erika Malchiodi, Jacob Devlin, David Stallard, Spyros Matsoukas, Richard Schwartz, John Makhoul, Omar F. Zaidan, and Chris Callison-Burch. 2012. Machine Translation for Arabic Dialects. In *Proceedings of North American Chapter of the Association for Computational Linguistics*, Montreal, Canada.

Unsupervised Word Segmentation Improves Dialectal Arabic to English Machine Translation

Kamla Al-Mannai[1], **Hassan Sajjad**[1], **Alaa Khader**[2], **Fahad Al Obaidli**[1], **Preslav Nakov**[1], **Stephan Vogel**[1]
Qatar Computing Research Institute[1], Carnegie Mellon University in Qatar[2]
{kamlmannai,hsajjad,faalobaidli,pnakov,svogel}@qf.org.qa[1], akhader@cmu.edu[2]

Abstract

We demonstrate the feasibility of using unsupervised morphological segmentation for dialects of Arabic, which are poor in linguistics resources. Our experiments using a Qatari Arabic to English machine translation system show that unsupervised segmentation helps to improve the translation quality as compared to using no segmentation or to using ATB segmentation, which was especially designed for Modern Standard Arabic (MSA). We use MSA and other dialects to improve Qatari Arabic to English machine translation, and we show that a uniform segmentation scheme across them yields an improvement of 1.5 BLEU points over using no segmentation.

1 Introduction

The Arabic language has many varieties, where the Modern Standard Arabic (MSA) coexists with various dialects. Dialects differ from MSA and from each other lexically, phonologically, morphologically and syntactically. MSA has standard orthography and is used in formal contexts (e.g., publications, newspaper articles, etc.), while the dialects are usually limited to daily verbal interactions. However, with the recent rise of social media, it has become increasingly common to use dialects in written communication as well, which has constituted the research in dialectal Arabic (DA) as a separate field within the broader field of natural language processing (NLP).

As DA NLP is still in its infancy, there is lack of basic computational resources and tools, which are needed in order to apply standard NLP approaches to the dialects of Arabic. For instance, statistical approaches need a lot of training data, which makes it very hard, if not impossible, to apply them to resource-poor languages; this is especially true for statistical machine translation (SMT) of Arabic dialects.

The Arabic language and its dialects are highly inflectional, and a word can appear in many more inflected forms compared to English. Consider the Arabic words تلعب, يلعب, لعبت, and يلعبون: they all belong to one root word لعب 'playing' /lEb/. Each morphological variation is derived from a root word with different affixes addressing different functions. This causes data sparseness, and covering all possible word forms of a root word may not be always possible. Considering the different variants of Arabic, the problem is exacerbated as dialects could use different choices of affixes for the same function. For example, the MSA word يلعبون /yalEabuwn/, meaning 'they are playing', could be found as يلعبون /ylEbuwn/ in Gulf, as عم يلعبوا /Eam yilEabuA/ in Levantine, and as بيلعبوا /biylEabwA/ in Egyptian Arabic.

One possible solution is to use a morphological segmenter that segments words into simpler units such as stems and affixes, which might be covered in the training set (Zollmann et al., 2006; Tsai et al., 2010). When applied to dialects, this may reduce the lexical gap between dialects and MSA by matching the common stems. Unfortunately, there are no standard morphological segmentation tools for dialects. Due to the difference in morphology, tools designed for MSA do not work well for dialects. Developing rule-based segmenters for each dialect might appear to be the ideal solution, but, as the orthography of dialects is not standardized, crafting linguistic rules for them is very hard.

In this paper, we focus on training an unsupervised model for word segmentation, which we apply to SMT for a given Arabic dialect. We train a pre-existing unsupervised segmentation model on the Arabic side of the training bi-text (and on some other monolingual data), and then we optimize its parameters based on the resulting SMT quality. Similarly, a *multi-dialectal* word segmenter could be developed by training on multi-dialectal data.

Proceedings of the EMNLP 2014 Workshop on Arabic Natural Langauge Processing (ANLP), pages 207–216,
October 25, 2014, Doha, Qatar.

In particular, we develop a Qatari Arabic to English (QA-EN) SMT system, which we train on a small pre-existing bi-text. As part of the development of the unsupervised segmentation model, we also collected some additional monolingual data for Qatari Arabic. Qatari Arabic is a subdialect of the more general Gulf dialect, among with Saudi, Kuwaiti, Emirati, Bahraini, and Omani; we collected additional monologual data for each of these subdialects, and we release this data to the research community.

We train an unsupervised segmentation tool, Morphessor, and its MAP model (Creutz and Lagus, 2007), using different variations of the collected Qatari data. We optimize the single hyperparameter of the MAP model by maximizing the translation quality of the QA-EN SMT system in terms of BLEU. Our experimental results demonstrate that the resulting unsupervised segmenter yields improvements in translation quality when compared to (i) using no segmentation and (ii) using an MSA-based ATB segmenter.

We further develop a multi-dialectal word segmentation model, which we train on the Arabic side of the multi-dialectal training data, which consists of Qatari Arabic, Egyptian Arabic (EGY), Levantine Arabic (LEV) and MSA to English, i.e., a scaled combination of all the available parallel data. We train a QA-EN SMT system using the segmented multi-dialectal data, and we show an absolute gain of 1.5 BLEU points compared to a baseline that uses no segmentation.

The rest of the paper is organized as follows: First, we provide an overview of related work on Dialectal Arabic NLP (Section 2). Next, we discuss and we illustrate the linguistic differences between different Arabic dialects in comparison with and with a focus on Qatari Arabic (Section 3). Then, we provide statistics about the corpora we collected and used in our experiments, followed by an illustration of the orthographic normalization schemes we applied (Section 4). We next provide a high-level description of our approach, which uses morphological segmentation to combine resources for other Arabic dialects in a QA-EN SMT system effectively (Section 4.3). We also explain our experimental setup and we present the results (Section 5). We then discuss translating in the reverse direction, i.e., into Qatari Arabic (Section 6). Finally, we point to possible directions for future work and we conclude the paper (Section 7).

2 Related Work

NLP for DA is still in its early stages of development and many challenges need to be overcomed such as the lack of suitable tools and resources.

Collecting resources for dialectal Arabic: Several researchers have directed efforts to develop DA computational resources (Maamouri et al., 2006; Al-Sabbagh and Girju, 2010; Zaidan and Callison-Burch, 2011; Salama et al., 2014). Zbib et al. (2012) built two dialectal Arabic-English parallel corpora for Egyptian and Levantine Arabic using crowdsourcing. Bouamor et al. (2014) presented a multi-dialectal Arabic parallel corpus, which covers five Arabic dialects besides MSA and English. Mubarak and Darwish (2014) collected a multi-dialectal corpus using Twitter. Unlike previous work, we focus on Gulf subdialects, particularly Qatari Arabic. The monolingual data that we collected is a high-quality dialectal resource and originates from dialect-specific sources such as novels and forums.

Adapting SMT resources for other Arabic dialects: Many researchers have explored the potential of using MSA as a pivot language for improving SMT of Arabic dialects (Bakr et al., 2008; Sawaf, 2010; Salloum and Habash, 2011; Sajjad et al., 2013a; Jeblee et al., 2014). This often involves DA-MSA conversion schemes as an alternative in the absence of DA-MSA parallel resources. In contrast, limited work has been done on leveraging available resources for other dialects. Recently, Zbib et al. (2012) have shown that using a small amount of dialectal data could yield great improvements for SMT. Here, we investigate the potential of improving the resource adaptability of Arabic dialects. Our work is different as we use an unsupervised segmenter that helps in improving the lexical overlap between dialects and MSA.

Building morphological segmenters for the Arabic dialects: Researchers have already focused efforts on crafting and extending existing MSA tools to DA by mainly using a set of rules (Habash et al., 2012). Habash and Rambow (2006) presented MAGEAD, a knowledge-based morphological analyzer and generator for Egyptian and Levantine Arabic. Chiang et al. (2006) developed a Levantine morphological analyzer on top of an existing MSA analyzer using an explicit knowledge base.

Riesa and Yarowsky (2006) trained a supervised trie-based model using a small lexicon of dialectal affixes. In our work, we eliminate the need for linguistic knowledge by training an unsupervised model using available resources. The unsupervised mode of learning allowed us to develop a multi-dialectal morphological segmenter.

3 Arabic Dialects

In this section, we highlight some of the linguistic differences between Arabic dialects and MSA, with a focus on the Qatari dialect.

3.1 Phonological Variations

The Gulf dialect often preserves the phonological representation of MSA, which is not the case with many other Arabic dialects. For example, in Egyptian (EGY) and in some Levantine (LEV) dialects, the MSA consonants ث /v/, ق /q/, and ذ /*/ are realized as ت /t/, glottal stop /'/, and ظ /Z/, respectively. While, their MSA pronunciations are preserved in Gulf Arabic.

In Gulf Arabic, there are some phonological differences between countries such as Kuwait (KW), Saudi Arabia (SA), Bahrain (BH), Qatar (QA), United Arab Emirates (AE), and Oman (OM). Here, we focus our discussion on Qatari Arabic, and we compare it to MSA and other dialects.

The QA dialect borrows two Persian characters namely چ /J/ and ڤ /V/. For instance, the MSA letter ج /j/ is converted to /J/ in QA, e.g., إجتماع 'meeting' is pronounced as /<jtimAE/ in MSA and /<JtimAE/ in QA. The Persian character چ /J/ is also used in place of ك /k/ in some MSA words when they are used in QA. For example, سمك 'fish' /samak/ is pronounced سمچ /smaJ/ in QA, while the EGY and the LEV dialects maintain the MSA pronunciation. The Persian ڤ /V/ is used to map the sound of the English letter 'v' in borrowed foreign words, e.g., فيديو 'video' is pronounced as ڤيديو /Viydyw/ as opposed to /fiydywu/; the form in which it is written in MSA.

The MSA consonant ض /D/ is not used in the QA dialect. It is substituted by ظ /Z/ in Qatari. For example, the MSA pronunciation /HaD/ of حض 'to encourage' is transformed to حظ /HaZ/ in QA, but it is maintained in EGY.

Meanwhile, the MSA consonant ظ /Z/ is realized as /D/ in EGY. For example, the MSA pronunciation /HaZ/ of حظ 'luck' is maintained in QA and transformed to /HaD/ in EGY. This change is consistent in all words within each dialect. However, such phonological variations between dialects have the potential to add ambiguity to dialectal Arabic.

The MSA consonant ج /j/ can be used to distinguish between different dialects, particularly Gulf subdialects. ج /j/ is pronounced as ي /y/ in KW, BH, QA, AE, ق /q/ in OM, much like in EGY, and ج /j/ in SA, much like in LEV. For example, the MSA word مسجد 'mosque' /masjid/ is pronounced as /masjid/ in MSA, SA, LEV, مسقد /masqid/ in OM, EGY, مسيد /masyid/ in KW, BH, QA, AE, while the MSA pronunciation is preserved in SA. This change does not apply to names. However, we should note that it is not consistent in QA, e.g., the MSA pronunciation of ج /j/ in جبل 'mountain' /jabal/ and برج 'tower' /burj/ is preserved in QA.

3.2 Morphological Variations

In Arabic, a root can produce surface wordforms by means of inflectional and derivational morphological processes (Habash, 2010).

An inflectional word form is a variant of a root word with the same meaning but expressing a different function, e.g., gender, number, case. It is usually formed by adding a prefix, a suffix, or a circumfix to a stem word. Note that Arabic dialects can make different lexical choices for affixations compared to MSA. For example, the MSA future prefix س /s/ is replaced by ب /b/ in QA and by هـ /h/ in EGY and LEV. Thus, the MSA word سيأكل 'he will eat' /say>kul/ becomes بياكل /biyAkil/ in QA and هياكل /hayAkul/ in EGY and LEV.

A derivational word form is formed by applying a pattern to a root word, e.g., 'player' is derived from 'play' using the pattern `noun + 'er'`. An example of an Arabic derivational form is تفعل 'do' /tafaEãl/. The root is فعل /faEal/ and it uses the imperative pattern فعل+ت. In EGY, ا /A/ is added as a prefix; so, it becomes اتفعل /AitfaEĩl/.

Meanwhile, the original form is preserved in QA.

Changing the structure of a pattern in a dialect will result in producing a new dialect-specific orthography for every word that is represented by the structure. For example, the MSA word تعلم 'learn' /taEalãm/ becomes اتعلم /AitEalim/ in EGY, while the MSA form is preserved in QA.

3.3 Lexical Variations

Lexical variations are among the most obvious differences between Arabic dialects. For example, the MSA word ماذا 'what' /mA*A/ would be found as شو /$uw/ in LEV, إيه /<yh/ in EGY, and شنو /$nuw/ in GLF. We can find lexical variations in subdialects as well. For example, the MSA negation word لن /lan/, 'not', is expressed as مب /mab/ in QA, as مو /muw/ in KW, and as مهب /ma-hab/ in SA.

3.4 Orthographic Variations

Due to the lack of orthographic standardization of dialectal Arabic, some MSA words can be found in dialectal text with both MSA and phonological spellings. For example, the MSA word جمعة 'gathering' /jamEap/ can be also spelled as يمعه /yamEah/, which is a phonetic variation in QA. Some dialectal words also vary in spelling due to variation in their pronunciation, e.g., أشوف /A$uwf/, a QA word meaning 'I see', can be also spelled as اجوف /Ajuwf/.

In dialectal Arabic, different orthographic forms are also possible for entire phrases. For instance, words followed or preceded by pronouns are commonly reduced to a single word, e.g., قلت لها /glt lahA/ 'I told her' is written as قلتلها. Also, commonly used religious phrases can be found written as a single unit, e.g., ما شاء الله /mA $A' Alãh/ 'God has willed it' as مشالله.

4 Methodology

In the section, we present some statistics about the Arabic dialectal data that we have collected. We processed it to remove orthographic inconsistencies. Then, we used a pre-existing unsupervised morphological segmenter, Morfessor, in order to segment the text.

Corpus	QCA	$AVIA_{QA}$	$AVIA_{O}$
Sents	14.7	0.9	2
Tokens	115	6.7	15

Table 1: Statistics about the collected parallel corpora (in thousands). $AVIA_O$ shows the statistics about the AVIA corpus excluding Qatari data.

4.1 Data Collection

We did an extensive search for available monolingual and bilingual resources for the Gulf dialect, with a focus on Qatari Arabic. Tables 1 and 2 present some statistics about the corpora we collected. More detailed description follows below.

Bilingual corpora:

– The **QCA speech corpus**, comprises 14.7k sentences that are phonetically transcribed from TV broadcasts in Qatari Arabic and translated to English; see (Elmahdy et al., 2014) for more detail. The corpus was designed for speech recognition and we faced several normalization-related issues that we had to resolve before it could be used for machine translation and language modeling. One example is the usage of five Persian characters to represent some sounds in Arabic words. Moreover, the English side had some grammatical and spelling errors. We normalized the Arabic side and corrected the English side of the corpus as described in Section 4.2. The corpus can be found at `http://sprosig.isle.illinois.edu/corpora/1`.

– The **AVIA corpus**[1] is designed as a reference source of dialectal Arabic. It consists of 3k sentences in four Gulf subdialects: Emirati (AE), Kuwaiti (KW), Qatari (QA), and Hejazi (SA).[2] The data consists of dialectal sentences that contain words commonly used in daily conversation.

Monolingual corpora: We further collected monolingual corpora consisting of a total of 2.7M tokens for various Gulf subdialects. The Qatari part of the data consists of 470K tokens. Most of the corpus is a collection of novels, belonging to the romance genre.[3] For the Qatari dialect, we also collected Qatari forum data.[4]

[1] `http://terpconnect.umd.edu/~nlynn/AVIA/Level3/`

[2] The website also contains small parallel corpora for MSA, EGY and LEV to English, but here we focus on Gulf subdialects only.

[3] `http://forum.te3p.com/264311-52.html`

[4] `www.qatarshares.com/vb/index.php`

Corpus	Novel						Forum
	AE	BH	KW	OM	QA	SA	QA
Tokens	573	244	178	372	412	614	69
Types	43	22	27	27	43	71	15

Table 2: Statistics about the collected monolingual corpora (in thousands of words).

To the best of our knowledge, this is the first collection of monolingual corpora for Gulf Arabic subdialects. It can be helpful for, e.g., language modeling when translating into Arabic, for learning the similarities and differences between Gulf subdialects, etc. Table 2 shows some statistics about the data after punctuation tokenization.

4.2 Orthographic Normalization

The inconsistency in the orthographic spelling of the same word can increase data sparseness. Thus, we normalize the Arabic text in the collected resources by applying the reduced orthographic normalization scheme, e.g., Tah Marbota is reduced to Hah. We also normalize extended lines between letters, e.g., سـكـر 'sugar' /sukar/ is changed to سكر, and we reduce character elongations to be just two characters long. In order to maintain consistency among different resources, we remove supplementary diacritics, e.g., عُقَد 'knots' /Euqad/ is normalized to عقد, and we map Persian letters to their phonological correspondences in Qatari Arabic[5], i.e., گ /G/ to ق /g/, ڤ /V/ to ف /f/, پ /P/ to ب /b/, and ژ and چ /J/ to ج /j/.

For the English texts, the orthographic variations were already normalized. However, the English side of the QCA corpus had some spelling and grammatical errors, which we corrected manually. On the grammatical side, we only corrected a subset of the data, which we used for tuning and testing our SMT system (see Section 5).

4.3 Morphological Decomposition

There is no general Arabic morphological segmenter that works for all variations of Arabic. The most commonly used segmenters for Arabic were designed for MSA (Habash et al., 2009; Green and DeNero, 2012). Due to the lexical and morphological differences between dialects and MSA, these MSA-based morphological tools do not work well for dialects.

In this work, we used an unsupervised morphological segmenter, Morfessor-categories MAP[6], an unsupervised model with a single hyperparameter (Creutz and Lagus, 2007). We chose Morfessor because of its superior performance on Arabic compared to other unsupervised models (Siivola et al., 2007; Poon et al., 2009).

The model has a single hyperparameter, the perplexity threshold parameter *B*, which controls the granularity of segmentation. The recommended value ranges from 1 to 400 where 1 means maximum fine-grained segmentation, and 400 restricts it to the least segmented output. We set the threshold empirically to 70, as shown in Section 5.1.

5 Experimental Setup

We performed an extrinsic evaluation of the variations in segmentation by building a Qatari Arabic to English machine translation system on each of them. We also tested Morfessor on other available dialects and on MSA, and we will show below how a uniform segmentation can help to better adapt resources for dialects and MSA for SMT. This section describes our experimental setup.

Datasets: We divided the **QCA corpus** into 1k sentences each for development and testing, and we used the remaining 12k for training.

We adapted parallel corpora for **Egyptian**, **Levantine** and **MSA** to English to be used for Qatari Arabic to English SMT. For MSA, we used parallel corpora of TED talks (Cettolo et al., 2012) and the AMARA corpus (Abdelali et al., 2014), which consists of educational videos. Since the QCA corpus is in the speech domain, we believe that an MSA corpus of spoken domain would be more helpful than a text domain such as News. For Egyptian and Levantine, we used the parallel corpus provided by Zbib et al. (2012). There is no Gulf–English parallel data available in the literature. The data that we found was a very small collection of subdialects of Gulf Arabic; we did not use it for MT experiments. However, we used the Qatari part of the AVIA corpus to train Morfessor.

Machine translation system settings: We used a phrase-based statistical machine translation model as implemented in the Moses toolkit (Koehn et al., 2007) for machine translation.

[5]This issue relates to the QCA corpus.

[6]This is an extension of the basic Morfessor method and is based on a Maximum a Posteriori model.

We built separate directed word alignments for source-to-target and target-to-source using IBM model 4 (Brown et al., 1993), and we symmetrized them using the grow-diag-final-and heuristics (Koehn et al., 2003). We then extracted phrase pairs with a maximum length of seven, and we scored them using maximum likelihood estimation with Kneser-Ney smoothing (Kneser and Ney, 1995). We also built a lexicalized reordering model, msd-bidirectional-fe. We built a 5-gram language model on the English side of QCA-train using KenLM (Heafield, 2011). Finally, we built a log-linear model using the above features.

We tuned the model weights by optimizing BLEU (Papineni et al., 2002) on the tuning set, using PRO (Hopkins and May, 2011) with sentence-level BLEU+1 optimization (Nakov et al., 2012). In testing, we used minimum Bayes risk decoding (Kumar and Byrne, 2004), cube pruning, and the operation sequence model (Durrani et al., 2011).

Baseline: Our baseline Qatari Arabic to English MT system is trained on the QCA bitext without any segmentation of Qatari Arabic. For the experiments described in this paper, we used the English side of the QCA corpus for language modeling.

5.1 Experimental Results

In this section, we first present our work on using Morfessor for segmenting Qatari Arabic. We tried different values of its parameter, and we trained it using corpora of different sizes to find balanced settings that improve SMT quality as compared with no segmentation and with segmentation using the Stanford ATB segmenter. We further applied our selected settings to segment MSA, EGY and LEV and used them for Qatari Arabic to English machine translation. Our results show that a uniform segmentation scheme across different dialects improves machine translation.

Morfessor training variations: We trained Morfessor using three corpora: (i) QCA, (ii) $AVIA_{QA}$ plus Qatari Novels, and (iii) a combination thereof. Table 3 shows the results for our SMT system when trained on the QCA parallel corpus, which was segmented using different training models of Morfessor with **B** = 40. The result for segmented Qatari Arabic is always better than the baseline, irrespective of the training model used for segmentation. We can see that the Morfessor model trained on a large monolingual corpus, i.e., on (ii) or (iii), yields better results.

Morfessor	BLEU	OOV%
Baseline	12.2	16.6
QCA	12.5	0.6
$AVIA_{QA}$, Novels	13.5	0.8
QCA, $AVIA_{QA}$, Novels	13.4	0.7

Table 3: Study of the effect of varying the training datasets for Morfessor on the Qatari to English SMT. "Baseline" shows the output of the MT system with no segmentation.

B	**10**	**40**	**70**	**100**	**130**
BLEU	13.3	13.5	**13.8**	12.9	12.6
OOV	0.3	0.8	1.4	2.8	2.8
			After merging		
BLEU	12.5	13.4	**13.7**	12.8	12.3
OOV	1.5	1.9	3.9	6.5	9.8

Table 4: The effect of varying the perplexity threshold parameter *B* of Morfessor on SMT quality. "After merging" are the results using the post-processed Qatari segmented data.

The high reduction in OOV in Table 3 is because of the fine-grained segmentation. We tried different values for the perplexity parameter *B* in order to find a good balance between better BLEU scores and linguistically correct segmentations. The first part of Table 4 shows the effect of different values of *B* on the quality of the machine translation system trained on $AVIA_{QA}$, Qatari Novels. We achieved the best SMT score at $B = 70$.

We further analyzed the output of Morfessor at $B = 70$ and we noticed that it tends to generate very small segments of length two and three characters long. The segmentation produces more than one stem in a word and does not generate legal word units. For example, the word والصناعة 'and the industry' /wAlSinAEp/ is segmented as PRE/و + PRE/ال + STM/ص + PRE/ن + PRE/ا + STM/ع + SUF/ة. We apply a post-processing step that merges all stems in a word and affixes between them to one stem. So, a word can have only one stem. For example, the word والصناعة would be segmented as PRE/وال + STM/صناع + SUF/ة. This yielded linguistically correct segmentations in many cases. The second part of Table 4 shows the effect of the post-processing on the BLEU score. We can see that it remains almost the same with an increase in OOV rate.

For rest of the experiments in this paper, we used a value of 70 for the perplexity threshold parameter plus the post-processing on segmentation. We trained Morfessor on the concatenation of QCA, $\text{AVIA}_Q A$ and Novels.[7]

Using other Arabic variations: In this section, we present experiments using MSA, EGY and LEV to English bitexts combined with the QCA bitext for Qatari Arabic to English machine translation. We explored three segmentation options for the Arabic side of the data: (i) no segmentation, (ii) ATB segmentation, and (iii) unsupervised segmentation using Morfessor.

The QCA corpus is of much smaller size compared to other Arabic variants, say MSA. It is possible that in the training of the machine translation models, the large corpus dominates the QCA corpus. In order to avoid that, we balanced the two corpora by replicating the smaller corpus X number of times in order to make it approximately equal to the large corpus (Nakov and Ng, 2009).[8] The complete procedure is described below.

In a nutshell, for building a machine translation system using the MSA plus Qatari corpus, we first balanced the Qatari corpus to make it approximately equal to MSA and concatenated them. For training Morfessor, the Qatari Arabic data consisted of QCA, Novels and AVIA_{QA}, while for SMT, it consisted of QCA only. In both cases, we balanced it to be approximately equal to MSA. We then trained Morfessor on the balanced (QCA, Novels, AVIA_{QA}) plus MSA data and we segmented the Arabic side of the balanced QCA plus MSA training data for machine translation. We built a machine translation system on the segmented data. We segmented the testing and tuning data sets similarly. We used the same balancing when we combined EGY-EN and LEV-EN with the Qatari Arabic – English data.

We also tried training multiple unsupervised models, but this yielded lower SMT quality compared to using a single model trained on multi-dialects. Using different models could result in having different segmentation schemes, which might not help in reducing the vocabulary mismatch between different variants of Arabic.

[7]We did not see a big difference in training Morfessor with and without the QCA corpus, and we decided to use the complete data for training.

[8]Due to the spoken nature of the QCA corpus, it contains shorter sentences. Thus, we balanced the corpora based on the number of tokens rather than on the number of sentences.

Train	NONE	ATB	Morfessor
QCA	12.2	12.9	**13.7**
'QCA,MSA	12.7	13.3	**14.6**
'QCA,EGY	13.0	13.5	**14.5**
'QCA,LEV	13.8	13.7	**15.2**

Table 5: BLEU scores for Qatari Arabic to English SMT using three different segmentation settings. 'QCA means the modified QCA corpus with number of tokens approximately equal to MSA, EGY and LEV in the respective experiments.

Table 5 shows the results. There are two things to point here. First, the SMT systems that used the unsupervised morphological segmenter, Morfessor, outperformed the systems that used no segmentation and those using the ATB segmentation. The Morfessor-based systems showed consistent improvements compared to the ATB-based systems over the no-segmentation systems. This validates our point that unsupervised morphological segmentation generalizes well for a variety of dialects and these SMT results complement that. The second observation is that adding a bitext for other dialects and MSA improves machine translation quality for Qatari–English SMT.

6 Translation into Qatari Arabic

Our monolingual corpora of Gulf subdialects could be also helpful when translating English into Qatari Arabic. We conducted a few basic experiments in this direction but without segmentation.

We trained an English to Qatari Arabic SMT system on the QCA bitext, using the same settings as described in Section 5. We then normalized the output of the translation system using the QCRI-Normalizer (Sajjad et al., 2013b).[9] As a language model, we used the Arabic side of the QCA corpus, novels and forum data, standalone and together. Table 6 presents the results of the effect of varying the language model on the quality of the SMT system. The best system shows an improvement of 0.22 BLEU points absolute compared to the baseline system that only uses the Arabic side of the QCA corpus for LM training.

The SMT system achieved the largest gain when adding QA forum data to the QCA data. SA and AE monolingual data also showed good improvements. This might be due to their relatively large sizes; we need further investigation.

[9]`http://alt.qcri.org/tools/`

LM	BLEU
QCA	2.78
QCA+QA-Novels	2.64
QCA+QA-Novels+BH-Novels	2.86
QCA+QA-Novels+KW-Novels	2.78
QCA+QA-Novels+AE-Novels	2.92
QCA+QA-Novels+SA-Novels	2.96
QCA+ALL-Novels	2.80
QCA+QA-Novels+QForum	**3.00**

Table 6: Results for English to Qatari SMT for varying language models. In all cases, the translation model is trained on the QCA bitext only.

Note the quite low BLEU scores, especially compared to the reverse translation direction. One reason is the morphologically rich nature of Qatari Arabic, which makes translating into it a hard problem. The small amount of training data further adds to it. We expect to see larger gains compared to Qatari Arabic to English machine translation when segmentation is used.

7 Conclusion and Future Work

We have demonstrated the feasibility of using an unsupervised morphological segmenter to increase the resource adaptability of Arabic variants. We evaluated the segmentation on a Qatari dialect by building a Qatari Arabic to English machine translation system. We further adapted MSA, EGY and LEV in the simplest machine translation settings and we showed a consistent improvement of 1.5 BLEU points when compared to the respective baseline system that uses no segmentation.

In the future, we would like to explore the impact of segmentation on both the translation model and the language model when translating into Qatari Arabic. This involves greater challenges, as a desegmenter is required for the translation output with every segmentation scheme.

References

Ahmed Abdelali, Francisco Guzman, Hassan Sajjad, and Stephan Vogel. 2014. The AMARA corpus: Building parallel language resources for the educational domain. In *Proceedings of the 9th International Conference on Language Resources and Evaluation*, Reykjavik, Iceland, May.

Rania Al-Sabbagh and Roxana Girju. 2010. Mining the web for the induction of a dialectical Arabic lexicon. In *Proceedings of the 7th International Conference on Language Resources and Evaluation*, Valletta, Malta, May.

Hitham Abo Bakr, Khaled Shaalan, and Ibrahim Ziedan. 2008. A hybrid approach for converting written Egyptian colloquial dialect into diacritized Arabic. In *Proceedings of the 6th International Conference on Informatics and Systems*, Cairo, Egypt, March.

Houda Bouamor, Nizar Habash, and Kemal Oflazer. 2014. A multidialectal parallel corpus of Arabic. In *Proceedings of the 9th edition of the Language Resources and Evaluation Conference*, Reykjavik, Iceland, May.

Peter F. Brown, Stephen A. Della Pietra, Vincent J. Della Pietra, and R. L. Mercer. 1993. The mathematics of statistical machine translation: parameter estimation. *Computational Linguistics*, 19(2), June.

Mauro Cettolo, Christian Girardi, and Marcello Federico. 2012. Wit^3: Web inventory of transcribed and translated talks. In *Proceedings of the 16th Conference of the European Association for Machine Translation*, Trento, Italy, May.

David Chiang, Mona Diab, Nizar Habash, Owen Rambow, and Safiullah Shareef. 2006. Parsing Arabic dialects. In *Proceedings of the 11th Conference of the European Chapter of the Association for Computational Linguistics*, Trento, Italy, April.

Mathias Creutz and Krista Lagus. 2007. Unsupervised models for morpheme segmentation and morphology learning. *ACM Transactions on Speech and Language Processing*, 4(1), January.

Nadir Durrani, Helmut Schmid, and Alexander Fraser. 2011. A joint sequence translation model with integrated reordering. In *Proceedings of the 49th Annual Meeting of the Association for Computational Linguistics: Human Language Technologies*, Portland, OR, June.

Mohamed Elmahdy, Mark Hasegawa-Johnson, and Eiman Mustafawi. 2014. Development of a TV broadcasts speech recognition system for Qatari Arabic. In *Proceedings of the 9th edition of the Language Resources and Evaluation Conference*, Reykjavik, Iceland, May.

Spence Green and John DeNero. 2012. A class-based agreement model for generating accurately inflected translations. In *Proceedings of the 50th Annual Meeting of the Association for Computational Linguistics*, Jeju Island, Korea, July.

Nizar Habash and Owen Rambow. 2006. MAGEAD: a morphological analyzer and generator for the Arabic dialects. In *Proceedings of the 21st International Conference on Computational Linguistics and the 44th annual meeting of the Association for Computational Linguistics*, Sydney, Australia, July.

Nizar Habash, Owen Rambow, and Ryan Roth. 2009. Mada+TOKAN: A toolkit for Arabic tokenization, diacritization, morphological disambiguation, pos tagging, stemming and lemmatization. In *Proceedings of the 2nd International Conference on Arabic Language Resources and Tools (MEDAR)*, Cairo, Egypt, April.

Nizar Habash, Ramy Eskander, and Abdelati Hawwari. 2012. A morphological analyzer for Egyptian Arabic. In *Proceedings of the 12th Meeting of the Special Interest Group on Computational Morphology and Phonology*, Montreal, Canada, June.

Nizar Y Habash. 2010. Introduction to Arabic natural language processing. *Synthesis Lectures on Human Language Technologies*, 3(1), August.

Kenneth Heafield. 2011. KenLM: Faster and smaller language model queries. In *Proceedings of the 6th Workshop on Statistical Machine Translation*, Edinburgh, UK, July.

Mark Hopkins and Jonathan May. 2011. Tuning as ranking. In *Proceedings of the Conference on Empirical Methods in Natural Language Processing*, Scotland, UK, July.

Serena Jeblee, Weston Feely, Houda Bouamor, Alon Lavie, Nizar Habash, and Kemal Oflazer. 2014. Domain and Dialect Adaptation for Machine Translation into Egyptian Arabic. In *Proceedings of the Arabic Natural Language Processing Workshop*, Doha, Qatar, October.

Reinhard Kneser and Hermann Ney. 1995. Improved backing-off for ngram langauge modeling. In *Proceedings of the IEEE International Conference on Acoustics, Speech and Signal Processing*, Detroit, Michigan, May.

Philipp Koehn, Franz J. Och, and Daniel Marcu. 2003. Statistical phrase-based translation. In *Proceedings of the Human Language Technology and North American Association for Computational Linguistics Conference*, Edmonton, Canada, May.

Philipp Koehn, Hieu Hoang, Alexandra Birch, Chris Callison-Burch, Marcello Federico, Nicola Bertoldi, Brooke Cowan, Wade Shen, Christine Moran, Richard Zens, Chris Dyer, Ondrej Bojar, Alexandra Constantin, and Evan Herbst. 2007. Moses: Open source toolkit for statistical machine translation. In *Proceedings of the 45th Annual Meeting of the Association for Computational Linguistics, Demonstration Program*, Prague, Czech Republic, June.

Shankar Kumar and William Byrne. 2004. Minimum bayes-risk decoding for statistical machine translation. In *Proceedings of the Human Language Technology Conference of the North American Chapter of the Association for Computational Linguistics*, Boston, MA, May.

Mohamed Maamouri, Ann Bies, Tim Buckwalter, Mona Diab, Nizar Habash, Owen Rambow, and Dalila Tabessi. 2006. Developing and using a pilot dialectal Arabic treebank. In *Proceedings of the 5th International Conference on Language Resources and Evaluation*, Genova, Italy, May.

Hamdy Mubarak and Kareem Darwish. 2014. Using Twitter to collect a multi-dialectal corpus of Arabic. In *Proceedings of the Arabic Natural Language Processing Workshop*, Doha, Qatar, October.

Preslav Nakov and Hwee Tou Ng. 2009. Improved statistical machine translation for resource-poor languages using related resource-rich languages. In *Proceedings of the 2009 Conference on Empirical Methods in Natural Language Processing*, Suntec, Singapore, August.

Preslav Nakov, Francisco Guzman, and Stephan Vogel. 2012. Optimizing for sentence-level BLEU+1 yields short translations. In *Proceedings of the 24th International Conference on Computational Linguistics*, Mumbai, India, December.

Kishore Papineni, Salim Roukos, Todd Ward, and Wei-Jing Zhu. 2002. Bleu: a method for automatic evaluation of machine translation. In *Proceedings of the 40th annual meeting on association for computational linguistics*, Philadelphia, PA, July.

Hoifung Poon, Colin Cherry, and Kristina Toutanova. 2009. Unsupervised morphological segmentation with log-linear models. In *Proceedings of Human Language Technologies: The 2009 Annual Conference of the North American Chapter of the Association for Computational Linguistics*, Denver, CO, June.

Jason Riesa and David Yarowsky. 2006. Minimally supervised morphological segmentation with applications to machine translation. In *Proceedings of the 7th Conference of the Association for Machine Translation in the Americas*, MA, USA, August.

Hassan Sajjad, Kareem Darwish, and Yonatan Belinkov. 2013a. Translating dialectal Arabic to English. In *Proceedings of the 51st Annual Meeting of the Association for Computational Linguistics*, Sofia, Bulgaria, August.

Hassan Sajjad, Francisco Guzman, Preslav Nakov, Ahmed Abdelali, Kenton Murray, Fahad Al Obaidli, and Stephan Vogel. 2013b. QCRI at IWSLT 2013: Experiments in Arabic-English and English-Arabic Spoken Language Translation. In *Proceedings of the 10th International Workshop on Spoken Language Translation*, Hiedelberg, Germany, December.

Ahmed Salama, Houda Bouamor, Behrang Mohit, and Kemal Oflazer. 2014. YouDACC: the youtube dialectal Arabic commentary corpus. In *Proceedings of the 9th edition of the Language Resources and Evaluation Conference*, Reykjavik, Iceland, May.

Wael Salloum and Nizar Habash. 2011. Dialectal to standard Arabic paraphrasing to improve Arabic-English statistical machine translation. In *Proceedings of the First Workshop on Algorithms and Resources for Modelling of Dialects and Language Varieties*, Edinburgh, Scotland, July.

Hassan Sawaf. 2010. Arabic dialect handling in hybrid machine translation. In *Proceedings of the 9th Conference of the Association for Machine Translation in the Americas*, Denver, CO, October.

Vesa Siivola, Mathias Creutz, and Mikko Kurimo. 2007. Morfessor and VariKN machine learning tools for speech and language technology. In *Proceedings of the 8th International Conference on Speech Communication and Technology (Interspeech)*, Antwerpen, Belgium, August.

Ming-Feng Tsai, Preslav Nakov, and Hwee Tou Ng. 2010. Morphological analysis for resource-poor machine translation. Technical report, Kent Ridge, Singapore, December.

Omar F Zaidan and Chris Callison-Burch. 2011. The Arabic online commentary dataset: an annotated dataset of informal Arabic with high dialectal content. In *Proceedings of the 49th Annual Meeting of the Association for Computational Linguistics: Human Language Technologies: short papers-Volume 2*, Portland, OR, June.

Rabih Zbib, Erika Malchiodi, Jacob Devlin, David Stallard, Spyros Matsoukas, Richard Schwartz, John Makhoul, Omar F. Zaidan, and Chris Callison-Burch. 2012. Machine translation of Arabic dialects. In *Proceedings of the 2012 Conference of the North American Chapter of the Association for Computational Linguistics: Human Language Technologies*, Montreal, Canada, June.

Andreas Zollmann, Ashish Venugopal, and Stephan Vogel. 2006. Bridging the inflection morphology gap for Arabic statistical machine translation. In *Proceedings of the Human Language Technology Conference of the NAACL, Companion Volume: Short Papers*, New York, NY, June.

Arabizi Detection and Conversion to Arabic

Kareem Darwish
Qatar Computing Research Institute
Qatar Foundation, Doha, Qatar
kdarwish@qf.org.qa

Abstract

Arabizi is Arabic text that is written using Latin characters. Arabizi is used to present both Modern Standard Arabic (MSA) or Arabic dialects. It is commonly used in informal settings such as social networking sites and is often with mixed with English. In this paper we address the problems of: identifying Arabizi in text and converting it to Arabic characters. We used word and sequence-level features to identify Arabizi that is mixed with English. We achieved an identification accuracy of 98.5%. As for conversion, we used transliteration mining with language modeling to generate equivalent Arabic text. We achieved 88.7% conversion accuracy, with roughly a third of errors being spelling and morphological variants of the forms in ground truth.

1 Introduction

Arabic is often written using Latin characters in transliterated form, which is often referred to as Arabizi, Arabish, Franco-Arab, and other names. Arabizi uses numerals to represent Arabic letters for which there is no phonetic equivalent in English or to account for the fact that Arabic has more letters than English. For example, "2" and "3" represent the letters أ (that sounds like "a" as in apple) and ع (that is a guttural "aa") respectively. Arabizi is particularly popular in Arabic social media. Arabizi has grown out of a need to write Arabic on systems that do not support Arabic script natively. For example, Internet Explorer 5.0, which was released in March 1999, was the first version of the browser to support Arabic display natively[1]. Windows Mobile and Android did not support Arabic except through third party support until versions 6.5x and 3.x respectively. Despite the increasing support of Arabic in many platforms, Arabizi continues to be popular due to the familiarity of users with it and the higher proficiency of users to use an English keyboard compared to an Arabic keyboard. Arabizi is used to present both MSA as well as different Arabic dialects, which lack commonly used spelling conventions and differ morphologically and phonetically from MSA. There has been recent efforts to standardize the spelling of some Arabic dialects (Habash et al., 2012), but such standards are not widely adopted on social media. Additionally, due to the fact that many of the Arabic speakers are bilingual (with their second language being either English or French), another commonly observed phenomenon is the presence of English (or French) and Arabizi mixed together within sentences, where users code switch between both languages. In this paper we focus on performing two tasks, namely: detecting Arabizi even when juxtaposed with English; and converting Arabizi to Arabic script regardless of it being MSA or dialectal. Detecting and converting Arabizi to Arabic script would help: ease the reading of the text, where Arabizi is difficult to read; allow for the processing of Arabizi (post conversion) using existing NLP tools; and normalize Arabic and Arabizi into a unified form for text processing and search. Detecting and converting Arabizi are complicated by the following challenges:

[1] http://en.wikipedia.org/wiki/Internet_Explorer

Proceedings of the EMNLP 2014 Workshop on Arabic Natural Langauge Processing (ANLP), pages 217–224,
October 25, 2014, Doha, Qatar.

1. Due to the lack of spelling conventions for Arabizi and Arabic dialectal text, which Arabizi often encodes, building a comprehensive dictionary of Arabizi words is prohibitive. Consider the following examples:

    (a) The MSA word تحرير (liberty) has the following popular Arabizi spellings: ta7rir, t7rir, tahrir, ta7reer, tahreer, etc.

    (b) The dialectal equivalents to the MSA لا يلعب (he does not play) could be مايلعبش, ميلعبش, مابلعبش, مابيلعبش etc. The resultant Arabizi could be: mayel3absh, mabyelaabsh, mabyel3absh, etc.

2. Some Arabizi and English words share a common spelling, making solely relying on an English dictionary insufficient to identify English words. Consider the following examples (ambiguous words are bolded):

    (a) Ana 3awez aroo7 **men** America leh Canada (I want to go from America to Canada). The word "men" meaning "from" is also an English word.

    (b) I called **Mohamed** last night. "Mohamed" in this context is an English word, though it is a transliterated Arabic name.

3. Within social media, users often use creative spellings of English words to shorten text, emphasize, or express emotion. This can complicate the differentiation of English and Arabizi. Consider the following examples:

    (a) I want 2 go with u tmrw, cuz my car is broken.

    (b) Woooooow. Ur car is cooooooool.

Due to these factors, classifying a word as Arabizi or English has to be done in-context. Thus, we employed sequence labeling using Conditional Random Fields (CRF) to detect Arabizi in context. The CRF was trained using word-level and sequence-level features. For converting Arabizi to Arabic script, we used transliteration mining in combination with a large Arabic language model that covers both MSA and other Arabic dialects to properly choose the best transliterations in context.

The contributions of this paper are:

- We employed sequence labeling that is trained using word-level and sequence-level features to identify in-sentence code-switching between two languages that share a common alphabet.
- We used transliteration mining and language modeling to convert form Arabizi to Arabic script.
- We plan to publicly release all our training and test data.

The remainder of the paper is organized as follows: Section 2 provides related work; Section 3 presents our Arabizi detection and reports on the detection accuracy; Section 4 describes our Arabizi to Arabic conversion approach and reports the accuracy of conversion; and Section 5 concludes the paper.

2 Related Work

There are two aspects to this work: the first is language identification, and the second is transliteration. There is much work on language identification including open source utilities, such as the Language Detection Library for Java[2]. Murthy and Kumar (2006) surveyed many techniques for language identification. Some of the more successful techniques use character n-gram models (Beesley, 1988; Dunning, 1994) in combination with a machine learning technique such as hidden Markov models (HMM) or Bayesian classification (Xafopoulos et al., 2004; Dunning, 1994). Murthy and Kumar (2006) used logistic regression-like classification that employed so-called "aksharas" which are sub-word character sequences as features for identifying different Indian languages. Ehara and Tanaka-Ishii (2008) developed an online language detection system that detects code switching during typing, suggests the language to switch to the user, and interactively invokes the appropriate text entry method. They used HMM based language identification in conjunction with an n-gram character language model. They reported up to 97% accuracy when detecting between two languages on a

[2] `http://code.google.com/p/language-detection/`

synthetic test set. In our work, we performed offline word-level language identification using CRF sequence labeling, which conceptually combines logistic regression-like discriminative classification with an HMM-like generative model (Lafferty et al., 2001). We opted to use a CRF sequence labeling because it allowed us to use both state and sequence features, which in our case corresponded to word- and sequence-level features respectively. One of the downsides of using a CRF sequence labeler is that most implementations, including CRF++ which was used in this work, only use nominal features. This required us to quantize all real-valued features.

Converting between from Arabizi to Arabic is akin to transliteration or Transliteration Mining (TM). In transliteration, a sequence in a source alphabet or writing system is used to generate a phonetically similar sequence in a target alphabet or writing system. In TM, a sequence in a source alphabet or writing system is used to find the most similar sequence in a lexicon that is written in the target alphabet or writing system. Both problems are fairly well studied with multiple evaluation campaigns, particularly at the different editions of the Named Entities Workshop (NEWS) (Zhang et al., 2011; Zhang et al., 2012). In our work we relied on TM from a large corpus of Arabic microblogs. TM typically involves using transliteration pairs in two different writing systems or alphabets to learning character (or character-sequence) level mappings between them. The learning can be done using the EM algorithm (Kuo et al., 2006) or HMM alignment (Udupa et al., 2009). Once these mappings are learned, a common approach involves using a generative model that attempts to generate all possible transliterations of a source word, given the character mappings between two languages, and restricting the output to words in the target language (El-Kahki et al., 2011; Noeman and Madkour, 2010). Other approaches include the use of locality sensitive hashing (Udupa and Kumar, 2010) and classification (Jiampojamarn et al., 2010). Another dramatically different approaches involves the unsupervised learning of transliteration mappings from a large parallel corpus instead of transliteration pairs (Sajjad et al., 2012). In our work, we used the baseline system of El-Kahky et al. (2011). There are three commercial Input Method Editors (IMEs) that convert from Arabizi to Arabic, namely: Yamli[3], Microsoft Maren[4], and Google t3reeb[5]. Since they are IMEs, they only work in an interactive mode and don't allow for batch processing. Thus they are difficult to compare against. Also, from interactively using Arabic IMEs, it seems that they only use unigram language modeling.

3 Identifying Arabizi

As mentioned earlier, classifying words as English or Arabizi requires the use of word-level and sequence-level features. We opted to use CRF sequence labeling to identify Arabizi words. We used the CRF++ implementation with default parameters (Sha and Pereira, 2003). We constructed training and test sets for word-level language classification from tweets that contain English, Arabizi, or a mixture of English and Arabizi. We collected the tweets in the following manner:

1. We issued commonly used Arabizi words as queries against Twitter multiple times. These words were "e7na" (we), "3shan" (because), and "la2a" (no). We issued these queries every 30 seconds for roughly 1 hour. We put large time gaps between queries to ensure that the results were refreshed.

2. We extracted the user IDs of all the authors of the tweets that we found, and used the IDs as queries to Twitter to get the remaining tweets that they have authored. Our intuition was that tweeps who authored once in Arabizi would likely have more Arabizi tweets. Doing so helped us find Arabizi tweets that don't necessarily have the aforementioned common words and helped us find significantly more Arabizi text. In all we identified 265 tweeps who authored 16,507 tweets in the last 7 days, containing 132,236 words. Of the words in the tweets, some of them were English, but most of them were Arabizi.

We filtered tweets where most of the words contained Arabic letters. As in Table 1, all the tokens in

[3] http://www.yamli.com/editor/ar/
[4] http://www.getmaren.com
[5] http://www.google.com/ta3reeb

Label	Explanation
a	Arabizi
e	English
o	Other including URL's, user mentions, hashtags, laughs (lol, , :P, xd), and none words

Table 1: Used labels for words

the set were manually labeled as English ("e"), Arabizi ("a"), or other ("o"). For training, we used 522 tweets, containing 5,207 tokens. The breakdown of tokens is: 3,307 English tokens; 1,203 Arabizi tokens; and 697 other tokens. For testing, we used 101 tweets containing 3,491 tokens. The breakdown of the tokens is: 797 English tokens; 1,926 Arabizi tokens; and 768 other tokens. Though there is some mismatch in the distribution of English and Arabizi tokens between training and test sets, this mismatch happened naturally and is unlikely to affect overall accuracy numbers. For language models, we trained two character level language models: the first using 9.4 million English words; and the second using 1,000 Arabizi words (excluding words in the test set). We used the BerkeleyLM language modeling toolkit.

We trained the CRF++ implementation of CRF sequence labeler using the features in Table 2 along with the previous word and next word. The Table describes each feature and shows the features values for the word "Yesss".

Table 3 reports on the language identification results and breaks down the results per word type and provides examples of mislabeling. Overall we achieved a word-level language identification accuracy of 98.5%. As the examples in the table show, the few mislabeling mistakes included: Arabized English words, Arabizi words that happen to be English words, single Arabizi words surrounded by English words (or vice versa), and misspelled English words.

4 Arabizi to Arabic

As mentioned earlier, Arabizi is simply Arabic, whether MSA or dialectal, that is written using Latin characters. We were able to collect Arabizi text by searching for common Arabizi words on Twitter, identifying the authors of these tweets, and then scraping their tweets to find more tweets written in Arabizi. In all, we constructed a collection that contained 3,452 training pairs that have both Arabizi and Arabic equivalents. All Arabizi words were manually transliterated into Arabic by a native Arabic speaker. Some example pairs are:

- 3endek → عندك (meaning "in your care")
- bytl3 → بيطلع (meaning "he ascends")

For testing, we constructed a set of 127 random Arabizi tweets containing 1,385 word. Again, we had a native Arabic speaker transliterate all tweets into Arabic script. An example sentences is:

- sa7el eih ? howa ntii mesh hatigi bokra → ساحل ايه ؟ هو انتي مش هتيجي بكرة
- meaning: what coast ? aren't you coming tomorrow

We applied the following preprocessing steps on the training and test data:

- We performed the following Arabic letter normalizations (Habash, 2010):
  - ى (alef maqsoura) → ي (ya)
  - آ (alef maad), أ (alef with hamza on top), and إ (alef with hamza on the bottom) → ا (alef)
  - ؤ (hamza on w), and ئ (hamza on ya) → ء (hamza)
  - ة (taa marbouta) → ه (haa)
- Since people often repeat letters in tweets to indicate stress or to express emotions, we removed any repetition of a letter beyond 2 repetitions (Darwish et al., 2012). For example, we transformed the word "salaaaam" to "salaam".
- Many people tend to segment Arabic words in Arabizi into separate constituent parts. For example, you may find "w el kitab" (meaning "and the book") as 3 separate tokens, while in Arabic they are concatenated into a single token, namely "والكتاب". Thus, we concatenated short tokens that represent coordinating conjunctions and prepositions to the tokens that follow them. These tokens are: w, l, el, ll, la, we, f, fel, fil, fl, lel, al, wel, and b.

Feature	Explanation	Ex.
Word	This would help label words that appear in the training examples. This feature is particularly useful for frequent words.	yesss
Short	This would remove repeated characters in a word. Colloquial text such as tweets and Facebook statuses contain word elongations.	yes
IsLaugh	This indicates if a word looks like a laugh or emoticon. For example lol, J, :D, :P, xD, (ha)+, etc. Smiles and laughs should get an "o" label.	0
IsURL	This indicates if a token resembles as URL of the form: `http`:/[a-zA-z0-9˙]+/. URLs should get an "o" label.	0
IsNo	This indicates if a token is composed of numbers only. Numbers should get an "o" label	0
Is!Latin	This indicates if a word is composed of non-Latin letters. If a word is composed on non-Latin characters, it is not "e".	0
WordLength	This feature is simply the token length. Transliterated words are typically longer than native words	8
IsHashtag	This indicates if it is a hashtag. Hashtags would get an "e" label.	0
IsNameMention	This indicates if it is a name mention. Name mentions, which start with "@" sign, should get an "o" label.	0
IsEmail	This indicates if it is an email. Emails, which match `[\S\.\-_]+@[\S\.\-_]+` should get an "o" label.	0
wordEnUni	Unigram probability in English word-level language model. The language model is built on English tweets. If a word has a high probability of being English then it is likely English.	-4
wordEnBi	Bigram probability in English word-level language model of the word with the word that precedes it. If the probability is high then it is likely that it is an English word that follows another English word.	-4
charEnNgram	Trigram probability in English character-level language model of characters in a word. This checks if it is likely sequence of characters in an English word.	-2
charArNgram	Trigram probability in Arabizi character-level language model of characters in a word. This checks if it is likely sequence of characters in an Arabizi word.	-13

Table 2: Used labels for words

Actual Tag	Predicted Tag	Count	Percent	Example (Misclassified Token Highlighted)	Analysis
a	a	1909	99.1%		
a	e	12	0.6%	tfker b2y **shy** be relax, **tab** 3 3ashan el talta tabta al **weekend** eljaay ya5i wow **be7keelk** the cloud covered	shy & tab: words that exist in English but are actually Arabic in context weekend: Arabized English words bt7keelk: sudden context switch before and after
a	o	5	0.3%	ya Yara ha call u @fjoooj eeeeeeh	ha & eeeeeeh: mistaken for smiles or laughs
e	e	773	97.0%		
e	a	21	2.6%	el **eye drope** eh ya fara7 **offtoschool**	eye & drop: sudden context switch offtoschool: misspelled English words
e	o	3	0.4%	4 those going 2 tahrir	4 & 2: numbers used instead of words
o	o	758	98.7%		
o	e	3	0.4%	URL's and name mentions	Could be fixed with either a simple rule or more training data
o	a	7	0.9%		

Table 3: Used labels for words

- We directly transliterated the words "isA" and "jAk" to "إن شاء اللّه" (meaning "God welling") and to "جزاك اللّه خيرا" (meaning "may God reward you") respectively.

For training, we aligned the word-pairs at character level. The pairs were aligned using GIZA++ and the phrase extractor and scorer from the Moses machine translation package (Koehn et al., 2007) . To apply a machine translation analogy, we treated words as sentences and the letters from which were constructed as tokens. The alignment produced letter sequence mappings. The alignment produced mappings between Latin letters sequences and Arabic letter sequences with associated mapping probabilities. For example, here is a sample mapping:

- 2r → قر (p = 0.459)

To generate Arabic words from Arabizi words, we made the fundamental simplifying assumption that any generated Arabic word should exist in a large word list. Though the assumption fundamentally limits generation to previously seen words only, we built the word list from a large set of tweets. Thus, the probability that a correctly generated word did not exist in the word list would be negligible. This assumption allowed us to treat the problem as a mining problem instead of a generation problem where our task was to find a correct transliteration in a list of words instead of generating an arbitrary word. We built the word list from a tweet set containing a little over 112 million Arabic tweets that we scraped from Twitter between November 20, 2011 and January 9, 2012. We collected the tweets by issuing the query "lang:ar" against Twitter. We utilized the tweet4j package for collection. The tweet set had 5.1 million unique words, and nearly half of them appeared only once.

Our method involved doing two steps:

Producing candidate transliterations: We implemented transliteration in a manner that is akin to the baseline system in El-Kahki et al. (2011). Given an Arabizi word w_{az}, we produced all its possible segmentations along with their associated mappings into Arabic characters. Valid target sequences were retained and sorted by the product of the constituent mapping probabilities. The top n (we picked n = 10) candidates, $w_{ar_{1..n}}$ with the highest probability were generated. Using Bayes rule, we computed:

$$\underset{w_{ar_{i \in 1..n}}}{argmax}\ p(w_{ar_i}|w_{az}) = p(w_{az}|w_{ar_i})p(w_{ar_i}) \quad (1)$$

where $p(w_{az}|w_{ar_i})$ is the posterior probability of mapping, which is computed as the product of the mappings required to generate w_{az} from w_{ar_i}, and $p(w_{ar_i})$ is the prior probability of the word.

Picking the best candidate in context: We utilized a large word language model to help pick the best transliteration candidate in context. We built a trigram language model using the IRSTLM language modeling toolkit (Federico et al., 2008). The advantage of this language model was that it contained both MSA and dialectal text. Given the top transliteration candidates and the language model we trained, we wanted to find the transliteration that would maximize the transliteration probability and language model probability. Given a word w_i with candidates $w_{i_{1-10}}$, we wanted to find $w_i \in w_{i_{1-10}}$ that maximizes the product of the transliteration probabilities (for all the candidates for all the words in the path) and the path probability, where the probability of the path is estimated using the trigram language model.

rank	count	precentage
1	1,068	77.1%
2	129	9.3%
3	49	3.5%
4	30	2.2%
5	19	1.4%
6	12	0.9%
7	5	0.04%
8	2	0.01%
9	1	0.01%
10	3	0.02%
Not found	68	4.9%
Total	1385	

Table 4: Results of converting from Arabizi to Arabic with rank of correct candidates

For testing, we used the aforementioned set of 127 random Arabizi tweets containing 1,385 word. We performed two evaluations as follows:

Out of context evaluation. In this evaluation we wanted to evaluate the quality of the generated list of candidates. Intuitively, a higher rank for the correct transliteration in the list of transliterations is desirable. Thus, we used Mean Reciprocal Rank (MRR) to evaluate the generated candidates. Reciprocal Rank (RR) is simply $\frac{1}{rank}$ of the correct candidate. If the correct candidate is not in the generated list, we assumed that the rank was very large and we set RR = 0. MRR is the average across all test cases. Notice that RR is 1 if the correct candidate is at position 1, 0.5 if correct is at position 2, etc. Thus the penalty for not being at rank 1 is quite severe.

For out of context evaluation, we achieved an MRR of 0.84. Table 4 shows the breakdown of the ranks of the correct transliterations in the test set. As can be seen, the correct candidate was at position one 77.1% of the time. No correct candidates were found 4.9% of the time. This meant that the best possible accuracy that we could achieve for in context evaluation was 95.1%. Further, we examined the 68 words for which we did not generate a correct candidate. Table 5 categorizes the 68 words (words are presented using Arabic script and Buckwalter encoding). Though there has been recent efforts to codify a standard spelling convention for some Arabic dialects (Habash et al., 2012), there is no commonly adopted standard that is widely used on social media. Thus, some of the words that we generated had a variant spelling from the ground truth. Also in other cases, the correct morphological form did not exist in the word list or was infrequent. In some of these cases, we generated morphologically related candidates that have an affix added or removed. Some example affixes including coordinating conjunctions, prepositions, and feminine markers.

Type	Count	Examples
no correct candidate	23	wbenla2a7 "and we hint to" - truth وبنلقح wbnqH oleely "tell me" - truth قوليلي qwlyly fsanya "in a second" - truth في ثانية fy vAnyp
spelling variant of word	17	online "online" - truth اونلاين AwnlAyn -guess انلاين AnlAyn betshoot "you kick" - truth بتشوط bt$wT -guess بتشوت bt$wt
morphological variant	17	bt7bii "you (fm.) like" - truth بتحبي btHby -guess بتحبين btHbyn tesharadeeni "you kick me out" - truth تشرديني t$rdyny -guess تشردين t$rdyn
English word	4	cute; mention; nation; TV
no candidate generated	4	belnesbalko "for you" - truth بالنسبلكم bAlnsblkm filente5abat "in the election" - truth فالانتخبات fAlAntxbAt
mixed Arabic & English	3	felguc "in the GUC" - truth فالGUC fAl-GUC ellive "the live" - truth الlive Al-live

Table 5: Analysis of words for which we did not generate candidates

In context evaluation. In this evaluation, we computed accuracy of producing the correct transliterated equivalent in context. For in context evaluation, if we used a baseline that used the top out-of-context choice, we would achieve 77.1% accuracy. Adding a trigram language model, we achieved an accuracy of 88.7% (157 wrong out of 1,385). Of the wrong guesses, 91 were completely unrelated words and 46 were spelling or morphological variants.

5 Conclusion

In this paper, we presented methods of detecting Arabizi that is mixed with English text and converting Arabizi to Arabic. For language detection we used a sequence labeler that used word and character level features. Language detection was trained and tested on datasets that were constructed from tweets. We achieved an overall accuracy of 98.5%. For converting from Arabizi to Arabic, we trained a transliteration miner that attempted to find the most likely Arabic word that could have generated an Arabizi word. We used both character transliteration probabilities as well as language modeling. We achieved 88.7% transliteration accuracy.

For future work, we would like to experiment with additional training data and improved language models that account for the morphological complexities of Arabic. Also, the lack of commonly used spelling conventions for Arabic dialects may warrant detecting variant spellings of individual dialectal words and perhaps converting from dialectal text to MSA.

References

B. Alex, A. Dubey, and F. Keller. 2007. Using foreign inclusion detection to improve parsing performance. In Proceedings of EMNLP-CoNLL

K. Beesley. 1988. Language Identifier: A computer program for automatic natural-language identification of on-line text. Proceedings of the 29th Annual Conference of the American Translators Association, 4754.

Kareem Darwish, Walid Magdy, and Ahmed Mourad. 2012. Language processing for arabic microblog retrieval. Proceedings of the 21st ACM international conference on Information and knowledge management. ACM, 2012.

T. Dunning. 1994. Statistical identification of language. Technical Report, CRL MCCS-94-273, New Mexico State University.

Y. Ehara, K. Tanaka-Ishii. 2008. Multilingual text entry using automatic language detection. In Proceedings of IJCNLP-2008.

Ali El-Kahky, Kareem Darwish, Ahmed Saad Aldein, Mohamed Abd El-Wahab, Ahmed Hefny, and Waleed Ammar. 2001. Improved transliteration mining using graph reinforcement. In Proceedings of the Conference on Empirical Methods in Natural Language Processing, pp. 1384-1393. Association for Computational Linguistics, 2011.

Marcello Federico, Nicola Bertoldi, and Mauro Cettolo. 2008. IRSTLM: an open source toolkit for handling large scale language models. Proceedings of Interspeech. 2008.

Nizar Habash. 2010. Introduction to Arabic natural language processing. Synthesis Lectures on Human Language Technologies 3.1 (2010): 1-187.

Nizar Habash, Mona T. Diab, Owen Rambow. 2012. Conventional Orthography for Dialectal Arabic. LREC, pp. 711-718. 2012.

Sittichai Jiampojamarn, Kenneth Dwyer, Shane Bergsma, Aditya Bhargava, Qing Dou, Mi-Young Kim and Grzegorz Kondrak. 2010. Transliteration Generation and Mining with Limited Training Resources. ACL NEWS workshop 2010.

Philipp Koehn, Hieu Hoang, Alexandra Birch, Chris Callison-Burch, Marcello Federico, Nicola Bertoldi, Brooke Cowan, Wade Shen, Christine Moran, Richard Zens, Chris Dyer, Ondrej Bojar, Alexandra Constantin, Evan Herbst, Moses: Open Source Toolkit for Statistical Machine Translation, Annual Meeting of the Association for Computational Linguistics (ACL), demonstration session, Prague, Czech Republic, June 2007.

Jin-Shea Kuo, Haizhou Li, Ying-Kuei Yang. 2006. Learning Transliteration Lexicons from the Web. COLING-ACL 2006, Sydney, Australia, 11291136.

J. Lafferty, A. McCallum, and F. Pereira. 2001. Conditional random fields: Probabilistic models for segmenting and labeling sequence data, In Proc. of ICML, pp.282-289, 2001.

Kavi Narayana Murthy and G. Bharadwaja Kumar. 2006. Language identification from small text samples. Journal of Quantitative Linguistics 13.01 (2006): 57-80.

Sara Noeman and Amgad Madkour. 2010. Language Independent Transliteration Mining System Using Finite State Automata Framework. ACL NEWS workshop 2010.

Hassan Sajjad, Alexander Fraser, Helmut Schmid. 2012. A Statistical Model for Unsupervised and Semi-supervised Transliteration Mining. ACL (1) 2012: 469-477

F. Sha and F. Pereira. 2003. Shallow parsing with conditional random fields, In Proc. of HLT/NAACL 2003

Raghavendra Udupa, K. Saravanan, Anton Bakalov, Abhijit Bhole. 2009. "They Are Out There, If You Know Where to Look": Mining Transliterations of OOV Query Terms for Cross-Language Information Retrieval. ECIR-2009, Toulouse, France, 2009.

Raghavendra Udupa, Shaishav Kumar. 2010. Hashing-based Approaches to Spelling Correction of Personal Names. EMNLP 2010.

A. Xafopoulos, C. Kotropoulos, G. Almpanidis, I. Pitas. 2004. Language identification in web documents using discrete hidden Markov models. Pattern Recognition, 37 (3), 583594

Min Zhang, A Kumaran, Haizhou Li. 2011. Whitepaper of NEWS 2012 Shared Task on Machine Transliteration. IJCNLP-2011 NEWS workshop.

Min Zhang, Haizhou Li, Ming Liu, A Kumaran. 2012. Whitepaper of NEWS 2012 Shared Task on Machine Transliteration. ACL-2012 NEWS workshop.

Author Index

Association for Computational Linguistics
209 N. Eighth Street
Stroudsburg, Pennsylvania 18360

CURRAN ASSOCIATES INC
proceedings.com

4th Workshop on Cognitive Aspects of the Lexicon 2014

(CogALex IV)

Held at COLING 2014

Dublin, Ireland
23 August 2014

ISBN: 978-1-63439-217-4